Understanding
People and Social Life

• • • • • • • • • • • •

Introduction to Sociology
Second Edition

Understanding
People and Social Life

· · · · · · · · · · · ·

Introduction to Sociology
Second Edition

H. Paul Chalfant
Texas Tech University

Emily E. LaBeff
Midwestern State University

·············· West Publishing Company

St. Paul   New York   Los Angeles   San Francisco

. . . .

Cover Image: Jeff Lowenthal/Woodfin Camp & Associates
Cover and Text Designs: Roslyn M. Stendahl, Dapper Design
Copyediting: Cindi Gerber
Composition: Parkwood Composition Service
Index: Sandi Schroeder
Art: The Asterisk Group
Credits: 4 Michael Hayman/Stock Boston, 8 George Malaue/Stock Boston, 16 Hazel Hankin/Stock Boston, 24 AP/Wide World Photos, 27 Spencer Grant/Stock Boston, 31 Peter Menzel/Stock Boston, Section 1 AP/Wide World Photos, 43 Marc and Evelyne Beinheim/Woodfin Camp & Associates, 48 Frank Siteman/Stock Boston, 54 AP/Wide World Photos, 61 Stock Boston, 67 AP/Wide World Photos, 77 Robert Eckert/Stock Boston, 87 Thomas Hopker/Woodfin Camp & Associates, 96 Judy Gelles/Stock Boston, 100 Joseph Schuyler/Stock Boston, Section 2 UPI/Bettmann Newsphotos, 118 George W./Stock Boston, 123 Michael Hayman/Stock Boston, 130 Frances M. Cox/Stock Boston, 150 UPI/Bettmann Newsphotos, 153 AP/Wide World Photos, 158 Peter Menzel/Stock Boston, 170 Eddie Adams/Woodfin Camp & Associates Photo, 172 Deborah Kahn/Stock Boston, 185 Elizabeth Crews/Stock Boston, Section 3 AP/Wide World Photos, 198 UPI/Bettmann Newsphotos, 203 John Maher/Stock Boston, 217 Stock Boston, 225 AP/Wide World Photos, 233 AP/Wide World Photos, 239 UPI/Bettmann Newsphotos, 250 Spencer Grant, III/Stock Boston, Research Application 11.1, Tables 11.2 & 3 are reprinted from STATE OF THE WORLD, 1987, A Worldwatch Institute Report on Progress Toward a Sustainable Society, Project Director: Lester R. Brown. By permission of W. W. Norton & Company, Inc. Copyright © 1987 by the Worldwatch Institute. 264 & 267 Reuters/Bettmann Newsphotos, Section 4/Kavanaghs, 274 Owen Franken/Stock Boston, 280 Peter Vandemark, 289 Michael Weisbrot/Stock Boston, 309 & 313 AP/Wide World Photos, 315 Roswell Angier/Stock Boston, 339 UPI/Bettmann Newsphotos, 343 AP/Wide World Photos, and Michael Hayman/Stock Boston.

COPYRIGHT ©1988   By WEST PUBLISHING COMPANY
COPYRIGHT ©1991   By WEST PUBLISHING COMPANY
                  50 W. Kellogg Boulevard
                  P.O. Box 64526
                  St. Paul, MN 55164-1003

Printed in the United States of America

98 97 96 95 94 93 92 91   8 7 6 5 4 3 2 1 0

Library of Congress Cataloging-in-Publication Data

Chalfant, H. Paul, 1929–
    Understanding people and social life: introduction to sociology /
H. Paul Chalfant, Emily LaBeff. — 2nd ed.
        p.   cm.
    Includes bibliographical references and index.
    ISBN 0-314-77342-8 (soft)
    1. Sociology.   I. LaBeff, Emily.   II. Title.
    HM51.C415   1991   90-40933
    301—dc20   CIP

•••••••• To Our Families

Contents

· · · · · · · · · · ·

········ Section 1   Understanding Order in Social Life   37

········ *Section* **4**   *Understanding Social Insitutions*   271

Preface

• • • • • • • • • • •

Our purpose in writing this second edition of *Understanding People and Social Life* remains the same as in the first edition and that is to present the basic concepts of sociology in a clear and interesting manner. We have, however, made many changes in this second edition. Two chapters have been added: one on research methods in sociology and the other on politics as a social institution. We added these chapters in response to suggestions from many different reviewers and with the realization that these topics are certainly important enough to be included in a brief text.

We have also added an epilogue, a kind of closing note, which we hope gives students a quick review of their semester and reminds them of the everyday usefulness of sociological study. As one reviewer noted, most texts just end without a final note to students.

Other changes have also been made with students in mind. A chapter outline now precedes each chapter in order for students to see the organization and flow of the topics. At the end of each chapter we have included questions for review rather than a brief summary. As a reviewer pointed out, summaries may too often be used as a substitute for reading the chapter. Our questions encourage students to actively review and study each chapter. We have also listed key concepts, now with page numbers for easy review, at the end of each chapter.

The 1990s promise to be a decade of remarkable international events, and greater cultural awareness among students is a necessity. To that end, more cross-cultural examples and discussions have been added to this text, particularly in reference to Japan, the Middle East, the Soviet Union, and developing nations.

Two types of boxed features have been maintained in the second edition. One boxed feature explains research methods in sociology by describing a published research study. The second type of boxed feature contains applications of sociological principles emphasizing the usefulness of sociology in understanding specific situations found in everyday life. More than half of the boxed features are new in this edition.

We want to acknowledge our debt to many people in this publishing endeavor. We are most thankful to the staff of West Publishing Company. Tom LaMarre, our acquisitions editor, was a cheerleader, gentle taskmaster, and good friend throughout this process. The production staff at West was also most helpful. Poh Lin Khoo was a hardworking, patient, and steady guide in moving the text through to actual production. We owe special thanks to her and to Tom LaMarre.

The many reviewers of this text have helped us a great deal: Prof. Roger Barnes, Incarnate World College; Dr. Peter Chroman, College of San Mateo; Prof. Robert Clark, Midwestern State University; Prof. Eleanor P. Godfrey, No. Illinois University;

Prof. Art Hill, Metro State University, St. Paul; Prof. Malcolm Holmes, University of Texas at El Paso; Prof. Andrea Landreth, MacMurray College; Prof. Martin Malone, Mount St. Mary's College; Prof. Benjamin Mariante, Stonehill College; Prof. Jack Niemonen, Augustana College; and Prof. Barbara Tomaskovic-DeVey, No. California State University. We took their comments and suggestions to heart, and they helped us make this second edition much more than just an update. We thank them for their efforts.

We also want to express our deep appreciation for the support our colleagues have given us. We want to thank Charles Chandler and Evans Curry of Texas Tech University, Peter Heller of Middle Tennessee University, and Marietta Morrissey of the University of Toledo. At Midwestern State we want to thank Robert Clark, Thomas Chaney, Elaine Purcell, Jackie Cuevas, Larry Williams, and Valerie Haines. We could not have completed this book without the help and support of colleagues—named and unnamed. While we take responsibility for content, we are grateful for their many suggestions and the great quantity of material and information they have furnished.

Finally, we wish to thank the hundreds of students in our introduction to sociology classes who have taught us so much. Their responses and input regarding this text have been invaluable.

H. Paul Chalfant
Emily E. LaBeff

Studying People and Social Life 1

Chapter Outline

It is the first day of an introductory sociology class at a southwestern university. The instructor walks in seemingly in control, professional, and experienced. She faces about forty students who are among the best of their generation. They seem to be serious-minded, reserved, and full of promise. However, a sociologist would not be content with these appearances. After some investigation, the sociologist might discover that the instructor is extremely nervous and makes every effort to hide it. The students also experience considerable pressures that rarely show on their faces in class. Intimate relationships, financial concerns, child care, lack of confidence in their academic abilities, lack of sleep from working late-night shifts, and fear at the thought of competing with so many other students are some of the issues the casual observer might not know. As sociologists Peter Berger and Hansfried Kellner (1981, 4) noted, "The world is not what it appears to be." Underneath the visible social world are dynamic forces waiting to be uncovered.

Sociologists attempt to reach a deeper understanding of people. An understanding beyond beliefs about the social world that are taken for granted. Sociologists are "intensively, endlessly, shamelessly interested" in the doings of people (Berger

1963, 18). Suspending the usual assumptions we make about our lives, sociologists use a special angle of vision and try not to rely on traditional, casual, or commonsense explanations. In this way, important but unnoticed and often intangible features of our social lives can be revealed—such as the hidden forces operating in the class-room. We ask you to take little for granted because things are not always what they seem. We invite you to step back, observe, think, and develop a fresh approach to understanding everyday life. Consider, for example, an analysis of the changing world of college freshmen.

College Students and the Relevance of Sociology

As a college student today, you may not be aware of how your attitudes and experiences have been shaped by the times in which you live. Who influenced you in deciding to go to college? What college major have you chosen? Are you one of thousands of nontraditional, older students returning to college in the 1990s? How are you paying for your education? What are your values and goals regarding education? While there are many individual answers to these questions, a sociologist would take a larger view in order to explain social trends.

When sociologists compare college students today with those twenty-five years ago, some striking differences appear. The types of people who go to college, their attitudes, choices of majors, and the education received are very different. It is difficult to account for such sweeping change as a result of the isolated choices of individual college students around the nation.

For example, today most college freshmen are women—more than 52 per-cent—compared with 43 percent in 1969. Attitudes about a woman's place have changed dramatically as well. In 1967, 57 percent of the freshmen believed that the activities of married women were best confined to home and family, while only 26 percent agreed with this point of view in 1988 (Astin, Green, and Korn 1987: *Chronicle of Higher Education* 1989).

Many other changes in the attitudes of college freshmen have been documented by surveys given to nearly seven million students over a twenty-five year period by the Cooperative Institutional Research Program at UCLA (1989). For example, the percentage of freshmen who cited "being very well-off financially" as "essential or important" increased from 40 percent in 1967 to 73 percent in 1988. Compared with students in the late 1960s, students today tend to be extremely career-minded and want careers that promise high material reward. They are much more likely to major in business, engineering, pre-law, computer science, or other high-salary fields than were students in the 1960s.

In contrast, interest in teaching as a profession has declined considerably. In 1968, 24 percent of the college freshmen planned to teach in elementary or secondary schools compared with 9 percent in 1988. Today's freshmen are also much less likely to major in the humanities, fine arts, performing arts, and social sciences. Interest in the physical sciences has declined by one-half since 1966. Departments of mathematics and statistics have lost more than three-fourths of their majors (Astin, Green, and Korn 1987, 7–24; *Chronicle of Higher Education* 1989, A33–34).

Changed attitudes toward careers have been accompanied by changed attitudes toward social issues, politics, and world affairs. In 1988, only one-third of the freshmen felt that it was important to keep up to date with politics; only 37 percent considered it important to have an influence on social values. In 1967, over 80 percent of the freshmen thought it was very important to develop a meaningful philosophy of life. In 1988, just over 50 percent of the freshmen said it was important (Astin, Green and Korn, 1987, 7–24; *Chronicle of Higher Education* 1989, A33–34).

Today's college freshman is less prepared academically for higher education. Nearly four million students enter colleges and universities each year, and anywhere from 25 percent to 50 percent need remedial work, particularly in English and math. The University of California at Los Angeles admits only the top 12 percent of high school graduates; *even so,* half of all entering students must take noncredit remedial English and math classes. Even Harvard University has had to institute catch-up programs for some freshmen. In addition, educators complain that many college students have few study skills and are not prepared for the long hours of concentration and effort needed to do well in course work (Innerst 1987, 58). This societal problem calls into question the institution of education and its effectiveness; it also manifests itself in the personal lives of millions of students.

Sociologists would explain these differences first by examining the historical contexts of students in the late 1960s and today.

In 1966, a college degree was considered a ticket to the good life, and students were less concerned about economic security. The United States had enjoyed unprecedented economic improvement and stability after World War II, and the country had not yet lost a war.

Despite this, the mid-1960s were a time of considerable social upheaval. The huge Baby Boom generation born between 1946 and 1964 was changing the face of America. It was a rebellious generation ushering in an age of rock music, psychedelic drugs, and social protest. Race riots in the nation's cities and student protests on college campuses deeply divided the nation.

Male students in 1966 faced the military draft and the prospect of fighting in Vietnam, willingly or not. Males who did not want to go to war tried to do well in college because college enrollment exempted them from the draft. Students complained that they could be asked to die for their country but could not vote in the presidential election because the voting age was still twenty-one. The spread of antiwar sentiment fueled more liberal attitudes.

A vigorous civil rights movement galvanized the country as blacks and women demanded equality. Segregation was still the rule in much of the country. Only a few blacks were found in predominantly white state universities, nor could women attend many all-male schools such as Yale, Harvard, or Texas A & M University.

It was extremely rare to see women in roles other than wife and mother or in occupations other than traditionally feminine ones such as teaching and nursing. In its infancy, the women's movement threatened many Americans of both sexes. In addition, the movement toward more sexual freedom, the advent of the birth control pill, resentment of the double standard for men and women, and liberal social attitudes helped fuel the sexual revolution. Couples experimented with living together, a shocking and largely unacceptable lifestyle then, but relatively common today.

The events currently shaping the lives of college students are far different. Today's students are not reacting against a controversial war half a globe away. However, they have seen the United States slip from world dominance as the country experienced periods of deep recession, high unemployment, lagging productivity, and cutbacks in social programs during the 1980s. Stiff competition from Japan and Korea mark today's economy. Consequently, students now feel less economically

These college students having a "love-in" in a park at the University of Nebraska in the late 1960s were typical of thousands of rebellious students of that era.

secure than their 1960s counterparts. To increase their sense of security, they look for careers with good prospects for employment and high income.

The evidence indicates that college students today experience considerable stress; students report a sense of being overwhelmed by the uncertainty of the economy, the competition for good colleges, the high cost of a college education, and the search for well-paying jobs. In addition, students now are conservative on issues such as capital punishment, perhaps because drug wars and high crime rates are given extensive media coverage. Fewer students consider themselves liberal; instead, most define themselves as "middle of the road" (Cooperative Institutional Research Program 1989).

Another major issue reflected in the different experiences of students today is the remarkable change in the position of women in the structure of modern society. More women than ever are in college and in the labor force. New opportunities in all career fields allow women much more choice than in the 1960s. Consequently, the number of women majoring in education, nursing, and secretarial science has declined.

The effects of the women's movement have not stopped there however. Women's desire to pursue careers has changed the agenda regarding sex roles and marriage. The strict division of labor at home between a husband's work and a wife's work has weakened considerably. The growing demand for daycare centers reflects the need of millions of mothers working outside the home.

Students today have also witnessed the country's highest divorce rate. There are more single-parent families, more families with stepparents and stepchildren, and more dual-earning couples. Many college students today grew up in homes affected by divorce, remarriage, and the stress accompanying periods of economic hardship.

Finally, the tragic AIDS (Acquired Immune Deficiency Syndrome) epidemic necessarily is changing the way students think about sex. The sexual freedom awakened in the 1960s and 1970s can be life-threatening to 1990s students. Time will tell if students will modify their sexual habits in response to a disease that already has claimed more lives than the Vietnam war.

In this brief discussion, we hope you can see what different worlds existed for college freshmen in the 1960s versus today. These different worlds resulted in remarkably divergent personal experiences, attitudes, values, and goals.

Such analyses are what sociology is all about. As a student today, you can perhaps identify with some of the issues: the changing economy, the new roles of women, lack of adequate preparation for college study, and changes in the American family. Sociological study has considerable relevance to everyday life. Such study offers a special vision in understanding ourselves and the social world. Research Application 1.1 gives additional information on the practicality of studying sociology.

Defining Sociology

Sociology can be defined simply. It is the disciplined attempt to understand society and social life. The disciplined approach is scientific in nature. Sociologists study patterns of interaction among people with an emphasis on group contexts and broad societal forces. Unlike psychology, the focus of sociology is on the group and the society, not on the individual. A basic premise in sociology is that people's actions are largely influenced by the groups to which they belong and by the interactions that occur within these groups. Clearly, the family, the neighborhood, the peer group, and the work group are extremely important in shaping our behavior. But how do we define and explain those larger social forces which affect us every day and guide the direction of our lives? C. Wright Mills's concept of sociological imagination can help provide an answer.

The Sociological Imagination

In his book *The Sociological Imagination,* sociologist C. Wright Mills (1959) clearly stated how sociology can be useful for an individual in understanding the social world. According to Mills, most of the time people see the world on a very personal level, restricted to what has been learned from individual experiences. This self-centered view of social life does not provide an accurate or sufficient understanding of how life actually works. Mills claimed that in relying on limited individual

Research Application 1.1

• • • • • • • Applying Sociology

Sociology is not a dry collection of facts and theories. It is a dynamic discipline that can be useful to students in every area of their lives. For example, the modern work world requires flexibility and adaptation to change perhaps more than any other attributes. As any successful executive knows, employees today must accept change as a constant. Sociology helps develop flexibility, awareness, and problem solving among students by encouraging them to look at things in new ways and from several different perspectives. Learning to reevaluate old assumptions and practices is an essential and practical skill today.

In the new world of a global economy, sociology encourages students to have a sense of other ways of life and to be aware of cultural differences in interpersonal interactions, as you will see in chapter 3. Even if you do not become an executive in the international marketplace, you may work in a hospital and have Vietnamese, Korean, Filipino, Mexican, Guatemalan, Czechoslovakian, and Pakistani patients. You may teach in a school with a diverse population of students, or you may be stationed overseas in the military. Sociology encourages students to be observant and nonjudgmental regarding other cultural groups, essential perspectives in the modern world.

In a more personal context, sociology provides insight into intimate relationships, successful marriages, and reasons for divorce. The enduring need for connection with others stimulates questions about how we know we are in love, about how our culture teaches us about love, and about how different men and women hold different views of love and sex. Chapter 12 covers these topics in some depth.

Change and diversity mark all lives and all intimate relationships. Love and hate, harmony and violence, wealth and poverty, order and chaos are familiar topics for sociology. Grappling with these issues, sociologists as well as students taking only one course in sociology learn to ask the crucial questions and to creatively search for answers.

• • • • • • •

experience people can see only a small part of the complex and richly textured world. People need a broader perspective from which to view their lives.

To use the **sociological imagination**, Mills argud that individuals must locate their personal biographies—their family and school experiences, their particular neighborhood and peer groups, their unique set of life events—within two broader contexts. First, they must analyze the historical conditions and events that have direct effects on their lives. These include economic conditions, depression and recession, war, the threat of nuclear annihilation, world political actions, prevailing social customs and beliefs, major technological advances, changes in family patterns, population changes, and many others. Second, they must locate themselves in the structure of society—where they fit with regard to social class, education, religion, racial or ethnic status, gender, occupation, urban versus rural lifestyle, and region of the country. Using these three elements of the sociological imagination—history, social structure, and individual experience—people can get a better grasp of personal events. This is what we attempted to accomplish in the earlier discussion of past and present college students.

A quote from Mills's book (1959, 10) is a forceful summary of the sociological imagination:

In so far as an economy is so arranged that slumps occur, the problem of unemployment becomes incapable of personal solution. In so far as war is inherent in the nation-state system and in the uneven industrialization of the world, the ordinary individual in his restricted milieu will be powerless—with or without psychiatric aid—to solve the troubles this system or lack of system imposes upon him. In so far as the family as an institution turns women into darling little slaves and men into their chief providers and unweaned dependents, the problem of a satisfactory marriage remains incapable of purely private solution. In so far as the overdeveloped megalopolis and the overdeveloped automobile are built-in features of the overdeveloped society, the issues of urban living will not be solved by personal ingenuity and private wealth.

Sociology and the Contemporary Scene

The element of change is characteristic of every culture; some cultures change slowly and some change at breakneck speed. The need to study the processes and structures of a society becomes most apparent when society is undergoing rapid change. In these periods, people are likely to feel uneasy or threatened. It is a time to ask questions.

The modern world is characterized by events that make us uneasy. American inner cities are decaying, and the sprawling urban areas surrounding them suffer from problems associated with rapid growth and change. Pollution and other environmental issues resulting from modernization plague the earth. Political upheavals in the Middle East and Soviet Union have had repercussions around the world. Americans face a national crisis in our public schools. Social conflicts continue over polarizing issues such as abortion, the treatment of AIDS patients, the disposal of nuclear waste, causes of unemployment, and the costs of welfare. Technological answers to some problems have also created unforeseen new difficulties. For example, some medical innovations have led to soaring costs in the area of health care and have actually resulted in a decline in health care for all but the wealthy.

The need for the sociological imagination is perhaps as strong today as at any time. Sociology was born at an equally critical time of rapid social change. It did not simply develop as another way in which scholars could ponder the social world in abstract fashion. Instead, it developed as students from several disciplines looked with concern at the prevailing social conditions in the world around them. Those social conditions faced by early sociologists are similar to the ones we face today. The following section discusses the historical parallels between their societies and ours and demonstrates the role of sociology in understanding societal crisis.

The Crisis of Society and the Beginnings of Sociology

The crisis that triggered sociological thinking was the **Industrial Revolution**, which referes to events beginning in the eigtheenth century that brought about an entirely different way of life as employment moved from farms to factories. The Industrial Revolution produced more change in one hundred years than has occurred in the rest of recorded history. Over a relatively short period of time, it changed the mode of production from the farm and cottage industries of rural England to the industrial factories which arose in such cities as London, Birmingham, and Leeds.

The technology that made an agricultural surplus possible made it necessary for the population to move from rural areas into the new urban areas. People moved

A child sits in the window of a slum apartment looking over a dirty, littered street. Such neighborhoods are common in the inner-city areas of our major cities.

to the cities in huge numbers and found that crowding, poverty, disease, and crime accompanied opportunity. They had little preparation to deal with the drastic changes. Rural values and traditions did not apply to conditions in the city. As a result, the majority of the people paid a very heavy price for European industrialization because it cost them the security of tradition and community. To make a hypothetical comparison, it would be as if residents of rural west Texas suddenly found themselves in New York City and were left to their own devices to survive.

During the Industrial Revolution, the machine became the central feature. People were put in service of mechanized assembly lines. Various forms of organization, such as artisans' guilds that had lasted for generations, were undermined by the new machines and manufacturing techniques. At the same time, science brought new ideas such as evolution, natural selection, and greater understanding of the earth and the solar system. Modernization tore apart the social fabric that had held together for many centuries. The world was being restructured, and people were confused, afraid, lost. Many were concerned that this disorder and confusion would lead to the destruction of human society.

Auguste Comte and the Birth of Sociology

A French scholar, **Auguste Comte** (1798–1857), gave the discipline its name. It comes from a combination of the Latin word for an association of individuals (*socialis*) and the Greek word meaning the study of some particular subject (*-logie*). In its root meaning, the term sociology stands for the study of the gathering of people or the study of groups.

The study of human relationships was not new when Comte introduced sociology. Philosophers and others had been pursuing it for centuries. Even before Plato and Aristotle raised basic questions about humanity, philosophers had been examining the quality of human interaction. But Comte believed their methods were inadequate for the present condition and could not lead society in new directions. Comte advocated the use of the **scientific method** as a means of salvaging a society he saw going out of control. The method of science is based on careful observation and measurement, not on personal, religious, or philosophical beliefs.

Put yourself in Comte's place. Or, better yet, practice your sociological imagination. Born soon after the French Revolution and the Reign of Terror, Comte lived through at least seven different political regimes in France including the reign of Napoléon. He was part of a generation of educated young French people who felt no strong sense of security for their future. Life was too uncertain. Only a short period before, France had seen mass beheadings at the public guillotine. Comte himself never found a stable academic appointment, and he died thinking his work was unrecognized.

In search of an answer to the problems of his day, Comte came to believe that the scientific method would give humans considerably more power over their lives and would help build a more satisfactory environment out of the suffering of his day. He felt that a science of humanity itself was needed. If, as Comte believed, social events were not the result of accident, then they could be rationally ordered and controlled through concerted effort. With the knowledge acquired through such a science, humans would be able to resolve the menacing social problems that had followed in the wake of the Industrial Revolution. Through his work, Comte laid the groundwork for the field of sociology as a science, although most of his efforts were ignored during his time. However, soon after Comte, several other important people took up the challenge of applying the scientific method to the study of society. They are discussed in the following section.

Three Sociological Pioneers

The sociological theories of **Karl Marx**, **Emile Durkheim**, and **Max Weber** were in large part results of their concern for a society threatened by industrialization. These early social thinkers were deeply concerned with the quality of life and the ability of society to survive the Industrial Revolution. These men turned to the new discipline of sociology to seek an understanding of the problems generated by the breakdown of the old society.

The sense that the "social glue" was dissolving, or that society was crumbling, was a strong feature in the works of these three sociologists. Although each was concerned with a particular aspect of the changing social order, and each viewed change differently, they were similar in their desire to comprehend and to explain what was happening in Europe just over a century ago.

Karl Marx and Human Alienation

Karl Marx (1818–1883) was born in Germany of middle class parents. Marx received an excellent classical education, but early on he developed a strong interest in revolutionary politics and was highly critical of the repressive German regime. Soon after earning his Ph.D., Marx was forced to leave Germany because the authorities reacted harshly to his radical writings. He spend most of his adult life in London observing, researching, and writing, as well as working for his revolutionary cause. Suffering long periods of poverty with his family, Marx experienced the underside of the Industrial Revolution. Many Americans hold a negative image of Marx, but few social scientists doubt his brilliance and his tremendous impact on all the social sciences.

For Marx, the type of economic system prevalent in a society determined the nature of relationships between individuals and groups. Consequently, Marx painstakingly analyzed the changes in the economy caused by industrialization. He paid particular attention to the conditions of the working class in London, and, like the writer Charles Dickens who lived at the same time, he did not like what he saw.

Karl Marx is considered the founder of the **conflict perspective**, one of the three major perspectives in sociological theory. Conflict theorists emphasize the importance of social change, competition and antagonism among social groups, the struggle for power, and the resulting conflict. According to Marx, one's relation to the means of production—whether one was an owner of production or a worker in production—was the decisive factor in determining one's life. The owners were called the **bourgeoisie** and the workers were called the **proletariat**. Conflict was inevitable between these groups because their interests were opposite.

Marx believed that humans were unique in their ability to work and produce goods and food which could ensure their own survival. To produce and to control what had been produced were essential features of human nature. To be cut off from this process—to be powerless, as were workers in factory assembly lines—was Marx's definition of **alienation**.

Marx believed an industrial, capitalist system destroyed the relationship between the individual and his or her own humanity. The individual usually worked on a small part of the finished product; thus, the very nature of production alienated the individual from the product made. The final product belonged to the bourgeois owner of the factory rather than to the many proletarians who had contributed to the finished product. The owners designed the workplace for profit and efficiency, not for the well-being or safety of the workers. In today's terms, Marx probably would say that much of the blue-collar work in his day was not only poorly paid labor but was also dehumanizing, destructive, and inherently meaningless to the individual except for the wages earned. However, he faulted the economic system, not the individuals who paid the price.

A critical question for Marx was why workers did not rebel against the system he saw as exploitative and unfair. He concluded that the proletarians were lulled into complacency by ideas fostered by the ruling class, ideas which explained the inequality as just, necessary, and inevitable. Using a variety of strategies including educational and religious training, the worker was led to believe that the system was necessary and proper. The worker came to believe that this was the way it should be and the only way it could be. Marx called this **false consciousness**. Marx wanted to free the workers from such inaccurate perceptions so that they would rebel, throw off the chains of alienating labor, and understand their true importance in society.

For Marx, the threat of the new order came from the belief that too many people experienced severe deprivations while a comparatively small number lived in excessive luxury. He was appalled at the poverty and powerlessness of the proletarians in contrast to the ever-increasing wealth among the bourgeoisie.

Emile Durkheim and the Threat of Societal Breakdown

Emile Durkheim (1858–1917) was born in France of middle class rural parents. Had he followed the traditional path of his family, he might have become a rabbi like his father and grandfather. But, characteristic of the times, Durkheim set out for a new way of life.

At an early age, Durkheim showed great promise as a student. Initially he entered the university in Paris to study mathematics. However, conditions in France at the time of the Industrial Revolution were unstable, and Durkheim felt that no area of study in the university dealt directly with the problems of society. There were no sociology classes because Comte had failed to gain support for the new discipline. Still, Durkheim took up the cause of sociology after studying Comte's and others' work, and he achieved acceptance for the new discipline. Unlike Marx, who advocated economic and political revolution, Durkheim simply advocated the development of the field of sociology as an academic science.

Durkheim is considered important in the development of another major perspective in sociological theory, functionalism. In many respects, **functionalists** hold a view of society opposite that of conflict theorists. Functionalists see society as a complex system of interdependent parts striving toward balance and harmony. For example, functionalists see the major institutions in society—the family, the school, the economy, and the government—as fulfilling important functions for the survival of the society. A change in one part affects all the others. For instance, a change in the economy has rippling effects on families when the breadwinner is laid off and on schools when taxes and budgets are affected.

Throughout his work, Durkheim's primary concern was the problem of social cohesion in industrial society. How is society going to stay together? Does it seem to you that we are no longer bound together in these times of rapid change? When conditions in society change drastically, Durkheim observed that a situation he called **anomie** developed in which people were lost and had no foundation on which to live. The social ground was shaking.

The breakdown of tradition and social cohesion became the focus of his writings. He felt that, in the past, traditions, common beliefs, and values held individuals and society together. He called this force of tradition and community **mechanical solidarity**. Also, Durkheim believed that the stronger the credo of a religious group, the more unified the group was likely to be, and therefore the better able to provide an environment that would effectively insulate its members from perturbing and frustrating experiences. But the era of traditional religious orientations seemed to be dying, and the participation in common religious rituals and activities that bound people together was less common. There were many religions, and many people in France doubted the necessity of religion altogether. Durkheim questioned whether the end of traditional religions would be a prelude to the breakdown of society's moral community.

However, Durkheim did not view all the effects of the change as negative. He believed the industrial society being built in France would maintain social cohesion through specialization, division of labor, and people's increasing interdependence. He called this complex division of labor **organic solidarity**. People were no longer necessarily linked by common beliefs, but they were linked by economic need for each other. However, the way of life would be very different, and the change to organic solidarity during the Industrial Revolution would be traumatic.

Moreover, Durkheim argued that the disappearance of traditional religion need not herald the dissolution of society. Instead, people would come to see that their interdependence was a function of the social order, as it always had been.

We will have much more to say about Emile Durkheim in this book. He occupies a central place in the development of sociology, and his contributions are worthy of ongoing consideration and evaluation.

Max Weber and the Iron Cage of Modern Bureaucracy

Max Weber (1864–1920) was a German intellectual whose background was upper middle class. His father was a dominating and unemotional Berlin bureaucrat. His mother was a selfless, devout Protestant who suffered some abuse from her husband. Thus, two extremely different influences affected Weber's life. His father represented the new world of modern bureaucracy, and his mother represented religious values that became a significant part of Western culture.

Weber studied a wide range of subjects, particularly law, economics, history, and sociology. He was convinced that one of the deepest trends in the modern world was the trend toward a bureaucratization of all phases of public activity. The basic principle of modern social organization is the reasoned and orderly method of conducting business. Rather than relying on persons of authority, **bureaucracy** relies on rules, regulations, red tape, and positions of authority. He also referred to bureaucracy as **legal rational authority**.

Weber saw bureaucracy being developed. From rule by the traditions of king and church, society changed to rule by bureaucracy. He was well aware of the results that would take place in the social world. Weber believed society would be governed by rational principles allowing little or no room for emotional concerns or individual differences. Social life would be dominated by rules and regulations rather than by people and by personality.

Weber recognized another form of power he called **charismatic power** which occurs when some people have extraordinary gifts and qualities that make others gravitate toward them and want to follow them. Such leaders have personal magnetism and can achieve a great deal as well as gain enormous power. But Weber believed such qualities of leadership are basically irrational and had no place in the rational world of modern bureaucracy.

While understanding the many benefits of bureaucratic organization, Weber also fully appreciated the dangers that bureaucracy presented for personal and intellectual freedom. The people would have to conform to the system of bureaucratic rules which could be stifling, repressive, and inhuman. The system's needs would take precedence over the human needs of people within it. Individual differences would not be a part of the equation. Large-scale corruption, mismanagement, red tape, and abuse of office were also features of the new bureaucratic lifestyle. Weber, however, pointed out that both the bureaucratic and the charismatic means of organization carried potential for social problems. Bureaucracy often creates too strong a sense of the impersonal and the cautious. Charisma opens the door to despotism.

Consequently, Weber dealt with another social problem, resulting from the Industrial Revolution. While Marx was concerned with economic inequality and Durkheim was concerned with the potential breakdown of the social and moral order, Weber was concerned with the transition to the bureaucratic society and the resultant potential pitfalls.

Sociology has a rich legacy of ideas from thinkers such as Comte, Marx, Durkheim, and Weber. In addition, sociology uses different perspectives to analyze elements of society. Two of these perspectives—conflict theory and functionalism—already have been mentioned in the discussions of Marx and Durkheim. However, we turn next to concentrated explanations of conflict theory and functionalism, as well as interaction theory, which has not yet been discussed.

Sociological Perspectives

Sociologists use a variety of perspectives from which to view the social world. It is usually necessary to organize what we see through our sociological eyeglasses. People often use the cliché, "Just give me the facts, ma'am," but facts do not explain themselves. A list of homicide rates from cities around the world might indicate that New York City has ten times the homicide rate of Tokyo. However, the figures do not tell *why* the cities have such dramatically different rates. Something else is needed to explain that Japanese and American cultures contain significantly different attitudes and patterns of interaction regarding violence.

The terms theory and perspective are often confused. **Theories are interrelated statements that attempt to explain.** Theories are attempts to explain a specific set of events such as certain types of crime. In contrast, **perspectives** are ways of seeing and understanding. They are broader in approach than theory. Keep in mind that both theories and perspectives attempt to go beyond description. They attempt to explain. A more detailed example of the major sociological perspectives is given in Research Application 1.2 on drugs in society.

Functionalism

Functionalism grew out of a nineteenth-century tradition that likened society to a living being. Like the human body, society is composed of specialized parts that work together in a complex and balanced system. A change in efficiency in one part of the body, say the lungs, inevitably affects other parts, such as the brain. Today, functionalism retains this emphasis on seeing society as a whole composed of parts.

Functionalists search for the effects the parts have on each other and on the whole. They ask such questions as: Why does this element exist? What role does it play? How does it contribute to stability or instability in the social system? Functionalists have looked at the functions of religion, the family, education, even deviance, assuming that these parts have important effects on the whole of society. You will see discussions of these functions throughout the text. For example, Emile Durkheim (1965 originally published 1912) analyzed the role religion played in maintaining social patterns. He theorized that religion contributed significantly to the stability of society by providing supranatural reinforcement for the group's way of life.

Three basic principles underlie functionalism. First, functionalists believe that every society faces problems that must be solved in order for the group to continue. Families must reproduce and care for their young. The young must be educated and trained to fit in society. Goods and services must be distributed to people through some form of economic system. Societal rules must be enforced by government. The social group must have a set of values that provides common bonds or social glue. In fact, according to functionalists consensus on basic values and beliefs is essential to society.

Second, social life is always in a somewhat precarious position because the various elements in society must be carefully balanced to ensure continuity. If this balance, or equilibrium, is jeopardized, the whole pattern of life may be threatened. When the lungs fail, the human body falters and without life-saving measures, dies. A decline in the educational institution affects the economy by not providing a capable workforce. It also affects government because an uneducated public may not effectively choose leaders or vote wisely. The uneducated, in turn, may not bring up children to be dependable social participants.

Third, social life is a system in equilibrium, and each segment of that system affects that equilibrium; however, each segment does not necessarily make a positive contribution. According to theorist Robert Merton (1968), some parts of the system contribute positively to the balance in society. He called these parts functional to the social system. On the other hand, some parts of the system may disturb the balance in society and are labeled dysfunctional. As an example, think of your college as a social system. It is composed of parts such as the student body, faculty, staff, the registrar's office, and the bookstore. The system must attract and retain students because enrollment is the main source of income. High enrollment is functional to the system. However, if faculty members wanted to increase academic standards and made their classes much more difficult, possibly more students would fail, and lower enrollment would result. The change in academic standards would then disrupt the balance of the system and be labeled dysfunctional.

In order to help you remember the main points of functionalism, keep in mind key words. Functionalists tend to use words such as system, balance, equilibrium, harmony, consensus, continuity, stability, specialization, patterns, common bonds, and social glue.

Given functionalism's emphasis on stability and consensus, these theorists often view change as disruptive to the system, which limits the usefulness of the perspective. In fact, the major criticism of functionalism is that it does not help account for the massive social changes going on in the world. Nor do functionalists necessarily see the need for change. People who use only this perspective tend to be blind to the positive, even essential aspects of social change. Conflict theory, in contrast, makes change a central issue.

The Conflict Perspective

The conflict perspective might be seen as being complementary to functionalist thought. From the conflict point of view, the processes of social life result from intense power struggles among various interest groups in society. Conflict replaces the harmonious balance of functionalism as the dominant aspect of social life. In conflict theory, the basic dynamic of life is the continual competition among groups for scarce rewards in society. To the conflict theorist, functionalism's emphasis on order and consensus is a selective perception that ignores the innumerable instances of conflict ranging from disagreements to outright violent protest. Any glance at the daily news indicates the pervasive nature of conflict in society. Two groups profoundly disagree over the issue of choice in abortion. White students are angry over perceived favoritism toward minorities in scholarship awards. Teachers' unions strike for better salaries and work conditions. Terrorist groups demand political concessions. Out of these conflicts comes social change.

Consider your campus again as an example. Faculty interests often oppose student interests regarding the difficulty of exams, attendance policies, and grading procedures. Students themselves may be divided along lines such as traditional versus nontraditional students, fraternity members versus independents, and commuters versus resident students. Nontraditional students may wish the university would spend money for quality daycare, while traditional students would like money spent for a better student-center theater. The key questions a conflict theorist would ask are "Who has the power to make decisions, and who benefits from these decisions?"

The conflict perspective draws its concept of struggle from the work of Karl Marx as discussed earlier. His original description of the ongoing struggle between classes in society provides the basis for viewing change. Modern conflict theorists have adapted and modified Marx's views to refer to conflicts between ethnic groups, between men and women, between young and old, between liberals and conservatives. To Marx, change inevitably results from these types of social conflicts; society is the stage for a constant power struggle for scarce resources such as money, prestige, and material rewards. Those who have greater control in society use social and political power to maintain a privileged position at the expense of other, less powerful groups. Therefore, dominant groups will exist in most societies. However, other groups inevitably rise to challenge the existing dominant group in order to get for themselves those things valued in society. The civil rights movement brought change as minorities demand equality. The feminist movement stimulated change in schools, the workplace, and in the family as women reacted to inequality.

The key words to watch for in regard to conflict theory are power, competition, inequality, interest groups, dominant groups, protest, authority, and exploitation.

In contrast to functionalism, conflict theory does deal well with social change, but it gives little attention to the fact that there is considerable consensus and stability in society in spite of the competition among groups. However, both theories are similar in one important regard: they take a large-scale view of society and have little to say about everyday interaction among people. They speak of elements of society, group conflict, or societal cohesion. They do not focus on human beings and human interaction. The next theory, symbolic interactionism, brings people back into the equation.

Symbolic Interaction

Interactionists concentrate on the everyday interrelations of people and on how people interpret their lives and the actions of others. Rather than concentrate on the big picture of society the way conflict theorists and functionalists do, interactionists are interested in people's actual behavior, how they develop meaning in life, and how they use language, symbols, and cues to communicate. This perspective is based on the idea that society is built and recreated every day by the interactions of individuals.

Symbolic interactionists delight in observing and accounting for the rich texture of everyday life. They are interested in how fashion, clothes, and hairstyle are used as symbols of communication about the self. They are interested in how close friends keep secrets from one another or in the way a stripper maintains a sense of self-worth in the face of strong social disapproval. They are interested in the way children learn by imitating their parents as they play house. They are interested in how a teenager first learns to smoke marijuana at the urging of friends, and how the friends

A guidance counselor and high school student look over the catalogues of various colleges. In their interaction both will make contributions to the concept of what getting a college education means.

teach him or her to recognize the effects of the drug. They are interested in how salespeople carefully rehearse a speech for customers the way an actor prepares for a stage play. No area of everyday life lacks interest to the symbolic interactionist.

A symbolic interactionist would look at campus life in an entirely different manner than either a functionalist or conflict theorist. The interactionist would want to study the interaction between faculty and students by asking how faculty and students view their respective roles in relation to each other. Do students and faculty put on an act for one another, given traditional expectations and college ritual? Another interactionist might study friendship patterns among students, particularly noting the labels given to different groups such as Greeks, nontraditionals, independents, geeks, brains, and so on. The interactionist would ask how such labels affect the self-image of the individuals. How do students assign status on the basis of labels? How do students nonverbally signify that they are members of one or another group? The interactionist would also notice symbolic communication in the not-so-subtle ways students have of "telling" the teacher it is time for class to end, for instance by rustling books and bags.

Symbolic interaction examines social life on a more personal level with emphasis on how symbols are formed and manipulated to produce routine patterns of interaction. From this view, we can only understand our social world by viewing its development in groups, for groups are essential in forming the individual's sense of self. In these groups, symbols are created which give meaning to social life for the group and which provide individual identity as well as meaningful interaction.

This perspective is based on the work of several important social thinkers. Charles Horton Cooley and George Herbert Mead both thought that the individual self was the product of experience and was constructed as a result of social interaction. (More information about Cooley and Mead can be found in chapter 4.) Both saw the self developing as individuals measured themselves and their behavior against the reactions of others to them.

Symbolic interactionists explain social life through its development in small, intimate groups. Social life results from the dynamic interplay of society and the individual. As the self develops through the manipulation of symbolic meanings, social life is organized and continued interaction is possible. Key words to watch for in regard to the interaction perspective are everyday life, the self, symbols, labeling, role-playing, self-concept, patterns of interaction, rehearsing, and staging behavior.

Symbolic interaction stresses the importance of the individual in social life. People are not merely the result of forces beyond their control. To the interactionist, people actually participate in the shaping of their lives. However, this perspective's rather narrow focus makes it difficult to deal with large-scale organizations and the embedded structures of society with regard to function and conflict.

Finally, it should be noted that throughout the text we will return to these perspectives for insights into social life. It is important that students have a clear, if basic, understanding of these points of view. It is also important to note that, while some sociologists are almost totally committed to one of these perspectives, most find it helpful to view various aspects of life from all three perspectives so they can get a more rounded picture of the phenomena in question. Research Application 1.2 on drugs and society demonstrates the usefulness of using all three.

Research Application 1.2

• • • • • • • Sociological Perspectives and Drug Use

Drug use and abuse are central issues in social life today. Opinion polls indicate that, for a majority of Americans, drugs are *the* central problem of our society, surpassing both general crime and communism. But the "drug problem" is frequently presented in banner headlines, scare stories, and a general aura of near hysteria. Such approaches do not help us solve the problem. Knowing there is a drug problem is one thing; understanding what it is really about is quite another.

Many sociologists are involved in the attempt to understand it. They approach the problem from different theoretical perspectives. Each of the three major points of view allows us to look at a different face of the drug problem.

Functionalism and Drugs

Remember that for functionalists the patterns of society, with their various parts, are seen as existing because they are functional to the ongoing life of the social group. Viewed from this perspective, the main question concerning drugs is whether drug use is functional or dysfunctional to the social system. The use of so-called recreational drugs, such as alcohol and marijuana, may help people relax and interact with one another more comfortably and, therefore, may be considered functional. Licit (legal) drugs, such as tranquilizers prescribed for the mentally ill, serve not only personal but economic functions. The introduction of mind-altering tranquilizers has enabled our society to reduce the number of patients in state and federal mental hospitals. Although many contend that patients are released too quickly and not given proper community care, others argue that a considerable amount of money is saved that could result in lower taxes or, more likely, in the use of this money for other publically-financed projects. Drug abuse can even serve the positive function of helping us define the limits of deviance: how much can or will our society tolerate in the way of misuse of what drugs?

Generally, though, drug use (seen simply as abuse) is defined as dysfunctional to the system and to smooth social life. In some cases even simple use of the drug may interfere with social functioning, as in the case of driving after using alcohol. Addiction to alcohol or other drugs obviously results in social loss; it also can result in economic loss to the system. Addicts to do not "pull their own weight" in the business of keeping society going and, further, use up valuable resources. Notice that functionalism does not focus on individual addict's problem but on the way in which addiction affects the balance in society.

Conflict Theory

Conflict theorists do not see a harmonious society but one in conflict over the "goodies" of power, prestige, property, and psychic gratification. From this perspective, a significant question concerning drugs has to do with how certain drugs come to be defined as bad (and illegal) or good (and legal). The actual effects and consequences of the drugs themselves appear to have little to do with the perception of their danger and the subsequent need to legislate against them.

Alcohol and nicotine, for example, are both highly addicting and account for far more deaths and much more injury than all of the illicit drugs combined. Yet they are not only legal but, in general, socially approved. They are the drugs most frequently used by members of the powerful elites in society and therefore are not defined as evil. Other drugs—cocaine, heroin, marijuana—originally were used by less-favored groups in society, groups which were potential economic and political threats to the established social order. These drugs are defined as bad and their use is illegal. Conflict theorists contend that this is so because the people who traditionally use them are not among the powerful elite and criminality is a way to keep these people "in their place."

For example, opium use was imported to this country by Chinese laborers brought here to help build railroads in the West. As long as their labor was needed for this task, opium smoking and opium dens were tolerated; it kept the laborers satisfied and quiet. However, the railroads were eventually completed and Chinese labor no longer needed for that purpose. The Chinese were still here, but now they comprised a labor pool in direct competition with the white working class. In such places as San Francisco, where there was a large Chinese population, considerable antagonism developed against the Chinese laborers, especially since they were willing to work for lower wages. To reduce the ability of Chinese to compete, cities on the West Coast began to pass laws making opium use illegal. Conflict theorists assert that these laws were aimed not at the drug but at the Chinese who used it. It made use a crime and the Chinese users criminal—and hence not employable.

Symbolic Interactionism

From the perspective of symbolic interaction, anything can be used as a symbol; symbols develop meaning through social interaction. Drugs, then, are viewed in terms of the way social groups perceive them. They can be used as symbols of almost anything so that the meaning of use and abuse lies in how they are defined in social life.

For many people today, alcohol use is a symbol of maturity and sophistication. This was not the case in the early part of this century when, for the dominant Protestant elite, alcohol use symbolized an improper lifestyle. Why? Again, the issue was not really the drug, alcohol. The real issue behind the movement that brought about Prohibition was the attempt to maintain the values, lifestyles, and dominance of rural Protestant America. These were threatened by the immigration into the country of Catholics and other groups who did not share the value system that had prevailed in the United States since its founding. In many cases, the new immigrants were Catholic rather than Protestant, and they were concentrated in urban areas where they displayed a lifestyle radically different from American tradition.

How could rural Protestant values be protected and remain dominant? The dominant group enacted into law a particular value—abstinence from alcohol. Abstinence became a symbol of respectability, hard work, and achievement orientation while drinking symbolized the opposite. The Volstead Act, which amended the Constitution to prohibit alcohol, became a very visible symbol of the continuing power of the old elite. Alcohol's effect as a drug was not the question. It was the symbolic nature of abstinence or use that was important.

Summary

In reading the above you may have found it difficult to totally distinguish between the views on drugs taken by the three theoretical perspectives. That is not surprising. There are similarities among them. The emphasis in each case, however, is different. The fact that similarities exist should tell us that it is really useful to look at our social world from each of these perspectives in order to get a full view.

Questions for Summary and Review

1. Explain how college students today are different from those in the 1960s. How did the times in which the students lived affect their personal lives?
2. Explain how C. Wright Mills's sociological imagination can help individuals understand themselves and the world around them.
3. Define sociology, and explain the special way the discipline looks at the social world.
4. How did the Industrial Revolution stimulate the development of sociology?
5. How is the Industrial Revolution similar to the times in which we now live?
6. What are the main contributions to sociology of Auguste Comte, Kark Marx, Emile Durkheim, and Max Weber?
7. Choose some aspect of social life, such as professional sports, and analyze it using the functionalist, conflict, and symbolic interactionist perspectives. Use Research Application 1.2 to help you.

Key Concepts

Alienation (p. 10)
Anomie (p. 11)
Auguste Comte (p. 8)
Bourgeoisie (p. 10)
Bureaucracy (p. 12)
Charismatic power (p. 12)
Conflict perspective (p. 10)

Dysfunctional (p. 14)
Emile Durkheim (p. 11)
False consciousness (p. 10)
Functional (p. 14)
Functionalism (p. 11)
Industrial Revolution (p. 7)
Karl Marx (p. 9)

Legal rational authority (p. 12)
Max Weber (p. 12)
Mechanical solidarity (p. 11)
Organic solidarity (p. 11)
Proletariat (p. 10)

Scientific method (p. 9)
Sociology (p. 5)
Sociological imagination (p. 6)
Symbolic interaction (p. 17)

References

1. Astin, Alexander W., K.C. Green, and W.S. Korn. 1987. *The American freshman: Twenty year trends.* University of California, Los Angeles: Higher Education Research Institute.

2. Berger, Peter. 1963. *Invitation to sociology: A humanistic perspective.* Garden City, N.Y.: Anchor Books.

3. Berger, Peter, and Hansfried Kellner. 1981. *Sociology reinterpreted: An essay on method and vocation.* Garden City, N.Y.: Anchor Books.

4. *Chronicle of Higher Education.* 1989. Survey of freshmen finds a growing level of stress caused by anxieties about money and status. (January 11):A32–A34.

5. Cooperative Institutional Research Program. 1989. *1988 Freshman survey results.* University of California, Los Angeles: American Council on Education.

6. Durkheim, Emile. 1965. *The elementary forms of the religious life.* New York: The Free Press.

7. Innerst, Carol. 1987. Freshmen: A study in unreadiness. *Insight* 3:58–59.

8. Merton, Robert K. 1968. *Social theory and social structure.* New York: The Free Press.

9. Mills, C. Wright. 1959. *The sociological imagination.* New York: Oxford University Press.

Researching Social Life 2

Chapter Outline

Suppose you take a summer job in a beef slaughterhouse because you need the extra money. You find the smell horrible and the job monotonous, dangerous, and dehumanizing. Although many workers claim they do not like the work, they have been there for years. Why do they stay?

In a history class studying Hitler's Third Reich, the instructor points out that many Nazi war criminals did not accept blame for the atrocities they committed in concentration camps because they were only following orders. Would very many people hurt someone if their bosses so instructed them?

Suppose you read an article in the newspaper about a man who is despondent over the loss of his job and commits suicide. The newspaper reporter concentrates on the man's emotional and personal crises. But this does not help you understand the approximately twenty-five thousand suicides that occur every year in the United States.

Sociologists are endlessly asking questions about social phenomena such as those above, which we will address later in this chapter. The sociological perspectives discussed in chapter 1 can help provide answers, but sociologists also need observations, data, and facts. With data, sociologists, like other scientists, can evaluate perspectives, develop and test theories, and provide some answers to the thousands of questions about life. The purpose of this chapter is to examine how sociologists get their data, how social research can be evaluated, and how students can apply this knowledge in their everyday life.

The Scientific Method

Auguste Comte's original definition of sociology as the science of society indicates that science has always been a fundamental aspect of sociology. The principles of research in sociology are based on the scientific method developed in other disciplines. The **scientific method** sets forth as its premise the idea that science is empirical, objective, tentative, and based on the principle of cause and effect.

First, science is, by its very nature, **empirical**. Empiricism means study based on observation. Scientific principles must be generated from data, not just from logic, thought, tradition, or common sense. In scientific study, all ideas must be tested through research and observation. However, not everything is accessible through observation (spiritual truths, for example); consequently, science cannot answer some questions.

Second, science strives to be **objective**. The scientist must take every possible precaution to avoid imposing his or her own values, judgments, prejudices, or personal wishes on the investigation. Personal bias is a particular concern for sociologists because often they must deal with emotionally-charged issues such as abortion, child abuse, rape, family stability, and many others. It is critical for sociologists to be aware of their own biases and their potential effect on their work.

Third, science is **tentative**. Nothing may be considered to be true without testing, retesting, evaluation, and continued research. Scientific results must always be open to question. Dogmatic acceptance of an idea runs counter to the ideal of science even though it is difficult to resist. The tentative and skeptical nature of science allows for progress, open-mindedness, and continual questioning and testing.

Finally, science is based on the principle of **cause and effect**. Fundamental to science is the belief that things do not occur randomly. There is order in the universe, and that order can be uncovered if searched out systematically. For something to occur, science holds that causes must have preceded the occurrence.

For the most part, the discipline of sociology adheres to these fundamental aspects of the scientific method. It is primarily the subject matter of sociology that differs from the natural sciences. Human beings are not necessarily as consistent in their behavior as other objects of scientific study. People are self-aware, they can make choices, and they can reflect upon events. As a result, any absolutes, such as the speed of light in physics, are hard to come by in the social sciences.

Just being observed or being part of an experiment may change people's behavior. The term **Hawthorne Effect** was coined to refer to the influence of the researcher on the subjects' behavior. The term originated during a study of the bank wiring room, an assembly line area in the Western Electrical Plant (Roethlisberger and Dickson 1939). Researchers were brought in to find a way to improve the productivity of the workers. They found that increasing the lighting improved productivity; but, to be safe, they decreased the lighting to see if productivity declined again. It did not. Finally, the researchers discovered that the workers were pleased to be "experimented on," to receive this kind of attention, and this was the main reason for the increase in their productivity.

Another concern in social science research involves necessary ethical restraints. Because the subjects of study are human, researchers must adhere to a rigorous and effective code of ethics controlling what they can and cannot do. Humiliating subjects, lying to subjects, or harming them in any way must never be tolerated in sociological research.

Sociology is a highly complex field because the study of people presents unique circumstances. The subject matter of sociology is people who are sense-making beings, unlike the subject matter of physics or chemistry. As symbolic interactionists have pointed out, sociologists must be alert to people's interpretation of things and to the meanings people assign. While the incorporation of the scientific method contributes a great deal to the study of people, it is not perfect. Remember that what you read about in this book is based upon knowledge obtained by the scientific method, rather than based on the personal beliefs of those who have obtained them. Thus it is essential, before you continue in this book, to get an overview of the methods of research used in sociology. How do sociologists get their information, and how reliable is it? The following section addresses these questions.

Methods of Research in Sociology

Much like detective work, sociological research requires creativity, careful attention to detail, logic, hard work, and long hours, but the endless possibilities for conducting research on social life make it an exciting enterprise. In this section, we will give a brief overview of four major ways to get information about people and society. Later, we give an overview of the entire research process in Research Method 2.1.

The mysteries of social behavior require more than one approach to unlock them. Each of the methods discussed here has both advantages and disadvantages and each lends itself to certain, but not all, tasks. In each of the following chapters, research method topics will detail specific methods of research by describing a specific sociological study applying one of those methods. In that way you, as students, will be reminded throughout the semester of the importance of research and of how it is conducted. The following should only be considered a brief introduction to research techniques.

Participant Observation

One way of getting information about a group of people or a social situation is to systematically observe it as it exists in the real world. All of us can act as participant observers in life, whether we watch people in the student center, in church, in the street, or at a party. It is an intuitively easy method to understand.

The premise of **participant observation** is that "in order to know our subjects, whether they be prostitutes or presidents, delinquents or Druids, popes or pimps, we must see them where they live and enter, as best we can, into their round of life" (Guy, Edgley, Arafat, and Allen 1987, 256). The participant observer must take care to approach the situation with reasonable objectivity and to systematically record, through notes or tapes, what is happening. Of course, there are varying degrees of participation. For some researchers, it may mean only a few months observing and talking with people in a bar; for others it may mean devoting two years of their lives to the research.

A good example of participant observation is William Thompson's (1983) study of work in a beef processing plant, where people must cope with dangerous, boring, routinized factory work. Thompson took the job for a summer to investigate factory life from the inside. He let the workers know that he was a sociologist who needed extra money, but he did not specifically say he was conducting a study. He was a complete participant in that he was a full-time worker like anyone else.

Hells Angels are a
good example of a
nonconforming group
not easily studied by
traditional research
methods. Here they
gather near a club in
New York to raise
money for their legal
defense fund.

By doing the same work and interacting daily with the "beefers," Thompson gained considerable insight into their lives and their views of the world. He discovered how they dealt with others' perception of beef processing as dirty work. He found that the workers minimized the smell and the blood, as well as the ever-present danger of major accidents or death. Workers daydreamed, joked around with other workers, and occasionally sabotaged the assembly line or the product in order to combat the excruciating monotony, physical exhaustion, dehumanization, and danger of their work, which consisted of processing 187 head of cattle per hour. Most important, Thompson discovered that, while many workers left after the first week, those who stayed caught themselves in a financial trap. They said they took the job for the summer to save up money to go to school, but they often stayed for twenty years or more. They trapped themselves by buying expensive status symbols such as motorcycles and stereos. The more they bought, the longer they had to keep the job to pay the bills.

One of the major advantages of participant observation is the firsthand nature of the research. Social scientists are fortunate in that they can identify with their subjects more so than can natural scientists. Field observation allows the researcher to "identify the distinctly human concerns of human beings, their feelings, emotions, loves, hates, and jealousies" (Guy et al. 1987, 255). Participant observation allows the researcher to gain a deeper understanding of the subjects. On the practical side, participant observation can be relatively inexpensive to conduct, and it is flexible in meeting the needs of the project (Babbie 1989, 285).

Another advantage is that, when using this approach, the sociologist can reach offbeat, unusual, nonconforming, or isolated groups. Such groups often refuse to take part in other forms of sociological research. Some classical sociological works have been participant observations of variant groups. William Foote Whyte (1955) and Elliot Liebow (1967) studied urban street corner men. In a controversial work, Laud Humphreys (1975) studied homosexual encounters in public restrooms. John Lofland (1966) spent the better part of two years with a religious cult in California in order to study how they converted new members.

There are, however, several disadvantages to participant observation. Foremost, the objectivity of field observation is often questioned. Can a researcher resist getting so involved with the subjects that he or she loses the ability to remain emotionally detached? Can the researcher keep his or her own biases and opinions from coloring the report? Certainly, the answers to these questions depend upon individual circumstances in each study, but safeguards can also be used to minimize subjectivity. The researcher can ask for input from other sociologists and can take care to distinguish empathy from sympathy. No piece of sociological research is going to be totally objective; we simply have less assurance with regard to this method (Babbie 1989, 286–288).

Another disadvantage of participant observation is that it is often limited in scope. It is difficult to conduct a massive participant observation of thousands of people. It is also difficult to generalize, with certainty, the results to other places, other times, and other people. For example, there is no guarantee that the results of John Lofland's study of a religious cult in California in 1966 would be the same as those of a study in Oregon in 1992. However, participant observation is useful in that its exploration of social life can offer direction to later research on the same topic and it can aid in generating theories or explanations about social life (Babbie 1989, 261).

The Laboratory Experiment

A second method of research used in sociology is the classic **laboratory experiment** conducted in an artificial setting, the laboratory. Almost any place can be a laboratory: a basement, a classroom, an office, or a highly sophisticated, technologically advanced set of rooms. The important point is that, unlike participant observation, the research does not take place in the real world of everyday life. The laboratory setting allows the researcher tremendous control over the conditions of the experiment. He or she can control who becomes a subject in the research, what the subjects experience, and how they experience it. The subjects can be carefully monitored and observed under the conditions set forth by the researcher.

Normally, the experiment includes two groups of subjects. Those who experience some condition, such as viewing a series of advertisements, are called the **experimental group**. Those who do not experience the condition are called the **control group**. Comparisons between the two groups often form the basis of a classic laboratory experiment. In the advertising example, the two groups would be compared on purchasing practices for the next week. However, depending on the design of the research, it is not necessary to have an experimental and control group. The following example of a laboratory experiment does not strictly have both groups; nevertheless, it is considered a classic in social science research.

In the 1960s, Stanley Milgram (1974) conducted an ingenious set of experiments testing obedience to authority. Over a period of time and using almost a thousand men who volunteered as subjects, Milgram systematically studied people's willingness to obey an authority figure who would bring harm to another person.

Milgram initially deceived the subjects by stating that the experiment was to test punishment's effect on learning. Will a person learn faster if threatened with an electric shock? The subject was to act as a teacher and was instructed to give a student an electrical shock whenever the student gave a wrong answer. The teacher-subject was seated at a set of control levers giving shocks up to 450 volts (noted "Danger: Severe Shock" on the controls.)

In one variation of the experiment, the student was put in another room, but the subject could hear the student cry out in pain, beg, and refuse to continue. In some cases, the student was said to have a heart condition. In reality, of course, the student was a **confederate** of Milgram's, someone working with the researcher unbeknown to the subjects. The confederate was not being shocked at all but was carefully told how to act out pain. The confederate-student was also instructed to be wrong enough times to force the subject to go all the way to 450 volts of electricity. Although many subjects anguished over hurting the student and said they could not do it, Milgram simply said, "The experiment requires that you go on" (1972, p. 339).

In Milgram's study, the experimenter represented authority. Much to Milgram's amazement and dismay, most of the subjects proceeded to go all the way to 450 volts even after hearing screams of agony from the student. In fact, 62.5 percent of the subjects were obedient to the researcher, although most of the subjects were considerably upset. After the experiment, Milgram debriefed the subjects, explained that no shocks were given, and told them that the real reason for the research was to study obedience. Professional counseling was available if the subjects needed it.

Milgram's research is an excellent example of what can be accomplished in a laboratory setting. The experiments tell us something about the context of behavior and how we define personal responsibility if someone in authority directs us to hurt others. As Milgram (1972, 327) himself said, "The situation in which one agent commands another to hurt a third turns up time and again as a significant theme in human relations. It is powerfully expressed in the story of Abraham, who is commanded by God to kill his son." Yet one serious question in Milgram's work is how it reflects social situations and pressures of authority in everyday life as opposed to a laboratory at Yale University.

The major advantage of an experiment lies in the control it gives the researcher. Compare this with the lack of control experienced by the participant observer, who must take life as it comes and may have to wait for things to happen. The experiment makes things happen. As a result, another advantage of the experiment is that it usually takes much less time. It is also less expensive than many other forms of

Using the survey
research method, a
market analyst
interviews a customer
in a Somerville,
Massachusetts
shopping mall. These
surveys are
increasingly common
in modern society.

social science research. In addition, experiments are easier to replicate (repeat the research with different groups of people) than most other research in sociology (Babbie 1989, 232–233). Finally, experiments are usually considered to be more objective than participant observation and other methods. The rigorous control and observation in an experiment help check the researcher's bias. Experiments are certainly not totally objective; researchers can indirectly influence their subjects in hundreds of ways (recall the Hawthorne Effect). Just the fact that people know they are part of an experiment can change their behavior. Nevertheless, experiments attempt to minimize bias by careful attention to detail and by scrupulous, statistical measurement.

The disadvantages of the experimental approach are significant in sociology. The major drawback is the artificiality of the laboratory and whether people's behavior in a university basement will be the same in the real world. In addition, experiments are limited in the number of subjects that can be included. As you will see, some research involves thousands of people, a number of people impossible to deal with in a laboratory. Finally, the experimental method is limited in scope for some central topics in sociology. For example, it is not possible to study the causes of poverty in America or the factors leading to a riot or a mass panic in a laboratory experiment. On the other hand, like all of the methods, the experiment has its important place in research. The logic and rigor of a well-designed, controlled experiment can go a long way in providing us with answers to the riddles of human behavior.

Survey Research

Most of us are familiar to some extent with survey research because it has become so prevalent in modern society. The U.S. government surveys the nation every ten years for the census report; politicians hire pollsters to tell about public attitudes and preferences; corporations use market surveys to test a new product; and the Nielsen Company surveys television viewers to find out which programs they watch.

Surveys are the most common method used in sociology because they can reach huge numbers and varieties of people. A **survey** is defined as the wide distribution of either questionnaires or interviews designed to get certain data from people. A **questionnaire** is a written set of questions which can be mailed or passed out to individuals. An **interview** is conducted in a face-to-face or telephone conversation with respondents.

The logic of surveys rests on the assumptions of random sampling. If researchers want to know about the drinking patterns of all adult Americans, it is not necessary to survey all of them. A sample of five or ten percent should reflect the values of all if that sample is selected randomly. For a sample to be a **random sample**, every

Research Application 2.1

• • • • • • Polls and Television Ratings

How do major network television executives decide which programs will remain on the air? They rely, in part, on national polls, a form of survey research. Public opinion polls are used by hundreds of organizations including the major network news agencies, newspapers, and news magazines. In political polls for these organizations, the results from fewer than two thousand respondents are used to predict who will win a presidential race. Such predictions are usually accurate within two or three percentage points (Babbie 1989, 163).

In producing Nielsen Ratings (technically referred to as Television Audience Research ratings), the Nielsen Company measures the size of the audience for a variety of TV shows. The company also details the age, sex, and education of people who watch various TV programs. However, nearly ninety million households in the United States have televisions (about ninety-eight percent of total households), and it would be quite impractical to survey even twenty percent of them. Consequently, in an average week the Nielsen Company surveys four thousand households, a tiny fraction of one percent of all U.S. households (Nielsen Media Research 1987).

Nielsen Company publications are careful to point out that the ratings do not measure the quality of TV programming. The numbers simply indicate what percentage of the sample watched all or part of a particular program. For example, a rating of seventeen for an evening program means that seventeen percent of the households had watched the TV show (Nielsen Media Research 1987, 9).

Advertisers are especially interested in various social characteristics, such as the income brackets, of those watching the programs because it helps them reach particular markets for products. Advertising revenue is a major factor in a television program's longevity.

Although the public is often skeptical about the accuracy of Nielsen ratings, the company is adamant in asserting that their careful random sampling provides more than adequate measures for the entire population. What is important is that the major network executives believe in the ratings and that advertisers across the nation buy TV time according to the ratings.

• • • • • • •

person in the larger population must have an equal chance of being selected; that is, the sample should be representative of the population at large. Consequently, any bias toward certain types or people should be eliminated or controlled.

At first, it may seem unlikely that a few thousand people would reflect millions of others, but the sophistication of sampling and polling today indicates its accuracy. For example, the network news organizations have become very proficient at sampling voting precincts and accurately projecting who will win a presidential election. The value of random sampling used in survey research by sociologists lies in its ability to represent vast numbers of people.

We will use a national study of family violence by Richard Gelles and Murray Straus (1988) as an example of survey research. It is no easy task to choose a sample that accurately reflects all United States families. Nor is it easy to get all the chosen family members to answer detailed questions about their private lives. However, through monumental efforts these researchers came close to their goals.

With help from the well-known national opinion research firm, Louis Harris and Associates, the researchers selected a nationally representative sample of 6,002 people to interview by telephone. The people were selected by randomly choosing telephone numbers from a library of telephone directories from throughout the fifty states of the U.S. They also selected an additional 508 black and 516 Hispanic households because these groups too often are underrepresented in surveys. About 84 percent of those selected cooperated with the researchers by answering up to 125 questions over the telephone in an average of thirty-five minutes. The questions asked were very detailed, structured questions about family life.

While their efforts resulted in a national sample, it was certainly not perfectly random because it was limited to those households with a telephone or with a listed telephone number (Gelles and Straus 1988, 209–212). Few studies can reach the perfection of random sampling, and many researchers settle for having a **representative sample** of the population. Representative means that the sample is similar in characteristics to the total population.

The results of Gelles and Straus's structured telephone interviews showed that slightly less than two percent of parents had violently abused their children. Slightly more than three percent of wives experienced severe beatings by husbands, while more than four percent of husbands experienced severe violence at the hands of their wives (Gelles and Straus 1988, 109). Surprisingly, when Gelles and Straus compared the results with those of their 1980 national survey on family violence (Straus, Gelles, and Steinmetz 1980), they found that both child abuse and spouse abuse had declined significantly. They speculated that, with the increase in negative attitudes and legal penalties regarding family violence, people were less likely to admit committing such violent acts, even to a researcher. They also noted that the previous research had been conducted in face-to-face interviews, and the change to telephone interviewing may have caused a change in the results.

The Gelles and Straus study indicates the breadth of survey research as well as the usefulness of the empirical approach in sociology. Before such research, many people would not believe that family violence was prevalent in our society. And yet, the results of such a study must remain tentative. Much more work in the area of family abuse is necessary; in fact, such research must be ongoing to keep pace with our changing society and family system.

The major advantage of survey research is its capacity to reach large numbers of people relatively quickly across a broad geographic area. A second major advantage is its ability to be representative of even larger numbers. Third, if surveys are highly standardized, the bias of the researchers can be minimized. Finally, surveys are especially well-suited for describing the characteristics of a large population. For example, surveys can efficiently tell us the marital status, age, sex, race, socioeconomic background, occupation, and income for millions of people.

The drawbacks of survey research are especially important to consider because this method is used so much in sociology. First, there is always the question of cooperation and motivation among respondents. Lack of cooperation can destroy a painstakingly chosen random sample. For example, if questionnaires are mailed to individuals, many will not return them. The respondents might not be motivated to fully answer the surveys or to give it the amount of thought necessary. Second, if the survey depends on the respondents' memories, then there is always the question of accuracy. In addition, people may not be willing to tell the truth, especially if the survey is very personal in nature, such as the case with family violence, despite the guarantee of anonymity. Third, surveys may be incredibly expensive to carry out. Interviewing more than six thousand people takes money, time, a large staff, and computer time, all of which can cost a great deal. The Gelles and Straus study cost more than $600,000 (Gelles and Straus 1988, 108). Finally, surveys are not always as penetrating as other methods. "Surveys are poor approximations of direct observations" (Guy et al. 1987, 250). For example, asking twenty or even two hundred questions about a couple's marital life does not necessarily delve deeply into their daily marital exchanges and experiences. Consequently, surveys are not enough if we want to get a full portrait of human societies.

The Use of Existing Data

The last of our four research methods, the **use of existing data**, is used more often today than ever before. Rather than go out and collect new data, a researcher may choose from a variety of material already available. Song lyrics, newspapers, magazines, television advertisements, trade journals, and, especially, government statistics provide a wealth of potential data for social researchers.

For a moment, imagine the amount of governmental data that exists about U.S. citizens. The census has been on record since 1890. Records of births and deaths, tax records, educational records, police records, city and county records, hospital records, FBI data on crimes and arrests, prison records, and personnel data are only a few among the many sources of information about people and society. A researcher may never have to leave the library, yet be able to put together a thorough analysis of crime rates over the past twenty years.

One of the best examples of a thorough analysis of existing data is also one of the earliest pieces of sociological research. Emile Durkheim's (1951, originally 1897) massive study of suicide in European societies at the turn of the century captures the essence and strength of analyzing existing data. Painstakingly, Durkheim collected data from governmental sources and analyzed the suicide rates over time. He also compared the suicide rates of certain social categories such as men and women, different age groups, and religious groups.

Durkheim discovered that men killed themselves four times more often than women, that Protestants killed themselves more often than Catholics, and that age groups varied in suicide rates. After analyzing the data, he explained his results by relying on a theory of suicide based on one's integration into social life and on the societal conditions of the times. (Recall Durkheim's concern with social breakdown discussed in chapter 1).

Computers have changed almost every aspect of life in contemporary society and have become a major factor in the conduct of social research. Such technology allows sociologists to deal with larger samples and to use more sophisticated statistical measures.

Durkheim theorized that individuals who were not sewn into the fabric of a social group were more likely to commit suicide. For example, single people, older people, and people without a strong involvement in a religious group had higher rates of suicide. He called this type of suicide **egoistic suicide** because it had to do with the self and lack of integration into a social group.

On the other hand, Durkheim discovered that a very strong integration into the group can also lead to higher suicide rates, a tendency he called **altruistic suicide**. For example, Japanese society traditionally has had a relatively high suicide rate because of the tremendous pressures to be a part of a group and not shame that group. Giving up one's life for the group was defined as honorable. The kamikaze pilots of World War II who intentionally crashed their planes into enemy ships were given high honor and respect by others. Their suicides were condoned and grew out of high group integration.

Finally, based on his data, Durkheim defined a third type of suicide which he called **anomic suicide**. Durkheim considered anomie a condition in society in which the equilibrium of the social world is upset. It comes about when too much change "pulls the rug out" from under people. Society must have a controlling effect on people; when that control is weakened, people are more likely to feel lost. The sense of being lost is strongest during any period of great change whether the change is for the better or for the worse. Examples of upsets in societal equilibrium include great financial disasters such as the stock market crash in 1929 and periods of great social change occurring in times of revolution. As Durkheim (1951, 246) put it, "Whenever serious readjustments take place in the social order, whether or not due to a sudden growth or to an unexpected catastrophe, men are more inclined to self-destruction."

Clearly, Durkheim's work is a remarkable achievement in using existing statistics. In addition, the empirical basis of *Suicide* was a springboard to a set of theoretical ideas that have had lasting impact in the field of sociology.

The major advantage of using existing data is the economy of time and money. In comparison to survey research, which can be enormously expensive, the use of existing data is quite inexpensive. Surveys require a great deal of time from the researchers, particularly if they are going to interview thousands of people; using existing data does not require such a monumental commitment of time. A second advantage of existing data is that it allows the researcher to do historical research and to compare the present with the past. For example, European suicide rates could be examined for nearly a hundred years in order to trace any changes over time.

The disadvantages of using existing data are significant. Most important, the existing data may be of questionable accuracy; one rarely knows for sure. For example, a continual problem with suicide figures is that some suicides are covered up to protect the family, or it may be impossible to know if an overdose of pills was accidental or intentional. Second, the existing data may not have exactly what the researcher needs. In a study of prison sentences researchers may know the length of an inmate's sentence, but that does not tell them how long the inmate will actually stay in prison because he or she may be granted parole at an undetermined time. Finally, relying on existing data distances the researcher from the social world as it is played out on a daily level. Studying people in the real world is a must for sociologists, a reminder of the value of participant observation. Nevertheless, using existing data is an important contribution to empirical research.

The four research methods discussed above are not the only methods in sociology, and you will see others in the research methods sections in each of the following chapters. For example, **content analysis** is a method under the heading of existing data. It is a specialized form of research analyzing any form of communication such as letters, diaries, country music lyrics, or modern poetry. Content analyses can provide considerable insight into social life. An example of it is on page 319. Other Research Method sections are listed in Table 2.1, in case your instructor wishes to discuss them in the context of this chapter.

●**Table 2.1**   List of Research Methods Illustrated in Chapter Features

●**Table 2.1**   List of Research Methods Illustrated in Chapter Features—*continued*

Finally, it is important not to view these methods as mutually exclusive. Often the best sociological research incorporates several different methods to get a full picture of some situation or phenomenon. It is also important to put these research methods in the context of the overall research process. Research Method 2.1 outlines the research process in sociology. You should study it carefully. Also, as you read each of the chapters in this text, take note of the Research Methods and Research Applications sections; they will give you a good feel for the way sociologists work.

Research Method 2.1

• • • • • • • **Stages in a Research Project**

Has the Double Standard for Men and Women Disappeared?

Because the scientific method requires careful procedures in conducting research, sociologists are expected to follow a standard blueprint in research, generally consisting of seven stages. These stages will be illustrated using research by Susan Sprecher, Kathleen McKinney, and Terri Orbuch (1987) on the double standard concerning male and female sexual behavior.

Stage 1: Choosing and Defining the Topic for Research

Sociologists are naturally curious, and thousands of questions are available for research. The difficulty is in narrowing the topic of study to a manageable form. It is of utmost importance to be clear and precise in defining terms. Such precise definitions, specifically created for research, are called **operational definitions.** Sprecher, McKinney, and Orbuch chose the double standard as their topic. However, they noted that the traditional double standard condemned premarital sex for women under any circumstances. The researchers felt that this definition of the double standard no longer applied since premarital sex had become common for both sexes. In fact, other sociologists had declared that the double standard was dead. Sprecher, McKinney, and Orbuch did not think that <u>all</u> types of double standards had disappeared. They were careful to restrict their topic to the "conditional double standard" which accepts premarital intercourse for both sexes but restricts women from engaging in the variety of sexual behavior allowed men. Men would not be condemned as much as women for having a variety of sexual partners before marriage or for having sex at an early age. Consequently, they operationalized their topic by carefully defining the conditional double standard.

Stage 2: Reviewing the Literature

It would be foolish to research any topic without first reading as much as can be found about the subject. The purpose of reviewing theories, other studies, textbooks, newspaper articles, and government data is to develop expertise on the topic. It is essential to know how other researchers have defined the subject, what results have been found in the past, and what other researchers have suggested for further study. Sprecher, McKinney, and Orbuch listed twenty-four books and articles that they reviewed. The first two pages of their eight-page article are devoted to reviewing the background literature and discussing previous studies going back to 1959.

Stage 3: Developing Hypotheses

Another purpose of reviewing the literature is to develop **hypotheses,** which are simply statements that the researcher expects to prove or disprove in the study. Hypotheses are like roadmaps: they serve as guides which give the researcher direction. Each hypothesis consists of an independent and a dependent variable. A **variable** is anything that changes or varies. Sex, age, marital status, crime rates all can vary and can serve as variables. An **independent variable** is used to explain a change in the dependent variable. The **dependent variable** is what the researcher is trying to explain. Independent variables are used to explain dependent variables. For example, if we speculate that studying produces higher grades, studying is the independent variable while grades are the dependent variable.

Sprecher, McKinney, and Orbuch developed two hypotheses. First, people will evaluate a woman more negatively if her first sexual experience is in a casual rather than a steady relationship, whereas the evaluations of a male would be less affected by the kind of relationship in which first intercourse occurs. Second, evaluations of a female will be more negative if she first engages in sex at an early age than they will be for a male who does the same. In both hypotheses, evaluations are the dependent variables. In the first, type of relationship (casual versus steady) is the independent variable. In the second, age of first intercourse is the independent variable.

It is important to note that not all sociological research includes this stage. Some projects, particularly those using participant observation, are more exploratory, and researchers will not want to confine themselves to specific hypotheses.

Stage 4: Choosing a Method of Research

The researchers now ask which method is most appropriate for the subject matter and which is most feasible given time and money constraints. Often it is best to use several methods. Sprecher, McKinney, and Orbuch decided on an experimental design. They devised a way to get subjects to evaluate a series of stories relating the first sexual experiences of various people. The sexual histories were designed to reflect differences in types of relationships and age in order to test the two hypotheses. The subjects would think they were evaluating real people's sexual histories. The experiment would be conducted in classrooms so that the researchers could maintain considerable control.

Stage 5: Collecting the Data

With the project carefully planned, the three researchers were ready to perform the experiment. The subjects included 320 females and 233 males at Oklahoma State University and the University of Wisconsin. The experiment took place in introductory and upper-level sociology classes so that freshmen through seniors would be represented. However, the researchers made no claim that their sample was random. The average age of the students was twenty-one.

As the experiment began, the students were told that they were reading a page from a high school or college student's personal questionnaire on sexual history. As part of a cover story to make the situation seem real, the subjects also were told that the impressions they formed of the student would be compared with actual information provided later. This, of course, was untrue since the researchers made up the sexual histories.

Stage 6: Processing and Reporting the Results

Sprecher, McKinney, and Orbuch next set about the complicated phase of analyzing the student responses collected during the experiment. Using statistical techniques, the researchers compared the evaluations of the fictional sexual histories to see if the college students negatively evaluated females who engaged in casual sex or sex at an early age. The data analysis indicated that actually males and females both were evaluated more negatively if their first sexual encounter was casual or at a young age. However, females were *more* negatively evaluated than males.

The data indicated, to some extent, support for the idea that a conditional double standard does exist. Next, the three researchers wrote up the report and sent it to a journal to be reviewed for publication. This process often takes months. If accepted, it is usually several more months before the article is published. In this case, the article was accepted by a prestigious journal published by the *American Sociological Association*.

Stage 7: Evaluating the Project and Suggesting Future Research

As part of their report, researchers are expected to clearly state the problems and drawbacks of their efforts. No research is perfect, and researchers often wish, in hindsight, they had done a few things differently. Detailing the pitfalls aids other researchers who might tackle the topic. For example, Sprecher, McKinney, and Orbuch point out that their sample is not random, so generalizing from the results is difficult. They also suggest that future researchers use a wider range of ages, in relation to both the age at first intercourse and to the age of people making evaluations.

Questions for Summary and Review

1. What is the scientific method?
2. What are the four characteristics of the scientific method?
3. Describe the four major methods of research in sociology, and give examples of each.
4. What are the advantages and disadvantages of each of the four major methods of research in sociology?
5. Why is it important to use a variety of methods in studying human beings?
6. Using Research Method 2.1, develop a research project on some topic of interest, such as dating patterns among college students. Follow the seven stages outlined in the Research Method section. Explain how each of the four research methods might be used to research your topic.

·················· **Key Concepts**

Altruistic suicide (p. 31)
Anomic suicide (p. 31)
Cause and effect (p. 22)
Confederate (p. 26)
Content analysis (p. 32)
Control group (p. 26)
Dependent variable (p. 34)
Egoistic suicide (p. 31)
Empirical (p. 22)
Experimental group (p. 26)
Hawthorne effect (p. 22)
Hypothesis (p. 34)
Independent variable (p. 34)

Interview (p. 28)
Laboratory experiment (p. 25)
Objective (p. 22)
Operational definitions (p. 33)
Participant observation (p. 23)
Questionnaire (p. 28)
Random sample (p. 28)
Representative sample (p. 29)
Scientific method (p. 22)
Survey research (p. 28)
Tentative (p. 22)
The use of existing data (p. 30)
Variable (p. 34)

References

1. Babbie, Earl. 1989. *The practice of social research*. 5th ed. Belmont, Calif.: Wadsworth.

2. Berger, Peter. 1963. *Invitation to sociology: A humanistic perspective*. Garden City, N.Y.: Anchor Books.

3. Durkheim, Emile, 1951. *Suicide: A study in sociology*. New York: Free Press.

4. Gelles, Richard J., and Murray A. Straus. 1988. *Intimate violence: The causes and consequences of abuse in the American family*. New York: Touchstone.

5. Guy, Rebecca, C. Edgley, I. Arafat, and D. Allen. 1987. *Social research methods: Puzzles and solutions*. Boston: Allyn and Bacon.

6. Humphreys, Laud. 1975. *Tearoom trade: Impersonal sex in public places*. Chicago: Aldine Press.

7. Liebow, Elliott. 1967. *Tally's Corner*. Boston: Little Brown.

8. Lofland, John. 1966. *Doomsday cult*. Englewood Cliffs, N.J.: Prentice-Hall.

9. Milgram, Stanley. 1974. *Obedience to authority*. New York: Harper and Row.

10. Nielsen Media Research. 1987. *What TV ratings really mean*. New York: A.C. Nielsen Company Publication.

11. Roethlisberger, F.J., and W.J. Dickson. 1939. *Management and the worker*. Cambridge: Harvard University Press.

12. Sprecher, Susan, Kathleen McKinney, and Terri Orbuch. 1987. Has the double standard disappeared? An experimental test. *Social psychology quarterly* (March):24–31.

13. Straus, Murray A., Richard J. Gelles, and Suzanne K. Steinmetz. 1980. *Behind closed doors: Violence in the american family*. New York: Anchor Books.

14. Thompson, William E. 1983. Hanging tongues: A sociological encounter with the assembly line. *Qualitative sociology* 6 (Fall):215–37.

15. Whyte, William Foote. 1955. *Street corner society*. Chicago: University of Chicago Press.

Section 1

· ·

Understanding Order in Social Life

· · · · · · · · · · · · · ·

3

Understanding Culture and Social Life

• • • • • • • • • • • •

Chapter Outline

●

Recently a group of American students from a Texas college was studying ancient history and culture in Egypt. At one point, an Egyptian guide made some reference to male and female circumcision as a longstanding cultural practice in Egypt. At first the Americans assumed he had simply made a mistake. But one curious student asked if he meant that females in Egypt were actually circumcised. The guide became uncomfortable discussing the topic and changed the subject. Later one of the American teachers in the group mentioned that female circumcision, also called clitoridectomy, is practiced in various parts of Egypt, the Middle East, and regions in Africa. The students reacted with shock and outrage at such a custom and could not imagine why any Egyptians would allow this type of barbarism. They found a book by researchers from the American University in Cairo who interviewed several Egyptian women about their circumcisions. One of the women is quoted below:

> I remember the time when I was circumcised very clearly. I was eight years old. I was to be circumcised along with my maternal first cousin and my sister. The night before

the operation they brought us together and stained our hands with henna. All evening the family celebrated with flutes and drums. We were terrified. . . . I heard the midwife come in about five o'clock the next morning. . . . They did the operation and then pounded an onion and salt mixture to put on the wound to cauterize it. When it was all over, they carried me and put me to bed. They told me to keep my legs straight in front of me and my thighs apart to keep the wound from healing over. . . . On the seventh day we got up (Atiya 1984, 41).

Although the practice of female circumcision is embedded in the web of historical and cultural tradition in Egypt, the unknowing American students were shocked by the practice. They experienced the severe jolts people can receive when coming into contact with a culture substantially different from their own. The phenomenon known as **culture shock,** the strong feelings of disorientation and stress that often accompany a radical culture change, became very real to these students.

The example of female circumcision illustrates the vast differences that can exist among cultures of the world. Such differences are especially significant today because of the ever-increasing contact with people of other cultural backgrounds. The world market requires Americans to work in Saudi Arabia, Japan, South America, Malaysia, China, and the Soviet Union. As one example, over eighty percent of Parker Pen's sales are outside the United States, and the company has offices in 154 countries (Axtell 1985, 105). Similarly, foreign companies, such as Toyota and Honda, have built factories in the United States and Canada and brought their executives and families to North America. The tremendous influx of Vietnamese, Koreans, and Hispanics into the United States continues America's rich tradition of cultural diversity.

Increased contact with people of other cultures creates the possibilities of barriers in communication, serious misunderstandings and misinterpretations of behavior, and difficulties in everyday interactions. Keep in mind that many cultural differences are often much more subtle than the example of female circumcision.

Unfortunately, people rarely consider the meaning and significance of culture in gaining a greater understanding of others. Comprehending cultural differences and grasping the cultural basis of our behavior is crucial to anyone in today's multicultural world. This chapter is designed to introduce you to the concept of culture and to its significance as well as its components, variations, and special complexities. It is hopeless to try to understand people without first knowing their culture.

Defining Culture

Culture is generally defined as everything which is socially learned and shared by a group of people in society. It refers to a way of life and the ideas which contribute to that way of life. One early anthropologist defined culture as "that complex whole which includes knowledge, belief, art, morality, law, custom, and any other capabilities and habits acquired by . . . a member of society" (Tylor 1871, xx).

Culture may be viewed as the way in which a group of people has come to solve problems which face any human group. Over time, people sharing a culture develop certain ideas about how to survive in their physical environment, about what is proper or acceptable behavior, about what is right and wrong, about how people should interact, and about how families and governments should be organized.

It is useful to think of culture, in a broad sense, as ideas shared by people which are reflected in their behavior. People create an ongoing way of life which provides solutions to their most basic societal and human needs including survival, adaptation to the environment, adaptation to each other, and perpetuation of the group. Perhaps author W. Somerset Maugham (1984, 8–9) most clearly summarizes the importance of culture in a passage from his novel, *The Razor's Edge:*

> . . . men and women are not only themselves; they are also the region in which they were born, the city apartment or the farm in which they learnt to walk, the games they played as children, the old wives' tales they overheard, the food they ate, the schools they attended, the sports they followed, the poets they read, and the God they believed in. It is all these things that have made them what they are and these are the things that you can't come to know by hearsay . . . .

Distinguishing Culture from Society

Before continuing the discussion of culture, it is important to understand the differences between the concepts of culture and society. While culture refers to a set of ideas creating a way of life, **society** refers to the people who share and enact that culture. A society has a definite geographic location, persists over time, is relatively self-sustaining and independent, and has organized relationships among the people. People can speak of United States society as opposed to Canadian society and know they are different and separate. Still, these two countries share many elements of culture such as language, religions, family lifestyles, patterns of interaction, and so forth. But there are many important differences between the two societies, including the fact that the people define themselves as different and separate.

It is helpful to think of culture as ideas and products of interaction, while society is defined as a body of people who see themselves as unique and independent. Culture can be called the script and society the body of people who act out that script. The structure of society is discussed further in chapter five.

Material and Nonmaterial Culture

It is also important to know that culture contains both material and nonmaterial components. **Material culture** refers to concrete objects that are produced by and typify a culture. For example, in United States culture we produce certain kinds of cars, houses, clothes, objects or art, or record albums which reflect our way of life and our concerns.

Much can be learned about a culture by studying its material objects; these objects are called **artifacts** by social scientists. As an illustration, the veil traditionally worn by Saudi women is a material artifact of Arabian culture concerning the place of women in society. It reflects the Arabic view that women must be covered, protected, controlled, and set apart from the public political and economic processes.

Nonmaterial culture, on the other hand, refers to the total body of ideas which construct a way of life for members of a society. Elements of nonmaterial culture are not concrete and tangible objects as are those in material culture. Religion, morality, values, and beliefs are part of nonmaterial culture. Most of the concepts in this chapter, including those in the following section on components of culture, are part of nonmaterial culture.

Components of Culture

Several features of culture are especially important in order to understand how people have attempted to meet basic social needs. Language and symbols, beliefs, values, and norms are essential components of culture. Without these, people would face chaos. People need to be able to communicate, to know what to believe and what to value. They also need to know how to act. Culture provides people with blueprints for behavior.

While human groups share these fundamental needs, different cultures, through their unique historical and evolutionary processes, meet these human needs in vastly different ways. No two cultures arrive at a solution to a social requirement in quite the same way. For example, to create and maintain a culture, people must be able to communicate, but hundreds of different languages and dialects exist around the world as solutions to that human requirement. People must have rules for behavior which help them survive in their environment, but various cultures contain vastly different sets of rules and customs to guide members. Such **cultural variability**, the wide range of different solutions to the same fundamental human needs, is evidence of the flexibility and creativity of humanity.

Another way to view the following components of culture is to use them as guides in analyzing a culture you soon may be visiting. If, for example, you might be transferred to Mexico, you could prepare by studying something about the language, beliefs, values, and norms of the Mexicans. Americans no longer can afford to ignore such basic preparations for travel or work in another country. The world market demands that people become sensitive to cultural differences. Research Application 3.1. illustrates some of these concerns in doing business in Mexico and Japan.

Research Application 3.1

• • • • • • • Cultural Factors in Doing Business with Japan and Mexico

Cultural factors such as language differences are often considerable barriers in American efforts to conduct business with people in other cultures. Not long ago, corporate officials at Chevrolet were discouraged by the low sales of the Chevy Nova in South America as compared to other countries. They finally discovered that Nova (no va) means "it does not go" in Spanish. American businessman Mark Zimmerman (1985, 41), who spent much time in Japan, noted that "for anyone who plans to have anything to do with the Japanese that is likely to be sustained and important, not learning the language was like trying to swim upstream with only one arm."

When American and Mexican business executives are conferring, it is common practice for the Mexicans to stand very close, too close by American standards, and to touch others a great deal. As a result, Americans often step back and become somewhat uncomfortable if not annoyed during the interactions. In contrast, the Japanese prefer even more space than Americans. Consequently, each appears rude to the other.

In Mexico and in Japan, codes of politeness and deference are different and are often misunderstood by Americans. In business, it is rare for either the Japanese or the Mexicans to call others by their first names. Americans are often perceived as disrespectful when they automatically assume a first-name basis; an American might work with someone in Mexico for years and not be on a first-name basis by Mexican standards. In addition, it is common practice for

Mexicans to shake hands much more than we do in the U.S. In Mexico, everyone shakes hands when they get to work. If you have already shaken hands in the morning and you see the person a few hours later, it is expected that you shake hands again. While the Japanese have adapted to the Western handshake, they prefer to bow in greeting. A handshake with a strong grip, valued among American men, is abhorrent to the Japanese, but they are unlikely to show their dislike of it.

Perhaps one of the most frustrating differences for Americans who are doing business in Mexico has to do with time. Americans are very conscious of time and put a great emphasis on schedules, deadlines, and arriving promptly at business meetings. In Mexico it is common practice to be late to meetings and to be less concerned with deadlines and schedules. A saying one hears in Mexico is that "A man must be a master of time, not time a master of him." On the other hand, punctuality is considered an absolute necessity to the Japanese who keep very tight business schedules.

To the Japanese, however, one must never be so in a hurry that one dispenses with etiquette. Introductions, elaborate by American standards, are quite important to them. The business card is essential in helping with these introductions. Gift giving, also elaborate by American standards, is a strong tradition in Japan; people in business must be very careful about gifts.

The Japanese are greatly offended by any behavior they perceive to be rude or insulting. Impatience, emotionalism, barely-disguised anger, pointing fingers, and raised voices are considered rude in business meetings with the Japanese although such things are not uncommon in American business meetings. The hard-hitting American style of conducting business is distasteful to the Japanese (Zimmerman 1985; 30–31).

Because of the Japanese concern with etiquette and proper behavior, it is difficult for them to say "No" directly to someone if it might be construed as rude. The Japanese word for "Yes,"—"hai"—will be used occasionally when the person does not really mean "Yes." In such a context, the nuances are what count, but it is difficult for Americans to know such nuances. The American hears "Yes," but the Japanese is sometimes simply acknowledging the question or statement. It is not unlike the American phrase, "I hear you" (Zimmerman 1985). Similarly, in Mexico if one does not want to say "No," he or she simply says "mañana" with the implication that "No" is meant. Mañana technically means tomorrow, but it is sometimes used as a polite convention for "No."

Americans in the business community often are unaware of the importance of cultural differences and are unfamiliar with other languages, but they are beginning to learn that such factors must be taken into account if they are to do well in foreign markets. As we come to rely more on foreign countries for much of our economic interests, we are learning that our way is not the only way to do business.

Language and Symbols: Communicating Ideas

A major component of culture is symbolic communication; cultures would not be possible without language. Symbols of various kinds, including **language**—a complex system of verbal and written symbols—are the most important elements of culture. Human beings must learn how to act, and this type of learning is, to a large extent, made possible by our capacity for language. Language helps transmit cultural ideas through time. It allows groups to store knowledge and contemplate writings from the past, including enormously important works in Western culture such as the Bible and the writings of the ancient Greeks.

Symbols reflect elements of culture and signify ideas to people. Flags, religious artifacts such as the Star of David or the Christian Cross, as well as many fraternity, sorority, and lodge symbols convey meaning because a number of people have come to a social agreement concerning these meanings. Symbols can be used to unify people or to command respect and devotion because the symbols communicate with power and directness.

An illustration of the use of symbols in a culture is the awareness and display of **status symbols** to convey information about the individual. The use of certain kinds of fashions, automobiles, and the size and apparent cost of a home can be interpreted as nonverbal symbols that communicate statements of wealth and status.

A Kikuyu tribesman, ready to step off a bus in Nairobi, Kenya, is carefully dressed to symbolically communicate his tribal affiliation during an independence celebration.

On the other hand, the avoidance of known status symbols may communicate that one is not interested in material possessions. One early sociologist, Thorstein Veblen (1902), asserted that the more wasteful the object, the more likely it was to be considered a status symbol in America because the individual could afford the waste. The gas-guzzling luxury automobile, the twenty-seven room mansion, $1,000 Italian silk suit, or the $17,000 watch may be used as examples of Veblen's assertion.

In addition to status symbols, other aspects of communication also are non-verbal. For example, gestures are frequently used to communicate and can vary markedly from culture to culture. The traditional United States gesture of thumb to forefinger means everything is okay, but it is an insulting gesture in France and Belgium and a vulgar gesture in Greece and Turkey. In Greece, the arm extended with palms forward and fingers splayed is a terrible insult, but in the United States this gesture simply means halt or stop (Ekman, Friesen, and Bear 1984). Travelers often are unaware of the remarkable cultural differences in interpreting gestures.

Beliefs: Ideas About What is True

Language and symbols are significant components of culture, but people must also learn what to believe. It is difficult to understand that different cultures can embody different conceptualizations about what is truth. People do not instinctively know what is true; they learn the beliefs of their culture which have evolved over time. These ideas are modified and transmitted from generation to generation.

Beliefs are ideas that are assumed to be true. They help to define reality. All cultures have accumulated many beliefs over time, and this accumulation provides people with a common basis for understanding their environment. For example, Americans have learned to believe the idea of individual achievement in which people are considered responsible for their own actions and are in control of their own lives. On the other hand, the Japanese are much more group-oriented and are uncomfortable if anyone is too different or independent from the group. An important saying in Japan is, "The nail that stands up must be hammered down." The Japanese teach intense loyalty and conformity within the family and work group; Americans less so.

Americans also have a strong belief in freedom, but the American definition of freedom is not the same as that in other cultures. For example, Russians define freedom as a society free of poverty, crime, and inequality and are less concerned with individual freedom of choice. It is important, then, to keep in mind that what people believe may be quite different in various cultures.

Values: Ideas About What is Good

Another component of culture is **values**, or standards for judging what is considered desirable. Values are criteria for evaluating behavior or actions and deciding whether they are good or bad (Williams 1968, 283–84). Cultural values help people make choices about their lives according to what is defined as right, worthwhile, and important. For example, Americans generally value achievement, equality, success, material reward, and independence. As a value, achievement may be reflected in judgments about a variety of social situations including winning in games or sports, making an important scientific discovery, or achieving an award for the highest number of sales at work.

People may not always act according to their values, and values often conflict with one another. For example, Americans may value freedom but have not always allowed everyone in the society to be free. In other words, values are not the only factor influencing people's behavior.

Of course, beliefs and values change during the course of history, and certainly not everyone in the society holds the same beliefs and values. Nevertheless, beliefs and values found in a culture provide meaning and a definite structure to people's lives. These core elements of culture provide people with a sense of security in knowing what is true and a sense of purpose in knowing how to judge what is worthwhile.

Norms: Ideas About How to Behave

Without culture, people would not know how to act. No one would know how to eat, talk, dress, or take care of children; in short, no one would know how to live. People must have rules for behavior that help create order. Each culture provides a huge repertoire of norms for its members. Quite simply, **norms** are rules for behavior. They are prescriptions for conduct that prevail within a group, and they range from expectations concerning proper clothing to commandments that people should not kill.

From the moment an infant is born, he or she begins to learn a vast and often changing storehouse of norms. By early adulthood most people find their culture's norms to be second nature. People are largely unaware of the massive number of norms to which they adhere.

In contrast to values, norms are specific prescriptions about behavior. Values are more general standards used to judge or guide actions. For example, the general value of equality might be used to develop norms regarding specific situations, such as a supervisor not showing favoritism to a particular worker. It is best to think of norms as more specifically tailored to direct actual behavior than values.

Because the word norms refers to so many rules, sociologists refer to three general categories of norms: folkways, mores, and laws. Each of these is discussed separately in the next sections.

Folkways: Norms for Everyday Life

Folkways are defined as routine habits and customs that guide our everyday lives (Sumner 1906). Folkways include expectations about what people should eat, how they should dress, how their breaths or bodies should smell, how they should greet one another, or how they should stand relative to others in an elevator. Folkways are informal (unwritten but still understood), socially-defined norms that guide our daily behavior.

It is intriguing to study folkways around the world. Consider some of the following. American women shave their legs and underarms, but Swedish, Norwegian, and German women do not, finding it an unnatural practice. Americans tend to smile a great deal and look people in the eyes; the Japanese are more reserved, and such overtly friendly behavior occurs mainly among family or close friends. The Chinese put their family names first and find it odd that Americans do not. There are no street names in Tokyo; the natives know where everything is. In many Islamic nations, people eat only with the right hand and are highly offended when Americans use the left. In the Soviet Union, close friends and family, including men, greet each other by kissing, often on the lips.

All cultures enforce folkways through a wide variety of responses from others and from self. These responses are called **sanctions**, defined as either rewards or punishments for conforming to or violating norms. Those who violate folkways often are met with teasing, laughter, raised eyebrows, or, sometimes, being cast apart from others. These are examples of **informal negative sanctions**. Any student can remember the ridicule some schoolmates received for their clothes, hairstyle, different interests, or unusual way of acting. On the other hand, people receive **informal positive sanctions** such as being accepted into the group and being liked when they conform. Folkways are most definitely socially enforced, even if subtly or informally.

A more detailed example of folkways is found in the research of Edward T. Hall (1959, 1966) who studied how we stand relative to one another within our zones of personal space, zones which vary by culture. Hall found that Americans consider the space from the body out to eighteen inches as **intimate distance**. Typically, only close friends and family members are allowed into that space. In everyday interaction, Americans prefer to stand approximately eighteen inches to four feet from another person; this is called **personal distance**. Check this when you are talking with an acquaintance outside of class or at work. In more formal situations—a job interview or discussions with a professor—Americans tend to stay about four to twelve feet apart. Hall referred to this as **social distance**. Finally, Hall noted that **public distance**, beyond twelve feet, was reserved for distance between a speaker and an audience, for example the distance between a preacher and a congregation.

Hall found it interesting to observe people's reactions when someone violated their standards of space. When someone stands very close in a casual conversation, people whose space is violated often become intensely uncomfortable. Typically, they shift their bodies, pull their elbows in, put a barrier such as a purse or books between themselves and the other person, or simply step back or leave. At the same time, they may not quite realize why they are so uncomfortable or angry. This demonstrates how norms become second nature and that people often are unconscious of them.

The most important point from Hall's research is that concepts of personal space vary by culture. North Americans may consider South Americans to be rude because of their tendency to stand closer than three or four feet. In Arabic cultures, people may stand much closer and are less likely to recognize the intimate-distance barrier that Americans take for granted. The Japanese tend to prefer more distance than Americans, and we often appear rude to them. Understanding such differences in folkways promotes understanding of others' behavior in the context of culture. Refer back to Research Application 3.1 for a discussion of the importance of folkways in international business dealings.

Mores: Norms Reflecting Morality

Mores (pronounced MOR-ays) are norms that are considerably more serious in nature than folkways. (*Mos* is the singular form for mores, although the term is rarely used.) Mores are norms which the culture defines as absolutely necessary to obey. Violations are forbidden and are severely and negatively sanctioned. Mores involve a sense of morality not found in folkways. Western mores include prohibitions regarding murder, incest, cannibalism, rape, child abuse, and other forms of behavior defined as dangerous to society.

Typically, people react to violations of mores with horror, anger, and revulsion. In reading accounts of mass murderers or a child molesters, we ask ourselves how it could ever be possible for anyone to do such things. Culture calls for strong, negative sanctions, such as long prison sentences, for such violators of mores. These sanctions are an expression of outrage and fear. They are the means by which culture provides some sense of safety for its inhabitants. A requirement for severe punishment for those who violate mores is related to a disturbance in a necessary sense of well-being in society. Severe sanctions help ensure that members of society will do what is expected of them most of the time.

Laws: Official Norms

The third type of norms, **laws**, are formalized norms. Laws are officially stated and enforced by some form of government. They may be either folkways or mores, or neither, although they usually are based on pre-existing folkways or mores. Official punishment is an example of **formal, negative sanctioning**. Official recognition for good work or good deeds is an example of **formal, positive sanctioning**.

Laws may be relatively minor traffic laws or they may be quite serious felony laws regarding homicide and robbery. In some cases, laws may contradict folkways or mores. The creation of the fifty-five-miles-per-hour speed limit was a contradiction of a folkway in that many Americans had longstanding traditions of driving considerably faster. As a result it is not a widely obeyed law. Not surprisingly, on interstate highways the limit has been changed to sixty-five miles per hour.

As societies have grown larger, more complex, diverse, and urbanized, emphasis on official enforcement of norms has become more prevalent while informal sanctions within a society have become less effective as the major means of control. However, societies continue to rely most heavily on the individual's acceptance of cultural norms so that he or she willingly conforms. This makes society possible. Short of totalitarian control, a large nation-state cannot control the behavior of millions of people through the threat of formal punishment alone. People who commit crimes often do not think they will be caught by the authorities. If, however, the individuals have been brought up to firmly believe in the rightness of norms, then they have internalized the norms of the group and will control their own behavior or feel remorse when they violate norms. This subject will be discussed more fully in chapter 4 on socialization.

Ethnocentrism and the Relativity of Culture

Because people are brought up to believe so fully in the rightness of their own culture, they tend to judge anything different as odd or crazy or inferior. This is especially apparent when people travel to another country. Some Americans think it strange and foolish for retailers in Athens, Greece, or Mexico City, Mexico, to close their stores for much of the afternoon. The Americans see only that the merchants are losing money; Americans may not appreciate the custom that allows people to go home for a nap or run errands before they reopen. It is an honored tradition for Greeks and Mexicans.

This pervasive tendency to see one's customs and traditions as best is referred to as **ethnocentrism**. It is the biased belief and ingrained assumption that one's own culture is superior to others. The American students' reaction to female circumcision demonstrated the tendency to be judgmental about others' cultural practices. The same students probably gave little thought to the routine American practice of circumcising male babies in what some physicians call a brutal procedure.

This Islamic woman's dress reflects the vast differences between East and West in cultural beliefs and practices regarding women.

All people have some feelings of ethnocentrism learned from their culture. People tend to think that their language is best, their religion is true, and their food is the most delicious. (How can they eat sheep's eye or gorilla meat?) For example, the Japanese have a word, *gaijin*, which means foreigner, and it is often used in a derogatory and insulting manner indicating a Japanese sense of superiority.

You can examine your own attitudes and perhaps come up with a number of examples of ethnocentric beliefs. If you were raised in a city, how do you feel about rural lifestyles and traditions? If you were raised in Louisiana, how do you feel about the customs and attitudes of people in New Jersey (even though you might never have been there and know little about it)? If you are American, how do you feel about the way of life in Mexico if you see children on the street begging for money? If you are from an Islamic nation, how do you feel about the way American women dress? There is a strong tendency to judge others by one's own cultural standards.

Ethnocentrism is both an advantage and a disadvantage in any culture. As an advantage, it reinforces patriotism and pride. Ethnocentrism helps create a sense of belonging, of being a member of a special society and living in a special place. It can help create a sense of satisfaction with one's life and home. A recurrent feeling of dissatisfaction would be quite likely if people believed that others were better off or had a more attractive and fulfilling way of life.

On the other hand, ethnocentrism can be a disadvantage when it retards change in a culture. If people are unwilling to consider new ways of doing things, the culture can become stagnant. Ethnocentrism can also become a major problem when diverse people come into contact with one another. Conflict can quickly arise when one group sneers at other groups or ridicules the other's food, dress, or social customs. Ethnocentrism can be a major factor in the misunderstandings that often develop among people of different cultural backgrounds.

To illustrate these points, consider the Europeans' encounters with Native American tribes in the 1600s. The Europeans often described the natives as dirty or unclean, even though at that time Europeans rarely took baths or washed their clothes, while the natives bathed routinely. It is likely that this stereotype of the unclean native resulted from European moral judgments about the Native Americans' lack of "proper" clothing. Also, the grease or paint used by some Native Americans was foul-smelling to the Europeans. One can imagine how the Europeans, who believed bathing was dangerous to their health, smelled to the natives. Another misunderstanding occurred concerning certain tribes whose livelihood depended on hunting. To Europeans, hunting was a sport. Therefore they viewed the natives as engaging in wasteful, leisurely activity rather than in constructive work. Finally, many Native American tribes had no private ownership of land. They believed owning the land was as ridiculous as owning a cloud or a plot of the sky. Consequently, Europeans and Native Americans violently clashed over ownership of the land.

Social scientists cannot afford to misunderstand cultures. They must be constantly alert to their ethnocentric tendencies, whether studying groups within their own culture or studying a different culture altogether. The term **cultural relativism** refers to the need to analyze any element of social life within the context of its own culture, instead of judging it from another point of view. Referring back to the discussion of female circumcision in Egypt, we personally may be appalled at this cultural practice just as Egyptians may be appalled at some of our customs. However, sociologists must attempt to be objective. They must analyze such a situation in the context of the culture and realize that the Egyptian people do not define the custom in the same way as did the American students.

The concept of cultural relativism is also a tool individuals can use to overcome their own ethnocentrism. To learn to appreciate cultural differences rather than to make ethnocentric judgments signifies a thoughtful and open-minded individual. This approach is particularly important today because many occupations require people to travel, to conduct business on the international market, or to deal with clients or customers of various cultural backgrounds. In order to understand and work with people, we must place them in their environmental context and realize that their behavior is relative to their culture, not to ours. Consider the following anecdote from a book written for executives who travel (Axtell 1985, 6):

> Watching a Chinese reverently placing fresh fruit on a grave, an American visitor asked, "When do you expect your ancestors to get up and eat the fruit?" The Chinese replied, "As soon as your ancestors get up and smell the flowers."

Cultural Diversity: When Ideas Differ

The concept of ethnocentrism becomes especially significant in a society with many different cultural groups because of the potential for intergroup prejudice and misunderstandings. All cultures have some variation in language, beliefs, values, and norms, although some cultures have a greater range of variation than others. In a large, rapidly-changing, postindustrial society like the United States, with its history of diverse ethnic, racial, and religious groups, a great deal of variability exists in folkways, mores, languages, customs, and lifestyles. Japan, on the other hand, is a relatively homogeneous culture with few ethnic or racial differences. While a dominant American culture exists, many other cultural practices coexist.

Cultural diversity refers to differences within a specific culture that add to the complexity of that culture and to the rich texture of social life. A remarkable array of cultural patterns exists in American society, and subcultures are the most significant feature in that cultural diversity.

Subcultures refer to groups that have cultural components significantly different from the larger culture. Subcultures may exhibit differences in language, custom, religion, and patterns of behavior. Nevertheless, most subcultures are a part of the larger society, and members of subcultures accept much of the dominant culture. It is useful to analyze American subcultures by placing them into five broad categories, which are discussed next.

Ethnicity as the Basis of Subculture

Ethnic subcultures include those with differences in custom due to national origin and identity. Such subcultures have always been a feature of American society. Members of ethnic subcultures often retain the language, food habits, celebrations, attitudes, and behaviors of their backgrounds. Jewish holidays are celebrated around the country, traditional Korean customs can be found operating in sections of many United States cities, and Spanish is spoken by about fifteen percent of our population. Research Method 3.1 is about a Mexican American subculture in Dallas, Texas. In addition, chapter seven contains much more detail about ethnic and other minority groups in America.

Religion as the Basis of Subculture

Subcultures that differ significantly according to religious practice and way of life are called religious subcultures. These subcultures have also contributed greatly to the spectrum of cultural variation in America. Because the United States was founded on religious freedom, many groups immigrated to this country in order to escape religious oppression. The development of our own unique religious groups also resulted from the freedom to practice religion. Religious subcultures include the Jews, Amish, Hutterites, Mormons, Shakers, and Quakers.

One unique religious subculture is the Old Order Amish, a Protestant sect descended from the Swiss Anabaptists. In his book on *Extraordinary Groups,* William Kephart (1987) described the markedly distinct lifestyle fostered by the Old Order Amish community in Lancaster County, Pennsylvania. The Amish prefer a simple, conservative way of life that has changed very little in 250 years. Religious conservatism dominates their entire way of life. In accordance with a strict interpretation of the Bible, the Amish oppose all "worldliness" and have carved out a way of life that conforms to their religious beliefs. To the Amish, worldliness is wickedness. They do not allow marriage to outsiders because the outsider might corrupt their way of life.

> Since they have specifically been chosen by God, the Amish take great pains to stay "apart" from the world at large. They do this not only by living apart, but by rejecting virtually all the components of modern civilization: automobiles, television, higher education, political involvement, movies, jewelry, electric lights, pictures, wristwatches, life insurance, musical instruments—the list goes on and on. Pressures come and pressures go—and when they come they may be severe—but the Amish simply will not conform to worldly ways (Kephart 1987, 3–4).

The Amish dress in mostly black clothes without ornamentation. Jewelry, including wedding rings, is strictly forbidden. On the coldest day, the Amish will not wear gloves. The women do not cut or curl their hair nor do they use any makeup. The Amish travel in horse and buggy and spurn even the telephone. They do not celebrate most American holidays, but they do celebrate Christmas and Easter without Santa Claus, Christmas trees, or the Easter Bunny. At Christmas, only children are given gifts.

The Amish are extremely hardworking people; their farms are among the best in the world. Because most of their work is done by hand, little time is left for leisure activities. Few smoke or drink, though some of the men chew tobacco.

The Amish are among the most devout religious groups in America, but they do not have churches, Sunday schools, or paid clergy. They worship every other Sunday by hauling benches to a designated house. Their communities have no formal laws, but all the Amish know what is expected of them. The most authoritative source is always the Bible. The most severe form of punishment is the *Meidung,* or ban, which is imposed by the bishop in cases where a major norm has been violated, such as marrying an outsider or buying an automobile without being repentant. The ban is total ostracism. No one is allowed to talk to the individual at all, not even the closest family members, or they could suffer the ban as well. Because the ban is a powerful threat, it is rarely used. Less severe negative sanctions are usually enough (Kephart 1987).

The ideas that shape the lifestyle of the Amish are unique in many ways. The Amish differ in each of the major components of culture. Their language, beliefs, values, and norms are unlike those of the dominant culture. Because of their differences, they are allowed some special statuses in our society. Their children attend public school only until the eighth grade, and they are given conscientious-objector status in the U.S. military. They would unquestionably refuse to serve in any capacity in the military because they endorse nonviolence. They also rarely vote. Because they would not accept any Social Security checks, the federal government has exempted them from paying Social Security taxes.

Research Method 3.1

• • • • • • • Participant Observation

Mexican Americans in a Dallas Barrio

By Shirley Achor

In the early 1970s, Shirley Achor, a doctoral student of anthropology at Southern Methodist University in Dallas, decided to conduct an in-depth study of a Mexican American neighborhood. She wanted to gain insight into this significant American subculture. Although she used a variety of methods in her study, the most prominent approach she took was participant observation.

In participant observation, the researcher attempts to immerse himself or herself into the everyday world of the people being studied. The researcher wants to see life from the point of view of the people. Involved in face-to-face relationships with those being studied, the researcher participates with them in their daily round of activities. Through interaction, trained study in techniques of observation, and careful, rigorous analysis, the participant observer develops an understanding of the particular social group and social environment.

Over a two-year period, Achor visited the Dallas barrio almost daily. She returned to update her research in the mid–1980s. The barrio was a predominantly low-income area not far from the center of Dallas. She established contacts and friendships by teaching free typing classes. After a while, this Anglo woman was no longer a curiosity in the Mexican American neighborhood. However, she felt that she needed to conduct full-time participant observation in order to get a complete picture of the social world of the barrio. According to Achor (1978, 6), "Prolonged, continuous, face-to-face interaction within the community could provide a more intimate perspective of barrio life and help me begin to see the residents' world through their point of view."

Achor and her husband moved into a rental house in the barrio, complete with rotted ceilings, decayed walls, moldy piles of trash, and hundreds of roaches. Building codes were not enforced, and the landlord refused to make any repairs; he said that he could easily rent the property to someone else. Achor discussed the culture shock she felt upon arriving in the barrio from her comfortable suburban home. She was not used to rats and roaches, the noise in the streets at night, and the complete unconcern of the landlord.

During her stay, Achor collected data by frequenting neighborhood shops, churches, and restaurants. She participated in informal neighborhood social interaction and attended parties, weddings, and public meetings. She also taught evening classes. Through the development of a number of particularly close relationships, she was introduced to the neighborhood. Everyone knew who she was. She did not hide the fact that she was a researcher and she tried to be as honest as possible when asked of her purposes for living in the barrio. Most of them accepted her as a neighbor, but she did meet resentment from a few people, a common reaction to researchers.

Here we can only give you a brief overview of the many insights provided in Achor's book. She discussed the high incidence of poverty coupled with the reluctance to apply for public assistance or go to public clinics, both of which could bring about loss of respect in the neighborhood. The barrio was the center of the social lives for most of the residents. Strong group solidarity existed in family and social relationships. Few close social relationships between Mexican Americans and Anglos existed even when they worked together. The residents were unlikely to contact the police when trouble erupted in the neighborhood, although it was fairly common for barrio boys to resort to violence. Considerable petty property crime existed in the area as well. Informal negative sanctions such as social exclusion and angry verbal expressions were typical social controls. When she returned to the barrio in 1986, residents were even more afraid of crime.

The family and the church were central to the lives of the residents. Work was less central in that it was viewed more as a means to an end—money. Male dominance was an important feature of family life, although Achor observed many exceptions. Contrary to beliefs and some sociological theories about Mexican Americans, the parents offered considerable encouragement to their children to get at least a high school education. Most indicated that they held achievement values and aspirations associated with the American Dream.

Finally, Achor categorized the responses of residents to life in the barrio into four types. First, some preferred to stay insulated in the barrio—apart from the outside world which was perceived as alien and hostile. Second, others took a path of accommodation, hoping eventually to enter the mainstream society. Third, some engaged in mobilization by organizing political action and protest. Finally, a small group felt a general sense of alienation. They felt powerless and hopeless in the face of day-to-day struggles as well as life crises. Deviant behavior in the form of theft, burglary, drug use, and fighting was most likely among this last group. She found these responses to be much the same in 1986.

It is unlikely that Achor could have accomplished her research goals without participant observation. However, any research method has drawbacks as well as strengths. The most common criticism of participant observation is that the researcher is more likely to lose objectivity than in other forms of research. After getting to know the people in the barrio and making good friends with many of them, was Achor less able to give an unbiased view of them? Another criticism of participant observation is that it is limited in place and scope. Can the results of Achor's study be generalized to barrios in other American cities? Most methodologists say they cannot. Finally, participant observation is criticized for lacking the scientific rigor of other methods. How does the researcher crosscheck and verify the results of the study?

Such questions can rarely be answered to everyone's satisfaction, but participant observation remains a valuable and important method of research. It allows the researcher into certain arenas of social life where other techniques such as survey research or the laboratory experiment would be useless.

Region as the Basis of Subculture

Ways of living also differ by region of the country. **Regional subcultures can be identified through the differing language usages.** Watch a person from Maine look puzzled when a Texan says, "My house is over yonder but I'm fixin' to go to town," or the difficulty a person from Wisconsin has in understanding a Louisianan who speaks in a Cajun dialect.

Patterns of interaction such as routine greetings, the preferred amount of personal space, styles of dress, folkways, and traditions all vary by region of the country, as any traveler knows. Certainly beliefs, often stereotypical and derogatory, about the differences between northern and southern lifestyles are common in American culture, and people expect to find such differences as they move from one region of the country to another. Many people from northern sections of the country migrating to the Sunbelt can give examples of the changes they find in folkways, beliefs, and values. Of course, such differences are not of the same magnitude as those found when moving to a society whose culture has an entirely different language and normative structure.

Occupation as the Basis of Subculture

Occupational subcultures include groups whose jobs unite them in a special lifestyle and set them apart from the larger society. For example, professional athletes lead lives very different from people in more traditional occupations in that their work season lasts six or seven months and they travel constantly during those months. This extensive amount of travel makes family life very difficult. Their careers are relatively short, and they risk physical injury which could prematurely destroy their careers.

The concept of occupational subculture is most appropriate when the occupational group perceives itself and is perceived by others to be markedly different. These differences are often reflected in a specialized slang, or **argot,** and in informal norms developed to guide individuals through situations unique to their occupation. For example, people in the professions also develop jargon that is mostly unintelligible to the uninitiated. Attorneys are especially criticized for their language of "legalese." Physicians use such terms as gomer (patient), tern (intern), lol (little old lady), nad (no apparent distress), zero delta (no change in a patient), cold (chronic

The living conditions of this Mexican-American family reflect the poverty discussed by Shirley Achor in her study of a Dallas barrio.

obstructive lung disease), and MFC (measure for coffin) (Safire 1983, 73). Much of this chapter is an effort to acquaint you with sociological jargon.

Opposition as the Basis of Subculture

A very special kind of subculture is called a counterculture because such groups not only differ from the larger society but are in conflict with it. A counterculture rejects many of the norms, values, and beliefs of the general culture, and it attempts to create alternatives for its members. Countercultures have flourished at certain times in American history and at other times have been relatively rare.

During the late 1960s and early 1970s in the United States, one could find many examples of countercultures among the young people of the Woodstock generation: the hippies who were pacifists and who were opposed to the traditional middle-class lifestyle; small, revolutionary groups such as the Weathermen or the Symbionese Liberation Army which kidnapped Patti Hearst; groups defiantly opposed to the Vietnam war; and communal groups who wanted out of mainstream society. Members of the larger society often are appalled and angry at such countercultural groups. Much anger was directed at the hippies because they appeared "dirty" to many traditional Americans, and they did not work but instead advocated free love and rejected material possessions gained through participation in the "rat race."

Such countercultural groups appear to be relatively nonthreatening when compared with countercultural terrorist organizations. The Red Army in West Germany and the Red Brigade in Italy are seriously and often violently opposed to the dominant culture.

Complexities of Culture

Cultures are quite complex because they are composed of hundreds of norms, values, and beliefs. Cultural diversity can contribute to ethnocentrism and result in conflict over norms, values, and beliefs. Such confusion is less likely in a small, homogeneous culture without much diversity. Cultures can indeed be complex, and they are not perfect.

Cultures are constantly changing and adapting to new ideas. **Cultural diffusion** refers to the exchange of elements among cultures and is one way in which cultures adopt new ideas. Elements of American culture can be found all over the world, whether it is a McDonald's in Tokyo or a pair of Levis in a remote African village or Soviet town. On the other hand, Americans borrow foreign dress styles, foods, words, and music. Culture also changes as a result of the innovative and creative efforts of its members in developing such things as television and the personal computer. In addition, the creation of knowledge and philosophy has given us such ideas as democracy and separation of church and state.

While cultural change seems very slow—and in many ways our basic and fundamental approach to living does not change perceptibly over time—many aspects of culture do change. Other parts of culture must respond to those changes. As sociologist William F. Ogburn (1922) noted long ago, material culture typically changes more rapidly than nonmaterial culture, and he used the term **culture lag** to refer to this lack of adjustment between the two. Norms and values, as parts of nonmaterial culture, rarely change as rapidly as scientific discovery. For example, advanced medical technology allows us to prolong life, but society has yet to deal adequately with the quality of life that is prolonged. Few norms exist concerning when or if a patient has the right to die or if the family has the right to prevent further medical treatment of a member who is in a persistent vegetative state.

Without norms or when we are confused over norms, we face uncertainty, and we are miserable. Being without normative guidelines is much like driving on a dark road without headlights, unable to see the stripes on the road or the road signs. Culture is the primary means by which we become certain about our environment. It provides us with road signs. Yet no culture is perfect; it may not always meet all human needs or provide the necessary guidelines to deal effectively with all situations. People face many circumstances in life without a norm to effectively guide us or with a norm that appears to have destructive effects.

Consider an example of a phenomenon called **bystander apathy** (Latane and Darley 1970; Latane, Nida, and Wilson 1981), in which individuals apparently see another in trouble but make no move to offer help. The sensational case of Kitty Genovese in New York City is a particularly painful example. One night the young woman was repeatedly stabbed and eventually killed in a middle-class neighborhood where at least thirty neighbors heard her screams. No one offered help or even called the police until she was already dying alone in the street. More recently, a screaming woman was gang-raped in front of cheering bystanders in a bar in Massachusetts. No one came to her aid.

While such situations are probably rare, they nevertheless cause us to question the extent to which people should refrain from interfering. Under certain situations, this norm of noninterference, or minding one's own business, has destructive effects if people refuse to help someone who is in danger. Perhaps society has become so urbanized and heterogeneous that people feel they must tolerate or ignore many unusual situations. Researchers (Latane and Darley 1968, 1970; Latane, Nida, and

Wilson 1981) have noted that ambiguity in defining the situation can contribute to bystander apathy. That is, when the situation is not clear, people are less likely to react. When they see a person lying on a downtown sidewalk, they might not know if that person is a skid-row drunk who has passed out or if he or she has had a heart attack. Another factor in bystander apathy involves the number of people who may be witnessing the event. Generally, the larger the crowd, the less likely any one of the crowd will step forward to help. Each may assume, or hope, that someone else will help. Also, some people think that they do not have time to assist others—another product of America's fast-paced cultural lifestyle.

Cultures may be quite diverse, may have conflicting elements, and may change over time. Cultures have enormous differences which cause difficulty in communication and understanding among people from different backgrounds. Cultures do not always meet all of the needs of their inhabitants and may indeed include destructive elements. However, without culture, we would be helpless.

· **Questions for Summary and Review**

1. Define culture and explain how the concept is different from society. Also, explain the difference between material and nonmaterial culture.
2. List and give examples of the four components of culture.
3. Explain the difference between folkways, mores, and laws. Give examples of each.
4. Define and discuss ethnocentrism. Give examples of ethnocentrism. Explain how cultural relativism is used to help overcome ethnocentric tendencies
5. Discuss cultural diversity and how it affects the United States.
6. Explain the concept of subcultures. List, define, and give examples of the five types of subcultures.
7. Discuss issues in the complexity of culture.

· **Key Concepts**

Argot (p. 53)
Artifacts (p. 40)
Beliefs (p. 44)
Bystander apathy (p. 55)
Counterculture (p. 54)
Cultural diffusion (p. 55)
Cultural diversity (p. 50)
Cultural relativism (p. 49)
Cultural variability (p. 41)
Culture (p. 39)
Culture lag (p. 55)
Culture shock (p. 39)
Ethnic subcultures (p. 50)
Ethnocentrism (p. 47)
Folkways (p. 45)
Formal negative sanctions (p. 47)
Formal positive sanctions (p. 47)
Informal negative sanctions (p. 46)
Informal positive sanctions (p. 46)

Intimate distance (p. 46)
Language (p. 42)
Laws (p. 47)
Material culture (p. 40)
Mores (p. 46)
Nonmaterial culture (p. 40)
Norms (p. 45)
Occupational subcultures (p. 53)
Personal distance (p. 46)
Public distance (p. 46)
Regional subcultures (p. 53)
Religious subcultures (p. 50)
Sanctions (p. 45)
Social distance (p. 46)
Society (p. 40)
Status symbols (p. 43)
Subculture (p. 50)
Symbols (p. 43)
Values (p. 44)

References

1. Achor, Shirley. 1978. *Mexican Americans in a Dallas barrio*. Tucson, Ariz.: University of Arizona Press.

2. _____. 1986. *Mexican Americans in a Dallas barrio: An addendum*. Commerce: East Texas State University.

3. Atiya, Nayra. 1984. *Khul-khaal: Five Egyptian women tell their stories*. Cairo: The American University in Cairo Press.

4. Axtell, Roger E. 1985. *Do's and taboos around the world*. New York: John Wiley and Sons.

5. Ekman, P., W. Friesen, and J. Bear. 1984. The international language of gestures. *Psychology today* (May) 18: 64–71.

6. Hall, Edward T. 1959. *The silent language*. New York: Doubleday.

7. _____. 1966. *The hidden dimension*. New York: Doubleday.

8. Kephart, William M. 1987. *Extraordinary groups. The sociology of unconventional lifestyles*. 3d ed. New York: St. Martin's Press.

9. Latane, B., and J. Darley. 1968. Group inhibition of bystander intervention. *Journal of personality and social psychology* 8:377–83.

10. _____. 1970. *The unresponsive bystander: Why doesn't he help?* New York: Appleton-Century-Crofts.

11. Latane, B., S. A. Nida, and D. W. Wilson. 1981. The effects of group size on helping behavior. In *Altruism and helping behavior: Social, personality, and developmental perspectives*, edited by J. P. Ruston and R. M. Sorrento. Hillsdale, N.J.: Erlbaum.

12. Maugham, W. Somerset. 1984. *The razor's edge*. New York: Penquin Books.

13. Ogburn, William F. 1922. *Social change with respect to culture and original nature*. New York: Huebsch, Inc.

14. Safire, William. 1983 Listening to what the doctor says. In *Sociology: Contemporary readings*, edited by J. and A. Stimson, 73. Itasca, Ill.: F. E. Peacock.

15. Sumner, William Graham. 1906. *Folkways*. Boston: Ginn and Company.

16. Tylor, E. B. 1871. *Primitive culture: Researches into the development of mythology, philosophy, religion, language, art, and custom, Volume I*. London: J. Murray.

17. Veblen, Thorstein. 1902. *The theory of the leisure class: An economic study of institutions*. New York: Macmillan.

18. Williams. Robin M. 1968. The concept of values. In *International encyclopedia of the social sciences, vol. 16*, edited by David Sills, 283–287. New York: Macmillan.

19. Zimmerman, Mark. 1985. *How to do business with the Japanese*. New York: Random House.

4

Socialization, the Self, and Interaction in Social Life

• • • • • • • • • • • •

●

In an interview with a foster mother, sociologist Ross Eshleman (1981, 484–85) reported the experience of a two-year-old boy who had been severely neglected before being placed in a foster home. The foster mother told Eshleman that the child was in terrible condition when he arrived, lacking almost all skills and social awareness. He had virtually no language abilities, and he had no understanding of what it was to sit at a table and eat a meal. Because he had never learned that meals might be regular occurrences, he gobbled up as much food as possible. He did not know what people were for because he had never had any real interpersonal involvement with others. "He could ignore a person like he ignored a piece of furniture." The foster mother also noted that it mattered little to the boy if he pleased her or anyone else. He had learned no feelings for others and did not appear to miss her or other family members when they left because he had no comprehension of family relationships or family closeness. In those first years with his foster family he did not respond to hugging, holding, or other signs of affection. He was afraid to go outside and would only stay out if made to do so. "He didn't know what a sandbox was for. He didn't know what toys were for. He had no idea what you did with a toy. We had to very patiently teach him all of this," and it took *years* of concerted effort on the part of the foster family (Eshleman 1981, 485).

Much has to be learned if we are to live in society. Through interaction with others, people learn enormously complicated languages, learn hundreds of folkways, mores, and laws that guide behavior, and learn what is considered necessary for the complex roles people play in society. The experience of the young, neglected boy indicates that humans must learn to be human, and that is what this chapter is all about.

What Do We Begin With?

Most social scientists insist that humans enter this world with few biological or genetic predispositions regarding behavior and personality. They emphasize the role of the environment in shaping the individual's behavior, personality, and ability. On the other hand, in recent years some scientists have returned to a biological explanation as a basis for much of our ability and behavior (Wilson 1975, 1979). The debate between those who emphasize biological determinants of behavior and those who emphasize the environment as the most important determinant of behavior is referred to as the **nature versus nurture debate**.

Sociologists traditionally have been on the nurture side of the debate, characterizing the individual as molded and shaped by social forces. But, as additional research is conducted, social scientists no longer can ignore the possibilities of biological influences in behavior. In a fundamental sense, biological forces have an impact on the person by dictating various physical attributes such as height, hair color, skin color, and facial features; these features are not important in themselves but are indirectly important in that the social group may define them as socially significant and react to the person very differently. For example, science gives virtually no support to the notion of biological differences due to race; however, as long as a society defines race as an important symbol and as long as people are treated differently because of their racial heritage, race will be a factor in that person's socialization.

Genetic factors in mental illness, temperament, aggression, and sex role behavior are also being extensively investigated, especially by psychologists. Some support is being found for genetic influences. For example, some forms of schizophrenia, a severe mental illness, appear to have biological bases, and some evidence indicates that shyness or aggression may be inborn traits for a small percentage of humans. However, a fundamental point remains: no amount of genetic information will matter if the individual is not allowed to develop in a supportive social and cultural environment (Hoyenga and Hoyenga 1979, Brooks-Gunn and Matthews

1979). Whatever biological blueprint we might have is either fostered, modified, or extinguished by the environment.

Defining Socialization

Socialization refers to the process by which people interact with others to learn the ways of their culture in order to function within it. At the same time (during socialization) people develop social selves and individual personalities. This process of social and personal development is made possible by the human's innate capacity to learn. Undoubtedly complex, the socialization process begins at birth and continues in various ways throughout life. People are constantly learning how to adapt to our physical, cultural, and social environments as we involve ourselves with others, take on new roles in family and work, grow older, face new ideas and inventions, and eventually confront death.

Types of Socialization

To get a better picture of what socialization is all about, it is useful to know four different kinds of socialization that occur in society. Because socialization begins at birth and continues throughout the life cycle, it is a process that takes different forms depending on the stage of life and the special environmental and situational problems that occur.

Primary Socialization

The most crucial learning for an individual occurs in the first years of life. In the early years of childhood, incredibly complex learning must occur, and it takes place relatively quickly. This early childhood socialization is referred to as **primary socialization**. It is called primary because it supplies the foundation for all other learning, and it must come first.

In primary socialization, the child learns the basic skills necessary to survive in our society. The child must master, or begin to master, motor skills involving coordination and control of the body such as learning to walk, to grasp, to feed himself or herself, and so on. The child also must master language and the understanding of symbols and gestures if any further learning is to take place. Most often, the child learns from the family through imitation, conditioning, and through reward for accomplishing the expected behavior. Consequently, interaction with others from birth is necessary for socialization.

Erik Erikson (1950), a noted psychiatrist, theorized that babies need to learn a sense of trust in their environment, a sense that their needs will be met, although this is not conscious thought in infants because they have no language in which to think. Soon after, according to Erikson, children begin to develop a sense of autonomy and independence in being able to walk and talk and do some things on their own. At about ages four to six, children have progressed enough both biologically and socially to develop a conscience—a sense of right and wrong—as well as a sense of initiative and creativity.

What happens if a child is denied interaction with others and is effectively denied primary socialization? Like the foster boy discussed at the beginning of this chapter, other cases of severely neglected children point to the overwhelming handicap of isolation. Perhaps the most notable cases of isolated children are those of

Kindergarten children have already experienced five years of primary socialization and are now learning how to interact with one another away from their family environment.

Anna and Isabelle, whose situations were similar. Anna was found in the late 1930s on a farm in the South. She was born illegitimately and her grandfather had locked her alone in a room for most of her first six years of life, apparently from the shame he felt at her illegitimacy. When she was found at the age of six, Anna could not walk, talk, or react in any way we would consider human. Although Anna was given good care after she was found, she died a few years later. She had learned to say a few words and feed herself, but little else (Davis 1947).

Also illegitimate and found soon after Anna, Isabelle was shut away in isolation with her mother, who was a deaf mute. Isabelle had the advantage of human contact. When she was found at about the age of six, she was able to walk and communicate in crude sign language, but she had learned little else. Interestingly, she did not react to sounds although she was not deaf, and she had not learned to make sounds from her vocal chords beyond a few grunting noises. She had the appearance of being a wild animal before strangers and she acted like an infant. Isabelle did survive and mature after receiving considerable attention and care from a team of specialists. With their expert and prolonged efforts, she went through the process of primary socialization at a relatively rapid rate (Davis 1947).

Humans appear to be adaptable and resilient under enormously adverse conditions (Kagan 1984). But at some point, primary socialization must occur; we do not know how long a child can be deprived and still develop into a reasonably healthy adult.

Anticipatory Socialization

One way of learning the roles we will play in our lives is to rehearse them. **Anticipatory socialization** refers to learning roles by practicing those roles we anticipate playing in the future. Many examples of anticipatory socialization can be found at various stages in our lives. In childhood, children play house; boys practice playing the father and husband roles while girls rehearse the behavior they see in their mothers. Children spend hours copying role models from television, books, and movies. Dolls provide children with an opportunity to practice playing parent to an infant. Other toys and games give children the opportunity to experience, through play, a taste of what they may do in the future.

Play is serious business. Games teach children about war, financial success, and various occupations such as doctor, firefighter, and teacher. Conformity is encouraged and children are quick to learn that some behaviors are not viewed by those around them as appropriate for a little boy or a little girl. Anticipatory socialization is a powerful learning process in which children observe and practice the subtleties of roles; they use the adults around them as role models on which to base their experiments and rehearsals.

In high schools and colleges, people formally rehearse roles through internships, student teaching, and apprenticeships. In informal ways, we also prepare ourselves for future roles by changing the way we dress and by altering our attitudes and behaviors as we anticipate some future role. Some students even practice being engaged through the use of promise rings, symbols that signal that the couple is "promised to be engaged."

Anticipatory socialization is a part of primary socialization but is not restricted to it. People continue to rehearse through much of their lives because rehearsal functions as a powerful learning tool. It serves as a means of preparation by which people gain some certainty and some confidence regarding their performances before others.

Adult Socialization

For many years social scientists concentrated their studies of socialization on children and emphasized the importance of primary learning. As a result, sociologists tended to overlook the significance of learning and adjustment that occurs throughout the life cycle, a kind of secondary socialization. Now we are also studying **adult socialization**, the learning that builds on and modifies primary socialization and is required of all people as they move into new stages of life and face a changing environment. People's lives are never static; learning is continual. For example, people may have learned the basic framework of marriage and parenthood from both primary and anticipatory socialization, but the actual adjustment to marriage and the ability to get along with your specific partner require some learning and adaptability. In addition, as societal expectations change regarding family and marital roles, divorce, and remarriage, many of us are forced to change as well.

Most people face changes due simply to predictable developments in the typical life cycle. For example, when the last child grows up and leaves, the parents must adjust to life without children in the home. The change may be difficult for parents who have geared their lives to raising the children. They find that they must develop new interests and concerns to fill the void left by the last child. The so-called empty nest also signifies that the parents are getting older.

In studying adult socialization, researchers have found typical stages of crises and adjustments faced by many adults in our society. Most adults must face predictable problems in a career, must adjust to aging in a youth-oriented society, and eventually must deal with the deaths of family members and friends, all issues in adult socialization. The specific stages in adult development will be discussed at length later in the chapter.

Resocialization

At times, some people are required to face a radically new environment or lifestyle for which they are unprepared. They must relearn the basics of how to act and how to survive. **Resocialization** is this process of unlearning past behavior and relearning to live in a very different way. A person who has been resocialized is sometimes characterized as having been "brainwashed" to perceive life and the environment differently, although the term brainwashing may be a bit too sinister to accurately apply to most kinds of resocialization.

Consider the example of a nineteen-year-old male who had been smoking marijuana, shooting speed, and smoking crack. He was caught several times and finally sent to the state department of corrections for a year. In prison he found a radically different set of rules for behavior imposed by the correctional staff. He also found a way of life among the inmates which differed from the staff's and from his own. In a short time, he had to adjust to the loss of freedom, constant supervision, routinization of the day, and the mass of rules imposed by the prison. At the same time, he had to learn the informal structure of the inmate subculture regarding leadership, group identification, gang affiliation, race, and ethnicity. He quickly had to learn how to maintain some sense of safety in a very dangerous place. His past ways of acting no longer worked in the prison environment (Braly 1976).

Sociologists characterize prisons, mental institutions, homes for the handicapped and aged, and monasteries as **total institutions** (Goffman 1961). Life in these institutions requires both a significant break with the past and the learning of a different way of living. Total institutions are cut off from the wider society, and the people in the institution live a closed, extremely supervised way of life. The nineteen-year-old had to be resocialized into a total institution; and, once out of prison, he had to face the reality of a new identity because he was now an ex-con and found a number of limitations regarding employment and personal relationships. He had dramatically changed his life in the span of one year.

A number of other illustrations of resocialization exist in society. Enlisting in the military and going through boot camp require a new identity and acceptance of new norms in different and sometimes restrictive environments. Joining a religious or fanatic cult requires radical alteration of self and behavior. Unlearning a way of life as an alcoholic or drug addict requires establishing an entirely new way of life that does not revolve around drugs. Learning to adjust to a physical handicap, such as paralysis resulting from an automobile accident, is a significant kind of resocialization. And, of course, moving to another culture altogether requires the learning of a new language, a new set of norms, and a new structure of roles and statuses.

Resocialization is sometimes confused with adult socialization, and it is important to be able to distinguish the two processes. It is helpful to think of adult socialization as the learning process required of all of us as we adjust to new stages in our lives. Resocialization, on the other hand, applies to situations which are more unusual and dramatic. It requires some break with a past way of life because that past way of life no longer works in the radically new situation. All people go through the process of adult socialization, while only some face the difficulties of resocialization.

Sociological Views on the Self and Socialization

Sociological theory brings a certain kind of perspective to the study of the social self and its development, a perspective different from the major trends in psychology. The sociological perspectives in this section present the unique approaches found in sociology and reflect the symbolic interactionist tradition discussed in chapter one. Symbolic interactionist theories are less concerned with cognitive or biological stages of growth or with the development of particular personality traits, which are the focus of much theory in psychology; rather, these interactionist theories emphasize the importance of the group context in socialization as well as the generalized view of the self as a social product.

Charles Horton Cooley and the Looking-Glass Self

Charles Horton Cooley (1864–1929) provided sociology with one of its most important concepts regarding the development of the social self. According to Cooley, the individual cannot exist without the group. The individual and the group are "two sides to the same coin." As we have seen, a person cannot develop without human contact and interaction with others. In addition, argued Cooley, a person cannot develop his or her individuality or unique personality outside the context of a group. A person has individuality only in reference to some group. Through interaction with others, then, we develop our sense of self and a sense of uniqueness based on what we learn from those around us. Other people essentially provide us with "social mirrors" in which we see ourselves and learn about ourselves. In other words, we get constant feedback about ourselves when interacting with others.

The concept of the **looking-glass self** contains the simple message that we see ourselves as reflected from others. Cooley's concept actually has three parts: "The imagination of our appearance to the other person, the imagination of his judgment of that appearance, and some sort of self-feeling such as pride or mortification" (Cooley 1964, 82–83, originally published in 1902). Notice that Cooley speaks of "our imagination" of how we appear to others and of others' judgments. We can never know exactly what others think, we can only imagine what they think based on their observable behavior in facial expressions, conversation, or actions. In turn, a person responds to others' judgments with some sort of self-feeling. Cooley implies here that people are profoundly concerned with the reactions of others.

The looking-glass self is a process in which people interact with others and learn about themselves along the way. For example, children develop ideas about themselves when they hear their parents or teachers or friends refer to them as bright or slow, talented or awkward, outgoing or shy. These ideas become integrated into the social self which in turn influences how the individual acts. A child who is treated as bright and talented incorporates that image and has more confidence to behave in a bright and talented manner. The looking-glass self becomes a very real product of interactions with others and helps stamp the person with various traits and tendencies. However, because it is a process, the looking-glass self changes over time as an individual's situation and group relations change. From birth, it is one of the most powerful processes in socialization.

George Herbert Mead: Two Parts to the Self and the Development of the Self

Another major contributor to the sociological understanding of socialization and the development of the social self is **George Herbert Mead** (1863–1931) who taught with Cooley at the same university for a short time. Like Cooley, Mead emphasized understanding the self and the social process of self development. Mead viewed the self as developing "in the process of social experience and activity" (Mead 1934, 135). However, in contrast to Cooley, Mead distinguished two conceptual or analytical phases of the self.

One phase of the self, the **me**, is the product of socialization whereby the individual has learned the organized attitudes, norms, beliefs, and values of the social group. As a "me," the person understands and incorporates what is expected with regard to thinking and behaving. Consequently, the "me" is the conventional, habitual, and conforming aspect of each of us as members of a group. Obviously, society depends on people acting predictably according to social expectations, and the "me" is socialized to conform so that the individual may be part of a group. The "me" is reflected in the fact that we can view ourselves as objects and try to see ourselves as other people see us in order to judge our own behavior. As a typical student, you sit in class, take notes, and carry out much of the required behavior to pass the class. As such, your "me" is present because you are conforming to the role of student according to social expectations.

However, we know there is much more to each of us than our routine, expected behavior. Each individual has his or her own reaction to the demands of the group. For example, individual students react differently to the social expectations for the role of student. According to Mead, the **I** is the unique and individual part of each person and represents the person's own response to the demands of the group. It refers to the unpredictable, innovative, creative, and impulsive phase of the self. The "I" represents self-expression, not necessarily group expression. While the "me" can be viewed as an object, the "I" is subjective; it acts, but it can never be completely predicted. In fact, Mead (1934, 174) said we also "surprise ourselves by our own action." Think of the times you have said to yourself, "I can't believe I did that," when you have surprised yourself with your own behavior. Mead theorized that we can never really know exactly what we are going to do in a given situation until the moment after we have done it. He gave the example of a baseball player who knows how he or she must act when the ball comes his or her way, but who can never know with certainty whether he or she will make a brilliant play or an error. Of course, we can practice and work in a number of ways to control what will happen, but some part of the situation, the actions of other people, and the individual's response will remain unpredictable. In turn, the person's action in the situation will influence his or her concept of self which becomes part of the "me".

The "I" and the "me" together comprise the self, but Mead was also interested in how this self develops in childhood. Consequently, Mead analyzed three stages in the socialization process. The first stage is **imitative** in that an infant first learns by mimicking and imitating others without any understanding of what the behavior means. For the first year or so of life, the child has no real consciousness of self as separate and distinct from others.

As the child reaches the age of one or two, play becomes the critical learning process instead of imitation. Calling this early childhood period the **play stage**, Mead said children play at various roles such as mother, father, doctor, or teacher, and they begin to have some understanding of what is expected of them in social life. However, in the play stage, children are not very organized, and their play is usually not governed by specific rules. They are free to play roles at whim, often taking on several roles in succession. A four-year-old may play mother, father, and sister, one after the other, and may talk back to the other roles. Yet the child is learning. In fact, Mead called this learning **taking the role of the other.** The children put themselves in another's place and attempt to act or to view the world as the other would. Taking the role of the other is a crucial social skill that we must use everyday and is necessary in order for the "me" to exist.

During the play stage, significant others in the child's life have a tremendous impact. **Significant others** are those people closest to us, including parents, brothers, sisters, best friends, and teachers. Although significant others remain important throughout life, children are especially aware of their reactions and their judgments. During the play stage, a child typically can take the role of only one person at a time, often the role of a significant other.

After the play stage—probably past the age of seven—children enter what Mead called the **game stage.** At this point they must learn to engage in organized play according to specific rules. For example, baseball players must understand each position on the team and what is expected of each. They must learn to be part of an organized group and to conform to abstract rules and expectations, also necessary for the "me." For Mead, games are a form of anticipatory socialization.

Mead took the game stage very seriously and pointed out that, through games, children learn to become fully functioning members of society by knowing what society expects. He used the term **generalized other** to refer to that awareness we have of what others—anonymous as they may be—expect us to do. The generalized other represents society in the individual. Through games, children learn to generalize rules and to be concerned with what society expects.

From Mead, we can learn that the self is actually a process involving both the "I" and the "me" and that the self develops gradually as children grow up. In addition, we can learn that some uncertainty about ourselves and our actions is a basic part of social interaction because the unpredictable "I" is inherent in human beings. Socialization is not a process that produces robots engaging in consistently predictable and routine behavior.

Erving Goffman: Many Selves for Many Situations

Also stressing the importance of interaction with others, **Erving Goffman** (1922–1982) developed an approach to understanding the social self that is often controversial. Goffman contradicts much of what we like to think about ourselves. Some say his approach is especially cynical. According to Goffman (1959), a core self in each individual does not exist in the traditional sense. Instead, each person has many selves. The self is situational. Depending on the interaction situation and the people involved, each of us acts very differently. In fact, Goffman believed that our most important requirement as social beings is to create a variety of acts that are designed to impress others. He called this process **impression management,** referring to the techniques people use to manipulate the impressions others have of us. Impression management is the art of putting on an act. Tactics in impression management include the use of costumes, makeup, props, settings, and rehearsals. We rehearse the use of various gestures, mannerisms, ways of speaking, styles of

As children enter adolescence, the peer group and pressures to conform are most important as illustrated by these young people in Stamford, Vermont.

dressing, and personal possessions in order to be more convincing and impressive to the audience.

Goffman compared life to the dramatic presentation of a play in a theater. In modern, anonymous societies, people are required to be actors playing roles, attempting to convince audiences that they are for real. For example, teachers stage their acts in front of the class, often very different from their acts at home or in front of their peers. Waiters and waitresses, sales people, politicians, and flight attendants have occupations that essentially require individuals to stage their behavior. A waiter or a flight attendant cannot often show behavior that would anger the customer even if the customer is being terribly difficult. Keep in mind, however, that Goffman assumed we all stage our behavior regardless of our occupations.

Goffman felt that a person really has no self other than what is acted out for others to see. The self is created in interaction, and it changes with interaction situations. For example, you might have one routine act for your family, another for your boss, another for those who work for you, another for customers, and another for a close friend. We create different kinds of selves depending on our audience. Which one is real? According to Goffman, they all are, if they are carried off. We have as many selves as we have situations. To Goffman, people are like onions; if you peel off all the layers, nothing is left. There is no core as there would be if we were like, say, an artichoke with its central heart. To Goffman, society is a dramatic show. We are each other's audiences, and the appearance of success in playing out the role is what counts in defining the actor. The socialization process teaches people how to put on acts.

The Settings for Socialization

So far in our discussion of socialization, we have mentioned in passing major socializers such as the family and peers. We now look at the major forces in socialization in more detail. Keep in mind the concepts of the looking-glass self, the "I" and the "me," and impression management as you examine the four most important socializers and the settings in which they act.

The Family as the Setting for Socialization

The family is the most important agent of socialization for a number of reasons. It provides the setting for primary socialization and is responsible for accomplishing the process. The family provides the earliest human contact for an infant and has the responsibility of giving the attention, love, and concern necessary for the child to thrive. As we saw earlier with the cases of Anna and Isabelle, families do not always live up to this responsibility.

In addition to nurturing the child, the family also gives the child its position in the social structure regarding social class, ethnicity, and religion. Most important, the location of the family in the class structure of our society—based on education, wealth, and prestige—has enormous effects on the socialization of the children. The educational level of the parents affects their overall approach to child-rearing, how they discipline the children, whether the children go to private or public schools, and what kinds of books, toys, and instructional materials are given to the children. The economic standing of the parents has several significant indirect effects on the process of socialization, too. The neighborhood in which the child grows up often determines the kinds of peers the child will play with and what kinds of schools will be attended. In turn, neighbors, peers, and schools have significant influences on the child's development or, for that matter, even survival.

Consider, for example, the early life of professional prizefighter Jake La Motta. In his book *Raging Bull* (1980), La Motta illustrates how life in a slum tenement affected his boyhood. He speaks of the smell, the rats, the cold winters without fuel, and the stifling heat of the summers. While he says he dreamed of what it would be like to have money and own a Cadillac, he "knew that all you would ever get would be what you could steal. . . . For me and the guys I knew, school was for the birds, the thing was to get the money. The guys who had the big cars and the broads, they weren't the ones going to school nights" (La Motta 1980, 3). La Motta goes on to relate how he learned to fight, first with an ice pick given to him by his father. La Motta was crying because he had been beaten by some bullies. His father slapped him severely several times, which was not unusual, telling him to use the ice pick to protect himself and to never cry again (La Motta 1980, 4–6).

The status of the parents and their ability to provide opportunities have an impact on their children's future by influencing a wide range of behavior relating to success, including academic ability, choice of college, and choice of occupation. Higher-status parents both directly and indirectly teach their children the necessary behavior to "get ahead." Poverty can be a major barrier for many children because they do not have the built-in opportunities available to children of the middle and upper classes. Differences in role models, educational opportunities, and things as fundamental as good health and diet are related to the social class of the parents.

The family, then, begins the process of socialization and is the first major setting in which the child interacts. Although parents are not solely responsible for the personality of the child—they are not sculptors able to create whatever they wish of the child—the parents do lay the foundation for the future of the child in direct and indirect ways. Without some sort of secure family environment, or with a destructive or neglectful family environment, children face far greater difficulties in both social and personal development.

Peers as the Setting for Socialization

In 1927, sociologist Frederic Thrasher, who studied the development of juvenile play groups and gangs, described children playing in crowded areas of downtown Chicago: "On a warm summer evening children fairly swarm over the areaways and sidewalks, vacant lots and rubbish dumps, streets and alleys. The buzzing chatter and constant motion remind one of insects which hover in a swarm. . . . This endless activity has a tremendous fascination and it would be a marvel indeed if any healthy boy could hold himself aloof from it" (Thrasher 1927, 23).

The quote from Thrasher illustrates that, very early in life, urban children begin playing with other neighborhood children and create a world for themselves apart from families and the adult world. With their peers, children are able to engage in democratic relationships without the ascribed differences found in the home. Although characterized as democratic, children's play groups quickly develop status arrangements. Leadership develops and children gain identities based on their background, ability, and behavior. For example, play groups often have to contend with the bully, the shy child, the spoiled child, or the bigger or more athletically developed child. Children quickly learn the power and the pain of ridicule from peers (and remember these episodes as adults); they feel the need to "fit in" and be like the others, as a result. Consequently, children are constantly learning new behavior and attitudes from other children. Sociologist Joseph Pleck (1976, 255) described the dreadful times in his own childhood when he was always the last boy chosen for a team because he had no athletic ability. The tremendous pressure from other boys and from his father left him with a strong sense of inadequacy.

Interactions within the peer group accomplish much in the establishment of identity and the looking-glass self. From other children, we learn how we are perceived by others outside our family, and those perceptions in turn affect how we perceive ourselves. Do the other children call me skinny or fat, fast or slow, smart or stupid, cute or ugly, friendly or unfriendly? Peers also provide role models for each other, as mentioned above in discussing Jake La Motta. He found that the boys who had status and recognition had material objects obtained through theft. He copied their behavior in an attempt to gain that status and recognition. Most parents can relate incidents when their children pleaded for something by noting that "all the other kids have it." Today, much of the pressure to wear the right clothes and do certain things stems from the role modeling of peers and the desire to fit in and be accepted. This desire to please the peer group becomes especially acute during the adolescent years when youths often feel a need to break away from the family and parental control.

The School as the Setting for Socialization

Once the child begins spending most of his or her time at school, a number of new issues develop in regard to socialization. Primarily we think of the school as teaching the intellectual skills necessary for effective participation in society. Certainly schools must accomplish this goal as part of the socialization process. But in school, children also receive the principle evaluations of their achievements in various intellectual, physical, and social skills. They come to see themselves as being a certain way, which in turn affects their emerging self-concepts. Schools channel children into various roles and often select the children's opportunities by tracking them into high-achieving or low-achieving routes. This, of course, has a great impact on their future opportunities (Elkin and Handel 1984, 156–57).

Sociologists are interested in the stated curriculum in schools regarding intellectual skills; they are just as interested in what we call the hidden curriculum in American classrooms and on school playgrounds. The **hidden curriculum** is concerned with molding and shaping what is considered to be proper social behavior. It teaches children to be neat and punctual, to respect authority, and to be patriotic citizens concerned with conserving the American way of life. On the other hand, some children learn that they are not good at being neat and punctual and that they do not fit into the mold prepared for them and that they are misfits. The hidden curriculum attempts to teach children conformity with regard to expected and conservative standards of behavior.

One major aspect of the hidden curriculum is the cultivation of traditional sex role behavior among boys and girls. Given different standards of conduct in school, boys are encouraged to be aggressive, athletic, and dominant. Girls are expected to be feminine, socially conscious, and submissive. In her book, Raphaela Best (1983), a reading specialist in a Maryland elementary school, noted that, very early on, boys learn to be strong, to fight, and to try to be first in all things. They learn that boys are not supposed to be sissies or crybabies, and boys are not to show emotion or affection or do housework. The boys were especially affected by strong peer-group pressure at school; rejection by the other boys was extremely painful. On the other hand, girls learn to be helpful, affectionate, and concerned with relationships. They were less likely to engage in fighting or in aggressive or competitive behavior. Research Method 4.1 illustrates research documenting the different ways teachers treat their male and female students, thus reinforcing traditional sex role socialization.

Research Method 4.1

• • • • • • Field Research: Sex-role Socialization in the Classroom

"If a boy calls out in class, he gets teacher attention. If a girl calls out in class, she is told to raise her hand before speaking. Teachers praise boys more than girls, give boys more academic help and are more likely to accept boys' comments during classroom discussions." Myra and David Sadker (1988, 191) found evidence of these significant differences in sex-role socialization in elementary school classrooms around the United States.

In order to study the possible differences in how teachers treat boys and girls, the Sadkers conducted a special kind of field research consisting of careful, systematic observation and recording of events occurring in schools in various areas of the United States. They sent trained field researchers into more than one hundred fourth-, sixth- and eighth-grade classes in the District of Columbia and four states. Half of the classes were in math and science, subjects in which boys traditionally excel, while the remaining half were in English and language arts, subjects in which females traditionally do better than boys. The classrooms reflected all varieties of American students and teachers including black and white, urban, suburban, and rural. The teachers included both males and females. The field researchers were instructed to carefully note which students spoke out in the classroom and how the teachers responded.

Field researchers are different from participant observers in that they do not get actively involved in the social situations they are studying in the way participant observers do (see Research Method 3.1 in chapter 3 for an example of participant observation). Instead, these field researchers were told to unobtrusively observe and record classroom behavior, without getting directly involved or affecting the routine situations of teacher and student interaction.

The Sadkers found that, in contradiction to teachers' assumptions that girls are more active in the classroom, boys actually dominated classroom interaction. Whether the class was in math or English, and regardless of the sex of the teacher or whether it was an urban, suburban, or rural school, boys participated more in class discussion than girls, and the boys' participation increased as the school year progressed. The researchers found that boys tend to be much more assertive in the classroom. While girls wait patiently with their hands raised, "boys literally grab teacher attention. They are eight times more likely than girls to call out answers" (Sadker and Sadker 1988, 192). When girls call out answers, they are more likely than boys to be reprimanded for interrupting.

The teachers observed by the field researchers tended to give more specific feedback to the boys and tended to focus more on their area of the room. Girls, on the other hand, tended not to receive as much encouragement or feedback from instructors.

Teachers are important significant others to children, and the impact of teachers' reactions to students on the basis of sex is enormous. The messages they send for both boys and girls are powerful in the socialization process. Boys learn to be strong and assertive while girls are penalized for behaving in such a manner. Consequently, the message is that girls should act like "ladies" and raise their hands, while boys are rewarded for being assertive and grabbing attention. "Sexist treatment in the classroom encourages formation of patterns such as these, which give men more dominance and power in the working world" (Sadker and Sadker 1988, 194).

The Sadkers found that the teachers were astonished with the results of the study. They had no idea that they had been treating their male and female students in such different manners. On the positive side, the Sadkers found that, with as little as four days of training, the teachers effectively eliminated their bias in the classroom. The teachers agreed that females need the same educational encouragement that boys receive.

The Mass Media as the Setting for Socialization

On an average day, a child in our society will be bombarded with information from the mass media. He or she is likely to spend at least five hours in front of the television. Reading comic books, listening to rock music on the radio, or going to the movies are also likely activities for the child. Almost all American homes have a television set in use almost every day. It has become another "person" in the home delivering messages at an incredibly rapid rate. On the average, only sleeping takes more of the child's time than watching television.

As one critic of television states, we have allowed the television industry to try "the first undertaking in mass behavior modification by coast-to-coast and intercontinental electronic hookup" (Goldsen 1979, 167). Many people criticize television because of its content, its pervasiveness, and the fact that it takes so much of the child's time which could be spent, they think, in more productive and important activities. Television is criticized for presenting a slanted view of reality, for implying that most people live at a comfortable upper-middle-class level. It is criticized for presenting unrealistic, derogatory, and stereotypical models of women and minorities. Some complain that television keeps children from reading more or from interacting more with others and gaining valuable social experiences. Many are concerned with the amount of violence portrayed on television both in prime time and in cartoons specifically designed for children. Others are more concerned with sexual content on television (Wright 1986).

What are the effects of television? Does it present a distorted view of reality? Does it function as one of the most important socializing agents? No firm conclusions can be drawn concerning the overall influence of television and other media, but we are beginning to find some trends regarding certain effects. Two areas of interest stand out: the effects of violence shown on television and the kinds of role models presented for children.

Much of the research on media influence is concerned with violence and its effects on the viewers. The evidence shows that television content is heavily concentrated with violent and aggressive behavior and that children are exposed to a large number of violent incidents. Some research indicates that viewing violence on television does increase the likelihood of aggressive behavior such as fighting or hitting or slapping among some categories of children (DeFleur 1983, 574). Moreover, people who view a great deal of television tend to overestimate the amount of crime in society and are more fearful of crime in general. Television programs also tend to give inaccurate pictures of crime and of the criminal justice system by overemphasizing both street crime and efficiency in the judicial process (Haney and Manzolati 1988).

Other studies show that the most important effects of the media have to do with presenting role models for children to admire and imitate. These role models are sometimes characterized as "dumb chic," implying that they glorify behavior that does not include doing well in school. In addition, television is criticized for presenting a narrow range of sex role images; children learn stereotypical and unrealistic expectations regarding the roles of men and women in our society, although less so than in the past. For example, female roles on television are usually less prestigious and important than male roles, and females are less likely to play the leading roles for a series. "In other words, television is a man's world in terms of both numbers and prestige" (DeFleur 1983, 569). Minorities are similarly presented—or rather, underrepresented—on television. With the exception of "The Bill Cosby Show," very few prime-time shows present a realistic image of black or Hispanic families, and advertising often ignores them altogether. Commercial advertising also reflects the stereotypes of women as being primarily responsible for housecleaning and cooking, while men are given more glamorous and interesting roles; men often have to come to the aid of women.

Television and other mass media are not necessarily designed to teach children the way our educational system is structured to teach. Prime-time programs are designed to entertain and perhaps teach indirectly. Because the media have no stated or vested interest in socializing children other than to get them to watch more television and buy various products, those who control media content need not worry about the consequences of their programming unless the public protests.

Nevertheless, the media's sheer pervasiveness has profoundly changed the socialization process simply because children spend so much time with the media.

Not all research, however, indicates that television's impact is necessarily negative. People are not necessarily passive receptors to the messages of television. In fact, people may interact with television and interpret what they see, rather than just accept the images. Television viewing can promote thinking and growth, especially when children watch television with their parents (Hodge and Tripp, 1986). As more research is conducted to identify media impact, we will have to judge carefully the effects on the socialization process.

Socialization Over the Life Cycle

As mentioned at the beginning of this chapter, socialization actually continues throughout a person's life. We now know that it is important to study both primary and adult socialization if we are to understand our lives. The processes in social looking-glasses continue, and the "me" is adaptable and modifiable. In some ways, we face new challenges each day and are confronted with changing situations and realities. We never reach a point at which we stop learning. Consequently, the purpose of this section is to give you an overview of the typical life cycle in American society.

Adolescence

We have already discussed the importance of primary socialization and the impact of the family, friends, schools, and media in setting the stage for childhood learning. But more needs to be said about adolescence, roughly the period from the age of twelve to the early twenties.

Special social and historical forces have created the life stage called adolescence in modern society. It was not until the late nineteenth century that adolescence received much attention at all. Before that, maturity had to come quickly to young people; they had to help on the farm or earn a living, often in harsh environments. But changes in work-force requirements meant that young people would have to stay in school longer to be trained for twentieth-century work. Longer training required longer time spent at home, governed by parents. At the same time, better diet and health lowered the age for the onset of puberty. Society created a kind of limbo for teenagers; physical maturity occurred earlier, but society required longer dependency on the family in order to be trained for modern work. The issues of dependency and social restrictions continue to be major problems for adolescents and their families.

Psychologist G. Stanley Hall (1904), published the first major work on adolescence. Hall developed the idea that the teenage years were especially difficult, calling adolescence a time of "storm and stress," when the individual is neither child nor adult. By the 1950s and 1960s, as the baby-boom generation entered adolescence, a youth subculture developed ushering in rock music and teenage rebellion.

Adolescence is still characterized as a period of limbo between childhood and adulthood, making it a time of possible confusion and instability. For one thing, adolescents must contend with major biological changes as their bodies begin to mature. They are beginning to learn how to interact with the other sex as they move into dating and intimate relationships, interactions which allow for potential feelings of insecurity and fears of rejection.

A double standard still operates in American society with regard to males and females (see Research Method 2.1, chapter 2). "For males the focus of sexuality may be sexual conquest. Young men who are nonexploitative or inexperienced are often labeled with highly negative terms like 'sissy.' On the other hand, peers often provide social reinforcement for stereotypical 'masculine' attitudes and behaviors. . . ." (Crooks and Baur 1990, 459). Females who engage in sex still risk losing their reputations as good girls. "Many girls face a dilemma. They may learn to appear 'sexy' to attract males, yet often experience ambivalence about overt sexual behavior" (Crooks and Baur 1990, 460). As one young woman reported (Crooks and Baur 1990, 460):

> Going out with boys is hard for me when it comes to making a decision about sex. I'm afraid if I don't hold out long enough they'll think I'm easy and if I wait too long they'll lose interest.

According to research by Zelnick and Kantner (1980) 69 percent of females and 77 percent of males have engaged in sexual intercourse before age nineteen. About one in ten sexually active teen females gets pregnant every year (Crooks and Baur 1990, 467). The problem of teenage sex and pregnancy in American society reflects the dual messages sent to youth. On the one hand, their bodies are signalling sexual maturity and, at the same time, television, movies, and advertising are saturated with explicit sexual imagery. On the other hand, teenagers usually are told it is wrong to engage in sex, if they are told anything at all at home. It appears that most American adolescents want their parents to provide sex education, but most parents do not provide adequate sexual information for their young sons and daughters (Crooks and Baur 1990, 488).

Erikson (1950) described adolescence as a time of experimentation with a variety of roles, and confusion over roles is a potential problem. It is a time when youth are more likely to experiment with various activities including sex, alcohol, drugs, disruptive behavior, running away, and delinquent conduct. The relatively high suicide rate among teenagers also indicates potential difficulties young people experience at that age. Although most do not run away, attempt suicide, or become seriously involved in drug use, a large enough percentage do—referred to as the significant one-third—to cause questioning and concern in society.

During the period of adolescence, the peer group moves into position as the most important agent of socialization, often promoting standards of conduct that conflict with those of parents. Young people often develop strategies for balancing the competing demands of peers and parents. They may listen to their parents more often regarding educational goals and future plans. However, they most often turn to their friends about issues such as dating, clothing, sex, and other things of immediate adolescent concern (Sebald 1989).

Typically, teenagers must contend with status arrangements at school. The cliques found in most high schools exercise considerable influence over members in expected school performance, extracurricular activity, and alcohol or drug use. Research Application 4.1 discusses the importance of peer group associations in a large, suburban high school.

Research Application 4.1

· · · · · · · **Cliques and Identity in American High Schools**

For most of those who attended American public high schools, regardless of how long ago, it is not difficult to remember the division of the student body into cliques. These cliques continue to be an integral part of the high school social scene. Membership in such cliques has a considerable influence on the adolescent's sense of identity and belonging, two strong needs common to teenagers in this society. Many sociological studies have documented the prevalence of group divisions in high school and have noted how clique membership and the resulting peer socialization affect the academic performance, as well as the goals and orientations, of the individuals.

Sociologist Ralph Larkin (1979) conducted an in-depth study of a large suburban high school in the United States. He found the existence of six major group divisions with a large number of students left out. Larkin called those who were left out the silent majority. The leading crowds, according to Larkin, were the "jocks and rah-rahs," the "politicos," and the "intellectuals."

The jocks and rah-rahs were so named because the group consisted primarily of cheerleaders, "athletes and their admirers and female students involved in more traditional roles of gaining success through the achievements of their boyfriends" (Larkin 1979, 69). This crowd formed the center of the school's spirit and was dominant in school social activities. They tended to be from upper-middle-class Protestant families and were expected to go to prestigious colleges.

Students in the second leading crowd, the politicos, were primarily involved in political offices on campus such as student body president or class officer. The student council activities interested them, and they were involved in other political and governmental bodies on campus. These students, like the jocks and rah-rahs, tended to come from privileged backgrounds but they were more likely to be Jewish.

Students in the third leading crowd, the intellectuals, were very bright students whose interests were in music, philosophy, literature, and mathematics. These students were seldom mocked by the other students and were respected for their talents and abilities.

Another crowd in Larkin's study included the freaks who were more likely to use drugs and who prided themselves on being anti-authoritarian and rebellious at school and in the community. Larkin also identified the greasers who modeled themselves after motorcycle gangs and developed a reputation for toughness and violence. While the freaks tended to come from middle-class families, the greasers were more likely to come from working-class backgrounds.

The high school in Larkin's study also had a small percentage of blacks who made up their own group and were not found to any extent in the groups mentioned above. Larkin characterized their existence at school as separate and unequal.

The bulk of students in the silent majority also had cliques centered on similar interests and common activities. Some were centered around religious youth-group activities while others were centered on similar interests at school such as computers, intramurals, or mechanics.

The significance of the various groups in high school is in the influence over the future direction of the respective members. Group membership influenced orientation toward education and whether the individual would go to college. The identity of an individual in a large high school is in large part a function of group membership. Not only other students but teachers and people in the

community tend to define the students according to their cohorts. Consequently, a student may be perceived as a poor student because he or she is known to associate with freaks or greasers, as such, he or she will not be accorded the status or privilege often extended to members of the leading crowds. In addition, while the importance of the peer group in the socialization process has already been discussed, the cliques found in high schools provide a clear example of how peers often provide the most important source of identity and belonging for adolescents.

Adolescence can be a difficult time of transition when experimentation is more common and when questions regarding identity and self-concept are more frequently asked. The peer-group standards become critical in helping define identity as well as in giving a sense of belonging and camaraderie. The pressure to achieve peer-group approval and live up to peer standards is at its height during the teenage years. As individuals reach their late teens and early twenties, however, they must face the transition to early adulthood and establish some independence and direction of their own.

Early Adulthood

As we move into a discussion of adulthood socialization, a word of caution is necessary. Research on stages in the adult life cycle is relatively recent and no definite agreement exists concerning even the existence of such stages tied to specific adult age categories. For example, as one author states, "because the adult years are so variable, we cannot assume that particular transitions will necessarily occur at specific ages" (Schlossberg 1987, 74). Consequently, the following discussion of adult stages must be viewed as very general, tentative, and subject to tremendous differences among individuals.

Although a person may be twenty years old or older, most people in our society do not define him or her as a full-fledged adult until he or she is self-supporting, in an occupation, and perhaps married. Even at work, the young college graduate is perceived as a novice, a beginner who has much to learn at work and in life, and is quite likely referred to as "the kid" by older workers.

Psychologist Daniel Levinson (1979, 1986) defines the twenties as the **novice stage** in early adulthood. The twenties are characterized as years of initial choices concerning marriage and family, occupation, lifestyle, and general direction in life. Young people in their twenties may have vague dreams of what they want out of life, but much of life seems to be in the future, and dreams are often unrealistic. There seems to be plenty of time to do whatever one wants in life. For some, it can be a rootless, transient time of exploring possibilities or putting off decisions; for others, it may be a time of premature commitment to a way of life without exploring alternatives. According to Levinson, both exploration and commitment are necessary for a stable life structure.

At about age thirty, although these ages vary with the individual, a transitional period is common, and many will experience it as a time of crisis. At about this age, one is no longer considered a novice, and suddenly it dawns on the individual that whatever choices made are "for real" (Levinson 1979, 58). The typical thirty-year-old will begin to ask many serious questions about career, family choices, and what he or she really wants out of life. He or she might feel it will soon be too late to change the direction of life or to reach the dreams left from the twenties.

A mother is clearly enjoying feeding her young child. Such intimate relationships form the basis for the deepest social learning that will last throughout the life of the child.

Their questions might include, "Do I want to do this kind of work for thirty-five more years? Why didn't I consider other choices regarding college or graduate school? What am I missing in life? Do I really love the person I've married? Is this what I hoped for?" Typically, the thirty-year-old has been married for five or ten years and now has bills to pay, children to raise; the honeymoon is definitely over. Often a difficult transitional period, these few years in the early thirties require the development of a realistic set of values and attitudes in life as well as either a revision or acceptance of these choices, which will govern the individual's adult life.

Journalist Gail Sheehy (1977) also wrote about "catch-30" in her book on adult socialization, *Passages*. From her series of interviews, she discovered that, at thirty, "almost everyone wants to make some alteration" (Sheehy 1977, 198). She noted that people in their early thirties tend to feel choking restrictions in their present way of life. As a result, they often make significant new decisions, and their commitments usually waver or deepen.

The late thirties are characterized as a "settling down" period in which the individual is primarily concerned with being successful at work and at home. The major concern is with recognition and advancement. During this time, the typical individual wants strong sociological anchors to family, friends, work, and the community. Soon—at about age forty, according to Levinson—the individual must face the transition to middle adulthood.

Middle Adulthood

The early forties may comprise another period of questioning, self-assessment, and searching according to both Levinson and Sheehy. At this point, people often begin to fear the effects of age: wrinkles, gray hair, balding, extra weight, or poor health. Our culture values a youthful appearance, and we fight aging and anguish over it. Aging may be particularly hard on women due to the sexual double standard which defines women as less attractive than men as they age. Sometimes this period in the early forties marks a fairly severe crisis for a person as he or she questions, "What have I done with my life now that it is more than half over?" The children may be grown, which often brings questions of whether or not one was a successful parent. At this point, they may review the past, regret mistakes, and worry about what has been accomplished at work or in life. The dreams never attained may now come back to haunt people.

Most people resolve these questions to some satisfaction during a period of adjustment; perhaps they make changes in the direction and meaning of their lives and then continue. The late forties and fifties mark a very creative period for those who have made peace with life. They may be more financially stable and have more time to do a variety of things such as volunteering in the community, returning to school, taking up a new career, or developing new interests and goals. Some find satisfaction in the **mentor role** at work. A mentor is an older person who takes a younger worker "under wing" and offers advice, training, friendship, and the enormous benefit of experience. Successful workers have often pointed to a mentor as an important key to their achievement. The mentor serves as an important agent of adult socialization at work and achieves the respect and admiration of the younger worker.

Late Adulthood and Death

Growing old and facing death are not issues many of us like to think about in this culture. We value life, youth, and vitality; we're deeply troubled when friends and relatives suffer chronic disabilities. Most people do not like to think about oncoming biological deterioration and declining health, but in those last years of life, people must learn to deal, not only with aging, but with the illnesses and deaths of husbands or wives and close friends. Retirement brings the loss of occupational status, which is a key factor in adult self-concepts, and financial difficulties are possible.

Often rejected by others, the elderly may find that they have no place or sense of purpose in society. The elderly are like adolescents in that neither group is given a definite place in our society. Members of both age groups are considered marginal to mainstream society. That is, they are not fully integrated into the occupational or adult social structure in our society. They exist slightly on the outside or on the fringe. Many occupations are closed to the elderly. Often their children do not want the elderly to live with them. Some families find that they cannot take care of an aged relative if there are significant health problems involved.

In addition, unlike in many other cultures, we tend to hold negative stereotypes about the elderly: that they are too slow, that they live in the past, and that they are senile. In a sense, we expect the elderly to disengage gracefully. **Disengagement** means letting go, slowly withdrawing from life in preparation for death. Yet, research shows that remaining active, which most prefer to do, is far more beneficial for the aged in terms of health, well-being, and a positive self-concept. Research also shows that being elderly does not automatically mean loss of memory or senility. Most people over sixty-five remain intellectually strong, alert, and capable. More about the elderly will be discussed in chapter eight.

Problem Areas in American Socialization

Several significant areas of concern in American society relate to the socialization process and are worthy of discussion in this chapter. For example, in the past ten years we have become increasingly concerned with violence in the family and more frequent reports of child abuse and neglect. Another problem area relates to the increasing use of daycare for small children. More dual-earning couples and single parents are more dependent than ever on day care for children. Children left at home alone and unsupervised while their parents work—latch-key children, as they are called—are also part of the reason for a growing concern about the socialization patterns brought about by both economic and social changes affecting the American family.

Violent Socialization

The disturbing figures regarding child abuse and neglect indicate that each year in the United States as many as one to two million children are beaten, tortured, kicked, belted, burned, bruised, sexually molested, or severely neglected. However, the public was not generally aware of such abuse until the late 1960s and early 1970s. Child abuse had to be studied, defined, and recognized as a social problem in order for the public to react. In fact, child abuse has not always been considered a crime. In American colonial times, children were viewed as the property of their parents, who could generally do what they wished with their children in terms of discipline and punishment. Vestiges of those ideas are still reflected in that some parents are outraged when authorities intervene in what they consider a private, family situation.

Today **child abuse** refers to actual physical violence by parents or caretakers. Sometimes it is difficult to decide at what point strict physical punishment stops being discipline and becomes physical abuse. Sociologists usually define child abuse as the intentional harm of a child beyond a mild spanking (Straus, Gelles, and Steinmetz 1980; Gelles and Straus 1988). Legally, more courts are now likely to concur with that definition.

Child neglect, more common than child abuse, means that the family does not provide the basic necessities of food, shelter, safety, emotional support, and attention. In both child abuse and neglect, the life of the child is often in danger. In a recent survey on family violence, Gelles and Straus (1988) found that 107 of every one thousand children aged three to seventeen experienced severe violence from parents in 1985. About two thousand children die every year from neglect and abuse.

The causes of child abuse and neglect are complex. The background and life experiences of the parents are important; if the parent was abused, he or she is more likely to abuse his or her child. Financial pressures on the family, immaturity of the parents, the belief in harsh discipline, isolation from others, and the inability to deal with anger or to express it without aggression have been found to be factors in child abuse.

What effects do such abuse and neglect have on the children? Recent research indicates certain trends. Victims of abuse tend to experience emotional problems and often have a very low opinion of themselves. They tend to feel guilty because they question what they have done to deserve such treatment. They sometimes suffer from depression and may have difficulty in establishing close emotional relationships. "They struggle, sometimes all their lives, to get the nurturing and the feeling of being cared for that they have never experienced" (Bartollas 1985, 245). To some extent, child abuse and neglect are also related to disruptive behavior in school, running away, alcohol and drug problems, delinquent or criminal behavior, and even homicide (Bartollas 1985, 245–47).

While we are becoming more aware of the problem and effects of child abuse, there is also room for hope. Children can be resilient, as in the case of Isabelle mentioned earlier in this chapter; they can go on to lead relatively normal, healthy lives, given some other source of stability and nurturance in the child's environment (Skolnick 1978). If the victims of abuse and neglect can be identified and helped, many of the problems mentioned above can be averted.

Day Care and Socialization

One trend in modern society—probably irreversible—is the increasing number of working women, including mothers of small children. The change has been dramatic. In the United States, fewer than 10 percent of all families have a father at work and a mother at home with the children. In 1950, only 12 percent of mothers with preschool children worked outside the home; today nearly 60 percent do. Of mothers with children younger than age 14, almost 70 percent are in the work force. More than 26 million children under age 14 have mothers who work outside the home in the United States, and most of these mothers work full time (U.S. Department of Labor 1988, 7–8).

Who takes care of the children while the parents are at work? Some working couples split shifts so that one can be with the child, but single mothers do not have that option. More than half of the children of all working mothers are cared for by relatives such as fathers, grandparents, aunts, uncles, or cousins. About 23 percent are cared for by nonrelatives—such as neighbors in private homes unregulated by the government—while 19 percent are in day-care facilities, nurseries, or preschool. Nearly 4 percent—the so-called latch-key children—simply stay home alone (U.S. Department of Labor 1988, 11).

Considerable concern has been expressed recently about the increasing number of infants and children placed in day-care centers or unlicensed homes of nonrelatives. While Americans are ambivalent about it, such child care arrangements have come to fill a significant need for many parents who have no one else to care for their children. Much of the concern for the increasing use of day care stems from the fact that it contradicts cherished traditions of family and child care in which the mother typically stayed home to care for the children. Change is often automatically perceived as threatening. We fret about the effects on the children and wonder if the fabric of the family is shredding. On the other hand, economic need draws both parents out of the home, if with a sense of guilt about leaving the children. Critics of increasing day-care use argue that children need the security and closeness of at least one parent at home. They assert that children growing up in other child-care arrangements miss the constant nurture and love that only a parent can give.

Research demonstrates that the critical variable in day care is the quality of the services (Kagan, Kearsley, and Zelaso 1978). If the day-care facility is an adequate one that meets children's needs for supervision, for emotional support, and for growth and learning, day care does not appear to be harmful to children by disrupting family ties or hindering children in social and emotional development. In fact, day care offers children a wider social network and gives them the opportunity to play in a structured environment with their peers.

The key issue lies in finding such quality day care at an affordable price. Quality care costs hundreds of dollars a month, and a single mother working for meager wages may find child-care costs overwhelming. In addition, the evidence indicates that quality child care is simply not available in many communities or may require a long commuting distance from the home. The United States lags behind other industrialized nations—all having a high percentage of women in the work force—in having a national child-care policy (Lubeck and Garrett 1990). The federal government has not been helpful in establishing day-care arrangements, and private industry is only slowly adjusting to the idea of day care provided at the workplace (Rhodes and Regan 1989).

In addition, parents may often find it extremely difficult to know from an initial contact whether the child-care facility meets the standards of the parents or the community. Adequate licensing and control of day-care centers is of utmost importance in our society as we come to rely on them more and more to help socialize our children.

Questions for Summary and Review

1. What is the nature versus nurture debate regarding human development? Explain.
2. Define socialization.
3. Explain the four types of socialization and give examples of each.
4. Discuss how Cooley, Mead, and Goffman view socialization and the self. What is the unique focus of sociologists regarding socialization?
5. Explain the imitative, play, and game stages discussed by Mead.
6. Discuss Goffman's concept of impression management and give examples from your own life.
7. What are the four major agents or settings for socialization? Discuss each and give examples of how they affect an individual as he or she is growing up.
8. Explain how socialization continues over the life cycle. Point out the features of socialization during adolescence, early adulthood, middle adulthood, and late adulthood.
9. Discuss the issue of family violence in America today. What are some of the causes and effects of child abuse?
10. Why is day care a major issue in modern society? Explain what changes have taken place that have made daycare an important social concern.

Key Concepts

Adult socialization (p. 62)
Anticipatory socialization (p. 61)
Child abuse (p. 79)
Child neglect (p. 79)
Disengagement (p. 78)
Game stage (p. 66)
Generalized other (p. 66)
I (p. 65)
Imitative stage (p. 65)
Impression management (p. 66)
Looking-glass self (p. 64)

Me (p. 65)
Mentor (p. 78)
Nature versus nurture debate (p. 59)
Novice stage (p. 76)
Play stage (p. 65)
Primary socialization (p. 60)
Resocialization (p. 63)
Significant others (p. 66)
Socialization (p. 60)
Taking the role of the other (p. 66)
Total institutions (p. 63)

References

1. Bartollas, Clemens. 1985. *Juvenile delinquency.* New York: John Wiley and Sons.

2. Best, Raphaela. 1983. *We've all got scars: What boys and girls learn in elementary school.* Bloomington, Ind.: Indiana University Press.

3. Braly, Malcolm. 1976. *False starts: A memoir of San Quentin and other prisons.* New York: Penguin Books.

4. Brooks-Gunn, Jeanne, and W.S. Matthews. 1979. *He and she: How children develop their sex-role identity.* Englewood Cliffs, N.J.: Prentice-Hall, Inc.

5. Cooley, Charles Horton. 1964. *Human nature and the social order.* New York: Schocken.

6. Crooks, Robert, and Karla Baur. 1990. *Our sexuality.* 4th ed. Redwood City, Calif.: The Benjamin/Cummings Publishing Co.

7. Davis, Kingsley. 1947. Final notes on a case of extreme isolation. *American journal of sociology* (March):432–43.

8. DeFleur, Melvin L. 1983. *Social problems in American society.* Boston: Houghton Miffin Company.

9. Elkin, Frederick and Gerald Handel. 1984. *The child and society: The process of socialization.* 4th ed. New York: Random House.

10. Erikson, Erik. 1950. *Childhood and society.* New York: Norton Press.

11. Eshleman, J. Ross. 1981. *The family: An introduction.* 3d ed. Boston: Allyn and Bacon.

12. Gelles, Richard J., and Murray A. Straus. 1988. *Intimate violence: The causes and consequences of abuse in the American family.* New York: Touchstone.

13. Goffman, Erving. 1959. *The presentation of self in everyday life.* Garden City, N.Y.: Anchor Books.

14. _____. 1961. *Asylums: Essays on the social situation of mental patients and other inmates.* Garden City, N.Y.: Anchor Books.

15. Goldsen, Ruth. 1979. Changing channels: How TV shapes American minds. *In Mass media and society,* edited by Alan Wells, 159–67. 3rd ed. Palo Alto, Calif.: Mayfield Publishing Company.

16. Hall, G. Stanley. 1904. *Adolescence: Its psychology and its relations to physiology, anthropology, sociology, sex, crime, religion and education.* 2 vols. New York: Appleton.

17. Haney, Craig, and John Manzolati. 1988. Television criminology: Network illusions of criminal justice realities. *In The social animal,* edited by Eliot Aronson, 120–131. 5th ed. New York: W.H. Freeman and Company.

18. Hodge, Robert, and David Tripp. 1986. *Children and television: A semiotic approach.* Cambridge, Mass.: Polity Press.

19. Hoyenga, Katharine B., and K.T. Hoyenga. 1979. *The question of sex differences.* Boston: Little, Brown and Company.

20. Kagan, Jerome. 1984. *The nature of the child.* New York: Basic Books.

21. Kagan, Jerome, R.B. Kearsley, and P.R. Zelaso. 1978. *Infancy: Its place in human development.* Cambridge, Mass.: Harvard University Press.

22. La Motta, Jake, with Joseph Carter and Peter Savage. 1980. *Raging bull.* New York: Bantam Books.

23. Larkin, Ralph. 1979. *Suburban youth in cultural crisis.* New York: Oxford University Press.

24. Levinson, Daniel. 1979. *The seasons of a man's life.* New York: Alfred A. Knopf.

25. _____. 1986. A conception of adult development. *American psychologist* 41:3–13, 287, 293.

26. Lubeck, Sally, and Patricia Garrett. 1990. Child care 2000: Policy options for the future. *In Social Problems 90/91,* edited by L.W. Barnes, 77–83. Guilford, Conn.: Dushkin.

27. Mead, George Herbert. 1934. *Mind, self, and society.* Chicago: University of Chicago Press.

28. Pleck, Joseph. 1976. My male sex role—and ours. *In The forty-nine percent majority: The male sex role,* edited by Deborah David and Robert Brannon, 253–69. Reading, Mass.: Addison-Wesley.

29. Rhodes, David W., and Margaret Regan. 1989. Managing child care in the 1990s. *The journal of business strategy* (July/August): 56–59.

30. Rosenthal, Robert, and Lenore Jacobson. 1968. *Pygmalion in the classroom: Teacher expectation and pupils' intellectual development.* New York: Holt, Rinehart, and Winston.

31. Sadker, Myra, and David Sadker. 1988. Sexism in the schoolroom of the '80s. In *Sociological footprints,* edited by L. Cargan and J. Ballantine, 191–194. Belmont, Calif.: Wadsworth.

32. Schlossberg, Nancy K. 1987. Taking the mystery out of change. *Psychology today* (May):74–75.

33. Sebald, Hans. 1989. Adolescents' peer orientation: Changes in the support system during the past three decades. *Adolescence* 24:937–945.

34. Sheehy, Gail. 1977. *Passages: Predictable crises of adult life.* New York: Bantam Books.

35. Skolnick, Arlene. 1978. The myth of the vulnerable child. *Psychology today* 2:56–65.

36. Straus, Murray, R.J. Gelles, and S.K. Steinmetz. 1980. *Behind closed doors: Violence in the American family.* New York: Anchor Books.

37. Thrasher, Frederic M. 1927. *The gang.* Chicago: University of Chicago Press.

38. U.S. Department of Labor. 1988. *Child care: A workforce issue, Report of the Secretary's Task Force.* Washington, D.C.: U.S. Government Printing Office.

39. Wilson, Edward O. 1975. *Sociobiology: The new synthesis.* Cambridge, Mass.: Harvard University Press.

40. _____. 1979. *Sociobiology.* 2d ed. Cambridge, Mass.: Belknap.

41. Wright, Charles R. 1986. *Mass communication: A sociological perspective.* 3d ed. New York: Random House.

42. Zelnick, Melvin, and John S. Kantner. 1980. Sexual activity, contraceptive use and pregnancy among metropolitan-area teenagers, 1971–1979. *Family planning perspectives.* 12:230–237.

5 *Understanding Organization in Social Life*

• • • • • • • • • • • •

Chapter Outline

•

Part of the complexity of life today is that we find ourselves in so many different and strange worlds. Our daily existence is filled with various experiences shared with any number of people from very diverse backgrounds. These many daily experiences happen in completely different settings. The intriguing thing is that usually we can make the transition from one experience to another with only minimal difficulty.

Mary Thomas rushes into class a few minutes late. She is late because her youngest child refused to finish breakfast and Mary had to take her children to the day-care center herself since they missed their ride. Once in class, however, she quickly opens her notebook, listens attentively, and takes notes on what her professor is saying. As soon as class is over Mary goes to her car and drives downtown where she works part-time as a secretary. There she types bills, answers the telephone, and does other tasks asked by her employer. After four hours at the job she again hurries on her way, this time to pick up her children and take them home. There her attention turns to preparing dinner for her husband and family. After dinner she and her husband talk over the activities of the day and make decisions concerning family affairs. Then she opens her books and begins preparing for yet another class she will attend on the next day.

For Mary, life is a series of rapid changes. In the course of one day she has gone from acting as a mother to being a student. Then she went to work where she performed as a good employee. From work she returned to her role of mother and, eventually, wife. Then she ended the day by returning to her activities as a student. Another day will bring the same shifting activities. She is constantly moving from one setting to another, reacting differently to other persons in each. The interesting fact is that she is able to make the numerous changes back and forth without difficulty; in fact, she makes them almost automatically.

Mary is not unlike the rest of us in having to make these continual shifts in behavior. We all do it many times a day. How is it that we can go from one situation to the next and grasp immediately what is expected of us? It is possible because our interaction with others is not unique to the particular situation. There is an organization or patterning to the way in which we relate to one another in any given social setting. For each new situation, such as a new job or a recent marriage, society has taught us expectations for our behavior and related expectations for the behavior of others.

The Patterning of Social Life

As we explained in the last chapter, humans adapt to their surrounding environment by cultural rather than physical evolution. Unlike other animals, humans do not have their behavior biologically preset for them. It is the culture of one's society that prescribes what behavior will be expected and proscribes what is forbidden. Sociologists use two general concepts to describe the way in which social life is patterned: status and role.

Status

Status refers to any of the hundreds of socially defined positions that members of a society may occupy. In this sense it has little to do with prestige, a term frequently used as a synonym for status. Rather, it signifies the many social spaces existing in society. These spaces are independent of the individuals who occupy them; they simply designate the positions necessary for the ongoing functions of a society: bank teller, lawyer, cleric, student, prisoner, mother, husband, and many more. Each individual will occupy a number of such statuses, though not all at the same time.

Consider your own life. How many different statuses do you hold? Right now you are occupying the status of student. You may also be a husband or wife, mother or father, friend, mechanic, secretary, or club member. Some statuses, such as man or woman, doctor or lawyer, are held for a long period of time; others, such as college student or spectator at a sporting event, are held for a much briefer time. All of us occupy a number of these long- or short-term positions in society at any given time.

We make an important distinction between two types of status: ascribed and achieved. **Ascribed statuses** are assigned to us by our society, generally at the time of our birth. Our gender, race, ethnic group, family heritage are all ascribed positions in society. Having a physical disability, such as blindness or lameness, can also be an ascribed status. In none of these instances do we work at having this position; it is a given with which we live.

A classic example of ascribed status is the Hindu caste system in the India of previous days. A Hindu was born into a particular caste and usually remained in that caste for life. The priest and warrior castes held the highest positions in the system. The occupational castes fell just below the priest and warrior. At the bottom were members of the society so lowly as to be outside the caste system altogether—the out-castes. In each case, caste position was designated on the basis of the parents' caste on the child's birth date. The caste system is no longer enforced in India; even so, children most often remain in the same status as their parents.

The United States is usually seen as an open society, one in which all are free to move from one position to another depending on our abilities. It is true that no rigid caste system exists, but we have come close to one in certain instances. The situation for blacks at one time was very much like that of a caste. Laws in the North as well as in the South restricted the activities and opportunities of those deemed to be of that race. Such limitations, based solely on an ascribed characteristic and enforced by law as well as custom, are reminiscent of the concept of caste; millions were held in a particular lowly esteemed status solely on the basis of birth. Today scholars such as William Julian Wilson (1972, 1987) contend that inequality is more a matter of socioeconomic status than race. Still, race continues to contribute heavily to that status.

So, even in contemporary society certain ascribed statuses are very important in determining the life chances of an individual. For example, gender often affects a person's earning power. Males have traditionally had an advantage in terms of occupational opportunities. Despite efforts to bring about equality, this advantage still exists; women earn only seventy cents for every dollar made by men.

Achieved statuses, on the other hand, are earned. They are attained as the result of some activity or accomplishment. The fact that you are in this sociology course means that you have achieved one thing—admission to a college or university and hence the status of college student. In turn, this and your other classes are steps toward another achieved status, that of college graduate and perhaps then teacher, business executive, or lawyer. In general, education is the single most important means by which individuals achieve more rewarding statuses in life.

Ascribed and achieved statuses are not independent. Some ascribed statuses may actually hinder an individual's achievement of occupational goals. For example, a female born to poor parents in the ghetto may dream of becoming a physician. The desire is not forbidden, but the chances that she will be able to get a decent education in ghetto schools, find the money to attend college and medical school, and graduate, are slim. Even if this individual should achieve the status of physician, positions at prestigious hospitals and practices may not be offered her.

Ascribed statuses can also help ensure that a cherished goal will be achieved. Imagine another young person, a male, who has a similar desire to become a physician. He is the son of a prominent banker and a graduate of a respected university. Assuming equal intellectual ability, it is much more likely that this person—because of ascribed class position and gender—will enter medical school and graduate, be accepted into one of the better residencies, and eventually join a prestigious practice.

Using the concepts of ascribed and achieved status helps us understand a basic goal of the various civil rights movements. Whether it is racial integration or equality of rights for women, the issue is the same—evaluations and rewards based on what individuals have done rather than on what they are. The continuing importance of ascribed statuses, illustrated by gender and race, leads to a consideration of how such positions can influence the total life of individuals.

Such statuses, as well as some that are ascribed, can be seen as **master statuses** which outweigh and influence all other statuses in the eyes of other people. For example, gender and race are master statuses. Women may become physicians, but they usually will be referred to as *women* doctors. Blacks may become university professors, but to many they will remain *blacks* first, professors second.

Not all master statuses are ascribed, however. Being labeled as deviant or homosexual, for example, can also become a status that affects the way in which others view everything you do. Obtaining a law degree or having exceptional talent will not erase, in the eyes of some, the deviant status (see chapter 9).

Occupation is another potential master status. Ministers, for example, are expected to be morally superior in all situations. Imagine the pastor who is playing golf with parishioners and misses a short putt. Most of us would at least utter a mild expletive. A short blast of profanity from the pastor, however, may be seen as

A Marine recruit takes on a new status as basic training begins at Parris Island, S.C.

out of character. The pastor is human, with a full array of emotions and needs, but first and foremost he is a *pastor*.

Some master statuses may have an especially negative influence on an individual. The status of mental patient or prisoner may be so encompassing that others view individuals who have occupied those statuses as mentally ill or as criminals for the rest of their lives. As a result, they may be denied access to profitable occupations, shunned by former friends, and suspected whatever they do. Indeed, some former mental patients have found that behaving normally is reinterpreted by others in terms of their illness.

Roles

Statuses are, in effect, positions waiting to be filled. Roles describe the behavioral expectations defined for statuses; they tell the occupant of a status how to behave and what to expect from others interacting with that position. Roles, then, are the rights and obligations that go with any status in society. Because there is general acceptance of the rights and obligations of most statuses, and agreement as to the roles involved, social interaction with strangers is possible. For example, you knew what was expected when entering your sociology class for the first time because your role as a student and the instructor's role as a teacher were known to you at least in broad terms.

A status with which most of us are familiar is that of being a sick person. Like all other statuses in society, that of being sick entails certain behavioral expectations. Even what may seem a purely pysiological position has its social side. People who attempt to play the sick role without meeting its conditions may be seen as malingerers.

Talcott Parsons (1951) made one early attempt to outline broadly the behavioral expectations of the role associated with being sick. In American society, according to this model, these expectations can be thought of in terms of two rights and two obligations. First, according to Parsons' model, the sick person has the right to expect to be excused from social responsibility in order to overcome the condition. The limits of this pardon will depend on the nature of the illness, but the purpose is to return the sick person to full participation in society. Second, the sick person has the right to not be held at fault for being ill. The individual is seen as suffering from a condition from which he or she cannot be expected to recover by simply pulling himself or herself together.

The two obligations associated with the role of being sick are particularly important because it is possible to misuse the rights of the status. You may remember trying to miss school by convincing your parents that you had a stomachache. You may also recall that your parents were quick to sense your delight in staying home from school, watching television, and being waited upon. When this pleasure seemed to outweigh your need to rest in order to get well, you were hustled back to school without delay. This is because a person who claims to be sick has the obligation to define the condition as undesirable *and* to have a corresponding desire to get well. Second, the sick person is obligated to seek competent help and cooperate with that help to get well. If absence from school or work is prolonged, you may need to show a note from a physician to indicate that you were working at overcoming your illness.

The various statuses of our lives all have attached expectations. Some variation is allowed in how these are to be met, but when an individual goes beyond acceptable limits to those variations, negative sanctions may be brought to bear. For example, professors are expected to teach their assigned classes, but they can take a number of approaches to teaching. Some lecture and expect students to simply take notes and be able to repeat the given material on exams. Others teach mainly through class discussion, while still others use a combination of both methods. However, there are limits. A course consisting of one videotape after another with little tying them together will probably earn the scorn of a faculty member's colleagues and, perhaps, the wrath of the administration. Continually dismissing the class early, although popular with some students, will result in the judgment that the professor has failed to meet the expectations of the role.

The power of role expectations in defining an individual is demonstrated by the fact that it is difficult for us to leave even those statuses that are purely achieved. To cease being a doctor, a nun, or a married person, among others, is not simple. Becoming an "ex" is a basic social process, referred to by Helen Rose Ebaugh as **role exiting** (see Research Method 5.1) and undergone by many individuals in our rapidly changing society. Disengagement from one status means a change in the role behavior, a change that is not always easy for us or those around us since some "hangover" from our previous roles continues to influence expectations for behavior.

Research Method 5.1

• • • • • • • Role Exiting and Becoming an Ex

Structured Interviews as a Method of Research

What is an "ex"? In her book, *Becoming an Ex: The Process of Role Exit*, Helen Rose Ebaugh (1988) presented the results of her research on those who have left one status to take on another and different status. She identified it as a common and important process in today's society. She put it this way:

> The experience of being an ex of one kind or another is common to most people in modern society. While people who lived in earlier eras usually spent their entire lives in one marriage, one career, one religion, one geographical locality, most of us today make at least one major shift in an area of our lives that we consider central to who we are. Some of us negotiate several major role changes in the course of our lives, sometimes simultaneously. It is quite common, for example, for a major shift in career to reverberate in one's marriage and result in divorce, or for the death of a spouse to cause a major change in career (Ebaugh, 1988: xiii).

She added that changing such a role is a process of disengagement that brings about the need to establish a new self-identity. How is this achieved?

To understand the process, Ebaugh conducted interviews with 185 individuals who had left one central role to take on another. Her sample included ex-nuns, ex-doctors, divorcees, and transsexuals, among others. She taped a structured interview, lasting two hours, with each respondent and then analyzed their interview to discover common patterns in the process. Ebaugh found three basic stages in the transition from the former role to the new one: initial doubts, the turning point, and creating a new role.

While she considered a variety of role changes, we will focus on only one—that of the ex-married. We will use that status to highlight the stages involved in role exit. The first step in role exiting is that of having **first doubts**. This period in the lives of those who will exit a role is one of reinterpretation and redefinition of their situation. What had previously been seen as a given takes on new meaning. Divorced people reported that their initial doubts about being married centered on disillusionment with the marriage, especially when comparing it with the American ideal of what a marriage is like. However, specific events usually trigger the doubt. Of the fifteen divorced individuals in her sample, for example, six came to question their marriages when they discovered that their husband or wife was having an affair.

Significant others also played a part in raising doubt. In one case, for example, a sister continued to suggest that a woman get out of what she considered the trap of her marriage. Her encouragement helped the woman to see that there were alternatives to remaining in her situation. Having seen potential options, the future exiters come to interpret subsequent happenings in a new light. For example, one woman's husband began bringing her presents after his affair was discovered. She did not take it as an apology; rather, she saw it as an offense and was angry that he would make these attempts.

As a result of the doubting, individuals began to compare their situation to some other. For divorced people it was mainly a tendency to look back on the earlier days of their courtship and marriage. Things just weren't what they used to be. Despite the negative reactions of others, they still reevaluated their marriages and saw how bad they really were. For some of the divorced people the admission that their marriages were bad and that they could get out of the marriages was a time of emotional relief. It took many a great deal of time to realize that divorce was a viable alternative but, once they did, they felt free. With this sense of freedom, the potential divorcees weighed the pros and cons of divorce and, having determined that they could put up with them, shifted their reference groups. They began to compare themselves with those who were free.

The second stage in exiting is **the turning point**. After the period of weighing the alternatives and identifying with new groups, a point comes when a firm decision to exit is made. According to Ebaugh, this decision usually comes at some turning point in the individual's life. Some event causes the person to see that the old role has failed or, for some reason, is over and the opportunity to start again is there. For one divorced woman that point came when her husband refused to buy a car for their daughter when she graduated from high school, although he had purchased one for their son the year before. This began an argument that led to consideration of even deeper issues in their marriage. For some of the divorced people, the turning point was the feeling that the marriage had to be ended if they were to maintain "their sanity."

After the final decision was made, two adjustment patterns were found. For some there was elation at being free again and the adoption of a singles life-style. Others, however, were shy about getting back into the dating game. They were reluctant to adopt the single role and had feelings of failure because their marriages had broken up. They felt as if they were in a vacuum. Neither single nor married, they felt caught between both worlds and confused and numb. All needed support from family or friends to form a bridge to the new status.

The third stage, **creating a new role** involved the process of developing a new status for themselves. Unlike those who had never been in the situation, their identity was still, to some measure, tied up with the expectations and norms of the role they were leaving. There was tension between the old and the new. There is a "hangover" identity from the previous status which poses a problem in creating a new role concept.

How were they to present themselves? Nearly all of the divorced saw that visible evidence of their new status was essential. New clothes, for example, were not only a psychological lift, they represented to others that the person had changed. This presentation was particularly important as most of the divorced still felt that social stigma was attached to being divorced. One way in which this way handled was by shifting their friendship networks. They became less involved with their old friends—those they had known in the marriage—and became closer to single and other divorced people. They even renewed old friendships that had been given up during marriage.

In summary, leaving one major role and assuming another is a major step. In our society such change is very common—so frequent, indeed, that it demands attention as a major social process. By conducting structured interviews with a relatively large number of individuals who had made such a change, Ebaugh has helped us see the steps through which the "exes" go in making the transition in their lives.

Role Sets

The roles we play are not acted out in isolation. They are defined in terms of the expectations we have for others and the expectations others have for us. For any particular status, our role is acted out in terms of behavioral expectations that are *complementary* to the rights and obligations of those with whom we interact.

Of the many different statuses we hold, we usually behave according to only one set of role expectations at a time while other potential roles remain dormant. When behaving as a student, for example, we will act according to the expectations of that role, although the dormant roles may influence our behavior. For example, a married student may be concerned about the health of child even while listening to a lecture. However, his or her behavior will center on those with whom the student is interacting directly. As a student you interact with the professor, your faculty advisor, fellow students in the class, student organization officers, and certain university officials, among others. These complementary roles all represent your **role set** for the status of student. You will behave a bit differently when interacting with each member of that set, but it will all revolve around your student role.

For each role there will be a different role set. For example, as son or daughter your role set may include parents, siblings, other relatives, and friends of the family. Again, each of these members of the set will evoke different reactions while affecting our behavior in that role.

Role Strain and Role Conflict

Role expectations are relatively well defined but they do not always provide for the separation of responsibilities between different roles or even within the same role. While strain and conflict can occur within and between roles, it is easiest for us to discuss them separately. Today, **role strain** is seen by most sociologists as occurring within one given role, while **role conflict** refers to the competing demands of two different roles.

Role Strain

The behavioral expectations of most statuses contain a great deal of ambiguity; no one set of expectations is clearly more important than the others. In most cases it is difficult, if not impossible, to fulfill all the expectations of a given status. Most students know the pressure of having three or four examinations on the same day. Strain is felt within the student role as the student attempts to study for all of the exams, especially if other aspects of being a student, such as earning tuition money, are also making demands.

Strain is felt by a busy executive who needs to complete an important report on the same day that she or he is scheduled to attend an important meeting in another city. Likewise, a secretary frequently experiences role strain when trying to balance the tasks of typing reports, scheduling an executive's time, making phone calls, and running errands for one or more superiors.

Teachers in public schools also often experience role strain. They are expected to follow the instructions of the principle, mollify parents, deal with sick children, and at the same time teach students. Too often, teachers are forced to forgo the last expectation in order to satisfy other demands.

The mother of several children, even if she does not work, will certainly experience strain within her role as parent. Small children can be very demanding and, when there is more than one such child, their competing demands can be the source of strain. Even the simple insistence of two children that the mother observe their activities at the same time can be stressful. If the family also includes a child in a middle school, the parental need to work with and be involved in that child's school activities are a further source of strain. Again, note that in this particular example we do not raise the more-than-likely possibility that the parent will hold a job in addition to the task of parenting. When occupational and parental obligations compete with one another, we generally speak of role conflict.

Role Conflict

Frequently it is impossible to fulfill the demands of all statuses we occupy; there is conflict among them as they compete for our time. The part-time student, for example, may experience conflict when an important business trip is scheduled on the same day as a midterm exam. If the same student is also a parent, child care may create an additional conflict. Certainly today's working mothers know the conflict occurring between their roles. The need to be in a business meeting in Chicago is in direct conflict with the urgent parental need to attend her child's first school pageant.

Studies (see Nelsen 1985, Chalfant et al. 1987) indicate that clergy experience considerable role conflict in their profession. In large congregations especially, the demands of the parish are often so intense that the pastor's entire waking time could be taken up with church activities. If the pastor is married, finding the time to fulfill the expectations of the role of spouse may be quite difficult. In fact, the role conflict often becomes so intense that it is generally blamed for an increasing divorce rate among ministers.

As intimated, role conflict can occur within a role as well as between roles. That is, it is not simply that the demands of the role place a strain on the individual but that conflicting demands are made within the same role. The increasing number of physicians who work as salaried employees of health maintenance organizations or hospital corporations experience this kind of conflict (Light and Levine 1988, Emmons 1987. McKinlay and Stoeckle 1988). As corporations take over medical care and physicians become employees rather than free professionals, they are expected to operate according to the policies and procedures laid out by their employers. However, long tradition in medicine has placed great emphasis on the autonomy of the physician as essential to good medical practice and to the personal and sacred nature of the doctor-patient relationship. The physician-employee is caught in a conflict between the demands of the bureaucracy and those of the profession.

Groups

Many American values center around the idea of individualism. Thoreau's *Walden* typifies both our need to be alone and the virtue of individuality. It paints an idyllic picture, but it does not correspond to the reality of human life. No person is an island; being human is being part of a group. Here we use the term **group** to refer to a number of individuals who identify with each other and act together according to established patterns of behavior out of a sense of shared interests. Even the most basic act separating humans from other animals—thinking—can be accomplished only through subvocal or internal speaking, or the use of language, which is the result of group interaction.

The Group as Agent of Humanity

Groups provide the protection humans need as well as an opportunity to share or divide the work of living. They also do much more. Only through the agency of the group do we become truly human. The experience of those who have worked with children isolated from most human contact during their early years, as well as research concerning the effects of isolation on adults, demonstrate the human's initial and continuing need for the experiences of the group in becoming and remaining a human being rather than simply the animal *Homo sapiens* (Davis 1947; Faris 1934).

This need for group experience extends beyond the early, formative years of life into later years, when group contact is necessary to maintain organization in a person's life. A number of sociologists have suggested that mental illness may result from the lack of adequate contact with groups. Robert Faris (1934) suggested that preschizophrenic individuals had experienced greater social isolation for longer periods than had nonschizophrenic individuals; as a result, they were unable to maintain contact with socially defined reality.

A steady stream of research supports this idea. As early as 1939 Robert Faris and Warren Dunham showed that the highest rates of schizophrenia were in areas of high mobility where numbers of one ethnic or racial group lived in sections dominated by members of another group. The resulting isolation provided a setting for the development of a schizophrenic personality. Later studies, such as those done by Srole and associates (1962) and Srole (1975) found that schizophrenia was far more prevalent among members of the lowest class in society where contact with groups occurred less often and where the contact tended to be less helpful in adjustment to general societal definitions of reality. Kohn (1974) has suggested that lower-class people have a far more limited range of life experiences and are thus less able to cope in stressful situations.

In another study, Edwin Lemert (1962) suggested that paranoia, another form of mental illness, may also result from the inadequate social learning that comes with limited social contact. Paranoids interpret the words and actions of others in ways that most people would not interpret them. This eventually leads to actual differential responses from others which increase the paranoid's feelings of persecution and further limits the ability to interact in an appropriate fashion.

The human being is totally dependent upon the group for anything approaching human-like behavior and life. The group is truly the "agent of cultural transmission" (Wilson 1971). Through the agency of the group, the preferences, norms, values, and role behaviors characteristic of the group are transmitted to the individual members. In a social sense, the group members are considered human only after they have assimilated the characteristics of the group.

But what is a group? We generally refer to any gathering of individuals as a group. We say there are groups at work, groups waiting for a bus, ethnic or racial groups living in one part of town, and so forth. However, a sociologist would not call each of these collections of people a group because some of them lack characteristics essential to the sociological definition of the word group. You may be better able to understand the concept of a group if it is distinguished from some gatherings of individuals that sociologists do *not* define as groups.

Nongroups

One nongroup is a category. A **category** is a set of people who happen to share some common characteristic. Categories of people are frequently used by sociologists, particularly those interested in the study of populations (demography).

A category can be the set of all females in the United States, of all college students, or of all owners of BMWs. Members of a category do not necessarily know one another or interact with one another in any way.

Another type of nongroup is an **aggregate**. This is a gathering of people in physical proximity who have come together temporarily but who lack any organization or lasting pattern of relationship. The crowd at the bus stop is an example of an aggregate, as is the audience at a movie or a play.

Social Groups

There are four essential characteristics of a **social group**: (1) regular and usually sustained interaction between members; (2) a sense of common identity; (3) shared interests; and (4) some patterns for organization of behavior on a regular basis.

From these characteristics we can move to a formal definition of a group. Sociologists are not in total agreement, but the following definition is generally accepted as standard: a **group** is a plurality of individuals who have contact, though not necessarily direct contact, with one another, who take each other into account in making decisions, and who have some sense of common identity as well as shared goals or interests.

Categories and aggregates are generally referred to as nongroups, but they can become groups. All farmers in the United Stated are a category. But farmers who are members of the American Farmers Union or the Farm Bureau can be said to form a group because they act together out of a sense of common purpose and express some loyalty to one another.

Similarly, passengers on an airplane are an aggregate, brought together for a limited period of time. They may chat with one another, although most will ignore each other. Should someone attempt to hijack the plane, though, the passengers may become a group as they face the collective task of dealing with the danger inherent in the situation.

All groups are not the same. They vary in terms of their size, the intensity of relationships between members, standards for membership, and the importance of the group to its members. It is useful to look at the various types of groups because they tell us more about how group life affects the individual and the society.

In-groups and Out-groups

The difference between an in-group and an out-group is as simple as it sounds. We think of some groups as "we" and of others as "they." Groups we think of as "we" are referred to as **in-groups**; the others are seen as **out-groups**. Within the in-group, an individual finds people of whom he or she approves and who have a corresponding sense of hostility toward those in the out-group. The characteristics of an in-group are that members identify with the group, feel a sense of loyalty toward the group, and feel as though they belong. The characteristics of an out-group are that its members are excluded, have a sense of being alien, and are treated with hostility.

An example of the in-group/out-group relationship was provided by Howard Becker (1963) in a description of the way dance band musicians felt about their customers. To a large extent, the musicians saw themselves as "we" and viewed their customers as "they." The musicians felt their customers forced them to play commercial music, which they disliked. Thus, these musicians formed a strong, cohesive group in which they stereotyped customers as unknowing and regarded them with suspicion and hostility.

Julian Roebuck and Woflgang Frese (1976) found a similar in-group/out-group situation between jazz musicians and their patrons at an after-hours club. Those musicians even regarded as outsiders customers who regularly stayed for their jam sessions and who appeared to appreciate their type of music. The jazz musicians believed that customers could not really feel the same way about music as they did.

Membership in some in-groups is dependent on the ability of the member to perform the tasks of the group in a satisfactory manner; for example, a trumpet player is included in the "we" of the band only as long as she can play the trumpet. When it becomes necessary to exclude a former member of an in-group—such as when the trumpet player loses her "lip" or ability to play—some way must be found to demonstrate social distance.

In a discussion of failure in professional sports, Donald Ball (1976) suggested two types of procedures used to establish and emphasize this distance: degradation and cooling out. An example of **degradation** is when a player who fails to make a professional sports team sees his locker being emptied and his name removed from it, and when former teammates treat him as a nonperson. When the **cooling out** method is used to emphasize social distance, the player's private and subjective estrangement from his teammates is less bitter. The establishment of distance is not as public, and attempts are made to explain the person's change in status and to help him gradually accept and adjust to it. In either case—abruptly or slowly—the effect is the same: the individual has been removed from the status of player.

Reference Groups

As we relate to our society we do so by identifying with groups in the society. These groups may be friendship groups, professional ones, socioeconomic status groups, and the like. Sociologists refer to these as **reference groups** because we refer to them in order to shape and maintain our behavior. We need not belong to the group with which we identify, but reference to it is essential in forming our self and defining appropriate behavior. There are two types of reference groups: normative and comparative.

We make decisions based on reference groups because they provide us with perspectives and norms that help us to view and organize reality. In the usual case one reference group will fulfill all of these functions. However, different groups may serve one or two of the functions. For example, while the normative reference group may be our family and our close friends, the comparative group may be one to which we aspire—for example, the members of a profession we hope to enter.

The term **normative reference group** is used to define any group or social category to which we refer in helping us define our beliefs, attitudes, and values. This type of reference group assists us in setting and maintaining the standards appropriate to our status in society. As a result of reference to the values of these groups, we internalize the values those groups hold.

We may use a wide variety of groups in gaining these perspectives. A reference group may be very distinct, such as the Republican Party, or it may designate only a social category which serves as a point of reference, such as the Irish. Thus, we may identify with being a Presbyterian, a Mason, a black, or a Chicano. The particular reference group that most will determine our values and our view of ourselves will depend on the relative importance of the group to us.

Reference groups may also shape our beliefs about the meaning of certain events in our lives. Edward Suchman (1964) demonstrated that reference groups influence the way in which people deal with illness. Individuals whose reference groups are provincial and who have a limited view of the world are more likely to try home remedies and folk medicines; those whose reference groups are cosmopolitan and who have a broad perspective of the world tend to be strongly dependent on modern medicine.

Helen Rose Fuchs Ebaugh (1988) suggests another way in which a group, or individuals representative of a group, may serve as a point of reference. She speaks

These three pre-teen boys are clearly very close friends, illustrating the concepts of primary group and in-group. Interaction in such groups help form the basis of our personalities.

of a gatekeeping function for the group. Using the example of a nun thinking of leaving her religious order, she contends that the decision to actually leave may be made by reference to either a group of individuals who approve or disapprove or by reference to a representative of the group, such as a priest.

A **comparative reference group** is one that provides us with an imaginary mirror by which we can "see" how we compare to those in the reference group. It is used to define any group or category to which we refer in judging how our behavior matches up to those who make up the group. If people in poverty evaluate their lot in terms of others in poverty, they probably will not evaluate their situation as negative. If they look at what the nonpoor in society have, however, they may see their situation as hopeless. (Mass media, particularly television, seems to have contributed to the dissatisfaction of the poor by showing them a vision of a better life.)

Primary Groups

Charles Horton Cooley introduced the term **primary group** and spoke of such groups as the "nursery of human nature" (1902, 23). In these small, intimate groups marked by face-to-face association and a common sense of identity, the most basic shaping of human character takes place. The very name of the group—primary—indicates something of its importance. It is primary in time, primary in intimacy, and primary in belonging.

Cooley used the term to describe groups that were characterized by close, intimate associations and cooperation. He saw such groups as primary in a number of ways, but principally in their "forming of the social nature and ideals of the individual" (1902, 23). In primary groups, the individual fuses with the commonality, so that the life of the group and that of the individual become virtually the same. The sense of group identity and loyalty is strong, involving the person deeply and resting upon mutual identification of members with one another, so that the group becomes an end in itself. Responses to one another tend to be to the whole person, rather than to some segment of an individual's personality, and communications are deep and extensive. Finally, group identification is often more important than individual needs.

The most concrete example of the primary group is the family. This group has the earliest and most fundamental impact upon the individual's development. Commitment to the family group is usually deep and will extend throughout life. It is here that most of us are taught the basics of being humn. The dedication to the roles and relationships of the family may be so deep and may become so important that group needs supersede the needs of the individual member.

In a discussion of the relationship between physician and patient, Samuel Bloom (1965) tells the story of Mrs. Tomasetti, a diabetic who was the grandmother in a large Italian family. The hospital staff saw her as a problem patient because she apparently refused to follow the necessary dietary regimen and time after time was brought back to the hospital in a coma. Most of the staff wrote her off as a "crock," but one sensitive intern finally discovered that Mrs. Tomasetti's diabetic diet interfered with the major role she held in the family, preparing the meals. Not being able to taste the pasta because of her diet meant she was unable to cook; being unable to cook, she felt she was no longer a member of the family. The need to be part of the primary group was so strong that she would risk diabetic coma rather than be cast out of her role in the family.

The family is not the only example of a primary group. The child's play group, the adolescent gang, and many friendship relationships in adult life may be classified as primary groups. Such groups are referred to as **peer groups**, that is, groups composed of individuals more or less equal to us. They are also vital to continuing humanization. The primary group not only forms and maintains human character; it also continues to form and reform that character throughout life. For adults, primary-group relationships are often established with close associates at work. Thus, some members of a university department may become close to one another and find the satisfaction and support they need from this friendship circle.

But why is the primary-group tie so important, even in adult life? The answer lies in the two basic functions of primary groups: socialization and individual sustenance. The primary group assists in the formation of basic human character and provides us with norms which we, in turn, internalize. While providing this education in socialization, the primary group also gives the member unconditional support (sustenance). Relationships outside the primary group tend to be dependent upon one's ability to perform. One can be a college student only as long as grades are maintained and bills paid. Failure on either count will result in being cast out of the role of student. On the other hand, membership in primary groups is not dependent upon performance, but on a covenant relationship in which one will be given support, even while being chastised for failing in some duty.

As we move into new roles and new situations in the world, we need to learn new skills and internalize new norms. The primary group is a place where these may be learned with little risk to personality. From the perspective of society and the individual, the primary group is the continuing agent of humanity and the constant support for our own identities.

When adults face new and strange situations, membership in a primary group can be important in adjustment. It has been suggested that this is one reason for the popularity of Pentecostal sectarian religion among Latin American migrants to urban areas. The members of these religious groups provide a close, family-like group for those cut off from traditional kinship ties. The small sect, with its emphasis on the importance of the group's norms, forms a bridge between the old life and the bewildering ways and activities of urban life. The "brothers and sisters" of the religious group are there to provide support and encouragement as the newcomers try to find their way through an unfamiliar maze.

This suggests that primary groups may also be important tools in the resocialization of individuals and in giving support during the transition from the status of heavy drinker to that of abstainer. Alcoholics Anonymous (AA) provides a primary group where this change can take place; the group is successful because of the essentially primary-group nature of its meetings. The active alcoholic needs to internalize a new norm of abstinence. The intimate nature of the AA group meeting becomes a primary group in which this norm can be learned. It is a place where members can safely undergo the resocialization that leads to internalization of the norm of sobriety.

Secondary Groups

As societies grow larger and more complex, the relative frequency of primary groups lessens. Most relationships between people are carried on in what are known as secondary groups. These groups are most simply defined as the opposite of primary groups.

There are four characteristics of the secondary group. First, the secondary group is of relatively larger size than the primary group. Second, the objectives of the secondary group are generally instrumental; that is, they have specific goals to attain, and the efforts of the group are directed at attaining them. Third, relationships within the secondary group are partial in that members tend to see only one or a few segments of the persona of their fellow members. Finally, relationships are basically contractual; members are expected to give something, perform some duty, or pay in some way for the privilege of membership.

Secondary groups are most prevalent in complex societies, and they tend to proliferate in societies such as ours. Most of our contact with one another is in the context of such groups: the sociology class, the company for which we work, our church, and so on. Although these groups do not provide the intensive socialization or support given by primary groups, they are essential to pursuing interests and completing tasks in modern society, and they provide socialization for these purposes.

The growing importance of secondary groups in American society concerns many. There is a feeling that when primary-group ties weaken and most of life is controlled by secondary groups, long-standing values will be less influential; this situation could lead to a number of problems in the society such as ineffective social control. This may be demonstrated by the effects which one type of formal organization, bureaucracy, has on our everyday life.

Bureaucracy

In discussing secondary groups it was noted that the larger, more impersonal group is becoming characteristic of more and more social relationships. Such groups are usually characterized by a type of formal organization referred to as a **bureaucracy**. In chapter 1 we discussed Max Weber's concern with what he saw as the "iron cage" of bureaucracy and its effects on modern society. With the Industrial Revolution came a shift in the source of authority, a shift from authority based on individuals to that supported by regulations and rules. Weber was among the first to call attention to both the benefits and dangers inherent in bureaucracies.

Formal organizations, with bureaucratic-like structures, were not unknown in previous times. Ancient China had a well-developed structure with most of the features of a bureaucracy (Eisenstadt 1971). Still, not until the Industrial Revolution did bureaucracy emerge as the dominant form of social organization. So far as American society is concerned, the study of formal organization is basically the study of bureaucracy, the rational-legal organization of groups.

Emerging Bureaucracy

In a sense, success is the origin of all bureaucracy. When a division of labor is initiated, the bureaucracy is in its infant stage. If the activity succeeds, the division of labor must be refined. In time, the positions in that division become permanent. This is the case even for movements that start with a devout belief in equality. The moment the group starts keeping records, elects officers, and makes a division of labor, it starts on the road to establishing a bureaucratic organization.

What occurs over time is that the group depends on someone to carry out a function which then becomes a permanent task, although the person performing the task may change (Downs 1967). Thus, the position of head bookkeeper of an organization may be essential, but the office can be filled by anyone with book-keeping skills. This formal description of work can lead to a sense of depersonal-ization for the laborer, which may result in a sense of alienation.

In time, even those groups that began in opposition to established formal orga-nizations and that depended on personal authority for guidance take on the trappings of a bureaucracy if they survive and grow. For example, the Church of Jesus Christ of Latter-day Saints (Mormons) was originally based on the revelation of one man, John Smith, and depended on his interpretations as the source of authority. Fleeing persecution in Illinois, the Mormons moved to Utah where they thrived. Indeed, they flourished and grew into a large and powerful organization. Today the religious group that was once led by the personal authority of one man is a highly organized bureaucracy with well-defined positions and duties for each position. A highly visible exhibit of this is the twenty-four story building containing the offices of the church which towers over even the Mormon tabernacle across the street.

The changes occurring in Western society at the end of the eighteenth century were characterized by an increasing rationality of organization. Basic to the devel-opment of an industrial society was what Weber (1946) referred to as instrumental rationality. This well-ordered approach to tasks involved a relatively complex di-vision of labor supported by a system of authority; authority was distributed along a hierarchy of power, guided by established routines and written regulations. Al-though such instrumental rationality could be directed toward irrational ends, We-ber suggested that a substantive rationality, focused on ends and goals, accompanied instrumentality to accomplish rational products.

Workers in a bureaucratic structure can find their work rational and efficient, but also invariably routine.

Principles of Bureaucracy

By centering on essential aspects of organizational form, Weber outlined the major features of a bureaucratic structure. Scott (1981) provided a useful approach to a discussion of these principles. He likened traditional organization to a system based on family or the rights of large landholders. Work units resemble large extended families with dependents. Members of the group rely on the authority of the "family" leaders. By contrast, bureaucratic organization is a special case of administration specific to the modern, industrial state. It differs from traditional styles of administration in several ways.

First, traditional organizations operate on the basis of assignments made by the "family" leader. The group functions on the basis of the wishes of that person, which usually are personal in nature. Bureaucratic organization, on the other hand, spells out activities in terms of official duties and necessary activities. Work is divided into areas, and activities are specified for those assigned to each specific area.

Second, authority in a traditional system is based on the loyalty of members to the group's leader; the power of that leader is diffuse, extending through every aspect of the unit. By contrast, bureaucracies are guided by an established hierarchy of authority which distributes responsibility to office holders in specific areas of the organization. Work is controlled by these officials, each of whom is responsible to the next higher level of authority for her or his area's effectiveness.

Third, there are no general rules or regulations in a traditional organization. The will of the leader determines which tasks will be done and by whom. Rules and regulations, however, are the lifeline of bureaucratic organizations. Rules tend to be more or less constant over time and determine almost all facets of the organization's work.

Fourth, in a traditional system property—even the means of production—really belongs to the individual leader, not to the organization. Personal property is not kept apart from the tools used in work. In bureaucratic structure, however, an often rigid distinction is made between these two kinds of property. The means of production are the property of the organization and do not belong to any single individual, regardless of office.

Fifth, workers in traditional groups are given work or tasks as a result of personal decisions made by the leader, not infrequently on highly personal grounds. Work and its rewards are basically granted by that leader. In bureaucracies, on the other hand, assignment to given offices and tasks is made on the basis of technical qualifications. Thus, positions within the bureaucratic structure generally will spell out minimal requirements to hold a particular office.

Finally, workers in a traditional system remain a part of the unit, and have employment, at the pleasure of the leader. It is simply the way of life for the members. In contrast, workers in the bureaucratic structure hold their positions supposedly on the basis of merit, and their employment is basically a career. That is, employment is a course of action taken by full-time employees to maximize their rewards; it is not simply granted or given to one.

Rationality and Efficiency

Ideally, the bureaucratic structure is the most efficient and rational way to divide tasks and accomplish goals. It is designed for execution or administration rather than for creativity and decision making. Bureaucracies have been described as organizations designed by geniuses to be run by fools; every effective bureaucracy has rationalized and compartmentalized its task so that many of the functions at the bottom of the structure can be accomplished with little training. That is why the established bureaucracy insists on simplicity, standardization, and conformity. New experience, innovation, and the unusual are too costly to tolerate.

Even the most efficient bureaucracies have problems. How does a creative or nonconforming person survive? What psychological problems exist? Money, advancement, prestige, and power can be rationally pursued only by the individual. Does the bureaucratic style of management provide the individual with the means for pursuing these goals?

Research Application 5.1

• • • • • • The rise and fall of an industry: U.S. Steel

Ramona Ford (1988) discussed the rapid growth and subsequent decline of the steel industry in the United States as an example of the problems created by the rigidity of bureaucratic structures. In particular she views the unwillingness to innovate as a major contributor to the decline of American steel in the world market.

The steel industry in this country developed rapidly at the end of the past century. Its main support was the railroad's need for steel as rail lines expanded across the nation. At one time the entire output of one plant, Bessemer Steel, went to the making of rails. Further, there was a close connection between the management of steel companies and the railroads; Andrew Carnegie served as a director of the Pennsylvania Rail Road before he began his own steel company. One hundred years ago the steel companies were highly competitive; they were forced to cut costs in order to compete, usually meaning that wages were lowered and working conditions not improved.

By the turn of the century, however, competition stopped. The assets of many steel companies were purchased by what became United States Steel. It has been estimated that at that time eighty percent of all the nation's steel came from that company, making it a virtual monopoly. The price of steel was set in "gentlemanly" fashion over lavish dinners, and the laws of supply and demand were virtually repealed. Prices went up regardless of market demand, wages paid, or any other factors.

Changes were to come. At mid-century, even as the giant steel industry was enjoying its war-time profits, trouble was in the making. By 1950 less than half of the world's production of steel (47 percent) came out of U.S. plants. This proportion had dropped to 26 percent by 1960 and fallen to 14 percent by 1980. Japan, West Germany, South Africa, South Korea, and Brazil were overcoming the dominance of the former giant steelmaker, the U.S. In fact, by the mid-1980s the United States was itself importing 22 percent of its steel. The situation would have been even worse if Japan and Germany had not accepted voluntary export limitations and if the U.S. had not placed heavy taxes on imported steel.

What happened? The steel industry was quick to find others to blame. It said foreign labor was too cheap given the wages unions forced companies to pay in this country. Industry leaders also said foreign governments subsidized their steel industries to lower the price of production. In truth, benefit packages made the lower Japanese salaries quite comparable. Further, foreign subsidization was not as extensive as the tax breaks given American companies. So where did the fault lie?

Two factors contributed heavily to the decline of the steel industry in this country, and both are related to the inability or unwillingness of a successful bureaucracy to adjust with the times.

First, the industry did not take advantage of new technologies in steel making. A more efficient and cleaner means for making steel had been invented which also provided for faster casting of steel. This new basic oxygen furnace (BOF) replaced the old open-hearth furnace that had been the U.S. standard for many years. European and Japanese companies quickly adopted the BOF, which worked ten times faster than the open-hearth furnace. Thus, they were able to provide steel at a lower price. Yet U.S. companies were still reluctant to adopt the new method; they preferred to take current profits rather than invest in "risky" new technologies.

Second, the demand for steel suddenly dropped just as the U.S. bureaucracies began to see the need to change. The recession of the 1970s further contributed to the decline in demand. In the end, the demand for old-style steel was replaced by a call for lighter weight construction materials. The U.S. companies could have answered that demand and been competitive and profitable once again but, again, the rigidity of the bureaucratic organization did not respond quickly enough.

Thus, the instrument which originally created the means for the growth of a great industry—bureaucratic organization—also caused its demise. The great giant of U.S. industry was felled, at least in part, by the industry's inability to make innovations and change with the time, an inability fostered by bureaucratic rigidity.

• • • • • • •

cording to Ford (1988) there are five disadvantages of bureaucratic organizations. First, *centralization of decision making* means that fewer and fewer individuals have responsibility over ever-extending areas of work and life. As the organization grows those in positions of central power may be making decisions about matters of which they have little knowledge. Second *the rigidity* of bureaucratic organizations implies that rules tend to become "set in concrete." While they may not apply in all situations workers face, they are nonetheless applied.

Third, bureaucratic organization can lead to *goal displacement* or the pursuit of goals that were originally intended as means to a greater end. For example, filling out the proper forms may become more the goal than getting a job done. Fourth, bureaucracy affects the *personality of workers* in sometimes destructive ways. These range from simple lack of initiative to a tendency to steal from what seems an impersonal structure. Finally, the *secrecy* of bureaucratic organizations can have a negative effect. Despite mountains of paper-work, workers hide things and try to keep mistakes from superiors and thereby exert more personal control over their work.

Rules designed to be impersonal may be perceived by workers in the system as constraining or stifling. When this happens the rules may get in the way of desired efficiency. Also, the fact that no two people are alike means each will react differently to the rules. Employees generally find ways to get around the formal rules and make their tasks less boring and burdensome.

This may work to the good of the company, as rules do not always fit a given situation. For example, hospitals set down very rigid guidelines to be followed by the nursing staff in caring for patients. These guidelines often work to the discomfort of patients. Nurses have learned a number of means for "staying within the law" while easing the burden on their patients. Simply calling something to the attention of the physician, thus not actually stepping over the boundary of authority, may work wonders for patient comfort.

On the other hand, informal or pragmatic rules developed by employees may result in sabotage of the company. In one factory it was an almost universal custom to stop work fifteen or twenty minutes before the noon whistle blew announcing lunch break. The extra time left the workers free to take a nap, go shopping, or attend to some other matter of personal business, all at the expense of thousands of hours of lost production daily. Those in positions of administration must be aware of and effectively use informal rules and norms and must guide the groups that implement them.

Questions for Summary and Review

1. What is meant by the term status?
2. Distinguish between ascribed and achieved statuses.
3. What is a master status, and how may it affect an individual's life?
4. What is a social role and how does it determine behavior?
5. What is meant by role sets?
6. Distinguish between role strain and role conflict.
7. How is a social group different from a nongroup?
8. What is the importance of social groups?
9. What is a primary group and what functions does it have?
10. What are in-groups and out-groups?
11. What are reference groups and how are they used?
12. Define a secondary group.
13. What are the characteristics of a bureaucracy?
14. List the disadvantages of bureaucracies.

Key Concepts

Achieved statuses (p. 86)
Aggregate (p. 94)
Ascribed statuses (p. 85)
Bureaucracy (p. 98)
Category (p. 94)
Comparative reference groups (p. 97)
Cooling out (p. 95)
Degradation (p. 95)
Groups (p. 93)
In-groups (p. 95)
Master statuses (p. 87)
Normative reference groups (p. 96)
Out-groups (p. 95)

Peer groups (p. 98)
Primary groups (p. 97)
Reference groups (p. 95)
Resocialization (p. 98)
Role conflict (p. 92)
Role exiting (p. 89)
Role sets (p. 91)
Role strain (p. 91)
Roles (p. 88)
Secondary groups (p. 98)
Social group (p. 94)
Status (p. 85)

References

1. Ball, Donald W. 1976. Failure in sport. *American sociological review* 41 (August):726–39.

2. Becker, Howard S. 1963. *Outsiders: Studies in the sociology of deviance*. New York: Free Press.

3. Bloom, Samuel. 1965. *The doctor and his patient*. New York: Free Press.

4. Chalfant, H. Paul, Robert E. Beckley, and C. Eddie Palmer. 1987. *Religion in contemporary society*. 2d ed. Palo Alto, Calif.: Mayfield.

5. Cooley, Charles Horton. 1902. *Social organization*. New York: Scribners.

6. Davis, Kingsley. 1947. Final note on a case of extreme isolation. *American journal of sociology* 52 (March):432–37.

7. Downs, Anthony. 1967. *Inside bureaucracy*. Boston: Little, Brown.

8. Ebaugh, Helen Rose Fuchs. 1988. *Becoming an ex: Role exiting*. Chicago: University of Chicago Press.

9. Eisenstadt, S. N. 1971. *Political sociology: A reader*. New York: Basic Books.

10. Emmons, D. N. 1987. *Changing dimensions of medical practice arrangements*. Chicago: American Medical Association, Office of Socioeconomic Research.

11. Faris, Robert E. L. 1934. Cultural isolation and the schizophrenic personality. *American journal of sociology* 34 (July):155–69.

12. Faris, Robert E. L., and H. Warren Dunham. 1939. *Mental disorders in urban areas*. Chicago: University of Chicago Press.

13. Ford, Ramona L. 1988. *Work, organization and power: Introduction to industrial sociology*. Boston: Allyn and Bacon.

14. Kohn, Melvin. 1974. Social class and schizophrenia: A critical review and reformulation. In *Explorations in psychiatric sociology*, edited by P. Roman and H. Trice, 113–37. Philadelphia: F. A. Davis.

15. Lemert, Edwin. 1962. The dynamics of paranoia. *Sociometry* 25:2–20.

16. Light, Donald, and Sol Levine. 1988. The changing character of the medical profession: A theoretical overview. *The Milbank quarterly* 66 (Suppl. 2):10–32.

17. McKinlay, John, and John D. Stoeckle. 1988. Corporations and the social transformation of doctoring. *International journal of health* 18(2):191–205.

18. Nelsen, Hart. 1985. Introduction to *The Protestant parish minister*, by S. Blizzard. SSSR Monograph Series, Washington, D.C.: Society for the Scientific Study of Religion.

19. Parsons, Talcott. 1951. *The social system*. Glencoe, Ill.: Free Press.

20. Perrow, Charles. 1986. *Complex organizations: A critical essay*. 3d ed. Glenview, Ill.: Scott, Foresman.

21. Roebuck, Julian B., and Wolfgang Frese. 1976. The after-hours club: An illegal social organization and its client system. *Urban life* 5 (July):131–64.

22. Scott, W. Richard. 1981. *Organizations: Rational, natural, and open systems*. Englewood Cliffs, N.J.: Prentice-Hall.

23. Srole, Leo. 1975. Measurements and classifications in socio-psychiatric epidemiology: Midtown Manhattan study I (1954) and midtown Manhattan study II (1974). *Journal of health and social behavior* 16:347–64.

24. Srole, Leo, T. S. Langner, S. T. Michael, M. K. Opler, and T. C. Rennie. 1962. *Mental health in the metropolis: The midtown Manhattan studies*. New York: McGraw-Hill.

25. Suchman, Edward. 1964. Sociomedical variations among ethnic groups. *American journal of sociology* 70:319–31.

26. Thoreau, Henry David. [1854] n.d. *Walden, or life in the woods*. Mt. Vernon, N.Y.: Peter Pauper Press.

27. Weber, Max. 1946. *Max Weber: Essays in sociology*. Edited by H. H. Gerth and C. W. Mills, New York: Oxford.

28. Wilson, E. K. 1971. *Sociology: Rules, roles and relationships*. Homewood, Ill.: Dorsey Press.

29. Wilson, William Julian. 1972. *Power, racism, and privilege.* New York: Free Press.

30. _____ 1987. *The truly disadvantaged: The inner city, the underclass and public policy.* Chicago: University of Chicago Press.

Understanding Structure
in Social Life

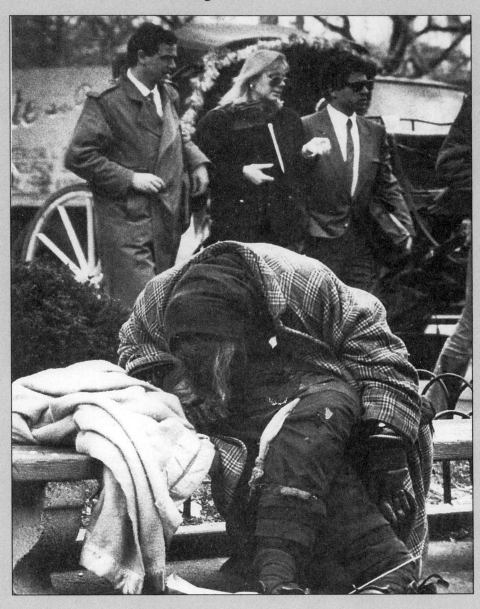

6

Inequality and Stratification in Social Life

• • • • • • • • • • • •

Chapter Outline

●

At the beginning of the 1990s, fewer than two hundred individuals and families in the entire world each held assets worth over a billion dollars. In the United States, fifty-five individuals and families were billionaires according to *Forbes* magazine (1989a). For example, San Walton and family, major owners of Wal-Mart and Sam's discount stores, were reputedly worth nearly nine billion dollars. Outside the United States, forty-one people in Japan and twenty in West Germany accounted for almost half of those worth over a billion dollars. They included Akio Morita, chairman of Sony corporation, whose family has had a prosperous business making soy sauce and sake dating back 324 years. West German billionaires included Erivan

Haub, the owner of Europe's largest supermarket chain and owner of the majority of stock in the A & P food chain in the United States. Interestingly, Haub made sure that his three sons were born in the United States so they could be American citizens as well as German citizens (*Forbes* 1989a, 1989b).

Worlds apart from Wall Street and international finance is a twenty-seven-year-old married beautician and mother of two. In the following quote, she discussed the economic hardships typical of early years of marriage in blue-collar families.

> When I was six months pregnant, I wasn't well, so I had to stop work early. Then, all of a sudden, Johnny got fired from his job. I don't think I was ever so scared in my life. After a while, things got so bad (I couldn't work, and he wasn't working) that we signed up for welfare. I'll never forget how ashamed I was (quoted in Rubin 1976, 73).

This family's situation is not uncommon in the United States, nor does it reflect the extreme poverty of American homelessness. More than thirty million Americans live below the official poverty level, comprising about thirteen percent of our population. Evidence also indicates that the gap between the richest and poorest families in the United States is greater now than at any time since the government began tracking the statistics (Goldstein 1990, 20). In addition, today it is more difficult to move up the income ladder. In fact, many are falling off the ladder to success in America (Goldstein 1990, Newman 1988).

As in America, Japan, or Germany, inequality persists in all societies around the globe. Consequently, it is a major focus of sociological research. Variously referred to as social standing, social status, or social class, it is probably the single most sociologically significant influence on an individual in a society; a person's social status affects almost every aspect of his or her life. It profoundly influences such fundamental aspects as life expectancy, health, medical care, employment opportunities, and educational opportunities. Our class background affects how we raise our children, where we live, how we talk, what we eat, what we value, the magazines we buy, the TV shows we watch, even our manners and concepts of etiquette. That is what this chapter is all about—understanding social inequality and its effects on people.

Social Stratification and Social Class

In the field of geology, the term stratification refers to the layering of the earth from bottom to top. Borrowed by sociologists, social stratification refers to the ranking or social layering of individuals in society according to some socially defined standard or measure. Put another way, **social stratification** is the uneven or unequal distribution of whatever people in society consider the good things in life. People are layered in **strata** or **social classes** according to their access to those good things in life. When a large number of people are approximately equal in rank and are differentiated from others, they are called a **social class** (Gilbert and Kahl 1987, 16). In Western societies like the United States, wealth, prestige, and power are defined as the good things and are usually scarce in society. These three dimensions of stratification will be discussed in more detail later. First, we look at the major theories concerning social stratification.

Why Does Stratification Exist?

Because the study of stratification is central to sociological inquiry, a number of important theories have been developed to explain the continuity of inequality in affluent societies. The purpose of this section is to familiarize you with the two most important theories.

The Conflict Theory of Stratification

Karl Marx was the first social scientist to rigorously analyze social stratification. His work originated the conflict perspective which focuses on the inequality of economic resources among classes. (See chapter 1 for an introduction to Marx's theory.) Marx believed there are two major classes in an industrialized society, the bourgeoisie and the proletariat. The bourgeoisie, or capitalists, own factories and industry and are motivated primarily by the acquisition of profit and power. Such power, derived from economic resources, allows them to dominate others in society through their manipulation of the major institutions in society such as education, government, the military, and the mass media. Self-interest drives them to maintain the status quo which continues their favored position. Their children grow up with special benefits and opportunities so that the system perpetuates itself. Stratification continues because scarce resources are concentrated in the hands of the few. Such privilege is not given up or shared without a struggle.

On the other hand, the proletariat are the industrial working men and women who sell their labor for wages. Because they do not own capital and have no control over the means of economic production, they have little, if any, power and influence in society. However, capitalists would have nothing but empty factories and offices without labor. Inevitably a struggle will result as the working class organizes to challenge the dominant class. To Marx, the conflict between these two classes for scarce economic resources was the key to understanding stratification and the social change that would occur as a result of class conflict.

Many theorists have elaborated on or reformulated Marx's ideas, making conflict theory a rich and detailed form of analysis and explanation in sociology. For example, C. Wright Mills (1959a) argues that members of the upper class have more opportunity to influence the actions of the government as well as the economy because of their enormous power and monetary influence—through campaign contributions, for example. He argues that this American power elite is composed of the top leaders in business, government, and the military and that they act together to protect their position in society from any challenge from other groups in society. So, inequality persists. (see Chapter 14 for further discussion of Mills and Domhoff).

Other sociologists, notably William Domhoff (1967, 1970, 1974, 1983), essentially agree with Mills that we have a self-perpetuating ruling or governing class in this society. Domhoff (1983) asserted that .5 percent of the population dominates political decision making as well as the corporate power structure in America. By holding key positions in industry and the political structure, they are able to influence if not control much of the direction taken by America. Domhoff (1970, 1974) also studied the social patterns of the elite in the United States. By intermarriage, socializing in exclusive clubs such as the Bohemian Grove in San Francisco, sending their children to private schools, and living in exclusive neighborhoods, the elite maintain a cohesiveness that enhances their power and influence.

Contemporary theorist Ralf Dahrendorf (1959) argues that Marx's emphasis on economic power is not the sole factor in stratification today. Instead, Dahrendorf believes that authority is the key variable. Authority flows from high managerial or political positions and is used to maintain a favored position in society. Such authority, made legitimate by the social system, allows the exercise of power for self-interest.

Other theorists point out that keeping a group of people in a state of poverty and powerlessness benefits the rest of the society in a number of ways. The poor provide a source of cheap labor to do the so-called dirty work in society that those in the middle and upper classes do not want to do. The poor provide a market for inferior goods and services. That is, they have no choice but to live in certain areas of town that have relatively low rent (yet slum landlords make considerable money from such buildings). The poor also reassure the working and middle classes that they are not the lowest in society; the poor provide those who are insecure about their class status a group to look down on and feel superior to (Gans 1972).

Other sociologists such as David Riesman (1953) theorize that both political and economic power are dispersed among a number of groups in society who are just as likely to compete with each other as they are to cooperate. Riesman believed that the powerful groups in society are pluralistic rather than unified. For example, political parties compete for power; labor unions compete with corporate powers; regional elites compete with one another; and we have elite groups in the corporate world that compete for profit. In other words, sociologists like Riesman believe that we have powerful interest groups that do not often share the same interests or goals and are less likely to cooperate in the way that a unified ruling class with centralized power and decision making would cooperate.

Conflict theory presents a view of stratification based on competition for scarce resources whether such resources are land, factories, political power, or legitimate authority. These theorists see inequality as unnecessarily extreme in modern societies. A very different and more harmonious point of view is evident in the next theoretical perspective.

The Functionalist Theory of Stratification

In contrast to the conflict perspective which stresses struggle among social classes, the functionalist point of view considers inequality inevitable in societies. (See chapter 1 for an introduction to functionalist theory.) Most fully presented by Davis and Moore (1945), the functionalist approach asserts that inequality is both necessary and positively functional for society. They point out that all societies are confronted with the problems of motivating people to do certain kinds of work in order to have a smooth division of labor in the system. All kinds of work must be performed or the system would break down. In addition, some work is more crucial to society's survival. These jobs require an especially long and arduous training period, or they require particularly scarce talents and abilities. For example, the role of physician entails a long and difficult training period for a complex, demanding, and highly skilled job. Other work such as food service requires comparatively little training and skill.

The social system must find a way to move the best qualified people into the most important positions. It must encourage individuals to vigorously strive for these jobs. In order to get the most qualified or competitive people into crucial jobs, the society must offer incentives and rewards in the form of money, power, and prestige. Davis and Moore assume that few would want to make the sacrifices necessary to become a physician if there were not significant rewards. "The result is, by definition, a system of inequality and stratification" (Rothman 1978, 29). A physician must earn more than a food service worker, but that is both necessary and positively functional for the survival of society. Davis and Moore argue that stratification promotes the efficient operation of the social system.

At first glance, the functionalist theory of Davis and Moore seems acceptable. A physician, who must undergo a long, costly, and difficult period of education and training, is worth more to society than those in many other occupations. In order to get the most qualified people into such important positions, society must pay them more and offer the respect and admiration of others.

Yet there are a number of criticisms of the functionalist theory (see, for example, Tumin 1953). First, it is not always easy to determine which jobs are more crucial for society's survival than others. A society needs food service workers, garbage collectors, construction workers, and teachers as well as doctors. Most occupations perform some service for society. The question then becomes, "Why does society make such a huge distinction between a physician and, for example, a teacher?" With the exception of the long training period, a good argument can be made that the teacher is as important to society as the doctor, yet the income gap is enormous between these two professions. Critics of functionalism argue that the gap is not justified on the basis of worth or training period.

Another criticism of the functionalist theory is that there are certain occupations in society that are highly rewarded but do not necessarily fulfill a survival function for society. Certain athletes, actors, and criminals have made an enormous amount of money and even have garnered great prestige, but one can argue that these people's occupations are not necessary for the survival of society.

Still another criticism of functionalism is that it ignores the factor of inheritance and the unequal distribution of access to a good education (to medical school, for example). It ignores the importance of personal contacts and having friends in the right places to help one get into certain schools or into certain jobs. These kinds of benefits are not evenly distributed in society, and the operation of these kinds of factors does not necessarily ensure that the most capable people are in the most important positions in society.

The functionalist theory based on the work of Davis and Moore cannot account for many important factors that influence how certain people attain certain positions. Nor does it provide us with a means of establishing which positions are critical to society's survival or of explaining why people in those positions must be rewarded so highly in comparison to others.

Both the conflict and functionalist theory offer insights into the existence of social stratification. They are not necessarily mutually exclusive, and it is important to keep both points of view in mind as we turn to a discussion of the dimensions of stratification in modern society.

The Dimensions of Social Stratification

Wealth

One of the most influential early sociologists, Max Weber (1978/1922) saw three dimensions in modern stratification systems: wealth, prestige, and power. Wealth is the dimension referring to money and property including ownership of corporate stocks, bonds, real estate, and other investments. Wealth is largely capital ownership.

Most American families do not hold much wealth other than the family home, automobiles, savings and their income, the latter of which is usually relied upon as a major source of wealth. Tables 6.1 and 6.2 show the breakdown of income and the distribution of income in the United States.

Many Americans associate material possessions with the idea of social class. "In this association, money is both cause and symbol. For many Americans, other considerations are comparatively inconsequential" (Coleman and Rainwater 1978, 29). One-third of the respondents in a survey of Kansas City and Boston residents mentioned only wealth when asked about social class. This attitude was especially strong among people of low to average income. As one factory worker in the study insisted: "Money, money, money, plain and simple—that's what's involved in social class. . . . You get the money, you can get all the class and prestige you want" (Coleman and Rainwater 1978, 29). People who have more material possessions are envied by many others for that alone, according to the study. Money brings visual symbols of success. The Boston residents repeatedly mentioned the symbolic importance of living on Beacon Hill, an undisputed upper-class neighborhood. They spoke of bigger cars, bigger houses, more cars, jewelry, expensive recreation, and long vacations.

Prestige

Weber, unlike Marx, was not willing to view wealth as the only dimension of stratification. His second dimension of stratification, **prestige**, refers to the respect, honor, and recognition received from others in society. Prestige is status and it is not a tangible thing, but evidence of its existence comes from how one is treated and viewed by others. Titles such as physician, president, or professor and awards such as the Nobel Prize or the Pulitzer Prize typically bestow prestige on an individual. Family name and background can bring prestige as in being related to the DuPonts or Kennedys, for example. Material possessions and status symbols are often used to signify prestige as well as wealth. Lavish expenditures on clothes, homes, and even on charity may be seen as attempts to establish prestige in the eyes of others.

Prestige is often associated with a person's social position or occupation. Positions such as physician or architect are often difficult to attain and require con-

●**Table 6.1** Percent Distribution of Family Income Levels

Income Level	Percent of Families
Under $5,000	6.2%
$5,000 to 9,999	10.8
10,000 to 14,999	10.3
15,000 to 24,999	18.6
25,000 to 34,999	16.0
35,000 to 49,999	17.3
50,000 to 74,999	13.4
75,000 to 99,999	4.2
100,000 and over	3.2

Source: U.S. Bureau of the Census. *Money Income and Poverty Status in the United States: 1988,* in Current Population Reports, Series P-60, No. 166, advance data from the March 1989 Current Population Survey, Washington, D.C.: U.S. Government Printing Office, 1989.

●Table 6.2   Percent Distribution of Total Income by Each Fifth of American
Families

Family Rank	Percent Received of U.S. Income
Highest fifth (above $52,910 in income)	43.7%
Second highest fifth (above $36,600)	24.1
Third highest fifth (above $25,100)	16.9
Fourth highest fifth (above $14,450)	10.8
Bottom fifth (below $14,450)	4.6
The top 5% of families (above $86,300 in income)	16.9

Source: U.S. Bureau of the Census. *Money Income and Poverty Status in the United States: 1988,* in Current Population Reports, Series P-60, No. 166, advance data from the March 1989 Current Population Survey, Washington, D.C.: U.S. Government Printing Office, 1989.

siderable education and expertise. Table 6.3 shows a recent ranking of occupations on the basis of prestige by a sample of Americans. Occupations given the most respect and honor by the sample include physicians, judges, lawyers, and other professional positions difficult to attain.

Power

Weber's third dimension of stratification is **power** which is critical to the perspective of conflict theory. Power includes political influence and the personal and official authority that Dahrendorf wrote about. Weber defined power as the ability to get one's way even in the face of opposition. It is the force a person has over others. Take, for example, power in the college classroom. By virtue of his or her position, the college professor on many campuses can throw a student out of a class for not having the proper attitude. The professor can choose from a multitude of testing and grading techniques that might be quite mystifying to students. The professor can stifle or encourage student discussion; the professor can humiliate a student before the class. Once the professor has tenure (usually granted to a faculty member after about seven years), it is extremely difficult to fire him or her.

What power do the students have even though they are essentially paying the professor for the class? In some universities, student evaluations are used, but it would be difficult to fire a tenured professor on the basis of negative evaluations alone. The students can complain to higher university authorities, campaign to get rid of the professor, attempt to humiliate him or her before the class, and avoid taking the professor's classes. As pointed out by the German social theorist Georg Simmel (1950), subordinate people—in this case, students—are never completely powerless. But the fact remains that the professor has considerably more power than the students.

An important source of power is a person's economic clout. Economic clout is expressed in campaign contributions and other attempts to influence politics by spending money. Economic clout is also expressed in attempts to manipulate markets by shifting, moving, or investing large sums of money. Keep in mind Marx's point of view discussed earlier.

In addition to economic clout, occupation is also an important source of power in that it grants the person the institutionalized authority and privilege, or lack of

● **Table 6.3**   Prestige Rankings of U.S. Occupations*

Occupation	Ranking	Occupation	Ranking
Physicians	82	Electricians	49
University teachers	78	Machinists	48
Judges and lawyers	76	Carpet installers	47
Dentists	74	Firefighters	44
Bank officers	72	Plumbers	41
Financial managers	72	Pipe fitters	41
Architects	71	Farmers	41
Psychologists	71	Carpenters	40
Airplane pilots	70	Blacksmiths	36
Clergy	69	Brick masons	36
Geologists	67	Airline flight attendants	36
Secondary school teachers	63	Mechanics	35
Registered nurses	62	Bulldozer operators	33
Authors	60	Hairdressers	33
Accountants	57	Bus drivers	32
Painters and sculptors	56	File clerks	30
Actors	55	Waiters	20
Computer programmers	51	Maids and servants	18
Athletes	51	Charwomen	12
Office managers	50	Shoe shiners	09
Bank tellers	50		

*The concept of prestige was defined as the respondents' estimation of the social standing of the occupations. The data are based on more than 20,000 completed interviews from 1972 to 1987.

Source: National Opinion Research Center. *General Social Surveys, 1972–1987: Cumulative Codebook*, edited by James A. Davis and Tom W. Smith. Chicago: National Opinion Research Center. 1988.

authority and disprivilege, attached to that role. An example is the professor given above. A corporate executive is paid to make decisions that might influence a large number of people. The executive wields more power than a receptionist or custodian in the same corporation.

The three dimensions of stratification are interrelated, and concomitant levels in each dimension tend to occur. Someone who has a great deal of property tends also to have high levels of power and prestige. Each is used to reinforce the other. For example, members of the U.S. Congress have considerable prestige and power which can be used to increase wealth. It is not surprising that they voted themselves the most lucrative retirement policy of any federal employees, a plan worth more than most retirement plans available in private industry.

We typically think that possession of money is the most important element of social class in our society, and it is extremely significant. Yet great wealth does not automatically qualify an individual for upper-class status because that individual may not be accepted by those in the upper class if he or she does not have the proper education, manners, or lifestyle to please the upper class. For example, in the 1920s Joseph Kennedy was not allowed entrance into the upper-class community of Boston even though he had amassed a great fortune. He did not have the proper background to please the wealthy establishment. Moreover, he was Irish and Catholic, traits not admired by the Boston elite of the time.

In contrast, some people with considerable prestige are not necessarily extremely rich, but they gain esteem from others in the community or society due to some accomplishment, personal talent, or quality. Albert Einstein or Sister Theresa would serve as examples here.

The American Dream usually contains some aspect of one or more of these three dimensions of stratification. Success is often defined by the acquisition of material objects, the ability to gain the respect and admiration of others, and the ability to acquire and use power.

The Measurement of Social Class

Because social class is such a pivotal issue, sociologists have developed various ways to empirically measure it. The two most common are the subjective and objective measures. The **subjective measure** of social standing relies on people's perceptions of their own and others' standing. Subjective measures are not as precise because people's perceptions are based on factors that vary from person to person. Aware of equalitarian ideals, most people tend to call themselves middle class, which presents a problem for researchers. Nevertheless, the subjective measure of social class is still important and is often used in combination with objective measures, discussed next (see Coleman and Rainwater 1978, for example).

The term **socioeconomic status** (often abbreviated SES) most often refers to an **objective measure** of social standing. In measuring socioeconomic status objectively, some combination of social and economic indicators is used to assess an individual's position in the stratification hierarchy.

Sociologists often employ an objective measurement of SES using a combination of occupation, income and education. Each of these variables is referred to as an indicator of SES because the three dimensions of stratification mentioned above (wealth, power, and prestige) are so difficult to measure or to get accurate assessments of directly. For example, it is very difficult to measure a person's power in a community, especially if he or she operates behind the scenes in exercising influence. People do not readily disclose such backstage maneuvering. In addition, a family's total wealth is often difficult to assess; income figures are much more accessible. It should be noted that, of the three objective indicators of social standing, occupation is, by itself, more useful than the other two. Knowing a person's occupation can give some indication of that person's income and level of education. Nevertheless, the three combined make a better tool for measuring social class, or, more accurately, socioeconomic status.

An Overview of the American Class Structure

Many Americans feel intensely uncomfortable with any discussion of social class. We have grown up with the ideals of equality and democracy expressed in such statements as, "No one is better than I am." Sociologist Paul Blumberg (1980) called class "America's forbidden thought." Journalist Benita Eisler (1983) referred to class as "America's last dirty secret." Yet within blocks of the Capitol in Washington D.C. one can find people trapped in poverty living in decaying urban slums.

The American class structure is an enormously complex system to study because our class lines are blurred. In a witty and satirical book on social class in America, Paul Fussell (1983, 3) pointed out, "Class distinctions in America are so complicated and subtle that foreign visitors often miss the nuances and sometimes even the existence of a class structure."

Numerous studies in sociology have attempted to delineate the American class structure (for example, Lynd and Lynd 1929, Warner 1936, Warner and Lunt 1941, Coleman and Rainwater 1978, and Wright 1987). While we will refer to these studies, the following discussion is based mainly on a recent analysis of the American class structure by Dennis Gilbert and Joseph Kahl (1987). They discussed six classes based primarily on the variables of education, occupation, and family income. As we view each of these social classes, we will include descriptions of lifestyles and important terms that relate to each class.

The Capitalist Class

About one percent of the American population is found in the **capitalist class**. These people are a "very small class of super-rich capitalists at the top of the hierarchy" (Gilbert and Kahl 1987, 331). They are the upper class. Although their numbers are small, they have vast power in society; they contribute huge sums to political campaigns, make business decisions and market investments that affect millions of jobs often on an international scale, and they own major media companies which can influence public opinion. It should be noted that sociological research on this small, elite group is limited for obvious reasons. It is difficult to gain access to their social situations and neighborhoods. Like most people, they prefer to maintain privacy, but members of the capitalist class have the power to ensure such privacy.

Some members of this class have great wealth that has been in their families for several generations; they form a kind of American aristocracy. Warner and Lunt (1941) referred to these people as members of the **upper-upper class**. These families have prestigious names such as Getty, Rockefeller, Mellon, Vanderbilt, Carnegie, or Ford. Their prestige is reinforced in the process of socialization through class custom and role modeling, highly selective private prep schools and universities, exclusive neighborhoods, exclusive men's clubs, and being in the Social Register (see Domhoff 1967, 1970, 1974, 1983, Persell and Cookson 1985, and Lapham 1988). Their lifestyle means that one has the proper manner, education, dress, outlook, and attitude. Being in this class requires a certain cultivated aristocratic behavior.

Other members of the capitalist or upper class lack such family background, proper education, and aristocratic manner. Warner and Lunt (1941) referred to these people as the **lower-upper class**, composed of people who are extremely, but recently, rich. Consequently the established rich tend to look down on these people as newcomers who lack the background to be socially respected and accepted even though these newcomers may have more money. In fact, the French have a term used to insult a person's social prestige. The term **nouveau riche**, literally translated to mean "newly rich," is a social slur meaning that a person lacks class, title, or elite background.

Given this seemingly arbitrary division of the upper class into two groups, it is not difficult to see that some class antagonism might potentially exist. The newly rich often resent being looked down upon by the others, while the old rich resent the inroads of the newcomers. Even Shakespeare, in the play *Romeo and Juliet,* subtly

One of the pleasures of immense wealth is the ability to purchase luxury items such as this Rolls Royce and be driven by a chauffeur. While it may be argued that this is a fine automobile and that it is comfortable to be driven by someone else, others, such as sociologist Thorsten Veblen, would contend that this is an instance of "conspicuous consumption." That is, such items become symbols of wealth.

referred to class conflict between two families, Juliet's family being the newly rich and Romeo's family being the established rich. Each family resented the other; thus the longstanding hatred developed between them.

Another example of these resentments between the two classes is illustrated in the life of Joseph Kennedy and his family. Born in 1888 Kennedy by no means had an impoverished background and had, early in his life, begun amassing a great fortune. As mentioned earlier, he was not accepted by upper-crust Boston society. In their biography of the Kennedy family, Collier and Horowitz (1984, 44) point out:

> Upper class New Englanders had reacted to the immigrant tide by creating caste institutions—exclusive prep schools and social clubs—which even respectable Boston Irishmen, about whom their were no rumors, couldn't buy their way into.... Rose was snubbed by the Cohasset matrons, and Joe was blackballed when he applied for membership in the Cohasset Country Club.... 'Those narrow-minded bigoted sons of ... barred me because I was an Irish Catholic and son of a barkeep.'

Perhaps another reason for the differences between the two classes is the tendency for the newly rich to engage in what sociologist Thorstein Veblen (1979/1899) called **conspicuous consumption**. This term refers to the tendency for people, when possible, to engage in an obvious, even flagrant, display of wealth. Perhaps more than most social critics, Veblen negatively reacted to the social concern with material objects as indicators of social worth. Certain material objects are generally known to cost a great deal of money, so an individual driving a Porsche or a Lamborghini is making a statement about wealth.

Veblen stated that beauty and desirability are equated with the price tag. When one builds a certain style of house or wears certain jewelry or certain clothes, one makes a social statement about status and wealth. Veblen argued that the more wasteful the object, and the less useful the object, the better it was in demonstrating status. The more rooms in the house, the more gas used by the car, the more expensive clothes and furs and jewelry, the more likely they will demonstrate money and status. That is their purpose. Maybe that was the intent of Imelda Marcos, wife of the deposed Philippine dictator, when she bought more than six thousand pairs of shoes.

Today's marketers in business are well aware of consumption patterns and have created many things that are disposable and wasteful. Through a variety of advertising techniques, businesses create a market for goods by appealing to people's need to demonstrate status through purchasing power.

Certainly, the newly rich have more stake in doing this—to prove that they now have money—yet conspicuous consumption is characteristic of all classes in the U.S. Americans tend to use material objects as status symbols to make social statements about themselves. The wealthy simply have more money and more resources to make their material consumption especially conspicuous if they wish.

The Upper-Middle Class

Consisting of about fifteen percent of the population (see Gilbert and Kahl 1987, 333 for example), people in the upper-middle-class are the professionals. They are the Americans most shaped by higher education; a college degree is a must and, often, advanced graduate studies are also required (Gilbert and Kahl 1987, 334). Physicians, lawyers, architects, bankers, executives, scientists, and mid- to high-level white-collar corporate and government professionals are examples of persons in this class. While most make a relatively high income, the range of income may be great. For example, a lawyer working as a public defender for the state may make less than $50,000 a year while a noted corporate attorney may make more than $500,000 a year. (See Tables 6.1 and 6.2 for income levels in America.)

The lifestyles of those in the upper-middle class are distinctive. They tend to be quite civic minded. They are involved in community politics and organizations such as the Lion's Club. The women often are in the Junior League or Women's Forum. They are the members of the country club along with the wealthy, although the upper-middle class is often excluded from the most prestigious and exclusive clubs of the rich.

According to Rothman (1978), members of this class have considerable social and economic resources allowing them much more access to power and influence than those in the classes below. Their professional associations, especially the American Medical Association and the American Bar Association, are very influential in legislation being passed in this country. "Because of their education, status ranking, and prestige they can occupy positions on school boards, public commissions, and Chambers of Commerce and in this way affect decisions at the state and local level" (Rothman 1978, 166). Because of their position in the structure of our class system, they command significant resources with which to influence the social and political systems.

The lifestyle of this class is often the one portrayed as the American Dream. A nice, large, comfortable home in a nice area of town with respected schools for their children and money for their college education, material success and security, and respect from others in the community and neighborhood. Even though this may be the American Dream, federal figures from the U.S. Census Bureau illustrate that this category includes a relatively small number of American families. Income figures for 1988 indicate that only 7.4 percent of American families had incomes of $75,000 or more. Obviously, this 7.4 percent includes those in the upper classes as well. (Refer to Table 6.1 on page 113 for a breakdown of family income levels for 1988.) Evidently, only a few truly achieve this version of the American Dream.

The Middle Class

Approximately one-third of American families fall into the category of the **middle class.** Occupationally, this class consists of white-collar workers whose jobs do not carry either the high prestige or high income of those in the upper-middle class. Such middle-class occupations include schoolteachers, small business owners, office managers, computer programmers, sales people, registered nurses, and mid-level white-collar employees in corporations and government. Many of these occupations do not bring large incomes—teaching school, for example. Table 6.4 gives the median incomes levels in the United States since 1967. Note that these income levels have not increased much in nearly twenty-five years.

White-collar workers in the middle class "supply the huge and essential work force that performs the everyday white collar routines of the corporation and distributes goods and services at the local level, but they are removed from the centers of decision making in the elite board rooms" (Vanfossen 1979, 320).

It appears that Americans generally tend to place higher value on white-collar occupations which require more education, are typically indoor, and do not require manual labor. This may be changing somewhat, however. Recent occupational prestige surveys revealed that certain clerical workers and white-collar workers are found to have about the same or sometimes even less prestige than skilled workers in blue-collar trades (Treiman 1977, Davis and Smith 1984). For instance, real estate agents and lower-paid sales personnel have slightly lower prestige rankings than electricians and machinists who are moving into the middle class.

It is likely that the first significant signs of discontent with work and with socioeconomic position occur in the middle class, possibly because they lack power and influence in decision making. Unlike those in the upper-middle class, they lack control over their work. Their jobs are more likely to be dead-end. For example, registered nurses might be considered well-paid semiprofessionals, but there is little upward movement available to them beyond head nurse. They would have to leave nursing to go into hospital administration or go back to college for advanced degrees to appreciably improve their positions. Consequently, they "neither prosper nor perish" (Vanfossen 1979, 324).

The lifestyle of the middle class is more likely to center around neighborhood, family, and church. They are somewhat less likely to be involved in community

●Table 6.4 Median Income Levels of American Families*

Year	Median Family Income
1967	$28,098
1970	30,084
1975	30,167
1980	30,182
1985	30,493
1988	32,191

*Based on constant 1988 dollars so that the figures are comparable.

Source: U.S. Bureau of the Census. *Money Income and Poverty Status in the United States: 1988,* in Current Population Reports, Series P-60, No. 166, advance data from the March 1989 Current Population Survey, Washington, D.C.: U.S. Government Printing Office, 1989.

politics and leadership than are people in the upper-middle class. They do not have as much influence. Membership in various community groups such as the Masons or the Elks and the Chamber of Commerce is common (Vanfossen 1979, 321–22). They tend to stress solid middle-class values with a special emphasis on respectability (Rothman 1978, 203). Given their position in the stratification system, they are sometimes given to "status panic" (Mills 1951) in that they have a fear of sinking down in the system. Some recent evidence supports the idea of a shrinking middle class (Rose 1986). During the late 1970s and 1980s, more than 600,000 middle management jobs disappeared due to changes in the economy (Goldstein 1990, 21). Research Application 6.1 discusses the issue of downward mobility among those in the middle classes who have fallen off the ladder to success.

Research Application 6.1

• • • • • • • Falling Off the Ladder: Downward Mobility in America

David Patterson worked his way up from a run-down neighborhood in Philadelphia to a high-level executive position in a computer firm. He and his family enjoyed a prosperous country-club lifestyle. Like many computer businesses, his company hit hard times, and his entire division was shut down, costing fifty-five people their jobs. David sent out hundreds of resumes for months, but he could not find a job. His wife's pay did not cover the bills. His family lost their home, their friends and their status. David lost his self-respect (Newman 1988, 1–7).

Jacqueline Johansen was married more than twenty years to a successful dentist. She had worked to put him through school but then left the work force to raise their three children. When her husband left her for a younger woman, she realized that, at age forty-seven, she had no college education and could only find a low-paying clerical job. Even with child-support payments, Jacqueline was falling out of the middle class (Newman 1988, 204).

Elena Morales worked for the Singer Sewing Machine Company in Elizabeth, N.J., for sixteen years, making her way up from the assembly line to a higher-paying position in quality control. However, Singer was facing stiff competition from abroad, and the working women of the 1970s and 1980s were less likely to buy sewing machines. While Singer diversified and is doing well in aerospace electronics, its sewing machine factory was finally closed, putting Elena and fifteen hundred other people out of work (Newman 1988, 179–181).

These three people reflect the experiences of millions of people each year in the United States. Downward mobility is more common today than at any time since the Great Depression, and it reflects the structural changes affecting mobility in our postindustrial society. Unemployment has been persistently high since the 1970s. "Unemployment in the United States is chronic and large, significantly larger than official rates would have it" (Rossides 1990, 177). The official rate of unemployment hovers around seven percent of the work force, but this does not include many people who are discouraged enough not to look for work at all.

There are a number of causes for unemployment and downward mobility. First, international competition has hurt a variety of industries causing mass layoffs and factory closings. Also affecting industry downturns are the shifting consumer needs and preferences in society. For example, there is simply less demand for sewing machines today.

Second, many of these lost jobs were relatively high-paying production jobs. However, many new jobs opening up are relatively lower-paying jobs. As sociologist Daniel Rossides (1990, 177) notes, "The inequality of jobs, already steep, seems to be getting more unequal with the bulk of new jobs coming in semiskilled and unskilled occupations." Without additional training, Elena Morales is unlikely to find a position that will pay as much as her factory job, just as David Patterson is less likely to find a job equivalent to his executive position. There are fewer well-paying jobs for new high school graduates today, as well.

Third, the high rate of divorce is also a factor in downward mobility, especially for women like Jacqueline Johansen. It usually takes two incomes in a family today to carve out a middle- or upper-middle-class lifestyle. A woman on her own has a difficult time earning enough money to support her children. Typically, women's average earnings, even in the same occupation, are less than men's (see chapter 8).

The issue of downward mobility indicates that America is reversing its previous history of an expanding economy. Consequently, "The United States appears no longer able to provide an expanding number of middle-income households" (Rossides 1990, 175).

The practical lesson to be learned from the experiences of David, Jacqueline, and Elena is that workers today must be aware. We must recognize that we live in a period of tremendous social change and that certainty is hard to come by. Flexibility as well as awareness and preparedness can help ease the pain. Keep in mind Mills's sociological imagination discussed in chapter 1. Historical circumstances play a key role in our personal lives. David, Jacqueline, and Elena might have bitterly blamed themselves, but Mills would say that is an inaccurate assessment.

Those in the middle class have some reason to fear an erosion of lifestyle, and therefore feel a strong need to demonstrate their status and respectability. When both husband and wife work, they are likely to have adequate incomes. Even though the members of the middle class cannot realistically afford the luxuries of those in the classes above them, they often feel considerable pressure from the economic system, from advertising, and from the need to impress others by spending beyond their means.

The Working Class

As mentioned above, the class lines between the middle and working classes are becoming more blurred as the higher-paying jobs of carpenters and plumbers gain in prestige while some routinized and lower-paying clerical jobs are now basically working-class occupations. Consequently, the traditional white-collar and blue-collar distinctions are no longer as useful as in the past. However, the bulk of the working class remains the semi-skilled factory workers such as machine operators, assembly-line workers, ironworkers, and construction workers. The working class makes up less than one-third of the population in the United States (Gilbert and Kahl 1987, 335).

Typically, members of the working class do not have much formal education beyond high school other than trade school or apprenticeships. But, in many ways, these people form the backbone of the labor force in our society. They do work that must be done whether it is collecting our garbage or repairing sewers or performing more so-called respectable jobs such as typist or retail sales clerk.

Several important facts stand out with regard to members of the working class in American society. First, their work is more dangerous. Each year in the United

Work for members of the working class is strictly instrumental. There is little personal statisfaction to be gained from standing for eight hours a day on the assembly line. But it provides the money to purchase the needs and pleasures of life.

States approximately 100,000 die in industrial accidents or from work-related illnesses, such as black lung disease among coal miners. Millions more are injured each year, many permanently disabled. As Levison (1974) points out, a major feature of their work in our society is "the simple fact that American workers must accept serious injury and even death as part of their daily reality while the middle class does not."

Second, the working class is more likely to face job instability as a result of the cyclical ups and downs of our economy. It is relatively rare for General Motors to lay off white-collar workers whereas industrial workers face repetitive layoffs depending on fluctuations in the industry and the economy. Other blue-collar workers such as those in construction must contend with occasional joblessness due to the weather or to local economic conditions. Recently the steel industry has been particularly hard hit partly as a result of strong competition from foreign steel makers. Consequently, American steelworkers have faced very long periods of unemployment. In fact, it is likely that a significant percentage will never regain their jobs after recent layoffs.

Third, related to the above example about steelworkers, many social scientists are saying that the number of working-class jobs is shrinking; they cite as causes our increasing automation (the growing use of robotics in assembly line work, for example) and computerization in industry along with growing competition from foreign countries such as Japan and Mexico. The shift in our society to a post-industrial, service-oriented economy means that many heavy-industry workers will no longer be needed. It is likely that many Americans will have spent a large part of their lives working in an industry and will soon find that their skills are obsolete in our rapidly changing economy. Since 1977, 2.5 million jobs in American factories have permanently disappeared (Goldstein 1990, 21).

A fourth feature of working-class life is that they, like many in the middle class, typically do not have the benefits that often accompany upper-middle-class occupations. Such benefits include expense accounts, stock options, better insurance coverage, and more flexibility in how they spend their time in the workplace. For example, if you work on an assembly line, your time and your work are controlled by the machinery and its pace. You do not take coffee breaks or bathroom breaks unless they are scheduled. Thompson (1983) noted that repetition and boredom on the assembly line are often excruciating. Fussell (1983) suggests that the degree of supervision a person experiences at work and the amount of freedom in how one spends time at work are better indicators of class than simply the amount of money one earns.

Finally, many members of the working class must face the fact that their jobs will seldom lead to advancement. That is, they are often trapped in certain kinds of work that do not have a specified means of advancement more typical of some middle-class and of all upper-middle-class occupations. Secretaries and other clerical workers as well as factory workers seldom have opportunities to climb the corporate ladder and significantly enhance their earning potential. While cost-of-living raises and labor union efforts to increase wages are common, they may not offset the effects of inflation and do not reflect the increases white-collar workers can achieve. For many in the working class, the best they can achieve is seniority on the job which can help insulate them against layoffs and other job insecurities.

Lifestyles in the working class are quite varied with the multitude of ethnic, regional, and occupational influences. While all classes show such diversity, it is more prevalent in the working class because newly arriving immigrants such as Vietnamese and Hispanics most often find jobs at this level. Generally, though, sociologists find that those in the working class are less likely to live in the suburbs and are less likely to be directly involved in politics and community organizations, even though they are indirectly involved through their union if they belong to one. Their incomes do not allow them to have the standard of living experienced by those above them in the class structure regarding the style of houses and other status symbols. They tend to be avid sports fans and have leisure-time activities that help make up for the boredom of their work. Thompson (1983), in his study of assembly-line workers in a beef processing plant, points out that many get caught in a kind of financial trap where they buy expensive material items such as stereos, motorcycles, and automobiles on credit which only makes them more dependent on their work and less likely to be able to return to school or look for other work.

On the other hand, members of the working class are quick to point out that they find benefits in their work. Unlike many upper-middle-class workers, they do not have to take their work home with them nights and weekends. When they leave the job, they are free. They also do not have to worry about keeping up the proper image as do many corporate and bureaucratic workers.

Finally, many blue-collar workers, especially the "blue-collar aristocrats" (LeMasters 1975) such as welders, have concrete results to show for their labor through which they feel a great deal of pride, unlike a mid-level manager whose work is often intangible.

The Working Poor

About 12 percent of our population falls into the category of **the working poor.** They include unskilled laborers, those in service jobs such as janitors or maids, and those in the lowest paying industrial jobs. Note from Table 6.1 (page   ) that 27.3 percent of American families have incomes of less than $15,000 a year. Often, the working poor face periodic unemployment, and their incomes may be at the minimum wage or less. In addition, their incomes often fall below the government's established poverty level depending on the nature of their work and the length of periods of unemployment. They are called the working poor because their incomes do not allow them to come close to the middle-class style of living in America (Gilbert and Kahl 1987, 336).

Comprising both poor and near-poor families, people in this class are caught in circumstances that are difficult to remedy without help. Many are female heads of households who cannot support children on a minimum-wage food service job or a five-dollars-an-hour position as a receptionist.

Consider this example. A student in one of our classes was recently divorced and received no support from her ex-husband for their three children. She had never worked during her fifteen-year marriage, but with the help of a federal tuition grant she earned a certificate as a Licensed Vocational Nurse not long after her divorce. Living in a relatively small town and lacking the resources to move to a larger city, she earned less than $14,000 a year. Soon she discovered that she could not house, clothe, or feed her children, nor could she pay for transportation, child-care costs, and medical bills. She finally turned to the state for help and received food stamps, which she considered humiliating because she had always heard negative comments about welfare. She recalled how she would refuse to check out at the grocery store if she saw anyone she knew. With assistance from federal programs, she returned to college and struggled for three years to become a Registered Nurse. She is now doing well, but she has bitter memories of those years as a member of the working poor. Her experience reflects those of millions of Americans caught in social and economic conditions that may take years from which to recover.

The Underclass

Sociologists have only recently begun to distinguish between the working poor and the underclass in our society. According to Gilbert and Kahl (1987, 337), the underclass are those in our society who "suffer long-term deprivation from low education, low employability, low income, and eventually, low self-esteem." They make up about twelve or thirteen percent of our population.

This class is sometimes referred to as the disreputable poor. Many of those in the underclass depend on welfare to survive and they face the harshest living conditions in our society. Ironically, like the upper class, the underclass tends to be invisible in that many people in our society do not realize the extent of such severe poverty.

In his study, Ken Auletta (1983, xvi) divided the underclass into four groups. The "passive poor" were the long-term poor on welfare who felt defeated and hopeless. The "hostile poor" were street criminals who often were school drop-outs, drug addicts, and those who terrorized others in urban areas. The "hustlers" earned their living in an underground economy selling drugs, running con games, and engaging in other nonviolent crimes such as prostitution. Finally, the "traumatized poor" were drifters, alcoholics, bag ladies, and the chronically mentally ill who roamed American streets, frequently collapsing from chronic poor health.

Roger Wilkins, historian and Pulitzer Prize winner, (1990) analyzed the situation of the urban underclass in Washington D.C. and pointed out five reasons for its existence. Although most poor people in America are white, in this area of Washington most were black and descendents of rural immigrants from the South who came to northern cities "with their soft, country ways" during the Great Migration from 1910 to 1970. They were looking for a better life than that of a sharecropper's in Alabama. At first these new immigrants found reasonable-paying industrial jobs that allowed them to support a family. But that soon would change.

Second, the civil rights movement of the 1960s provided the opportunity for the best-educated and luckiest residents of impoverished areas to move out of the inner city because of desegregation laws. That left the poorest and least educated in the ghetto areas, and they had lost the role models of the black bank owner, minister, and other professionals who had moved to the suburbs. The loss was devastating in that young, poor blacks had few neighbors who could infuse hope and middle-class values into the ghetto.

Third on Wilkins's list was the dramatic economic downturn in the U.S. beginning in 1973. Many industrial jobs were no longer available, and inflation and recession took their toll on blue-collar incomes. Service jobs that were available, such as food handler at McDonalds, would not support a family.

Fourth, the Reagan administration of the 1980s cut federal assistance programs that provided job training and educational benefits for the poor. America seemed to turn its back on those who appeared not to benefit from desegregation and the war on poverty. As Wilkins pointed out, Americans appeared to consider inner-city residents as the throwaway people.

Fifth, and finally, the crack epidemic hit D.C. streets in 1985, and the effects were catastrophic. Not only were there no longer any middle-class role models in the neighborhood, now the major role models were drug dealers who made much money. The price, of course, was that one-third of the men in the neighborhood were in jail before age thirty. Several hundred were murdered in drug wars. America began to take notice. However, as yet, the United States has not begun to formulate a policy to deal with the entrenched poverty of the urban underclass. In fact, poverty in America is a much misunderstood phenomena.

Poverty in America

Defining poverty is no easy task. With the constantly changing features of the modern economy as well as the conceptions of what is necessary and what is not in modern life, it is difficult to establish who is considered poor. Some researchers prefer a relative approach whereby poverty is defined in relation to the standard of living in society. For example, it has been suggested that we consider the bottom twenty percent of the population as poor; others have suggested that poverty should be defined as one-half the median income level in society. Using the relative approach usually guarantees the existence of a certain amount of poverty regardless of the improvements or downturns in the economy.

An alternate approach to defining poverty, the absolute approach, assumes that an income level exists below which a family cannot maintain a minimal standard of living (Rothman 1978, 136–37). Today the most widely used definition of poverty is the federal government's establishment of yearly income levels depending on family size and rural or urban location. Below these levels families cannot meet the minimal demands for food and shelter. Although the government uses an absolute approach, the cutoff level for poverty changes from year to year in response to inflation and, particularly, to variations in the cost of food. The federal poverty level is also extremely important in determining who is eligible for government aid. Figures 6.1 and 6.2 give some descriptive information about those who fall below the poverty level in the United States.

Based on data regarding the federal poverty level, there is no question that poverty in the United States has increased since 1980 even though, until recently, it had showed a steady decline since World War II. Since 1985 the poverty rate has again declined, though very slightly. The United States has proportionately more poor people than most Western European and industrialized nations. How is it that in this country, as wealthy as it is and with its ideology of equality and opportunity, more than 30 million citizens live in poverty and even more live in near poverty?

The question is difficult to answer. A recent Gallup poll indicates that nearly forty percent of Americans think poverty is the result of an individual's lack of effort. More than a third of those surveyed believed that poor people prefer to remain on welfare, and almost two-thirds felt that the current welfare system makes people dependent (*The Gallup report* 1989, 2–7). Many Americans believe that opportunity exists for those with the motivation and the drive to seek it out. In our university classes and in grocery store lines, we often hear people complain about "welfare cheats" who misuse food stamps or defraud the government. However, more than seventy percent of those surveyed in the Gallup poll indicated that they were more sympathetic to the poor than they were five years previously; nearly one-fourth had a close relative living in poverty (*The Gallup report* 1989, 2–7).

A statistical breakdown of the poor (see Table 6.5 as well as Figures 6.1 and 6.2), or those falling below the federally established poverty level, will help overcome some of the stereotypes about poor people in our society. First, fully two-thirds of the poor are, for a variety of reasons, unable to work or find it extremely difficult to work. This two-thirds includes children under age 16 (we have child labor laws in most states that restrict the work children and teenagers can do) and the elderly over age 65. This two-thirds also includes the handicapped such as the blind, the disabled, the mentally ill, or the retarded, and those suffering from chronic illnesses such as emphysema, heart disease, or cancer. Also included are students who find it difficult to make enough money to rise above the poverty line and still attend school. Consequently, most of the poor are people who are not necessarily lacking in motivation or ambition but whose social circumstances make it very difficult for them to make more money. It is notable, if not tragic, that one in every four children under six is poor in this country (U.S. Bureau of Census 1989).

Of the remaining third who fall below the poverty level, many are working but are in jobs that do not pay enough to rise above the poverty line or are in jobs that are seasonal or part-time. For example, among those at the lowest income levels in our society are migrant workers who pick our fruits and vegetables. In Florida, it is not unusual for them to be paid less than the minimum wage for backbreaking labor. One might question why someone would stay at this job. Typically, their parents were migrant workers who traveled a great deal making a good education for the children difficult. Often the children are kept out of school for long periods to help in the fields. Consequently, many never even reach high school. The school drop-out rate for children of migrant workers is eighty percent.

●**Figure 6.1** Percentages of Poverty Rates for Persons with Selected Characteristics: 1988

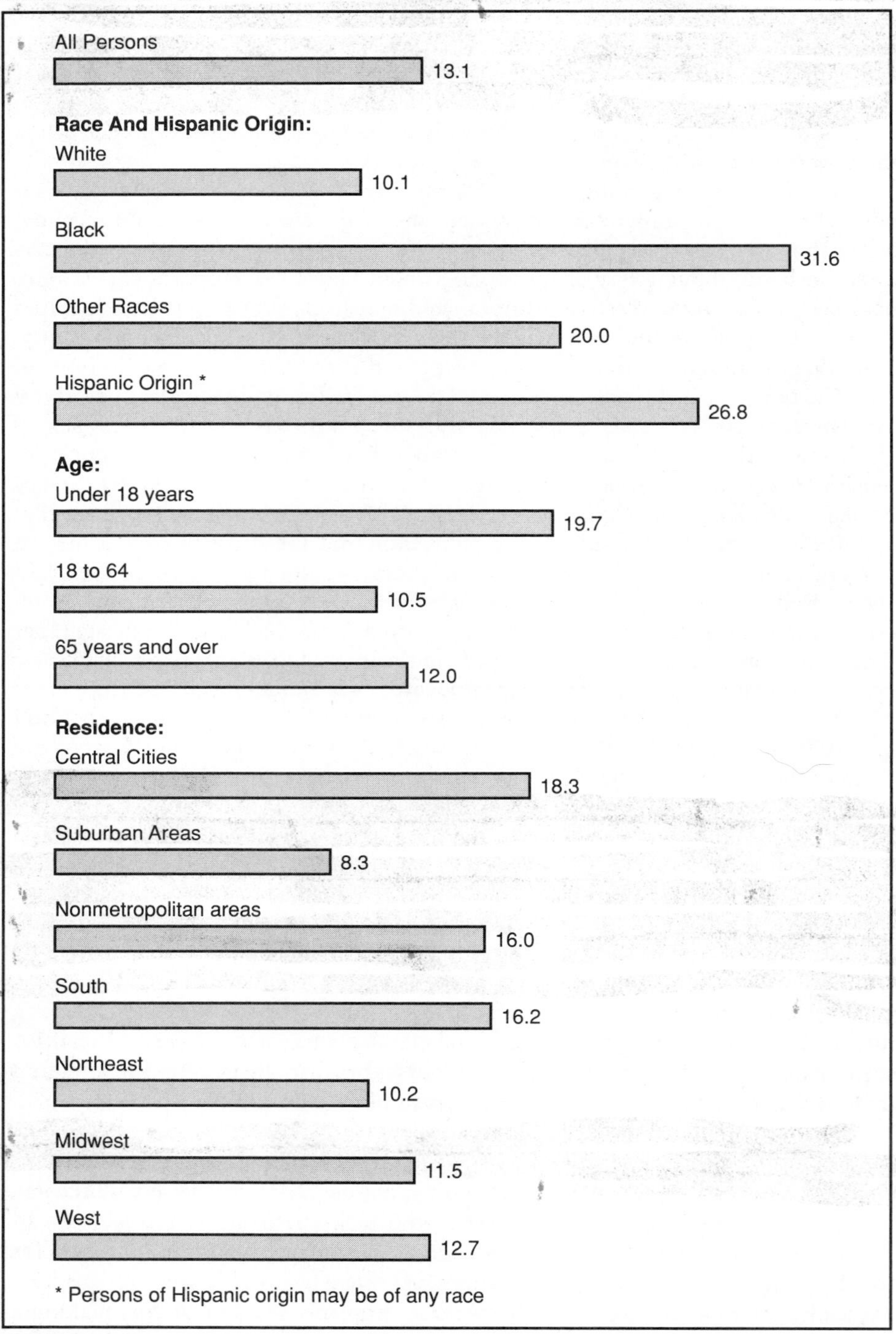

All Persons
13.1

Race And Hispanic Origin:
White
10.1

Black
31.6

Other Races
20.0

Hispanic Origin *
26.8

Age:
Under 18 years
19.7

18 to 64
10.5

65 years and over
12.0

Residence:
Central Cities
18.3

Suburban Areas
8.3

Nonmetropolitan areas
16.0

South
16.2

Northeast
10.2

Midwest
11.5

West
12.7

* Persons of Hispanic origin may be of any race

Source: U.S. Bureau of the Census. *Money Income and Poverty Status in the United States: 1988*, in Current Population Reports, Series P-60, No. 166, advance data from the March 1989 Current Population Survey, Washington, D.C.: U.S. Government Printing Office, 1989.

•**Figure 6.2** Percentages of Poverty Rates for Families with Selected
Characteristics: 1988

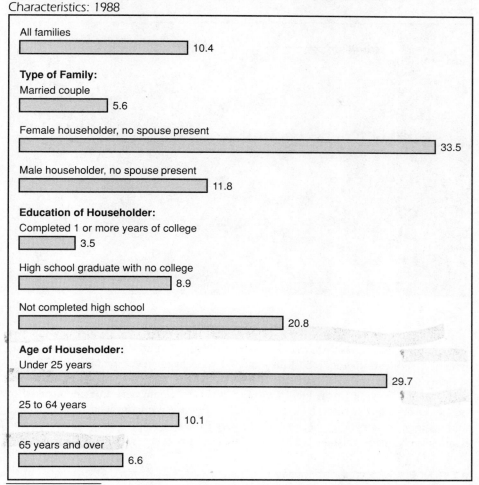

All families
10.4

Type of Family:
Married couple
5.6

Female householder, no spouse present
33.5

Male householder, no spouse present
11.8

Education of Householder:
Completed 1 or more years of college
3.5

High school graduate with no college
8.9

Not completed high school
20.8

Age of Householder:
Under 25 years
29.7

25 to 64 years
10.1

65 years and over
6.6

Source: U.S. Bureau of the Census. *Money Income and Poverty Status in the United States: 1988*, in
Current Population Reports, Series P-60, No. 166, advance data from the March 1989 Current Population
Survey, Washington, D.C.: U.S. Government Printing Office, 1989.

In addition, migrant workers lack access to any kind of power or influence; they
may move too often to even establish residency in order to vote (NBC News 1981).

For the most part, migrant workers are invisible in our society, yet the work
must be done. As members of the underclass, these workers and others like them
find it extremely difficult to get better paying jobs. Their lack of skills and education
is not the only problem. They cannot leave work to look for other jobs because
they cannot afford to lose the money for that day. They lack the clothes and the
proper presentation of self for many middle-class employers to consider them for
jobs. Some are recent immigrants to the United States and may not speak English
adequately for certain jobs. Thus, they tend to remain at the lowest income levels
of society. Recall from our earlier discussion of the conflict theory of inequality
that it is also likely that many in society benefit from keeping the underclass at low
income levels.

Amid the plenty of modern American society there are those who share in little of its wealth. These homeless men in Philadelphia get what little comfort they can from the warmth of a trash fire.

Finally, the majority of the poor who do not work tend to be female heads of households. That is, they are women with children who find day-care too expensive, who lack education and job skills, and who perhaps never planned to have to support a family. In fact, over half—53 percent—of all poor families are headed by women. Growing up in the 1950s and 1960s, women were not encouraged to be career oriented as often as they are today; they were encouraged to get married and become homemakers. Some married very early to escape family situations, and some simply made mistakes. The fact remains, however, that three of every four

●**Table 6.5** Facts about Poverty in America

Most poor people are white. 29.6% of all poor people are black.

53% of poor families are headed by females. 75.6% of black poor families are headed by females. 47.9% of Hispanic poor families are headed by females. 43.5% of white poor families are headed by females.

The average number of children in poverty families is 2.25.

Poverty rates are consistently higher for adult females than for adult males. This is true for all races and ethnic groups, but the effect is greater for black women.

50.4% of the poor are either under age 18 (39.5%) or over age 65 (10.9%).

Only 9.5% of the female heads of households who are poor worked full-time year round in 1988.

Of adult householders, 18 years of age or older, classified as poor, 48.3% worked full- or part-time during 1988. The majority of those not working were women staying home with their children.

Of those adult householders who did not work full-time in 1988, about one-third were ill or disabled.

Source: U.S. Bureau of the Census. *Money Income and Poverty Status in the United States: 1988,* in Current Population Reports, Series P-60, No. 166, advance data from the March 1989 Current Population Survey, Washington, D.C.: U.S. Government Printing Office, 1989.

persons living in poverty are female. This phenomenon is sometimes called the feminization of poverty in the United States. More than one in three female-headed families fall below the poverty line while only one in ten married-couples families are below the poverty level (U.S. Bureau of the Census 1989).

Another fact to consider about poverty is that most people who are poor are white, but minorities such as blacks and Hispanics tend to have disproportionately more poverty (see Figure 6.1). In 1989, for example, 31 percent of blacks and 29 percent of Hispanics were below the poverty level compared to 10 percent of whites. The high rate of poverty among minorities is in part attributable to the past and present discrimination in education, hiring, and advancement these minorities experienced. In addition, the high rate of single-parent families among minorities contributes to their income difficulties. A more detailed discussion of this problem follows in chapter 7.

More than one-third of the poor live in the South, particularly in the rural areas of Appalachia and the Rio Grande Valley of Texas. Another fact to consider is that many poor people do work their way out of poverty. They may receive welfare for a year or two while they are taking advantage of a job training program or getting the equivalent of a high school diploma. Yet, as they slowly move out of poverty, others unfortunately move in due to loss of job, disability, illness, or a host of other reasons (Duncan et al. 1984). We do have a hard-core group of poor who tend to pass the lifestyle of poverty on to their children much like upper-middle-class families tend to pass on that style to their children. Such effects of poverty are part of our next discussion on the overall consequences of inequality.

The Consequences of Stratification

Perhaps most important to any sociological discussion of social stratification is the understanding of the consequences of inequality for individuals in the social system. As mentioned earlier in this chapter, an individual's social class background has wide-ranging effects on the individual. In this section, we are going to look at these most significant consequences. Another way to view it is that a person's opportunities in life are, to a large extent, influenced by social class. Life chances are defined as social opportunities and the probabilities of whether an individual will benefit from the stratification system.

Life Expectancy

One of the most basic effects of class inequality has to do with expected length of life. Not surprisingly, the higher the class the longer the life expectancy in the United States. The figure commonly given is that poverty takes ten years off a person's life. As another example, the average life expectancy of a migrant worker in this country is 49 years. Compare that with the overall life expectancy in this country of 75 years. The differences in life expectancy can be explained by the unequal access to high-quality medical care. For example, the rural poor can rarely afford to travel to urban centers where medical care is likely to be more advanced and specialized. The lifestyle and living conditions of the poor, particularly with regard to work and dangerous conditions, make them more likely to die in industrial accidents. The homicide rate is greater among the poor. They are more likely to be murdered (and to murder) than any other income group. The infant mortality rate is greater among the poor. Consequently, even length of life is affected by one's position in the stratification system.

Health

For many of the same reasons, a person's chance to live a healthier life is greater in the higher classes in our society. People who have trouble making ends meet to pay for rent and food are more likely to put off trips to the doctor for regular checkups. Even when they do get ill, they tend to wait longer to go to the doctor thus increasing the chances that their illnesses will worsen. Often fearing the cost of a hospital stay, poorer people and even many middle-class people will put off the trip to the doctor. And, as mentioned above, the work environment has a great deal to do with the kinds of illnesses and dangers that an individual will face. Serious mental illnesses are also more common among lower socioeconomic groups and in part may be related to the work environment (Link, Dohrenwend, and Skodol 1986).

For white-collar workers, stress and a high-pressure environment along with lack of proper diet and exercise may eventually take their toll. However, recent figures from the American Heart Association show that heart disease increases as income decreases. In addition, more immediate dangers are faced by coal miners who risk black lung disease and mine disasters. Other industrial workers risk death or disablement daily. Many are aware of the risk and often dismiss it or minimize it. On the other hand, some workers are unaware of and have no choice over dangers to which they are exposed. For example, there is some evidence that executives in the Johns-Manville Corporation (now called Manville) apparently knew that asbestos in their industrial plants posed hazards of lung disease for the workers long before the company publicly acknowledged those hazards. Evidence exists that Johns-Manville, Pittsburgh Corning, and other companies were aware of the dangers faced by their plant workers yet did not take measures to curtail the danger until years later (Ermann and Lundman 1989).

Family Stability

Most studies of divorce and family instability indicate that the lower the class, the higher the rate of family instability. Divorce rates are higher in the lower classes as is separation and desertion. There are more single-headed households, mostly female-headed, among the poor than among the other classes, as was mentioned earlier in our discussion of poverty. On the other hand, family stability is strongest in the higher social classes. Sociologists give several reasons for these statistics. First, and most important, the economic difficulties of life in the lower classes—especially among poverty groups—causes considerable strain among family members (see South 1985, for example). With our philosophy of individualism in this country, the blame and thus the guilt of not being able to support a family brings resentments and arguments. As C. Wright Mills (1959b) pointed out, we often do not look at the larger forces operating on our private lives and instead look around for someone to blame. A family member, a husband, or a wife is usually the one to receive the blame.

In addition, health problems, alcoholism, and other troubles more common among the poor bring a terrible strain to the family. Poor people often do not have the resources characteristic of those in the upper and upper-middle classes to deal with the problems they face. Not only the lack of financial security, but lack of education, community support, and a wider network of interests and involvements contribute to the difficulties of lower socioeconomic status families. The role models parents present for their children and their socialization process in general can act as a barrier. Research Method 6.1 discusses research on marriages in relationship to class.

Research Method 6.1

· · · · · · · Intensive interviews

Worlds of Pain: Life in the Working-Class Family
by Lillian Breslow Rubin

Believing that social scientists should talk not about *the* American family but about the *variety* of families, Lillian Breslow Rubin wanted to discover the distinctive features of life for working-class families. In her sociological analysis, Rubin was determined to get to the heart of the marital experience of couples in the working class. She wanted to analyze the trends in this marital experience in the early, middle, and later years of the couples' lives. Focusing on economic constraints, she wanted to discover what roles work, leisure, and sex played in husband and wife experiences. She also wanted to investigate the different perceptions of life and marriage found among husbands and wives.

In order to get the data for her study, Rubin conducted an intensive study of fifty white working-class couples. The husbands were employed in traditional blue-collar work, the wives were under forty, neither husbands nor wives had more than high school educations, and at least one child was in each home. Since she was "dominantly concerned with class differences" (Rubin 1976, 9) among American families, Rubin also studied twenty-five upper-middle-class families, similar to her working-class families except that they had college educations and professional careers. These upper-middle-class families served as a basis for comparison and contrast so Rubin would not attribute characteristics to working-class families that might also be true of families that are more economically secure (Rubin 1976, 9–10).

All seventy-five couples in the study participated voluntarily in intensive, in-depth interviews conducted by Rubin. The interviews lasted up to ten hours for each person, often over several visits. The families lived in various communities in the San Francisco Bay area. Rubin preferred to interview each husband and wife separately. She wanted each to feel free to speak candidly about his or her life without the constraints or influences possible with a spouse present. This was especially important when discussing sensitive topics like sex and the quality of the marriage.

Rubin entered the homes armed with tape recorder—the indispensable tool of an in-depth interviewer—and with a general set of questions and probings for the individuals. In-depth interviews are much like long conversations, unstructured in the sense that questions do not have to be asked in a specified manner or order. The researcher is allowed to probe for more information and clarification from the subjects.

Rubin noted that she felt more welcome in homes of the working-class families than in the upper-middle-class homes; the professionals more often suggested Rubin's office as a place to meet. The working-class couples, typically living in smaller homes, were very cooperative in that the spouse not being interviewed would voluntarily leave the home for however long Rubin needed. Rubin did note that she often interviewed the wife first, who then encouraged her husband to cooperate.

When she finished her book, Rubin wanted the men and women to read her manuscript to see if they felt she captured a fair and honest picture of their lives. In general, Rubin reported that they said she achieved an almost painfully accurate portrait.

Characterized by her title, *Worlds of Pain*, Rubin found that life is often difficult for families in the working class. The couples typically married quite young, and the early years of marriage were particularly difficult. Serious conflicts, pressures, and drinking problems were not uncommon. Except for the "blue-collar aristocrats," many of the men were found to be bored, resigned, alienated, and even bitter in their work lives. Financial pressures were, at various times, quite severe. Layoffs, economic downturns, and bouts of unemployment were common for the working-class couples and rare for the professional couples. The working-class couples purchased much on credit and soon discovered that bills never seemed to get paid. When added together "the car payment, appliance payments, mortgage payments, payments on charged purchases, perhaps payment for a truck, a camper, a small boat, add up to an enormous chunk of family income" (Rubin 1976, 205). When asked about fantasies of inheriting a million dollars, they answered without hesitation that they would pay off their bills to rid themselves of that "nagging anxiety."

Although they hoped their children would do better in life, the working-class parents were not sure if their children would go to college. "If they want to," they said (Rubin 1976, 207). Most realized they could not afford to give their children more; they could not pay for four years of college for one or more children. Rubin suggested that our system ensures that a large work force will continue as these parents directly and indirectly prepare their children for lives like their own. These realities contradict the comforting American illusion about large-scale upward mobility (Rubin 1976, 211).

Rubin's use of in-depth interviews as a method of research is open to much criticism by many social scientists. She did not use a random sample, which makes generalizations suspect. The use of anecdotal data taken from conversations may not be representative of the working-class family experience. But Rubin defended her work by noting that sociology has a wealth of important representative studies about attitudes and behaviors. She wanted a sense of connection and rapport with the people she interviewed. In this way, she felt she was able to give "flesh and blood" to the people discussed in her book. She wanted a picture of the richness of living from within the families of working-class men and women (Rubin 1976, 13–14).

Educational Chances

Educational opportunity, the quality of the schools attended, and the chance for a college degree are all affected by parents' social background. Because social standing in part determines in which part of the city a family lives, children of different social classes have varying opportunities to attend better public schools, which tend to exist in upper-middle-class areas. The parents, as a child's most important role models, also indirectly influence the child's orientation to and appreciation of education. And, in a more basic sense, a child from a very poor family may be affected by lack of adequate diet and nutrition, which obviously interferes with success in school.

Other Life Chances

In addition to life expectancy, health, family stability, and education, a number of other important life chances are affected by socioeconomic status. For example, the criminal justice system in part discriminates against those in the lower socioeconomic strata because their crimes are more visible. Their offenses are more likely to be street crimes like robbery and burglary. On the other hand, in the higher socioeconomic strata, the crimes (often referred to as white-collar crimes) are less visible and considered less threatening; such white-collar crimes include embezzlement, income-tax evasion, and corporate criminal activity. The poor are less likely to have access to successful lawyers and are more likely to be labeled criminal because of their appearance, their background, or their lack of prestige. This topic will be discussed more in chapter 9 on crime and deviance.

Those in the lower socioeconomic classes are more likely to be victims of crime as well. They are more likely to live in crime-prone areas of large cities and are less likely to have adequate means to protect themselves. Typically in our society the poor commit crimes against the poor. In addition, those from lower socioeconomic backgrounds are more likely to serve in the front lines in the military and are more likely to be killed in war.

In a variety of other ways, social class affects our lives and our opportunities. It may affect our outlook on life, whether or not we define ourselves as happy, how we raise our children, and how we view ourselves. Our system is structured so that not everyone can succeed. Wealth, prestige, and power are scarce. As mentioned by Fussell (1983), it is not enough to succeed, others must fail.

Social Mobility: Who Gets Ahead?

Class and Caste

In the study of social inequality, sociologists make a distinction between those societies that allow members to change their positions in the social system and those that maintain a strict set of fixed boundaries allowing no change from one rank in the system to another. A society allowing little or no social mobility is considered a **closed** or **caste** society where social caste is an ascribed status—one given at birth that cannot be changed. Work, education, and lifestyle are determined as a result of a person's caste at birth. A caste system also has social barriers inhibiting people from interacting equally with others in different castes. India was a caste society for a very long time. While they have made strong attempts to discard the highly unequal caste patterns, the Indian people are still highly stratified. It continues to be difficult for people of different castes to socialize together in India. It is even more difficult to marry someone of a higher or lower caste. Such traditions are deeply embedded in the Indian historical tradition, their social fabric, and their Hindu religion.

If a society allows change in social rank, it is called an **open** or a **class** society, and the movement from one class to another is called **social mobility**. For example, let's say that someone is born into a working-class family but becomes an architect or a physician. That person has moved out of one class and into another. Theoretically, in class societies the individual is allowed to rise or fall in the stratification system according to his or her achievement. The individual is not constrained at any particular level because of birth.

No societies are purely open or strictly closed. Generally speaking, there are few large societies left with a rigidly enforced, politically approved caste system of stratification. However, there are many societies with elements of a caste system. South Africa has a rigid system based solely on race. The Soviet Union has elements of caste based on ethnic background. In Japan, about two percent of the population are called Burakumin but are indistinguishable ethnically from other Japanese, yet they have been treated as outcasts for centuries. Historically, the Burakumin were considered unclean by Buddhists because the Burakumin slaughtered cattle and worked leather, much as they still do today. Such practices were violations of ancient Buddhist mores. If a Japanese has any hint of a Burakumin background, it is extremely difficult to move into other neighborhoods or get corporate jobs. Inquiries are made before marriage to make sure neither party is Burakumin. (Christopher 1983).

The United States still has elements of caste with regard to race and poverty. As we saw in the section on poverty, the United States has a semipermanent, core group of poor people in the underclass. As we shall see in chapter 7, race and minority status in America also reflect elements of caste.

Social Mobility in the United States

In the broadest sense, social mobility occurs when an individual moves from one position to another or from one job to another. However, sociologists are more interested in movement that results in a change of social class. Consequently, we define vertical mobility as the up or down movement from one social class to another. For example, a steelworker moves up by going back to school and becoming a personnel manager in a corporation. One can move down in social class as well. It is increasingly common to see a well-paid professional lose his or her job due to an economic downturn, unable to find a job equal in status and pay (Newman 1988). Both are examples of vertical mobility. However, a change in job that does not appreciably affect one's social class is called horizontal mobility. That is, there has been no change in social class although there has been a change in jobs.

Sociologists are especially interested in intergenerational mobility. This concept refers to the comparison of social class between parents and children. If one is born into a lower-class family and goes on to greater achievement than the parents, it is an example of intergenerational upward mobility. Intergenerational mobility is an important concept because it allows us to study the influence of background and parental social class on the children's future success.

In the past twenty years, sociologists have concentrated a great deal of research on social mobility and on how people climb the socioeconomic ladder. For example, we have discovered that much of the social mobility that occurs in our society is in the middle ranges of the hierarchy and may be slowing. The most common kind of intergenerational mobility occurs when children of the working class move into the middle class or when children of the middle class move into the upper-middle class. Most upward mobility is a small step up. Huge leaps are rare. Downward mobility is becoming increasingly significant today as well (Newman 1988, Rossides 1990).

Furthermore, sociological research has pointed out that much of this inter-generational mobility is a result of social and economic changes that bring about more opportunity in some areas while decreasing opportunity in others. Called structural mobility, it means that opportunity for upward mobility depends as much on the economic conditions of society as it does on individual talent and personal effort. In other words, the conditions of the economy create or eliminate opportunity for large numbers of people.

As our society advances technologically, more white-collar and service jobs are being created while the number of manufacturing jobs is shrinking. Consequently, children of blue-collar families may find it more possible to move into white-collar occupations than did their parents. Or, they may find that higher-paying factory jobs are not available while lower-paying service jobs such as food service worker are more common. In our society we experienced increased opportunity for upward, intergenerational mobility from the 1930s to the 1970s, primarily as a result of the changes in the economy and the labor market. However, in the past fifteen years, new changes in the economy such as the increase of foreign competition and the decline of various industries, primarily in manufacturing, have restricted this mobility. Such facts contradict the American ethic of individual achievement (Rossides 1990).

Although it is extremely important, structural mobility is not the only factor that affects upward or downward movement. Family background is also quite important in influencing one's chances of being successful. Recall from chapter 4 that the family is the most important agent of socialization. Parents act as role models for their children and often pass on their occupational interests to their children. Parents can actively encourage and reward educational achievement, typical of middle- and upper-middle-class families. One researcher noted the significant differences in middle- and working-class socialization patterns. Middle-class parents tend to instill greater independence and initiative in their children while working-class parents emphasize obedience and following orders (Kohn 1959). Note in Research Method 6.1 that the working-class parents did not actively encourage their children to go to college because they realized they did not have the resources to pay for it.

So far, then, we have noted two important influences on social mobility. What else affects a person's chances for upward mobility? Certainly, educational attainment has proven to be important. The importance of parents' values and encouragement, as well as economic resources, on their children's educational achievement is well-documented (Duncan, Featherman, and Duncan 1972). So, while education is important, it is difficult to study the effects of education apart from family background.

In addition, race and ethnic status have acted as major barriers in upward mobility. The discrimination in education, hiring practices, and promotion experienced by minorities has been documented over and over. Prejudicial attitudes are still strong among many in our society, and such attitudes often act as a barrier in accepting minorities in a variety of occupational positions. Chapter 7 goes into more detail on the issues of prejudice and discrimination experienced by minorities in America.

Other factors that have some effect on upward mobility are the individual's aspirations, expectations, and drive with regard to success. Individual determination is a powerful factor in upward social mobility, but the factors that influence such determination are often difficult to document in research. Moreover, the ability or willingness of the individual to defer gratification—for example, to put off rewards until one has finished a long educational career—is also an important variable. Finally, we cannot discount other factors that may occasionally play a role in upward mobility such as talent, appearance, and good luck. But note that these factors are circumscribed by the structural conditions in the economy as well as family background and educational attainment.

In this chapter we have covered many concepts and ideas which are extremely important to the study of society. It is useful to remember that the key concept in this chapter is inequality. By definition, a stratification system is characterized by inequality. No matter how one explains that inequality, the fact remains that in our society we see a great range of statuses from the very rich to the very poor.

Questions for Summary and Review

1. Define social stratification and social class. Explain why they are such important concepts in understanding social life.
2. Explain the conflict and functionalist theories concerning social stratification. Compare and evaluate the two theories. How can they be combined to explain social inequality?
3. Define and explain the dimensions of social stratification. Give examples of each.
4. How do sociologists measure social class?
5. Discuss the six social classes in America and describe the lifestyles of each.
6. How do the underclass and the working poor differ? Why do we have an underclass?
7. Poverty is defined in what two ways? Give a clear description of those who are poor in the United States.
8. What are life chances? How are they affected by one's social class?
9. Explain the difference between caste and class?
10. What are the major types of social mobility? Give an example of each.

Key Concepts

Absolute approach to poverty (p. 126)
Bourgeoisie (p. 110)
Burakumin (p. 136)
Capitalist class (p. 117)
Caste systems (p. 135)
Class systems (p. 135)
Conflict theory (p. 110)
Conspicuous consumption (p. 118)
Functionalist theory (p. 111)
Horizontal mobility (p. 136)
Intergenerational mobility (p. 136)
Life chances (p. 131)
Lower-upper class (p. 117)
Middle class (p. 120)
Nouveau riche (p. 117)
Objective measures of social class (p. 116)
Power (p. 114)

Power elite (p. 110)
Prestige (p. 113)
Proletariat (p. 110)
Relative approach to poverty (p. 126)
Social class (p. 109)
Social mobility (p. 135)
Social stratification (p. 109)
Socioeconomic status (p. 116)
Structural mobility (p. 136)
Subjective measures of social class (p. 116)
Underclass (p. 125)
Upper-middle class (p. 119)
Upper-upper class (p. 117)
Vertical mobility (p. 136)
Wealth (p. 112)
Working class (p. 122)
Working poor (p. 125)

References

1. Auletta, Ken. 1983. *The underclass.* New York: Vintage Books.

2. Blumberg, Paul. 1980. *Inequality in an age of decline.* New York: Oxford University Press.

3. Christopher, Robert C. 1983. *The Japanese mind.* New York: Fawcett Columbine.

4. Coleman, Richard, and Lee Rainwater. 1978. *Social standing in America: New*

dimensions of class. New York: Basic Books.

5. Collier, Peter, and David Horowitz. 1984. *The Kennedys: An American drama.* New York: Summit Books.

6. Dahrendorf, Ralf. 1959. *Class and class conflict in industrial society.* Stanford: Stanford University Press.

7. Davis, James A., and Tom W. Smith. 1984. *General social surveys, 1972–1984.* Chicago: National Opinion Research Center.

8. Davis, Kingsley, and Wilbert E. Moore. 1945. Some principles of stratification. *American Sociological Review* 10:242–49.

9. Domhoff, G. William. 1967. *Who rules America?* Englewood Cliffs, N.J.: Prentice-Hall.

10. _____. 1970. *Higher circles: The governing class in America.* New York: Vintage Books.

11. _____. 1974. *The Bohemian Grove and other retreats: A study in ruling class cohesiveness.* New York: Harper and Row.

12. _____. 1983. *Who rules America now?* Englewood Cliffs, N.J.: Prentice-Hall.

13. Duncan, Greg, Richard Coe, Mary Corcoran, Martha Hill, Saul Hoffman, and James Morgan. 1984. *Years of poverty, years of plenty: The changing fortunes of American workers and families.* Ann Arbor, Mich.: Institute for Social Research, University of Michigan.

14. Duncan, O.D., D. L. Featherman, and B. Duncan. 1972. *Socioeconomic background and achievement.* New York: Seminar Press.

15. Eisler, Benita. 1983. *Class act: America's last dirty secret.* New York: F. Watts.

16. Ermann, M. David, and Richard J. Lundman. 1982. *Corporate deviance.* New York: CBS College Publishing.

17. *Forbes.* 1989a. A wealth of billionaires. 144 (July 24):117–308.

18. _____. 1989b. The Forbes 400. 144 (October 23):145–358.

19. Fussell, Paul. 1983. *Class: A painfully accurate guide through the American status system.* New York: Ballantine Books.

20. Gallup Poll. 1989. *The Gallup report,* (August) no. 287. Princeton, N.J.: The Gallup Poll Organization.

21. Gans, Herbert J. 1972. The positive functions of poverty. *American journal of sociology* 78:275–89.

22. Gilbert, Dennis, and Joseph A. Kahl. 1987. *The American class structure: A new synthesis.* 3d ed. Homewood, Ill.: Dorsey Press.

23. Goldstein, Mark L. 1990. The end of the American dream? In *Annual editions: Social problems, 90/91,* edited by LeRoy W. Barnes, 20–23. Guilford, Conn.: Dushkin.

24. Kohn, Melvin L. 1959. Social class and parental values. *American journal of sociology* 64:337–350.

25. Lapham, Lewis H. 1988. *Money and class in America.* New York: Ballantine.

26. LeMasters, E. E. 1975. *Blue-collar aristocrats: Life styles at a working class tavern.* Madison, Wis.: University of Wisconsin Press.

27. Levison, Andrew. 1974. *The working class majority.* New York: Penguin Books.

28. Link, B. G., B. P. Dohrenwend, and A. E. Skodol. 1986. Socio-economic status and schizophrenia: Noisome occupational characteristics as a risk factor. *American sociological review* 51:242–258.

29. Lynd, Robert S., and Helen M. Lynd. 1929. *Middletown.* New York: Harcourt Brace Jovanovich.

30. Mills, C. Wright. 1951. *White collar: The American middle classes.* New York: Oxford University Press.

31. _____. 1959a. *The power elite.* New York: Oxford University Press.

32. _____. 1959b. *The sociological imagination.* New York: Oxford University Press.

33. NBC News. 1981. The migrants, 1980. Produced for television by NBC News, New York.

34. Newman, Katherine S. 1988. *Falling from grace: The experience of downward mo-*

bility in the American middle class. New York: The Free Press.

35. Persell, Caroline H., and Peter W. Cookson. 1985. Chartering and bartering: Elite education and social reproduction. *Social problems* 33:114–129.

36. Riesman, David. 1953. *The lonely crowd.* New York: Doubleday.

37. Rose, Stephen J. 1986. *The American profile poster.* New York: Pantheon Books.

38. Rossides, Daniel W. 1990. *Comparative societies: Social types and their interrelations.* Englewood Cliffs, N.J.: Prentice-Hall.

39. Rothman, Robert A. 1978. *Inequality and stratification in the United States.* Englewood Cliffs, N.J.: Prentice-Hall.

40. Rubin, Lillian B. 1976. *Worlds of pain: Life in the working-class family.* New York: Basic Books.

41. Simmel, Georg. 1950. *The sociology of Georg Simmel,* edited by Kurt Wolff. New York: The Free Press.

42. South, Scott J. 1985. Economic conditions and the divorce rate: A Time Series analysis of the postwar United States. *Journal of marriage and the family* 47:31–42.

43. Thompson, William E. 1983. Hanging tongues: A sociological encounter with the assembly line. *Qualitative sociology* 6:215–37.

44. Treiman, Donald J. 1977. *Occupational prestige in comparative perspective.* New York: Academic Press.

45. Tumin, Melvin, 1953. Some principles of stratification: A critical analysis. *American sociological review* 4:387–94.

46. U.S. Bureau of the Census. 1989. *Statistical abstract of the United States, 1989.* 109th ed. Washington, D.C.: U.S. Government Printing Office.

47. _____. 1989. *Money income and poverty status in the United States: 1988.* Current population reports, series P–60, no. 166. Advance data from the March 1989 current population survey. Washington, D.C.: U.S. Government Printing Office.

48. Vanfossen, Beth E. 1979. *The structure of social inequality.* Boston: Little, Brown and Company.

49. Veblen, Thorstein. 1979. *The theory of the leisure class.* New York: Penguin Books.

50. Warner, W. Lloyd. 1936. American caste and class. *American Journal of Sociology* 6:215–37.

51. Warner, W. Lloyd, and Paul S. Lunt. 1941. *The social life of a modern community.* New Haven, Conn.: Yale University Press.

52. Weber, Max. 1978/1922. Class, status groups and parties. In *Weber: Selections in translation,* edited by W. G. Runciman, 43–56. Cambridge, Mass.: Cambridge University Press.

53. Wilkins, Roger. 1990. The Throwaway people. *Frontline* documentary series. Produced for Public Broadcasting System. February 13.

54. Wright, Erik Olin. 1987. *Classes.* London: Verso.

Racial and Ethnic Minorities 7

• • • • • • • • • • • •

Chapter Outline

•

B rawls involving matters of racial antagonism have been reported between black and white students at several universities. At other schools black students have been verbally abused, even physically assaulted. Student organizations at other colleges sponsored social events which had as their underlying theme the denigration of black students—racial slurs, racist slogans, and crude jokes. Graffiti appeared on dormitory walls which promoted the Ku Klux Klan and proclaimed "Death to the Niggers." Black students were even "thrown out" of their dormitory rooms solely on the basis of race.

These are only a few examples of conflict between whites and blacks on American campuses. They sound as if they came out of the south in the 1950s or 1960s. They did not. They all occurred in nonsouthern schools and took place within the past few years (Farrel 1988, Wiener 1989). Furthermore, analysis of the incidents indicates that they are not confined to college campuses. They appear to be part of a conservative trend in the nation which includes an increasingly negative evaluation, by whites, of blacks and the resurgence of a kind of racism many thought had been vanquished.

These incidents are extreme forms of action but they underscore the results ethnocentrism can have in society (see chapter 3). Ethnocentrism is present, to some extent, in every society. It also exists among subgroups within societies. We tend to feel that people who are different from us are less human than we are—that they are not as intelligent, cultured, or able. Thus, we may prejudge all members of out-groups and consider them less worthy of the valued but relatively scarce rewards society has to offer.

Such feelings lead to invidious distinctions between groups. The dominant ethnic or racial group defines others as unequal and undeserving of equal access to the rewards of the society. Thus a system of **ethnic stratification** arises in which some groups are defined as less deserving than the dominant group. Such groups are called **minorities**. They are identified in terms of special characteristics and receive a lesser share of society's rewards.

What Is a Racial or Ethnic Minority Group?

Common usage defines a minority as any group that is numerically smaller than others. Sociologists, however, employ a definition in which group size is not of primary importance. In sociology a **minority group** is one that has been assigned an inferior status in their society. In this status they are given less than what would be their proportionate share of the power, income, and social prestige the society provides. Another way of putting the matter is simply to note that the minority group is always subordinate to a **majority group** which is dominant in society. Yetman (1985) has suggested that we can equate the term minority group with the word subordinate and, similarly, the term majority group with dominant. As we shall see, minority status may be determined on the basis of a variety of factors, although in this chapter we will be looking at two features—race and ethnicity.

Using this definition, blacks in many parts of Mississippi and Alabama are a minority despite the fact that numerically they outnumber whites who are the dominant or majority group. The greater number of blacks in the population is not significant because they lack the political, economic, and social power to obtain even an equal share of the resources of their society. In South Africa, blacks, "coloreds" and Indians make up eighty-nine percent of the population, but the small proportion of whites in the population constitutes the majority or dominant group. Even with recent changes in the status of blacks in that country, whites continue to dominate all aspects of life. Such subordination means that the life opportunities or chances of minority group members are limited. Regardless of personal intelligence and ability, individual members of minority groups find that occupational success, wealth and self-gratification are less open to them.

In a sociological sense minorities are not so much social groups as they are categories (see chapter 5). While they almost always possess a sense of being part of the group and have contact with it, this is not essential to being treated as a minority group member. For example, a black youth raised by white parents in a white suburb will still be considered a black and subjected to minority-group treatment despite lack of ongoing contact with other blacks. It is the characteristics of individuals as well as the way in which they are treated that determine minority status. Several key characteristics apply to all groups that are defined as minorities.

Key Characteristics of Minority Groups

Subordinate in Power and Resources

A major factor in understanding the position of a minority group in society is that it is subordinate to the dominant group and lacks the power and resources to gain an equal place in society. As groups, minorities are at a disadvantage because they do not have the same access to the political, social, and economic resources as does the dominant group. Indeed, majority group members often enjoy many advantages in society at the expense of the minority group and continue to have access to those advantages because of their dominance.

This advantage is often reinforced by law. Discrimination supported by legal measures is referred to as *de jure* discrimination. The experience of blacks in the South following the Civil War provides an example of the use of legislative power on a minority. After the withdrawal of federal troops, a series of laws were passed that were specifically intended to prevent blacks from achieving any political or social power. The so-called Jim Crow laws were drafted and passed by the dominant group, the white anglos. The laws prevented blacks from voting, from holding public office, from going to school with whites, and so forth. Blacks were unable to fight against these laws because the overwhelming power of white sheriffs, judges, juries, and even state militia enforced the laws. As a result the blacks were left with inferior education, a lack of access to well-paying jobs that could improve their economic situation, and no political or social avenue for pleading their case.

While such Jim Crow laws were found to be unconstitutional, this by no means indicates that discriminatory practices disappeared. The negative attitudes toward blacks, combined with their actual disadvantaged situation, interact with one another and lead to negative evaluation of blacks and others. In numerous ways segregation and other forms of *de facto* discrimination, that which results from practice not law, continue to affect the nation's black population (Jaynes and Williams 1989). Unequal access to employment, schooling, and residential neighborhoods still keep the majority of blacks separated from the dominant white group.

The pressure on blacks to conform to dominant group norms in order to make any gains is strong. In a major study of blacks in American society (Jaynes and Williams 1989), the significance of black conformity with white attitudes and behavior was underscored as a major factor in black advancement. The authors reported that those blacks who have been able to gain economically and socially, despite being minority group members, are those who were best able to take advantage of civil rights legislation, antipoverty programs, and an expanding economy. In short, blacks who were able to rise in status had the education, the attitudes, the values, and behavior which promoted success. That is, they conformed most closely to what white society expected.

This pressure to adopt the ways of the dominant group in American society is referred to as **Anglo-conformity**. The majority culture of the United States is basically a version of the British culture brought to this country by the first European settlers. Their dominance having been established, they expected members of all other groups to conform to their ways. Our language, as well as our social structure and culture, is basically still that of white, northern Europeans (Farley 1988). To advance in society has meant to become as much like that group as possible.

Distinguished on the Basis of Physical and Cultural Differences

Almost any visible attribute of a group can be used as the outward symbol of minority status: gender, sexual preference, race, ethnic identification, or religion, among others. The mark, however, must be readily identifiable by others in the society. In this chapter we are concerned with those groups that are distinguished on the basis of physical characteristics (race) and cultural practices (ethnicity). Such distinguishing physical characteristics or cultural practices mark those who possess or practice them as different from the majority and inferior in all they do.

For example, college professors, especially at elite private schools, hold high status in our society, but when a black professor at the University of Chicago attempted to move into an all-white suburb of Chicago, the community was appalled. The fact that the man was on the faculty of one of the most prestigious universities in the nation and that he possessed several higher degrees and held a number of academic honors did not matter. All the residents of the suburb saw was the black face. That mark provided sufficient stigma to make an otherwise desirable neighbor unwanted.

Cultural differences, such as accent, dress, or darker skin color, are the signs marking members of an ethnic minority group. While many ethnic cultural traits are acceptable, such as popular food items, others can be seen as justification for unequal treatment. For example, a preoccupation with being on time for appointments and other activities is part of an Anglo middle-class, majority culture. If another cultural group—for example, Latin Americans—does not have a similar concept of punctuality, members of that group may be characterized as irresponsible, lazy, and unambitious. These accusations may become an excuse to perceive members of these groups as unfit for more responsible jobs.

Religion is a cultural characteristic that distinguishes certain groups and sets them off as different. The early settlers of the United States were Protestant and believed theirs to be the only true religion. When Catholics began to arrive in some numbers, Catholics from Ireland being the first, they were treated as inferiors and subjected to very negative treatment. Their religious practices marked them as different and they were seen as a threat to American traditions (Anglo-conformity). Catholics were even seen as part of a foreign conspiracy, based in Rome, to undermine the liberties of the nation.

More than harsh words were directed at them. Catholics in the last century and the early part of this were treated unequally with regard to the rewards of the society. In Boston in the nineteenth century it was not uncommon to see signs saying "Help Needed—Micks (a derogatory term for Irish Catholics) *need not apply!*" This discrimination extended to all aspects of the lives of Catholics in that city at that time. Majority attitudes toward the Catholics were so embedded by 1850 that an anti-Catholic political party, known as the Know Nothing party, got twenty-one percent of the presidential vote; anti-Catholic feelings also were part of the doctrine of the Ku Klux Klan (Schaefer 1984).

Today much of the hostility expressed against religious cults may be explained by cultural differences. Cults related to the more general Anglo-Christianity of our society are more acceptable than those that derive their beliefs and rituals from Asian culture. Thus the Hare Krishnas and Moonies are more scorned than cults based on modifications of Protestant fundamentalism.

Perceived and Treated as Different and Inferior

Minority group members are identified and singled out as different. They are also viewed as inferior in a number of ways and are thus judged as less deserving of their share of society's rewards. In short, they are discriminated against in the competition for the resources of their society.

Minority group members in the United States have been subjected to various forms of discriminatory treatment. Perhaps the mildest form is **derogation**: jokes, derisive names, and prejudicial statements about minorities. You may have heard, and possibly told, stories in which the humor fixed upon some supposed inferiority of an ethnic or racial group. Perhaps you laughed, thinking there was little harm in the humor. Likewise you probably have heard degrading nicknames applied to others, and you have not thought a great deal about their use. However, jokes and derisive names are means of reminding both majority and minority group members of the latter's inferiority. Imagine yourself in Japan. You are riding a train and as people pass you they mutter the word *Gaijin*. The word means foreigner but it carries with it the connotation of ignorance and inferiority. It is an insult. Being called by this name makes you feel uncomfortable and, in some measure, unworthy. Words may not break bones but they can, indeed, hurt.

Research Application 7.1

• • • • • • Institutionalized Racism: The English Language Is My Enemy

I stand before you, a little nervous, afflicted to some degree with stage fright. Not because I fear you, but because I fear the subject.

The title of my address is, "Racism in American Life—Broad Perspectives of the Problem," or, "The English Language Is My Enemy."

In my speech I will define culture as the sum total of ways of living built up by a group of human beings and transmitted by one generation to another. I will define education as the act or process of imparting and communicating a culture, developing the powers of reasoning and judgment and generally preparing oneself and others intellectually for a mature life.

I will define communication as the primary means by which the process of education is carried out.

I will say that language is the primary medium of communication in the education process and, in this case, the English language. I will indict the English language as one of the prime carriers of racism from one person to another in our society and discuss how the teacher and the student, especially the Negro student, are affected by this fact.

The English language is my enemy.

Racism is a belief that human races have distinctive characteristics, usually involving the idea that one's own race is superior and has a right to rule others. Racism.

The English language is my enemy.

But that was not my original topic—I said that English was my "Goddamm" enemy. Now why do I use "Goddamm" to illustrate this aspect of the English language? Because I want to illustrate the sheer gut power of words. Words which control our action. Words like "nigger," "Kike," "sheeny," "Dago," "black power"—words like this. Words we don't use in ordinary decent conversation, one to the other. I choose these words deliberately, not to flaunt my freedom before you. If you are a normal human being these words will have assaulted your senses, may even have done you physical harm, and if you so choose, you could have me arrested.

These words are attacks upon your physical and emotional well being; your pulse rate is possibly higher, your breath quicker; there is perhaps a tremor along the nerves of your arms and your legs; sweat begins in the palms of your hands, perhaps. With these few words I have assaulted you. I have damaged you, and there is nothing you can possibly do to control your reactions—to defend yourself against the brute force of these words.

These words have a power over us; a power that we cannot resist. For a moment you and I have had our deepest physical reactions controlled, not by our own wills, but by words in the English language.

A superficial examination of Roget's *Thesaurus of the English Language* reveals the following facts: The word "whiteness" has 134 synonyms, 44 of which are favorable and pleasing to contemplate. For example; "purity," "cleanness," "immaculateness," "bright," "shiny," "ivory," "fair," "blonde," "stainless," "clean," "clear," "chaste," "unblemished," "unsullied," "innocent," "honorable," "upright," "just," "straightforward," "genuine," "trustworthy,"—and only 10 synonyms of which I feel to have been negative and then only in the mildest sense, such as "gloss-over," "whitewash," "gray," "wan," "pale," "ashen," etc.

The word "blackness" has 120 synonyms, 60 of which are distinctly unfavorable, and none of them even mildly positive. Among the offending 60 were such words as "blot," "blotch," "smut," "smudge," "sullied," "begrime," "soot," "becloud," "obscure," "dingy," "murky," "low-toned," "threatening," "frowning," "foreboding," "forbidding," "sinister," "baneful," "dismal," "thundery," "wicked," "malignant," "deadly," "unclean," "dirty," "unwashed," "foul," etc. In addition, and this is what really hurts, 20 of these words—and I exclude the villainous 60 above—are related directly to race, such as "Negro," "Negress," "nigger," "darkey," "blackamoor," etc.

If you consider the fact that thinking itself is subvocal speech (in other words, one must use words in order to think at all), you will appreciate the enormous trap of racial prejudgment that works on any child who is born into the English language.

Any creature, good or bad, white or black, Jew or Gentile, who uses the English language for the purposes of communication is willing to force the Negro child into 60 ways to despise himself, and the white child, 60 ways to aid and abet him in the crime.

Source: Ossie Davis, "The English Language is My Enemy," *IRCD Bulletin 5* (Summer 1969), p. 13. (The above are Davis's words directly quoted.) Reprinted by permission of *American Teacher*, American Federation of Teachers.

A more direct method of dealing with minority groups involves **denial**: practices that forbid minority members access to institutions and positions that would provide opportunities for advancement in social status. Denial occurs in a variety of situations. It can mean being denied entry to a school, a club, or an occupational group. In certain occupations, minority status may mean lack of opportunity. For example, until recently, black physicians were not allowed to join the American Medical

Association (AMA). They formed an alternative, the National Medical Association, but because it was all black it possessed little of the power held by the AMA.

Segregation of the minority group, whether it exists in a school, a neighborhood, or a job, is a form of denial. The minority group is denied access to societal resources that would lead to the possibility of getting ahead. For example, living in a middle-class neighborhood usually means better schools and thereby an education that will prepare the student to compete in the labor market. Being denied access to such schools, by living in a segregated neighborhood, significantly handicaps a minority group member in the search for success.

Violence is the most extreme treatment minority groups may receive. The history of native Americans is one of forced displacement and violent aggression after the coming of "the white man," treatment designed to lead to genocide or the extermination of a whole people. Such an approach was also common as the British settled both Australia and New Zealand. Aggression against the original inhabitants of Australia, the aborigines, was efficiently and relentlessly applied in an effort to implement a governmental policy of extermination. Like the native Americans, the aborigines were systematically hunted down and finally, in the "ultimate solution," sent to reserves. There they could die off and fulfill the British prophecy that they were, after all, only a doomed race (Evans, Saunders, and Cronin 1988).

The lynching of blacks that occurred in the South during the last century and the early part of this one are another example of such violence. Similarly violence was used as United States citizens invaded that part of Mexico called California. As they gained power and freedom from Mexico, the former Mexican landowners and leaders of the region were reduced to a propertyless and powerless group viewed as inferior and were relegated to menial jobs.

Riots centering on racial and ethnic differences have been common in this country for more than a century. They have occurred in places as diverse as New York, Los Angeles, Tulsa, Oklahoma, and Detroit. In each case whites attacked blacks, and deaths and injuries resulted for both groups (Farley 1988). As recently as 1980 riots in Hispanic neighborhoods occurred in Miami (Porter, Dunn, and Portes 1984). More recently, ethnic conflict has occurred in the Soviet Union. In February of 1990 the usually peaceful city of Baku, capital of the Soviet Republic of Azerbaijan, was the scene of bloody riots. When the natives, an ethnic minority within the broader Soviet system, attempted to gain power they were met with government gunfire as tanks ran through the streets of the city.

An Ascribed Status

In almost every case, members are born into a minority group. It is not usually a status about which one makes a decision or has control. We cannot arrange our skin color, our sex, our age, or the nationality or religion of our parents.

Some minority group members can pass as members of the dominant group. For most, however, the attributes of that status cannot be shed. They remain throughout their lives as symbols of discrimination. By working much harder than members of the majority group, some individuals will achieve positions of higher status and power. Even then, they generally will lag behind their majority counterparts. More effort or more education does not necessarily grant minority group members better jobs or more pay for the same jobs (U.S. Bureau of Labor Statistics 1985). Black physicians, for example, seldom attain the prestige or income of their white counterparts.

In general, minority group members are aware that they are excluded from full participation in society and know the stigma attached to their status. For some, this realization begins early as they attend school and interact in the community; for others, living in a ghetto may protect them from awareness but only for a time. The negative feelings of others toward them are internalized and can convince minority people of their "inferiority."

Race, Ethnicity, and Racism

Race

Perhaps no term has more problems associated with its definition than does race. From a scientific perspective, the term has little or no significance. At one time scientists diligently tried to determine how many human races there were and how they differed, but they have been completely unable to agree on these matters. Estimates of the number of races have ranged from the customary three (black, white, and yellow) to as many as thirty-four (Dobzhansky 1962). The whole range of human beings is actually one species sharing many genetic traits (Simpson and Yinger 1985). What differences that do exist have little direct influence on social behavior. We simply cannot classify human beings into meaningful categories according to skin color or other physical attributes (van den Berghe 1978). The amount of interbreeding among various groups adds further confusion to the concept of race.

Nevertheless, people do react to one another on the basis of race. Race may be only a social construction, but it is significant because people make it so. In this sense race is an administrative category usually based on physical features or social customs of the group as perceived by others and by the group itself as distinct. As Farley (1988) notes, the concept has two aspects: physical and social. However artificial the scientific distinctions may be, social distinctions lead to categorizations that assign some people to lower status on the basis of race.

Ethnicity

An ethnic group is a collection of individuals that defines itself, and is defined by others, as having a unique cultural system, a system that distinguishes it from others in the society. Language, dress, and religious beliefs are the most frequent characteristics of ethnic groups. Ethnic groups have both objective and subjective aspects. The objective features are those visible customs and behaviors that anyone can see. The subjective aspects of ethnicity, such as common beliefs and attitudes about health, are generally only available to members of the group itself. The differences between an ethnic minority and the dominant group may seem minimal, but they are sufficient to bring about the discrimination that goes with minority status.

America is often termed a land of immigrants, and so it is. Large numbers of people have come to this country from Europe and other parts of the world as voluntary immigrants. They sought a new world of opportunity. Others, whom we can term involuntary migrants, such as blacks, were brought here against their will. And two groups, the Mexican Americans and native Americans, were conquered as the Anglos colonized this new world. Regardless of how they came to have minority status, each group has met with unequal treatment at the hands of Anglos. The Irish of Boston were stereotyped as shiftless and drunken when they arrived there in the nineteenth century. They were denied access to jobs and other societal resources. Similarly, the Italians who settled on the lower east side of New York City were subjected to unequal treatment as were the Chicanos of Texas who were forbidden to use their language in the public schools and generally could find only "stoop labor" to make a living.

Racism

There are many definitions of racism. Farley (1988) suggests that a broad definition best helps us understand the concept. Accordingly, we can define racism as any type of action or attitude, individual or institutional, which recommends or implements exploitative behavior toward a racial or ethnic group. Whether the attitude or behavior is intentional or unintentional is not the issue. Rather, if the results lead to exploitation we have an instance of racism. Expanding on this broad definition Farley lists four aspects of racism: (1) attitudinal racism or what is commonly called prejudice; (2) ideological racism, the culturally based beliefs concerning innate inferiority among a group; (3) individual racist behavior leading to discrimination; and (4) racism which has become institutionalized in a society or social group.

Racial Prejudice: An Attitude

Prejudice is the irrational dislike for or negative image of members of another group. Prejudice tends to be rigid; it is resistant to change even in the face of evidence contradicting the prejudice. It is basically an attitude or a set of attitudes. Prejudice tends to be irrational in that it is not necessary for a prejudiced person to know any member of the disliked group in order to hate the entire group. As an example, one study listed a large number of ethnic groups and asked respondents whether or not they would accept working with, living next door to, or going to church with members of certain groups. The list included two fictional groups. The researchers found that people who tended to be prejudiced against other groups were also prejudiced toward the two groups that did not actually exist.

Understanding the difference between prejudice and discrimination is central to the study of inequality in society. We will look at individual acts of discrimination later. Here it is important to recognize that, while prejudice is an attitude, discrimination is an act. An individual may hold a deep prejudice against, say, "bikers." Without any power to enforce this attitude it will not be possible for the person to act on that prejudice and discriminate against such people.

Racist Ideology: A Cultural Belief

The term racism has been used to refer to a system of beliefs among a group of people to support and endorse racial inequality. That is, racism endorses the view that some races are biologically superior to others and that inferior groups should not be allowed to participate fully in society. Hitler's idea of the Master or Aryan race is one example of the extreme nature of racist ideology. Although Hitler committed suicide in 1945, the bigotry he preached is not dead. The American Nazi party and the so-called skinheads who espouse similar racial hatred are very much alive. The news media rather regularly reports on the ways in which these groups express their racist ideology not only through propaganda but also in direct action.

Racism begins in the belief that physical or cultural characteristics, such as skin color and facial features or cultural practices, are directly related to levels of intelligence and to social attributes such as morality and reliability. These invidious comparisons are widespread in societies such as ours, where numerous racial and other groups differ from the dominant group. Racism—as opposed to ethnocentrism, which is universal—has been particularly virulent among European colonial powers and in North America. In such cases, it results from the colonial expansion that characterized dominant Western ideology in the nineteenth century (van den-Berghe 1978). In the settlement of both Australia and New Zealand racist ideology was invoked to justify the treatment of the native population. In New Zealand beliefs about the native Maori's inferiority were so strong that, when the Maoris did win battles in the New Zealand Wars, their victory had to be explained. It was unthinkable that such primitive people could defeat the superior British forces. The victories were eventually laid to unfair tactics on the part of the Maoris or imitation of British techniques by the natives (Belich 1986).

It is possible for minority groups to hold a racist ideology concerning the majority group. Many, though not all, Black Muslim groups have preached just such doctrine (Lee 1988). Whites are portrayed in the most negative and derogatory terms and are the subject of fierce hatred. However, the racist beliefs of the minority group remain only an attitude. They lack the power to act out their prejudice.

These are slave laborers in the Buchenwald Concentration Camp near Jeone. Many had died of malnutrition when U.S. Troops arrived from the 80th Division and entered camp. Elie Wiesel is the man whose face can be seen on the far right of the center bunk.

Racist Discrimination: An Individual Act

Discrimination refers to an action taken by an individual or groups. An action is discriminatory if it causes members of the majority group to receive preferential treatment while it restricts the opportunities and life chances of minority group members. The key to discriminatory action is the denial of access to the valued but scarce goods that are taken for granted by members of the dominant group.

Discrimination today is usually more subtle than it was in the past, but it can be just as vicious. For example, it may be against the law to deny blacks the opportunity to live in an apartment complex, but the apartment manager may simply say there are no vacancies when a black family seeks an apartment. It is difficult to investigate and sue the manager in such a case. It is also impossible to successfully prosecute the real estate agent, who, so very subtly, steers customers to the "right" neighborhoods.

In sociology, prejudice and discrimination are considered to be related but do not necessarily occur together. In other words, it is not necessary to be prejudiced in order to discriminate, and it is not necessary to discriminate if you are prejudiced. Robert Merton (1949) outlined four types of relationship between the two. He noted that a **nonprejudiced discriminator** is someone who feels he or she does not actually harbor negative feelings toward those against whom he or she discriminates. For example, suppose the owner of a restaurant does not feel prejudiced or does not wish to discriminate against blacks. At the same time, the owner believes that white customers would not patronize the restaurant if blacks were served. To keep the white customers, then, the owner may refuse to serve blacks or may give them such slow, poor service that they understand they are not welcome.

A **prejudiced nondiscriminator** is prejudiced but has no way of putting the prejudice into action. The police officer who holds negative views of minorities may be constrained by department rules from acting out these feelings. Laws have been passed over the past quarter of a century which make discrimination more difficult, but they do not take away the prejudice held by some. At least one federal employee insists on going to work on a holiday—Martin Luther King's birthday—as a protest but no one is hurt except him.

There is less inconsistency in the relationship between prejudice and discrimination for the other two types. The **unprejudiced nondiscriminator** is described as a person who will not discriminate in any case. Referred to as all-weather liberals, such individuals hold no prejudice and are dedicated to refraining from any intentional acts that lead to unequal treatment for others. On the other hand, the **prejudiced discriminator**, or the all-weather bigot, follows through on his or her prejudices at every opportunity and is not deterred from using available measures to ensure the inequality of the minorities against which he or she is prejudiced.

Joseph Hraba (1979, 150–51) suggests that more than prejudice or its absence affects whether discrimination exists. The extent to which there are social pressures for nondiscriminatory or discriminatory behavior will affect how individuals behave toward members of minority groups. Lyle Warner and Melvin DeFleur (1969) point out that, where there is strong support for discriminatory behavior, even the most nondiscriminatory person may be led to behave negatively toward minority group members. On the other hand, where there is strong pressure not to discriminate, even a bigot may be forced to behave in a nondiscriminatory fashion.

Institutional Racism: A Societal Act.

A more insidious form of discrimination is referred to as **institutionalized racism** or **institutionalized discrimination**. In this case, discrimination results from the structural prejudices built into the fabric of society rather than from individual purposeful acts. Because our history in part determines the present, centuries of discrimination become a part of the way our society and its institutions operate. For example, many jobs have only recently been opened to minorities; thus, minorities have little seniority in many companies. Most employers operate according to the seniority system: last hired, first fired. When there is a layoff or an operational cutback, many minorities lose their jobs first. This form of discrimination exists because of the rules of the system.

There are many forms of institutionalized discrimination in our society. If a significant number of minorities live in a poor section of the community, they probably do not have a large tax base for their schools. Consequently, they probably will not have the best teachers or the best environment for learning compared with a school in an upper-middle-class neighborhood with greater financial resources and a community environment more conducive to learning and success. An inferior education in turn limits employment opportunities, which limit the opportunity to move to another area with a better school for future generations.

One can argue that no one intends for this to happen—yet it does. In effect, then, society and its institutions have been structured over time by the dominant group, which benefits most from the society's arrangements; members of the majority group tend to vote against any kind of change that would reduce the way in which laws and custom benefit their group.

Source of Prejudice and Discrimination

How do members of different groups come to be prejudiced against one another? Why does prejudice become ingrained and lead to discrimination against minority groups? These are complex questions. To answer them, sociologists suggest that there are three periods in the relationship between majority and minority groups.

In the first stage, prejudice and discrimination emerge and are stabilized into racist attitudes. The second stage involves the maintenance of unequal power. In the third stage, the ability of the dominant group to maintain power breaks down and leads to either assimilation or cultural pluralism.

Emergence and Stabilization

Contact is the first essential step in the emergence of intergroup relationships. If no people ever migrated from one place to another, no intergroup contact would take place. For centuries Japan remained isolated from the immigration of other ethnic or racial groups (Bowen, 1986). To this day, as underscored by the ethnocentric attitudes recently displayed by a former Japanese prime minister, that nation's population is extremely homogeneous. For the most part the issue of intergroup relationships within the country simply has not arisen.

When migration does occur it presents a significant problem for the group. It requires that scarce goods and other rewards be shared. This directly affects how residents and newcomers perceive one another. A contest arises over the rewards of the society as each group struggles for power or dominance in the allocation of those rewards. In some cases the newcomers dominate the natives, as with American Indians and the Australian aborigines. In others, as in the case of Italians, Jews, and others in the United States, the dominant group exercises its power to reduce the new group's share. The result of intergroup contact may have several different consequences.

Aggression

The initial pattern of interaction often takes the form of acts of aggression. **Aggression** or violence frequently erupts between groups in this contest for power and eventual dominance. The potential for violence becomes greatest when groups are unequal in power. In such cases, violence demonstrates emphatically the extremes to which the struggle to dominate can go. Fortified with unequal power, and gaining legitimacy through ethnocentric stereotypes of the minority, the dominant group's battle to gain control can be bitter and bloody (Noel 1968).

In a familiar variation of this pattern, the majority group leads planned attacks on the minority. American history has provided numerous examples of such attacks. In the years between 1863 and 1943, whites attacked black minority group members in a number of cities across the United States. For example, in New York in 1863 a mass attack on blacks by whites resulted in the deaths of two-thousand people. In 1919, following the First World War, whites attacked blacks in Chicago and Washington D.C. as well as other cities, and Los Angeles and Detroit were the scene of interracial fighting. Twenty-five blacks and nine whites were killed in Detroit riots (Farley 1988).

Riots also occur within the minority-group community. Violence is often considered the last resort of those without power or without the belief that they are being heard. In the United States the urban conflicts of the 1960s forcefully called attention to the problems of blacks and other minorities in society. Ghetto riots

Members of the skinheads take part in a Ku Klux Klan parade in Pulaski, Tennessee to protest the celebration of Martin Luther King's birthday. This was the first time the skinheads participated in the annual Klan demonstration.

were symbols of frustration and despair over the effects of racial and ethnic discrimination. The assasination of Dr. Martin Luther King in April of 1968 triggered inner-city violence among blacks across the nation. Large sections of such major cities as Chicago and Detroit were literally burning as the sadness and anger of decades of deprivation were expressed. More recently Hispanics have reacted against the effects of discrimination on their lives with the violence of riots in the Cuban neighborhoods of Miami in 1980.

Extermination

A more extreme and systematic form of violence is that which aims at the extermination of the minority group. This action is referred to as **genocide**, that is, the total elimination of the members of a minority group. After the settlement of America by the English and during the conquest of the frontier, this approach to dealing with the natives or Indians was put into action. The long death marches from their homelands to the West had exterminated large numbers of native Americans. As many as one quarter of the Cherokee nation was eliminated during such a forced march (Josephy 1968, 323). In one reservation officials issued to the native Americans blankets that came directly from the wards of smallpox hospitals.

As we have pointed out, the British who came to Australia followed a similar pattern. They attempted to eliminate the native population, the aborigines. Such action was deemed necessary to ensure the dominance of the European settlers. It was viewed as a final solution to the problem of how the land and its goods should be shared.

Some may have forgotten how recently genocide was seen as a solution to intergroup competition in Europe, but it is only half a century since the Nazis in Germany sought to exterminate the Jewish population wherever its armies held power. Auschwitz and Buchenwald, two of the most notorious death camps of Hitler's regime, stand as eternal symbols of this attempt. More than six million Judaic people died in The Holocaust, and many more millions would have suffered a similar fate had the Third Reich not been defeated and its policy of non-Aryan extermination ended.

It is ironic that in many cases those who, as members of a minority group, suffered such violence themselves engage in similar aggressive acts when their status has changed. For example, a number of the Irish in Boston, once a reviled minority, were prominent in violence against blacks during school desegregation struggles in that city. Also, more extreme groups in Israel now propose policy toward the Palestinians that appear to have genocide as their aim.

Physical Segregation

Where violence or extermination is not carried to ultimate extremes, a common pattern of intergroup relations is the **physical segregation** or separation of minority and majority groups. The United States has had extreme forms of such segregation. The history of our treatment of the native Americans again provides an example. When extermination was either not possible or finally viewed as too extreme, Indians were forced from their homelands and settled on reservations located in land thought worthless by the settlers. There more than half of the remaining native American population remain, separated from the mainstream of American life and living in poverty and despair.

Though Jim Crow laws in the South functioned to separate blacks from the white population in a number of ways, residential segregation has been more absolute in the North and in the emergent urban South. While such segregation is officially illegal in the United States, it continues to exist. Jaynes and Williams (1989) noted that residential segregation is one of the major barriers and disadvantages facing blacks in our society. According to them, residential separation of blacks and whites—at least in metropolitan areas—has not been significantly reduced in the 1980s when compared with 1960s. In the twenty-nine U.S. cities with the highest proportion of black population, residential areas remained eighty percent segregated.

Separation for blacks is twice that for Asian Americans and is generally greater than is segregation for Hispanic Americans. While advances were made between 1940 and 1960, they may have created a more difficult situation for the blacks who remain in segregated residences. The outward movement of blacks with higher status has left such areas with a social structure that contains numerous problems. The reduced tax base of such areas, for example, means less money for essential educational and welfare services as well as lowered opportunity for employment.

Maintenance of Unequal Power

Once the dominant group establishes power over others, the group tries to maintain its power. How does the dominant group continue the definition of the minority as undeserving of societal rewards? We can look at two different aspects of this process. The first is concerned with the development of negative stereotypes and attitudes toward the minority. The second concerns the structure of competition between the majority and minority groups and the question of who benefits most from restricted competition.

Maintenance of unequal power is supported by the development of negative attitudes towards those who are different. As Noel (1968) pointed out, ethnocentrism is the basis of the negative attitudes which support the continuing application of unequal power to reduce competition from minority groups. Theorists hypothesize that prejudice arises and is sustained by frustration and aggression. It is the result of the frustration felt by a group or individuals when they can find no other adequate outlets for built-up aggression.

In many cases prejudice comes from those who are powerless to attack the real source of their frustration—their boss, their family, coworkers with more power, or politicians. Not being able to make a direct attack on the source of frustration, the individual seeks solace in some other direction. Such action is called **scapegoating**. In sociology, this term means that the frustration is not taken out on the real cause of the feeling but on some group in society that is even more powerless, such as blacks, Hispanics, or the Jewish community.

According to the scapegoating theory—sometimes called the frustration-aggression theory (Vander Zanden 1983)—members of all groups have certain needs they feel should be met. However, circumstances usually mean that all of these cannot be met. This leads to a sense of frustration, which must be relieved in some manner. If it cannot be met by direct confrontation, the aggression is displaced to individuals or groups over which the frustrated individuals have some dominance.

By expressing their feelings of frustration on weaker groups and minorities, members of the dominant group can vent the anger that builds up within them. In doing so, they develop numerous rationalizations that support their feelings. The derogation so prominent in attitudes toward minority groups is simply a means whereby the majority is able to displace its frustration and aggression and feel justified in doing so.

Another prominent theory contends that certain personality types are more likely to exhibit prejudice than are others. Right after the end of World War II, one research group (Adorno et al. 1950) sought to find the elements that were common to the prejudiced person and attempted to put these into one personality type, which they referred to as the **authoritarian personality**. This approach suggests that people with an authoritarian personality are extremely conventional in their attitudes, which means that they are submissive to authority and aggressive in the name of that authority. Further, such individuals are unlikely to think deeply in terms of their own feelings. They are guided more by superstition and stereotypes than by thinking through the complexity of a problem. Concentration on power and toughness and a projection of extreme puritanical and moralistic feelings concerning sex also characterize this attitude.

Competition

Another approach to maintaining power focuses on the nature of competition between the two groups. When extermination, aggression, or segregation cannot be maintained, dominant and subordinate groups find themselves in **competition** with each other. In such cases, patterns of **ethnic stratification** take place. This term refers to a style of intergroup relations in which the dominant group limits the access of subordinate groups to societal resources, including wealth, power, and prestige.

Ethnocentric feelings that lead to discrimination may be based upon the competition that exists between various groups. When two groups come into competition with one another, the dominant group uses ethnocentric stereotypes to justify placing the minority-group individuals in a status that denies them the good things of the society. For example, it is in the interest of better-paid workers to define minorities as unfit to hold high-paying jobs and thereby relegate them to marginality in the labor market. This reduces competition for the desirable jobs and helps ensure that wages will not be driven down by minorities willing to work for less.

Essentially, the majority group uses its power and position to dominate minority group members and to benefit its own status. For example, immigrants or minority group members may be forced to take only certain jobs (usually menial and requiring hard physical effort) for low pay. The majority benefits in two ways: its members do not have to do the work and they do not have to pay high wages to get the work done. Migrant workers have been exploited in this manner for years.

We can view such competition from two aspects. One is the differential ability of minorities to compete with the majority group for the good things of the society. Blauner (1972) proposes a theory of **internal colonialism** which makes an important distinction between those minorities that have been conquered—the **colonized minority**—and those that have willingly entered a country—the **immigrant minority**. This distinction is significant because it is real in its consequences.

He classified blacks, Chicanos, and native Americans as colonized minorities. That is, they have been subjected to subordinate status totally against their will. While blacks were not conquered in this country, they were subdued and forcibly brought to this country. The experience of these groups stands in contrast to that of the immigrant minorities, especially those from Europe and particularly northern

Europe. The main point to be made is that the colonized minorities are at a significant disadvantage when compared with immigrant minorities. The historical difference in the way they came to be in the country continues to affect their treatment. The colonized minorities are subjected to more discrimination and social disadvantage than the immigrant minorities.

The other aspect of this has to do with the economics of competition. From a strict functionalist perspective, when competition results in discrimination against one group in the labor market it is dysfunctional to the society because it places the employers at a disadvantage. Bonacich (1972) claimed that employers lose because they cannot take advantage of the lower-cost labor that would be available if minorities were admitted to jobs held by majority group members.

The argument is that business owners recognize that discrimination is dysfunctional and would prefer not to discriminate. They really want to get the cheapest labor. Therefore it is logical to suppose that it should gradually disappear since it does not serve the needs of the employer or society. Firms that do not discriminate have a comparative advantage over those that do. While this has happened to a limited degree, it is far from common in part because an interest group, white laborers, forces them to discriminate.

Another approach, which views the matter from the conflict perspective, sees competition as the clash of different interest groups over the distribution of societal resources. This has been called the split labor theory (Bonacich, 1972, 1975, 1976). Edna Bonacich (1972, 1975) contended that, on the economic level, competition between groups leads to the development of a **split labor market**. In the split labor market, significant differentials between the price of labor develop along ethnic or other lines of stratification. In other words, the dominant group will command higher salaries while minorities will receive less for the same labor. This division in wages underlies antagonism between groups.

Bonacich focuses upon the divergent interests of three key groups: employers (usually white), higher-paid workers (usually white), and lower-paid workers (usually nonwhite). The employers are seen as wanting to replace higher-paid labor with a labor supply that is cheap and docile so that they can compete effectively with other employers.

When a group sells its labor at rates substantially lower than the prevailing group's, higher-paid labor faces severe competition to maintain its economic advantage. If the lower-paid workers are of a different racial or ethnic group, the resulting class antagonism typically takes the form of racism. The antagonism then focuses upon ethnic or racial issues, although at root the conflict is one of class. The more expensive labor force resists displacement by trying to exclude the less expensive labor force or by imposing a form of economic caste system. Both approaches can secure victory for the higher-paid workers by preventing further undercutting of their jobs and wages.

A more Marxian approach suggests, however, that both white and black laborers lose in this competition as a result of discrimination. According to this approach it is the capitalists who gain and the white workers who lose. Racial antagonisms are seen as dividing workers from their real interests. Michael Reich (1972) claimed that the system causes employers to benefit and both sets of laborers to lose: the profits gained from the existence of a lower strata of labor go to the employer. From the perspective of minority groups it matters little whether the benefits go to the upper-strata laborers or the employers. Either way, the system of prejudice and discrimination built into the structure of the labor market leaves them with few of the rewards of the economy.

When Power Cannot Dominate

When the majority group cannot fully manipulate exclusion or control intergroup competition, it must turn to other forms of relationship. Two possibilities are assimilation and pluralism.

Assimilation

Assimilation is the process by which diverse ethnic and racial groups come to share a common culture and have equal access to the opportunity structure of a society. The assumptions are that (1) ethnic evolution in America results in the assimilation of the nation's ethnic groups and that (2) assimilation results from natural history or is a product of societal modernization—an outcome of industrialization, occupational diversification, urbanization, and the spread of mass education and literacy.

Assimilation is often thought to be the goal of our nation; the melting pot theory envisions many different groups joining to form a new, unique society. In sociology, assimilation refers to the incorporation of members of minority groups into the dominant ethos. To do so, the minority group must abandon its distinctive culture. For many European groups that has been an achievable goal. Generally it took about three generations for assimilation to occur; thus, although many Americans today trace their roots to European origins, they do not feel different from the dominant groups of Americans.

In the United States, assimilation has been less difficult for lighter-skinned minorities. Visibility is a major factor in preventing assimilation. For example, the dark skin of blacks is itself a major barrier to assimilation. It remains to be seen if the visibility of Asian groups will pose a similar barrier. To this time, Asian minorities have fared better than other minorities of color. This does not mean that Asian

Placing children with diverse heritages together, as seen at this Nashville day care center, is one step toward assimilation.

Americans have not felt the sting of discrimination; they have. However, there is mounting evidence that their cultural values have helped them overcome the worst effects of discrimination.

In the ultimate example of assimilation, the groups would simply merge into one another. This is referred to as **amalgamation**. Generally such assimilation occurs through marital assimilation. When intermarriage between groups becomes common, the separate groups cease to exist and former distinctions are disregarded.

Pluralism

As a pattern of intergroup relations, **pluralism** refers to a situation where the majority and minority groups maintain cultural differences but participate equally in society. In other words, the minority group does not suffer social, economic, or political disadvantage because of its customs. Very few situations of true pluralism exist. One example is Switzerland, where people of French, Italian, and German backgrounds maintain language and cultural differences but no group is treated as a minority.

In the United States, Hawaii is an example of pluralism. In the other states, pluralism has existed only with certain groups and in certain areas. The Amish of Pennsylvania and other states have been left to continue their unique way of life. However, if they were brought into a situation of conflict or competition with the dominant group, their pluralistic privilege might vanish.

The assumptions are that relations among ethnic and racial groups evolve, but this evolution does not necessarily bring about the assimilation of the groups into a single, monolithic entity. As relations among ethnic groups evolve, the expressions of ethnicity change. In America, ethnic boundaries have generally grown more inclusive and less restrictive, and ethnic identity and its cultural expression have become more domestic and less foreign. Pluralism is buttressed by the nation's tolerance for many other ethnic groups and by the ability of racial and ethnic groups to obtain sociopolitical power.

Minority Group Experience

The existence of numerous minority groups in the United States raises the questions of how such groups are treated and how they came to be defined as minorities. Native Americans, various European immigrants, blacks, Hispanics, and Asians all have experienced prejudice and discrimination. Full discussions of the minority experience of various groups can be found in a number of texts (for example, Yetman 1985, Farley 1988). In this section we look at only two examples of how discrimination affects two minority groups as illustrations of how such prejudicial action affects individuals in such groups.

Three points need to be made before beginning this discussion. First, the following sections look at only two correlates of being a minority group member— income/employment and education. These are the most crucial impacts of discrimination on the daily lives of minority group members. However, it is important to remember that many other facets of minority group members' lives are affected by their status. Some of these, such as crime and family life, are discussed in other chapters.

Second, the two correlates of minority-group status discussed here are related, just as all of the various correlates of minority group status are interrelated (Chalfant

1974). For example, income is a function of education; therefore residence in segregated minority areas may lead to lower income because poorer education is usually offered in such areas. Such residence may further lead to a lower level of health, which affects the ability of an individual to earn a living. In short, minority group members experience a wide range of effects related to the two correlates discussed here.

Third, the following sections deal only with the two largest minorities in the United States, blacks and Hispanics. This is not because these groups are affected more by discrimination. The major reason for focusing on these two minority groups is that they represent the largest such groups in our country. Further, they have been minorities for hundreds of years without greatly changing their life chances. Although there are significant differences between their experience and that of other groups, such as the Asian Americans, they do serve as the most appropriate models of minority experience.

Income and Employment

The story of discrimination against minorities can begin with differential rates of unemployment. Rates of unemployment remain considerably higher for blacks and Hispanics than for whites. Blacks are unemployed about two and one-half times as often as whites, and Hispanics have an unemployment rate about twice that of whites (U.S. Bureau of Census 1989). There has been little advance for blacks and Hispanics since 1955. Unemployment is actually higher for all groups than in the mid-1970s. This supports the suggestion of Jaynes and Williams (1989) that the fate of minorities is tied to the general economy more than to attempts to improve the status of minorities. As the economy has slowed, so have opportunities for minorities and other low-income groups to improve their position and to gain employment.

Unemployment is a particularly severe problem for minority youth. More than one-third of Mexican Americans (34 percent) between the ages of 20 and 24 are unemployed. Similarly, 42 percent of Puerto Rican youth are unemployed as are 46 percent of blacks in this age group (Children's Defense Fund 1990). On the average, white youth earn about $9,000 per year while Hispanics earn only slightly more than $7,000 and blacks about $5,500.

The chance of being unemployed is higher for blacks and Hispanics even as they obtain more education. For example, black college graduates have twice the chance of being unemployed as do whites. The chance for Hispanics to be unemployed is higher than that for whites at all levels of education. To some extent, as seen in Research Method 7.1, a combination of education and fluency in English aids Hispanics in gaining employment, but it is the combination and not education alone that is effective. The U.S. Bureau of Labor Statistics (1985) estimates that, on the average, black college graduates earn only about the same as white high school graduates. Such differential earnings are to be found at most levels of education, making it understandable that getting an education can seem unimportant to minority students.

Research Method 7.1

• • • • • • • **Secondary Analysis: Occupations of Hispanic Men**

Ross M. Stolzenberg (1990) studied the occupational differences between Hispanic and non-Hispanic men by the secondary analysis of existing data. He had three concerns in his investigation. First, he wanted to study differences in occupational attainment for these two groups and the influence of differences in education, English fluency, and related work characteristics. Second, he was interested in the effects of geography on occupational differences, that is, the extent to which being in areas with a high proportion of Hispanic males affected occupational attainment. His final interest concerned the possible effects of subcultural differences within the Hispanic group on occupational success. Does being Mexican American as opposed to, say, Puerto Rican make a difference in level of occupation?

To address these concerns, Stolzenberg drew data from the Survey of Income and Education (SIE) which was conducted by the U.S. Bureau of Census. The national survey had a response rate of 95.4 percent. About 160,000 households were included in the sample. The survey included such details as English fluency, Hispanic ethnicity and group membership, and amount of schooling, as well as economic and demographic data. Samples were conducted separately in each state; in his study, Stolzenberg concentrated on analysis of the nine states in which there was data on at least two hundred Hispanics in the labor force. The states selected actually had about eighty percent of the Hispanic population in the country at the time of the study. The final analysis used several specific variables: education, potential years of labor-market experience, foreign birth, language fluency, Hispanic ethnic group, race, and occupation.

The strategy of the analysis was the use of a procedure known as a two-way analysis of covariance. The statistic was applied to each of the dependent variables. First it was used to analyze occupational attainment and then to examine subgroup differences. Finally, occupational differences were subjected to analysis.

Stolzenberg had expected to find that both geographic distribution of Hispanics and differences between Hispanic subgroups would account for varying occupational achievement. However, the analysis revealed a quite different pattern.

What he found was what he called a pattern of *conditional occupational assimilation*. In other words, he found that a great deal of the inequality in occupation between Hispanic and non-Hispanic men could be attributed to two factors: differences in years of school completed and fluency in the English language. When the Hispanic men spoke English "very well" and, in addition, had at least finished high school (or twelve years of education), inequality in occupational success virtually disappeared. Hispanic men who were fluent in English and had at least high school education competed favorably, at least in the nine states studied, with non-Hispanic men.

Stolzenberg's study found that the assimilation of Hispanic males into the work force, given language fluency and education, was not affected by either the men's subgroup or the amount of work experience, nor was it influenced by the state in which the Hispanic males lived. Only Cuban Hispanics seemed to fare better than other subgroups and this could well be explained by the difference in higher socioeconomic status of many Cubans who immigrated to this country after Castro took power in Cuba.

It is a condition of their minority status that blacks have generally tended to work at less prestigious, lower-paying jobs (Farley 1980). Since the end of World War II, the average income of two-parent black families has grown from 64 percent of the average income of white families to 85 percent. However, for the most rapidly increasing segment of the black population, female-headed families, earnings were 31 percent of those for white families, a decrease of 2 percent since 1964. Overall, the median income for blacks was only 56 percent of that for whites, an increase of only 2 percent since 1964.

General figures on differentials in income are shown in Table 7.1. Here we see that while 22 percent of the white population has a family income of more than $50,000 per year, only 8.8 percent of blacks and 10.2 percent of Hispanics have this level of earnings. On the other end of the economic ladder, only 3.5 percent of white families in the U.S. have incomes of less than $5,000; for blacks the figure is 14.0 percent and for Hispanics, 8.7 percent. Again, Puerto Ricans were most often found in this income bracket with 17.7 percent of families earning less than $5,000 per year.

Other figures support the existence of a poorer economic situation for blacks and Hispanics. Between 1947 and 1982 the gap in income between blacks and whites actually widened; the absolute-dollar gap (the difference in income when the dollar is held constant in value) between the median incomes of the two groups grew larger during those thirty-five years. While black income had improved in dollar figures, the black population was relatively less well off (Weeks 1987). This gap continues. In 1987 the median family income for whites was $30,809, while the corresponding figure for blacks was $17,604 and for Hispanics, $19,995. In considering median income for blacks we should remember the low income of the large number of female-headed households among blacks. Also, with regard to Hispanics not all sub-groups have similar fates. For Puerto Ricans, for example, the median family income is only $14,584 (Bureau of Commerce 1989).

Again, there is support for the findings reported by Jaynes and Williams (1989). The overall state of the economy affects both majority and minority groups. When the economy is slow, those in the lower strata of society have little chance of improving their situation. Given the fact that the majority of blacks and Hispanics began in this strata, they remain at the lower income level. The power of the

●Table 7.1 Total Family Income by Race, 1986, by Percentage

Annual Family Income	White	Black	Hispanic
Less than $5,000	3.5	14.0	8.7
$ 5,000–9,999	6.7	16.1	14.6
$10,000–14,999	9.1	13.8	15.2
$15,000–24,999	19.5	20.2	22.4
$25,000–34,999	18.6	14.7	16.5
$35,000–49,999	20.6	12.4	12.5
$50,000 and more	22.0	8.8	10.2
Median income	$30,809	$17,604	$19,995

Source: U.S. Bureau of the Census. *Current Population Reports, Series P-60, No. 159,* Washington, D.C.: U.S. Government Printing Office, 1986.

dominant group operates, as discussed in this chapter, to restrict the distribution of economic resources, especially when those resources are becoming increasingly scarce.

Education

Begin by looking at the differences in number of school years completed by whites, blacks, and Hispanics (see Table 7.2). The median number of school years completed is higher for whites than for blacks and Hispanics. In 1987, 20.5 percent of whites had four or more years of college education while only 10.7 percent of blacks had attained this level of schooling and 8.6 percent of Hispanics. While the percentage of blacks and Hispanics completing four or more years of schooling has increased since 1970, it has not kept pace with the increase in educational attainment for whites (U.S. Bureau of Commerce 1989).

The educational level for minorities has been and continues to be substandard (Vander Zanden 1983). A major problem is the high rate of school drop-outs among minority youth. Joan Moore and Harry Pachon (1985, 69) have shown evidence that the percentage of high-school drop-outs is much greater for minority groups than for whites. They report that Mexican Americans and Puerto Ricans are two to three times as likely to drop out of high school as are whites. Later figures sustain this finding and extend it to black youth. In 1986, 24 percent of blacks and 40 percent of Hispanics failed to graduate from high school whereas only 17 percent of whites did not graduate. For the Hispanic population, in particular, only 20 percent of young adults had more than nine years of education as of 1988 (Children's Defense Fund 1990).

Clearly this situation places the minority population at a serious disadvantage with regard to employment and especially employment above the poverty level. Given the importance that American society places on formal schooling and the need for academic credentials to get jobs that pay a decent wage, why are black and Hispanic youth leaving school earlier and at a higher rate than nonminorities?

One reason, which we have already mentioned, is that education simply does not pay off for blacks and Hispanics as it does for whites. Even when formal academic credentials are earned, the chance of using that education for job success is lessened

● **Table 7.2** Years of School Completed, 1987, by Percentage (Persons 25-years-old and Over)

Level of School Completed	White	Black	Hispanic
Elementary school			
0–4 years	2.0	5.0	11.9
5–7 years	4.1	8.0	15.2
8 years	5.9	5.3	18.2
High school			
1–3 years	11.0	18.2	13.9
4 years	39.2	37.1	29.0
College			
1–3 years	17.2	15.7	10.7
4 years or more	20.5	10.7	8.6
Median years completed	12.7	12.4	12.0

Source: U.S. Bureau of the Census. *Current Population Reports, Series P-20, No. 426*, Washington, D.C.: U.S. Government Printing Office, 1987.

by discrimination (Horowitz 1983). Minority status remains a stigma that denies access to better job opportunities despite school achievement. Clearly this discourages blacks and Hispanics from working hard to achieve in school.

Another aspect of the problem is that most of these minority youth attend schools that are of low quality. In 1986 about two-thirds of black and Hispanic youth (63 and 70 percent, respectively) were enrolled in predominantly minority schools. For Hispanics the schools were frequently more than 90 percent minority (Children's Defense Fund 1990). The importance of this fact is that such schools seldom allow students to achieve their potential; thus, those who finish school are not well prepared to enter the job market. This clearly contributes to the fact that education for these minority groups does not lead to better employment and that students are more likely to drop out. Again, there seems little encouragement to remain in school since it is not seen as providing a means of upward mobility.

In this chapter we defined a minority group as one that has an inferior status in the society and which, because of that status, does not have a proportionate share of the good things the society has to offer—money, social status, and power. This is true because the majority or dominant group is able to systematically discriminate against the minority, subjecting them to unequal and unfair treatment. Such treatment clearly invades every second of minority life. As the gap between those who have and those who have not, including many poor who are not minority group members, continues to widen, our society will be faced with a major problem, one that cannot be ignored if the structure of that society is to remain stable.

Questions for Summary and Review

1. Define the terms minority group and majority group.
2. What are the key characteristics of a minority group?
3. What forms has discrimination taken in the United States?
4. What do we now believe that the term, race, means?
5. What is the difference between a racial and an ethnic minority group?
6. What is racism?
7. Distinguish between prejudice and discrimination.
8. How are prejudice and discrimination related to each other?
9. What is meant by institutionalized racism and institutionalized discrimination?
10. What are the stages in the development of majority-minority group relations?
11. In what ways do majority groups maintain their dominance over minorities?
12. What is meant by assimilation and pluralism?
13. What are the economic consequences of minority status for blacks and Hispanics?
14. How are educational opportunities limited for blacks and Hispanics?

Key Concepts

Aggression (p. 153)
Amalgamation (p. 159)
Anglo-conformity (p. 144)
Assimilation (p. 158)
Authoritarian personality (p. 156)
Colonized minority (p. 156)
Competition (p. 156)
Contact (p. 152)

De facto discrimination (p. 143)
De jure discrimination (p. 143)
Denial (p. 146)
Derogation (p. 145)
Discrimination (p. 151)
Ethnic group (p. 148)
Ethnic stratification (p. 142, 156)
Genocide (p. 154)

References

1. Adorno, T.W. et al. 1950. *The authoritarian personality.* New York: Harper and Row.

2. Belich, James. 1986. *The New Zealand wards.* Auckland, New Zealand: Penguin Books.

3. Blauner, Robert. 1972. *Racial oppression in America.* New York: Harper and Row.

4. Bonacich, Edna. 1972. A theory of ethnic antagonism: The split labor market. *American sociological review* 37:547–59.

5. ———. 1975. Abolition, the extension of slavery, and the position of free blacks: A study of split labor markets in the United States, 1830–1863. *American journal of sociology* 81:601–28.

6. ———. 1976. Advanced capitalism and black/white relations in the United States: A split labor market interpretation. *American sociological review* 41:34–51.

7. Bowen, E. 1986. Nakasone's world-class blunder. *Time* (October 6):66–67.

8. Chalfant, H. Paul. 1974. The correlates of poverty. In *The sociology of American poverty,* edited by J. Huber and H.P. Chalfant, pp. 193–203. Cambridge, Mass.: Schenkman.

9. Children's Defense Fund. 1990. *Latin youths at a crossroads.* Washington, D.C.: Children's Defense Fund.

10. Dobzhanky, Theodosius. 1962. *Mankind evolving.* New Haven, Conn.: Yale University Press.

11. Evans, Raymond, Kay Saunders, and Kathryn Cronin. 1988. *Race relations in colonial Queensland.* St. Lucia, Australia: University of Queensland Press.

12. Farley, John. 1980. The long road: Blacks and whites in America. *American demographics* 2:11–17.

13. Farley, John E. 1988. *Majority-minority relations.* 2d ed. Englewood Cliffs, N.J.: Prentice-Hall.

14. Farrel, Charles S. 1988. Black students seen facing "new racism" on many campuses. *Chronicle of higher education* (January 27):2, 36.

15. Horowitz, Ruth. 1983. *Honor and the American dream: Culture and identity in a Chicano community.* New Brunswick, N.J.: Rutgers University Press.

16. Hraba, Joseph. 1979. *Racial and ethnic minorities.* Itasca, Ill.: Peacock.

17. Jaynes, Gerald David, and Robin M. Williams, Jr., eds. 1989. *A common destiny: Blacks and American society.* Washington, D.C.: National Academy Press.

18. Josephy, Alvin M., Jr. 1968. *The Indian heritage of America.* New York: Alfred Knopf.

19. Lee, Martha F. 1988. *The nation Islam, an American millenarian movement.* Lewistown, N.Y.: Edward Mellen Press.

20. Merton, Robert M. 1949. Discrimination and the American creed. In *Discrimination and national welfare,* edited by E.

MacIver, pp. 99–126. New York: Harper and Row.

21. Moore, Joan, and Harry Pachon. 1985. *Mexican-Americans*. 3d ed. Englewood Cliffs, N.J.: Prentice-Hall.

22. Noel, D.L. 1968. *The origins of American slavery and racism*. Columbis, Ohio: Merrill.

23. Porter, Bruce, Marvin Dunn, and Alejandro Portes. 1984. *The Miami riots of 1980: Crossing the bounds*. Lexington, Mass.: Lexington Books.

24. Reich, Michael. 1972. Economic theories of racism. In *Schooling in a corporate society,* edited by M. Contry. New York: McKay.

25. Schaefer, Richard T. 1984. *Racial and ethnic groups*. 2d ed. New York: Random House.

26. Simpson, Richard, and Milton Yinger. 1985. *Racial and cultural minorities*. 5th ed. New York: Harper and Row.

27. Stolzenberg, Ross M. 1990. Ethnicity, geography, and occupations of U.S. Hispanic men. *American sociological review* 55:143–154.

28. U.S. Bureau of Census. 1989. *Statistical abstracts of the United States*. Washing-

ton, D.C.: U.S. Government Printing Office.

29. U.S. Bureau of Labor Statistics. 1985. *Handbook of labor statistics, 1985*. Washington, D.C.

30. Van den Berghe, Pierre. 1964. *Minorities in the New World: Six Case Studies*. New York: Columbia University Press.

31. _____. 1978. *Race and racism: A comparative perspective*. 2d ed. New York: Columbia University Press.

32. Vander Zanden, James W. 1983. *American minority relations*. 4th ed. New York: Knopf.

33. Warner, Lyle, and Melvin DeFleur. 1969. Attitude as an interactional concept: Social constraint and social distance as intervening variables between attitudes and actions. *American sociological review* 34:133–69.

34. Weeks, Paul. 1987. *Population*. Palo Alto, Calif.: Mayfield.

35. Wiener, John. 1989. Racial hatred on campus. *The Nation* (February 27): 260–64.

36. Yetman, Norman R. 1985. *Majority and minority: The dynamics of race and ethnicity in American life*. 4th ed. Boston: Allyn and Bacon.

Women, Men, and the Elderly: Sex and Age in Social Life

8

Chapter Outline

Women belong at home. That is what the Japanese will say, but the reality in Japan is quite different. More than half of all Japanese married women work, although they generally work in clerical positions offering little advancement. They earn about fifty-five percent of what Japanese men earn, and they are still expected to do all "wifely" duties at home. Very few women are in positions of corporate authority despite the fact that many have a university education. A Japanese woman who remains single past the ideal marriage age of twenty-five is a source of embarrassment and shame for her employer as well as her family (Tasker 1988).

The Japanese also have a long tradition of honor and respect for the elderly. However, in parts of Japan, forcible euthanasia of old women was a practice in the nineteenth century. Today, the Japanese government provides little for the elderly because the family is supposed to care for them. However, in the modern world of longer life expectancies, small mobile families, and high costs of living, it is much more difficult for Japanese families to provide for the aged whose pensions usually do not suffice (Tasker 1988). In short, just as Westerners have discovered, Japanese women and the Japanese elderly are discovering that tradition does not necessarily suit them for the late twentieth century.

Throughout history people have attributed a great deal to a person on the basis of his or her sex and age. All cultures make a distinction between men's work and women's work, although the actual content of the work may be vastly different from place to place. In the U.S., we tend to think of physicians as males while in the Soviet Union they most often are females, although Soviet physicians have less prestige than American physicians. Cultures also vary according to the prestige and respect given to the older members of the group. In youth-oriented America, we tend to ignore the abilities, contributions, and potential of the elderly.

Age and sex are pervasive aspects of life, and they shape others' views of us as well as our own self-concepts. This chapter will explore these two significant ascribed statuses, beginning with a discussion of men and women.

Men and Women: Some Lessons from History

Several important historical traditions have influenced our beliefs about men and women. In Western history, men have been the favored sex. For example, in ancient Athens women were not allowed to vote; they were rarely formally educated and remained in the home, responsible for domestic chores. Married women could not even observe the fabled Olympic games. On the other hand, ancient Greek play-wrights gave Western culture some enduring visions of strong women including Antigone who defied king, family, and tradition in attempting to bury her brother and to care for her blind father, Oedipus (Kitto 1957). This ambiguity, this tendency to be contradictory about women, is an important element of the Western tradition.

According to O'Kelly (1980), the subordination of women reaches its greatest peak in agrarian-agricultural societies such as ancient Greece and many Third World nations today. Rural women worked long, hard hours, but much agrarian work required the brute strength of men to clear the land, plow, and irrigate. Women were to bear and rear children, to work at weaving, sewing, and maintaining the food supply. The tendency of these societies to engage in warfare and militarism, emphasizing male bravery and aggression, also contributed to the relatively low status of women.

Similar to Greek tradition, the Judeo-Christian ethic in Western culture endorsed a system of male dominance and female submissiveness. The Judeo-Christian tradition also included contradictions. On the one hand, the Virgin Mary represented purity and blessedness. On the other, women were seen as the source of evil drives in men. Millions of women were killed as witches during the Middle Ages. Chalfant and associates (1987) pointed out that Western religion underscored a status system that denied equal opportunity to women. Today, the continuing debate over female priests and pastors is evidence of the controversy over women's place in the church. While a number of Protestant churches now officially allow women into the clergy, the Catholic church has remained steadfast in its tradition of "men only" priests.

As industrialization transformed Western societies in the 1800s, economic activity gradually became separated from the home. People went to work in factories and offices apart from home. Over time, a rather rigid sex role division of labor developed. The husband took on the breadwinner role and the wife was responsible for the management of the home and the socialization of children. The home became a haven away from the vicious world of grimy industrial work and cutthroat competition. Women, particularly middle- and upper-class women, became associated with a set of virtues: domesticity, purity, morality, piety, and submission. This view of women is called the **cult of true womanhood**, and it developed in the Victorian Age. The cult of true womanhood separated women from life outside the home; they were to remain innocent, chaste, and child-oriented (Welter 1978). Such beliefs encouraged society to put women on a pedestal. Of course, these beliefs were irrelevant to working-class women crowded into sweatshops or working as maids; they always had to work; and, too, thousands of men worked miserably long hours in hot and dangerous factories to support their families.

The pedestal of true womanhood, however, exacted a high price for all women. Consider that no women were allowed to vote, they were barred from most universities except those exclusively designed for women, they could not own property in their own name, they were barred from most occupations, they were almost completely dependent on their husbands for economic support, and they were not permitted to get divorces. They were the property of their husbands, and they were, formally, powerless. For many, their informal source of power was to work through their husbands. Their source of pride was often derived from the successes of their husbands.

During World War II, millions of women worked in factories that fueled the war, and their successes were well-documented. However, when the men returned from war to their jobs, the women were sent home, and a period of conservatism and traditional sex role division returned. Betty Friedan (1963) noted a cult similar to that of true womanhood which she called **the feminine mystique**. Middle-class women were isolated in their private homes in the suburbs and told that their responsibility was to raise children and maintain the home. They were the mothers of the Baby Boom generation, the people born between 1946 and 1964. These women were financially dependent on their husbands and most could not afford the consequences of divorce. As a result, those who had married young and were not happy saw no way out of bad marriages. Those who were college educated rarely got jobs equal to their level of expertise.

Dissatisfaction among some of these women fueled a new women's movement in the 1960s and 1970s. Other factors also contributed to the development of this movement. Labor-saving equipment in the home potentially reduced the time needed for housework. The decrease in the birth rate, typical of industrialized societies, reflected the fact that women were having fewer children to rear. The lengthening of life expectancy gave women about thirty years after the children were grown to do other things. Technological changes meant that most jobs no longer required brute strength. A greater proportion of women were attending college yet finding few economic opportunities. These college-educated women were more receptive to the issue of women's rights. Growing economic pressures in the economically difficult 1970s encouraged wives to work to help support the family. Finally, a rising divorce rate meant that large numbers of women could not rely on support from men. All of these factors combined to change how men and women lived in America (Chafetz 1978). While few people argue that opportunities for men and women are equal in the United States, most would agree that the status of women has improved.

Sex, Gender Roles, and Sexism

People often confuse the terms sex and gender, so it is necessary to make a distinction between the two. **Sex role** is defined as one's biological sex at birth reflecting one's chromosomal, anatomical, hormonal, physiological structure and behavior, and roles in childbearing (Richardson 1981, 5). Sex role uses the labels male or female. On the other hand, **gender role** is the set of culturally defined expectations regarding how one should act on the basis of one's sex. Gender role determines the range of acceptable behavior for each sex. These gender expectations influence the social opportunities, occupations, familial roles, and prestige allowed men and women. Gender role uses the labels masculine or feminine. Stereotypes regarding social and personal attributes are a deeply ingrained part of our images of men and women, but masculinity and femininity are culturally prescribed and vary from culture to culture. Gender roles are more important for sociologists because they focus on the cultural, social, and political creations of social role expectations.

The term **sexism** refers to the whole complex of prejudice and discriminatory treatment based on sex, much like the term racism was used in the previous chapter. Sexism occurs when people unconsciously carry stereotypical and negative images of people solely on the basis of sex. Sexism occurs when a woman is denied a job or an education mainly because she is a woman. It occurs when a man is ridiculed for crying or showing emotion because he is a man.

Until lately, much of the research in sociology dealt with sexism directed at women; more recently, we have developed a greater awareness of the sexism experienced by men (see, for example, Farrell 1986, Doyle 1989). Nevertheless, in the social and political sphere, there is little question that women are the second sex having experienced a wider range of discrimination, prejudice, and other blocks to full participation in society.

Fifteen years ago, this female second lieutenant in Quantico, VA, would not have been allowed to train with male Marines.

Sex Stratification and Its Consequences

Sex stratification refers to the unequal access to property, power, and prestige according to sex. Just as people are stratified into social classes, they can be stratified by sex. Women have been called a minority group; one writer called women the "oppressed majority" because women make up fifty-one percent of the U.S. population (Whitehurst 1977). Much evidence exists to support the idea that a good deal of sex stratification exists in our society. The socialization process encouraging girls and boys to conform to traditional expectations of masculinity and femininity is extremely powerful. Change in these long-accepted roles is threatening to a strong sense of security. In this section, we will explore the socialization of men and women, sex stratification in the workplace, and the consequences of this stratification.

Sex Stratification and Socialization

From the moment of birth, family members begin a never-ending process of differing socialization patterns for sons and daughters. Parents will describe their child according to gender role stereotypes almost immediately after birth. They describe sons as stronger, more active, and bigger while describing daughters as smaller, less active, sweeter, and weaker. Biological evidence mostly supports the opposite conclusion about newborns and their behavior. On average, male babies are smaller, weaker, and more prone to health problems (Brooks-Gunn and Matthews 1979).

In our society parents go to great lengths to show the sex of their baby by dressing the child in either pink or blue, using bows and ribbons for girls, and choosing baseball T-shirts for baby boys and frilly dresses for baby girls. These gender advertisements call out different behavior from others who interact with the child (Baker et al. 1980). In addition, a baby whose clothing does not identify the child as a boy or a girl will often cause confusion among adults; one of their first questions will be to ask the sex of the child (Seavey et al. 1975).

This systematic socialization process results in considerably different behavior for boys and girls by school age, although there are some notable exceptions. For example, in many rural areas, daughters are brought up performing physically demanding "man's work." Remember Charles Horton Cooley's concept of the looking-glass self in chapter 4. Cooley said we tend to see ourselves as we think others see us. These self-concepts, in turn, influence on our behavior. Boys are expected and encouraged to be aggressive, active, exploratory, independent, and strong. Girls typically are encouraged to be submissive, dependent, less active, less aggressive, and more concerned with getting along with others. Girls are allowed more expression of emotions.

Remember, too, George Herbert Mead's emphasis on the play and game stages of childhood socialization in which children learn and practice social roles. Learning and playing at gender roles are pervasive during childhood. Sex-typed toys such as guns, simulated war equipment, trucks, and footballs for boys, and dolls, miniature refrigerators, and toy vacuum cleaners for girls reinforce the difference in expectations for sons and daughters. Boys' play is more likely to provide them with a wider range of experiences and teaches them a variety of skills which may be useful in the work world. Girls' play tends to emphasize the roles of mother and homemaker. Boys' games are more likely to teach leadership, independence, and competition. Girls' games tend to play up nurturance and cooperation rather than competition (Lever 1976). A daughter is told to be a little lady; a boy is told to be a man. By the end of infancy, the toddler knows that gender is the most important dimension of the world and that he or she is, along with everyone else, either one or the other. The toddler also knows that certain activities are for males and others for females (Brooks-Gunn and Matthews 1979, 95).

Gender role socialization serves not only to perpetuate the traditional behavioral differences between the sexes; it has other consequences as well. Socialization makes it more difficult for boys than girls to adjust to the strictness of primary-grade classrooms. On the other hand, socialization of boys better prepares them for the occupational world, for competition, and for assertiveness. Girls brought up traditionally may have more trouble adjusting to the work world because certain feminine behavioral expectations such as submissiveness and dependence do not serve them well. Women tend to have more problems with self-esteem and self-confidence. They are less certain that they can accomplish various tasks either because they have been told that they are less capable or because they lack experience and the reassurance that they can succeed. On the other hand, men are considerably restricted because they lack the opportunity to express emotions and fears. Members of both sexes may suffer from the square-peg-in-a-round-hole syndrome when they feel they cannot live up to gender role expectations. Boys especially find it painful to be ridiculed as a sissy or a bookworm by their more physically active and stronger peers. It is particularly noticeable that boys are taught to disdain anything that is remotely feminine. "No sissy stuff" is a cardinal rule of boyhood (David and Brannon

This father, a single parent, has learned to take on many household and child care duties including making snacks for his children and their friends.

1976) Sociologist Joseph Pleck (1976, 256) recounted his own experience in the ninth grade as a square peg and the pain he felt in not meeting his father's expectations for him to be physically strong and athletically coordinated. Pleck wrote:

> I remember most of all a father-and-son picnic and softball game in my homeroom when I was a freshman. I knew this wouldn't be a good experience, but I was not strong enough to refuse to participate in it, as several other people in the homeroom did. After my father and I arrived, things got right down to business with the softball game. I was the only person on both teams, the fathers and the sons, not to get a hit; I struck out every time. I don't think I have ever felt so ashamed of myself as I felt then, or felt that anyone else was so ashamed of me as my father was then. In the picnic which followed, my father and I avoided each other completely. Driving home with him was excruciating. I didn't attempt anything even remotely athletic on my own initiative for about five years after that experience.

Gender role socialization is sometimes described as the making of cages which restrict full development of human beings. For example, Table 8.1 illustrates some of the drawbacks faced by men in society.

Feminists, counselors, and therapists have argued that an individual, whether male or female, should not be caged by rigid expectations of gender behavior. People should be allowed to express a wide range of behavior regardless of whether it is defined as unbecoming for their sex. The term **androgyny** refers to this freedom from gender stereotypes. The androgynous person does not restrict his or her life on the basis of traditional social expectations. Those arguing for androgyny claim that it creates flexibility not rigidity (Bem 1974, 1979). The androgynous person is free to choose from both masculine and feminine behavior. For example, an androgynous male allows himself to be more comfortable with his feelings, and an androgynous female allows herself to be assertive and confident.

On the other hand, it is difficult for men and women to be involved with one another without traditional gender expectations and inequality as major mitigating factors. For example, Research Application 8.1 discusses the power imbalances of single women and married men involved in sexual affairs.

● **Table 8.1**   *Men Are Not Equal Either*

Females, on the average, are expected to live about 7 years longer than males in the United States.

Males are 4 times more likely than females to be victims of homicide in the United States.

Males are 3 times as likely as females to commit suicide in the United States. The difference increases considerably with age. At age 85, males are 10 times more likely to commit suicide.

Males are more than twice as likely as females to die in accidents in the United States. About half of these accidental deaths occur in automobile wrecks.

Males are three times more likely than females to die of lung disease. However, rates of lung disease for females are increasing because more women smoke than in the past.

Of the estimated 10 million problem drinkers, about 80 percent are males.

American males have a cancer death rate that is nearly 30 percent higher than females. This is mainly a result of smoking and greater exposure to pollution in the workplace. Experts assume that females will begin to catch up to men in cancer rates as their stress and lifestyle at work become more like those of males.

Sources: Adapted from Henslin, James M. 1990. *Social Problems.* 2nd Ed. Englewood Cliffs, N.J.: Prentice-Hall, and Bogue, Donald J. 1985. *The Population of the United States: Historical Trends and Future Projections.* New York: Free Press.

Research Application 8.1

• • • • • • • **Married Men and Single Women: Inequality in Affairs**

It is estimated that between eighteen percent and thirty-five percent of single women become sexually involved with married men at some point in their lives (Richardson 1986). While some are brief sexual encounters, other affairs develop into very intimate, long-term relationships.

What are the special features of long-term love affairs between married men and single women? Laurel Richardson's (1988, 212) major study of these kinds of affairs found that "the man's marital status creates a context of privacy, time constraints, and expectations of temporariness that encourage revealing secrets about the self."

The affairs she studied lasted at least one year, although many lasted as long as five years. Because the relationship was not expected to last, those involved felt free to reveal more to each other and created a very special secretive and shared intimacy. Richardson (1988, 214) quoted one of the women, "I still marvel that he considered me worthy enough to know him that well. His wife may have had his name, but I had his soul."

People might think that the single woman involved with a married man holds considerable power because she can destroy his life by making the affair public. In fact, in Richardson's in-depth interviews with sixty-five women who had been involved with married men, she found that they never revealed the affairs or even threatened to do so. The single woman had as much or more to lose than her married lover. First, all of these women reported being very much in love. Each described the affair as incredibly intense, "uniquely intimate," or "emotionally pure" (Richardson 1988, 212). While many of them realized that her lover would not leave his wife, each nevertheless wanted to do nothing to endanger her relationship with him, and threats to disclose the affair would clearly be destructive to the trust and intimacy in the relationship.

Second, threatening to tell the wife was not in the single woman's best interest because it required "acknowledging the wife's existence" (Richardson 1988, 214). The single woman preferred to psychologically deny the wife's importance and status. This way, the lovers could build a private and secret world of their own.

Third, if she worked with her married lover, the single woman risked her job status because others would accuse her of using sex to advance her career. Also, if she publicly disclosed the affair, she could be labeled "home wrecker" (Richardson 1988, 214). Quite often, given today's sex role prescriptions, the woman is held more to blame than the man. The double standard regarding sex has not disappeared, and social expectations still require the woman to be the "sexual cop" and be more responsible for control of sexual involvements than the man.

Richardson noted the inequality in the affairs, particularly when the single women reported reconstructing their lives to suit the schedules and opportunities of the married men. One of the women in her study commented, "In a normal relationship you usually don't have to give up who you are. In my relationship, I gave up my family, my identity, my culture, the theater, the arts . . ." (Richardson 1988, 216).

The essential feature of these relationships is the imbalance of power. Part of that imbalance results from the fact that the man is married, and a married woman in an affair with a single man would have similar advantages. In addition, an older, married man tends to have higher socioeconomic status than a younger, single female, adding to the status and power imbalance between

them. The physician has more power and influence than the nurse; the professor more than the student; and the vice-president more than the accountant.

Finally, an important part of the power imbalance is the issue of gender. "Because women tend to value relationships more highly than men, work more to sustain them, and feel more responsible for their outcomes, women are likely to care more about having and preserving a relationship than men are" (Richardson 1988, 210). So she works very hard to please him and, in return, she feels loved.

• • • • • • •

Sex Stratification in the Workplace

As women have moved into the paid labor force in record numbers during the past thirty years, they have experienced a wide range of problems. They have faced income inequality and have met employers unwilling to hire them or unable to believe that women are capable. They have shouldered the overload of demanding work on top of being wives and mothers because women still carry the major burden of homemaking duties. They have found it difficult to provide adequate economic support as a single parent, and they have faced sexual harassment on the job. Sex stratification has had mostly negative effects for women; the work world remains designed for men and tends to benefit men.

Of these problems, the issue of income inequality has perhaps received the most attention. On the average, women make approximately sixty-six percent of what men make. This difference in earning power has remained virtually the same even though millions of women have entered the paid labor force. Even within the same occupation, the average salary of women is almost always lower than the average salary for men. Table 8.2 shows the differences in pay for men and women for selected occupations. Table 8.3 shows the differences in pay according to educational level.

● **Table 8.2**   Median Income for Men and Women in Selected Occupations*

Occupation	Men's Median Income	Women's Median Income	% Difference
All occupations	$26,656	$17,606	66
Professional specialties	37,490	25,789	69
Executive, administrative, and managerial positions	36,759	23,356	64
Administrative support, including clerical	24,399	16,676	68
Sales	27,022	15,474	57
Precision production, craft, and repair positions	25,746	16,869	66
Machine operators, assemblers, and inspectors	21,382	13,289	62
Service occupations	18,648	11,032	59
Farming, forestry, and fishing	14,300	9,926	69

*Refers to year-round, full-time workers for the year 1988.

Source: U.S. Bureau of the Census, *Money Income and Poverty Status in the United States: 1988,* in *Current Population Reports,* Series P-60, No. 166, Advance data from the March 1989 Current Population Survey. Washington D.C.: U.S. Government Printing Office, 1989.

●Table 8.3 Median Incomes* According to Educational Level by Sex

Educational Level	Men's Median Income	Women's Median Income	% Difference
8 years or less	17,190	11,358	66
1–3 years high school	20,777	13,104	63
4 years high school	26,045	16,810	65
1–3 years college	30,129	20,845	69
4 years college	36,434	25,187	69
5 or more years college	43,938	30,136	69

*Refers to full-time, year-round workers.

Source: U.S. Bureau of the Census, *Money Income and Poverty Status in the United States: 1988,* in Current Population Reports, Series P-60, No. 166, Advance data from the March 1989 Current Population Survey. Washington, D.C.: U.S. Government Printing Office, 1989.

Part of the explanation for income inequality lies in the different jobs men and women typically hold. Most women work in service-sector jobs that are low-paying and dead-end. Such jobs include waitressing and clerical positions. In fact, more than one-third of all working women are found in clerical positions such as secretaries, file clerks, receptionists, and typists while only six percent of males are in these jobs. Less than one-fourth of all professional, managerial, and technical jobs are held by women, and most of these are in schoolteaching. Table 8.4 lists occupations that are predominantly female and others that are predominantly male.

When women are found in traditional masculine professions they are often referred to as "lady lawyers" or "women physicians" just as men in a traditionally feminine job are referred to as "male nurses." Women are rarely found in higher paying blue-collar jobs such as carpentry, masonry, and other crafts. More than half of all women workers are employed in traditionally feminine occupations. These traditionally female jobs include secretaries, nurses, teachers, and telephone oper-

●Table 8.4 Sex Stratification in the U.S. Labor Force

Occupations	% Female	Occupations	% Male
Receptionists	97.5%	Firefighters	98.0%
Librarians	85.6	Carpenters	98.7
Registered nurses	95.1	Mechanics	97.3
Secretaries	98.1	Truckers	96.0
Bank tellers	90.6	Police officers	89.2
Cashiers	83.0	Engineers	93.8
Dental assistants	98.0	Dentists	93.8
Waiters and waitresses	85.1	Architects	89.2
Child-care workers	96.0	Physicians	84.0
Cleaners and servants	96.0	Lawyers and judges	83.8
Data entry keyers	87.2	Commodities sales representatives	83.3
Hairdressers	89.3	College and university teachers	73.4

Source: U.S. Bureau of the Census. *Statistical Abstract of the United States, 1989.* Washington, D.C.: U.S. Government Printing Office, 1989.

ators. The salaries for such jobs are, on the average, lower than the typically masculine jobs of steelworkers, dentist, engineer, business executive, and electrician (Baker et al. 1980).

There are several reasons why, in the past, employers traditionally did not pay women as much as they paid men. First, women were less likely to complain; such an action was unfeminine. Second, it was assumed that women were working for a second income and that men needed more money because they were the primary breadwinners of families. Finally, women had few legal rights to challenge the system. If they did complain, they could simply lose their jobs. As certain jobs came to be defined as female, the wages typically remained low. For example, before the twentieth century most secretaries were male, and the job had more prestige and better pay before it was occupied mostly by females.

On the other hand, statistics also tell us that even in the same occupation with the same amount of education and experience, women, on average, do not make as much as men (see Tables 8.2 and 8.3). Typically, the higher the education, the closer women come to making as much as men, but the gap remains in every occupational field.

This income gap is caused by several factors. First, women tend to be newer entrants into fields such as law and medicine and have yet to reach positions of seniority and better pay.

Second, some women work on an intermittent basis, shaping their jobs or careers to fit with their husbands' jobs and with bearing and rearing children. Some women drop out of the labor force while their children are young; when they do go back to work they have lost those years that would have gone toward advancement. They have also lost seniority to others younger than themselves. Third, men are more likely than women to have jobs that permit overtime work. This increases their incomes on average. And, fourth, women are more likely to work part-time.

Finally, discrimination toward women on the part of employees and institutions continues to be a highly significant barrier. Women are discriminated against in the hiring phase by being hired at a lower level of their expertise than an equally qualified man. An example would be a college-educated woman hired as a secretary in comparison to a college-educated man hired as a manager trainee. Moreover, women may be passed over for promotion a number of times in favor of a male who may better suit the traditional image of the business or occupation. Employers may feel that women are less stable employees and may be less willing to pay them higher wages even though the evidence is to the contrary (Baker et al. 1980).

Although laws have been passed to make such forms of discrimination illegal, they often are not rigorously enforced. In most cases, the woman must take the time and spend the money for a lawsuit before a company is forced to change informal practices of sex discrimination. Sex discrimination is also difficult to prove in court.

As women move into traditionally masculine jobs, they must also face potential resentment for upsetting the status quo or for contradicting accepted notions regarding gender-role stereotypes. For example, Martin (1980) found that male police officers in Washington, D.C., reacted with resentment and hostility to women entering patrol. The men feared they were in more physical danger either when working with a female partner or when a female officer responded as a backup to a crisis situation. Martin noted that the women were highly visible, much talked about, feared as competitors, and excluded from the informal social world so central to the police role. The women were pressured into feeling a sense of inferiority by a variety of verbal and nonverbal cues including the phrases used to describe them, the joking, gossip, traditional gender-role etiquette, and sexual harassment. Such negative male reactions acted as a barrier to full acceptance and cooperation and were perhaps the most serious problem faced by the female officers.

In her study of women at work in a large corporation, Kanter (1977) found that similar problems faced white-collar women. They were more likely to be perceived and treated as tokens rather than as coworkers. They stood out and were more noticed and judged for their physical appearance. In interacting with coworkers and clients, they felt themselves to be treated more like wives or dates rather than professionals. They were often excluded from the camaraderie of the work force. Research Method 8.1 offers more detail on Kanter's study.

Research Method 8.1

• • • • • • • Men and Women of the Corporation

The Use of Multiple Methods

At times the best approach to a project in sociology is to use several methods of research. Rosabeth Moss Kanter did just that in her detailed study of an American corporation. Kanter had several goals in her work. She wanted to take a long, close look inside a large corporation which often appears forbidding and mysterious to outsiders. She wanted to focus on two groups of workers who spend most of their lives in offices. One group was made up of professionals and managers including elite executives. "Far below them in status and class position," but close in physical proximity, were members of the second group: clerks, secretaries, data processors, and record keepers (Kanter 1977, 4). Kanter was especially concerned with women who were moving into management level jobs. How were their lives, their choices, and their behavior influenced by the roles imposed by the corporation? How did women "fit" into work roles previously acted out only by men? How were they treated and accepted by others?

In order to take this in-depth look, Kanter spent five years consulting for the corporation and conducting her research. Conforming to ethical principles in sociology, she never gave the real name of the company or of anybody in it. She listed ten sources of data for her study.

1. She designed a mail questionnaire for more than two hundred men in the sales force.
2. She interviewed the first twenty females to begin work in the sales force.
3. She used a survey of more than a hundred people on attitudes toward promotion in the company.
4. She conducted a content analysis of performance evaluations of clerical workers, mostly secretaries. She also interviewed bosses and secretaries in relation to the evaluations.
5. She recorded group discussions and meetings. One set of discussions was with twelve husbands and wives and took place over a two-day period.
6. She used participant observation in corporate meetings.
7. She also observed and participated in company training programs.
8. She studied a large set of company documents, booklets, annual reports, and newsletters.
9. She took part in many individual conversations among staff.

10. She relied on various individuals in the corporation with whom she grew especially close to act as informants; they helped Kanter understand the inner workings of the corporation.

Kanter argued that a combination of methods was the most valid way to get an understanding of the complex reality of the corporation. Results of each could be checked against the other for reliability and consistency (Kanter 1977, 293–97).

It would take too much space to review all of Kanter's results. Since much of Kanter's concern was with women in the corporation, we can review her results about secretaries and women in management.

The dominant feature of a secretary's work was that she was "office wife" for her boss. (All of the secretaries were female.) Not only was the secretary expected to do her clerical work, she was expected to keep the boss's office clean and to buy Christmas presents or birthday cards for his family. The secretary was judged as much by her physical appearance and dress as by her clerical skills. Her status in the corporation was determined by the rank of her boss. She was allowed to be more emotional than any of the men in the corporation, but she was expected to be extremely loyal to her boss. Attachments between secretary and boss were often strong; one secretary said leaving her job was like getting a divorce. Kanter noted that there were younger secretaries who refused to run personal errands and clean the office. However, Kanter characterized them as a new kind of wife, but still a wife. Most secretaries were rewarded for being relatively timid and nonassertive. They did not see themselves as highly skilled although many had trained several bosses. The secretaries tended to be "praise addicted," relying on substantial verbal approval from their bosses in order to feel that they were doing a good job (Kanter 1977, 89–97).

In contrast to the secretaries was the small number of executive women. The most dominant feature of their work world was that there were so few women; as a result, they stood out. They faced the loneliness of being different but had the advantage of being highly visible. The executive woman did not necessarily have to perform to have her presence noticed, but she did have to work hard to have her abilities and achievements noticed (Kanter 1977, 216). Performance pressures on her were great; at the same time, she also had to be loyal to her male peers and not outperform them too much or she could face greater isolation. In some cases she took on a role that was in keeping with traditional views of women. For example, some women took on the mother role. "Mother" would be a comforting and understanding listener to whom the men could take their problems. The "pet" was a mascot or cheerleader for the group; she would laugh with and admire the men from the sidelines. The "seductress" was sexually attractive and might seem available to the men; a man would often act as her protector. The "iron maiden" was considered tough and dangerous; she was isolated and not trusted. The iron maiden is a stereotypical role in which strong women are often placed (Kanter 1977, 233–36).

Kanter's book has become well known in sociology. Her careful, rigorous analyses based on multiple methods illustrate how much a sociologist can contribute toward understanding complex social environments. On the other hand, no one can be sure how representative this study is for other corporations, nor can anyone know exactly how much personal bias Kanter may have expressed in her work. Nevertheless, her book stands as a significant achievement in the study of the corporate work world and the entrance of women into that world.

Before we leave our discussion of sex stratification, it is important to recognize that considerable gains have been made by women. In just the past ten or fifteen years we have seen the first woman on the U.S. Supreme Court, the first female vice-presidential candidate, and the first American woman in space. In the past twenty-five years many laws have been passed that support equality for women including the Civil Rights Act in 1964, the 1974 Educational Amendments Act, and the 1978 Pregnancy Discrimination Act (Sapiro 1986). Nevertheless, the Equal Rights Amendment, which was designed specifically to prevent sex discrimination, was never passed. Today, few argue that opportunities for men and women are equivalent. It will be interesting to see, twenty years from now, what a sociologist will say was not possible for women in the 1990s.

The Aged in America

More than ever, the elderly make up a significant proportion of our society. The number of older people in our society has grown significantly and is expected to continue to grow. Table 8.5 shows the percentage of people aged 65 and over in America. Yet, considerable ambivalence exists toward aging and the elderly. There is little question that America is a youth-oriented society and that the elderly are often ignored or pushed aside in our modern, work-oriented, fast-paced society.

The most common age used to define one as elderly is 65. No clear-cut reason for this exists other than that it was socially defined as old age, and it became a convenient marker used by demographers and census takers. In Japan age 55 was used until recently (Barrow and Smith 1983). As shown in Table 8.5, more than one in ten Americans is 65 or older. In 1790, at the time of the first U.S. census, only two percent of the population was 65 or over. By the year 2000, it is projected that more than thirty million people, or close to fifteen percent of the population, will be in this age group. The percentage of the elderly in other industrialized societies is similar to or greater than that in the U.S. For example, West Germany and Sweden report fifteen percent of their populations in this age group while Japan and Canada report eight percent. These figures are in stark contrast to the relatively small percentage of elderly people in Third World nations. Mexico and India report three percent of their populations to be 65 or older (Atchley 1985, 20, 25).

●**Table 8.5**   The Percentage of People Aged 65 and Older
in the U.S. Population

Year	Percent 65 and Older
1930	5.4%
1940	6.8
1950	8.2
1960	9.2
1970	9.8
1980	11.3
1984	11.9
1987	12.2
2000 (Projected)	13.0

Source: U.S. Bureau of the Census. *Statistical Abstract of the United States, 1989.* Washington, D.C.: U.S. Government Printing Office, 1989.

The reasons for the increase in the proportion of the elderly in industrialized societies are quite clear. Most important, technology allowed control of infectious diseases through the use of clean water and sewage control. In addition, the control of localized famines was achieved through the establishment of fast transportation systems to distribute food. Finally, modern medicine introduced vaccines and antibiotics which also helped to control the diseases that could devastate large numbers of people—typhoid, plague, smallpox, cholera, and polio (Atchley 1985, 23). Life expectancy was thus increased. Moreover, as we will see in chapter 12, when populations industrialize, birth rates fall as children become an economic liability rather than an economic asset. Consequently, over time industrialized societies develop a population structure having a larger percentage of older people.

One of the problems in **gerontology**, which is the systematic study of the aged in society, is that chronological age is not always the most useful or accurate measure of age. In other words, aging is relative; it varies from person to person and from society to society. "Aging is not one process, but many," and it has both positive and negative outcomes (Atchley 1985, 5). The use of the age 65, then, is somewhat arbitrary in nature as a measurement for old age. For example, a football player is old at 35 or 40 while a U.S. senator is relatively young at 50. The male-female double standard applies here as well, because many people view a woman as old at 40 but a man is still considered relatively young at that age. Some individuals remain quite healthy and active into their 80s while others seem much older at 60. Still, chronological age continues to be viewed as important because it determines when one can receive Social Security and other financial benefits.

A Brief History of Aging in America

Western culture has always contained ambivalent attitudes toward the elderly, but at earlier times in American society the aged were given more status and respect. According to Fischer (1978), in our earliest colonial times the oldest male members of the communities sat in positions of high status and authority both politically and socially. Long life was interpreted as a sign of God's favor. In addition, because sons could not inherit wealth or the family farm until after the father's death, it was in the sons' best interests to respect the father. Significantly, the poor who were old and women, particularly indigent widows, did not fare as well as middle- and upper-class men. Class, race, and sex have always divided America.

One historian (Fischer 1978) characterized the period from 1780 to 1970 as one of growing **gerontophobia** (a fear and dislike of the aged). Negative terms for the elderly such as codger and geezer began to show up in the early 1800s. Many sociologists believe that modernization and industrialization brought an overall lowering of the prestige of old age. Industrial times brought a premium on younger, stronger workers, and young adults were less dependent on their parents for economic support. As mentioned at the beginning of this chapter, even in Japan, which has a long tradition of respect for age and a religion incorporating ancestor worship, a decline in the status of the elderly is apparent (Barrow and Smith 1983).

Through modernization, the twin variables of increasing length of life and decreasing need for the elderly in the labor force combined to help lower the overall position of the aged. Economically, they were worse off; socially, they were less respected.

By the Great Depression, conditions for the aged were quite bad, and people in America first became aware of a growing problem. The **Social Security Act of 1935** was the major governmental response to the problems of forced retirement, age discrimination, and poverty experienced by the elderly.

During the 1960s and early 1970s, greater government support came in various programs for social and economic aid. **Medicare**, which aids those 65 or over in paying medical bills, was instituted during this period. However, recent federal budget problems and resulting spending cuts have already begun to undermine these support programs for older Americans.

On a more optimistic note, Fischer (1978) suggested that this country may be moving into a period of better living conditions for the aged. This would echo the trend found in some other Western nations, particularly the Scandinavian countries. Denmark, Sweden, and Norway offer much more welfare assistance than the U.S. In Sweden, for example, full health care is available to the elderly at practically no cost, regardless of the length or type of illness, although many question whether the health care is up to the standards expected in America. Swedish citizens can choose to ease into retirement between the ages of 60 and 70. They can continue to work part-time if they choose. Free home-help services including nursing, cleaning, shopping, cooking, and even help in bathing are offered to the elderly. Many of these Scandinavian governments sponsor fitness programs and vacations at no cost as well. These programs allow the elderly greater independence, but they are paid for by taxes. However, even in Scandinavian countries, stereotypical, negative attitudes about the old are found among the young (Barrow and Smith 1983, 392–95).

Ageism

Prejudice and discrimination against the elderly are referred to as **ageism**. Ageism may take many forms in society, ranging from mandatory retirement laws to verbal slurs such as old fogeys, geezers, fossils, codgers, biddies, and old maids (Nuessel 1982, 274). Ageism "reflects a deep seated uneasiness on the part of the young and middle-aged—a personal revulsion to and distaste for growing old, disease, disability; and fear of powerlessness, 'uselessness,' and death" (Butler 1978, 43). It is important to note that ageism is not a direct result of the existence of the elderly. It is a complex form of discrimination affected by changing family patterns, technology, industrialization, rapid social change, and generational differences. Ageism is created and institutionalized by historical, cultural, and social forces; it is not created by the elderly or their behavior (Barrow and Smith 1983, 7).

Most societies develop **age norms** which indicate how people are required and allowed to act according to their age. Age norms are based loosely on what people are capable of doing at various ages and on what is assumed to be appropriate for them. The assumptions underlying age norms are often discriminatory. Older people may not be hired because it is assumed that they are less capable of being trained or are physically weak. Consequently, the older one becomes the narrower the range of options open to him or her (Atchley 1985). Much research shows, however, that individual differences among the elderly are great and that people's ability to learn as well as their strength are not determined only by age. Although age tends to result in a slowing of responses, it does not necessarily cause loss of knowledge or of the ability to learn (Meer 1986).

Ageist attitudes and stereotypes are related to age norms and are also an important factor in setting up additional hurdles for the aged. Particularly among adolescents and young people, stereotypes tend to emphasize the changing physical condition of the aged and include a wide range of negative images such as wrinkled, slow, helpless, dependent, sickly, thin, deformed, or having stooped shoulders and false teeth. While certain personality traits of the elderly are seen as positive, such as being kind and friendly, the most common negative feature associated with the aged is senility. Moreover, many people think of the aged as living in institutions for the old. These last two stereotypes are particularly damaging, and they are quite inaccurate. Less than five percent of the aged live in institutions and less than ten percent suffer from senility (Barrow and Smith 1983, 31–33, *Newsweek* 1989). Research Application 8.2 focuses on research that contradicts stereotypes about dating and romance among the elderly.

Research Application 8.2

· · · · · · · **Dating Among Elderly Singles**

Do people in their 70s fall in love and experience those same mysterious feelings people feel in their 20s? Do they find each other physically attractive? When they do get involved, what do elderly singles do on dates? In a recent study, Bulcroft and O'Conner-Roden (1986) examined these and other questions about aging and singlehood. The researchers suggested that many people in our society assume that romance and passion were not—or should not be—part of the lives of the elderly. People assume the elderly will only be interested in companionship, not sex and dating. The researchers also pointed out that the social situation of the elderly could actually promote dating. There are more people over age 65 than ever before in America, and they are healthier as well. Many are single as a result of divorce or widowhood, and retirement allows them more leisure time.

Bulcroft and O'Conner-Roden interviewed forty-five men and women ranging in age from 60 to 92. Each was widowed or divorced and had been dating for the previous year. One major drawback of the study was that most of the forty-five were middle class and all were white. The researchers asked the people how they met their dates, what they did on dates, and how significant romance and sexuality were in their relationships. They also asked about the reactions of family and friends.

Results of the study showed that age is mostly irrelevant when it comes to love. One 64-year-old woman said that people always search for the thing we call love. The respondents said that the dating relationship was extremely important in their lives. They tended not to be casual in dating like younger singles; they had little interest in playing the field. Dating to the elderly was a long-term commitment, and it was not considered just a friendship. They favored the direct, "no games" approach, and as a result their relationships did tend to progress more quickly than those of young people.

The feelings experienced by the elderly when they fell in love were quite like those experienced by a person of any age in America. These older daters talked of sweaty palms, racing hearts, a lack of concentration, and not wanting to be apart from the other. Romance for this group of elderly was defined much as young people define it. They enjoyed candlelit dinners and gifts of candy or flowers. Like younger males, the men in this study were more likely to link romance with sex.

What did the elderly do on dates? Again, it was much the same as what people of any age do on dates in this society, except their activities tended to be more varied. They went to movies, ate out, and danced. They also went camping or to the opera or, finances permitting, would even fly to Hawaii. Intimacy and sex were also important aspects of almost all of the relationships, but most felt they had to hide intimacy for fear of the disapproval of others. The researchers noted one difference, however, in that the older daters placed more value on touching and hugging than young people.

Finally, these older daters said that they had faced few problems with their families or friends in reaction to their dating. Family members, especially, were glad that their elder relative was happy, and the date was often accepted into family gatherings. Occasionally, friends would be jealous, but, for the most part, they were also supportive.

Interestingly, few of these older daters planned to marry. They said they had less incentive to marry, and many wanted to maintain some independence. Others were afraid of health deterioration and what that would do to the new relationship. Most were content with their situation.

Overall, then, results of Bulcroft's and O'Conner-Roden's study may help dispel the idea that dating and romance are in the past for the elderly. We should remember, though, that the study included only middle-class people. Situations may be very different for those who are poor, in ill health, or who are isolated and alone.

Special Problems Faced by the Elderly

In his textbook on aging, Atchley (1985) noted a number of role changes that face the elderly in society. These changes are shaped by the social contexts of growing old, age norms, and the life cycle. Three of the most significant of these role changes include retirement, widowhood, and dependency.

Retirement

Retirement is a relatively recent social invention because it is closely tied to the decreasing demand for labor in industrialized society and to the increase in life expectancy. Although the United States has abolished mandatory retirement ages, about eighty percent of men and ninety percent of women over age 65 in our society are not working in an occupation. They live on pensions, savings, and Social Security depending on the type of job held, the planning for retirement, and the economic standing prior to retirement.

Retirement inevitably brings many changes in life. After spending the majority of their lives in occupational settings, many find the adjustment to retirement a crisis regardless of how well they liked their jobs. Retirement requires a self-sufficiency that can be difficult to accept. It requires rearrangement in the lifestyles of married couples as well. Evidence shows that about one-third of those who retire find it a period of great difficulty and characterize it as "a world turned upside down" (Atchley 1985, 121). Our society tends to evaluate a person according to what one does. A retired person is often seen as no longer productive. Retired people often report financial problems, missing one's job and work associates, health problems, and more negative attitudes toward retirement (Barrow and Smith 1983, 149).

Our youth-oriented society frequently overlooks the contributions the elderly have made and continue to make to a society. Here a small child is learning from an elderly man and experiencing the warmth of a meaningful relationship.

Widowhood

Widowhood is the second social role change commonly found among the elderly. In fact, "There is probably no loss greater, no emotion more searing and numbing, than the death of a loved one," such as a husband or wife (Weeks 1984, 279). Because women, on the average, live longer than men, widowhood is more common among women; more than half of women over 65 are widows compared to less than twenty percent of the men. In addition, women appear to be better able to handle the grief and loneliness that come with widowhood. Women are allowed to express their emotions more so than men, and they may receive more social support from friends and relatives.

At first, the widow or widower feels shock and numbness followed by intense and acute grief. Denial, anger, guilt, and depression also make their assault on widowed individuals. They must contend with the loneliness and loss of sexual involvement. Research shows that they must eventually break with the past, readjust to a new environment, and form new relationships if they are to overcome their grief (Schulz 1978). With time and with the social support of friends and family, most of the widowed adjust to their new life situation.

Dependency

Dependency is the third social role change often faced by the aged. With the American emphasis on independence and individualism, being dependent on others for financial support or for physical needs as a result of illness can be humiliating and excruciatingly painful. To be dependent also means that you are expected to defer to those on whom you depend and to be ever grateful. Dependency means to be no longer in control of one's everyday life. Resentment and anger followed by guilt are often experienced by those older people who have to rely on their children, and it is just as difficult for their children who must rearrange lifestyles and finances to accommodate aging parents (Atchley 1985, 122). Certainly, not all of the elderly become dependent on their children; in fact, many may help their children financially.

Health Problems

Although major health problems are not an inevitable part of old age, the physical aging process takes its toll in a number of ways. Actually, eyesight and hearing begin to decline quite early, in the 30s and 40s. Various organs of the body no longer operate as efficiently as in youth, and it takes longer for the body to recover from illness or trauma. The body's immune system is not as effective. The skin wrinkles. The body tires more easily and quickly and becomes less erect, and the bones weaken. However, social and environmental factors play a role in this general deterioration process. Diet, smoking, lifestyle, and work environment can negatively affect health but can masquerade as the aging process (Barrow and Smith 1983).

The leading causes of death among people over age 65 are heart disease, cancer, strokes, and Alzheimer's disease. These are chronic conditions rather than acute illnesses such as pneumonia and influenza. Chronic diseases last over a period of time, have high medical costs, and signify dependency, as discussed earlier.

Of the four leading causes of death for the elderly, none is more complex than **Alzheimer's disease**, a degenerative brain disorder. Often thought of as senility or as the loss of memory and ability to function, Alzheimer's disease is at the moment incurable. Strokes, alcoholism, and other diseases also can bring on senility, but these are not related to Alzheimer's. The disease kills 120,000 in our society each year and severely afflicts about ten percent of those over 65; almost half of those over 85 have the disease. It is not at all accurate to assume that senility is inevitably associated with old age. Many elderly people remain intellectually and physically strong. Nevertheless, for those who suffer from Alzheimer's and for their families, the illness is devastating. Lasting anywhere from six to twenty years, the disease is portrayed as killing its victims twice. First, it kills the mind by destroying nerve cells and chemical transmitters in the brain so that eventually even the smallest task is impossible. The victim will not recognize members of the family or remember how to eat. Second, because of the brain degeneration, Alzheimer's slowly destroys the body (*Newsweek* 1984, 1989).

Consider the situation of one American family. Alzheimer's disease struck a 50-year-old mechanical engineer. Within two years this man who worked on the Atlas rocket project could not add three plus three. His wife must help him brush his teeth, shave, dress, and eat because he has forgotten how. His wife must also support the family economically. The man gets out of the house only twice a week; mostly he tinkers in his repair shop or just sits. His friends rarely come to see him, and his children find it terribly painful to see him degenerate. One family member said he would probably be better off dead. Many people with Alzheimer's end up in nursing homes which can be an economic burden; the cost averages $1,400 a month. Other alternatives are day-care centers or other places designed to care and treat those with Alzheimer's. Research may eventually find a cure or an effective treatment to slow the disease, but for now nearly two million people and their families suffer with little hope (Colt 1986).

Other health issues facing the elderly are accidents, arthritis, and diabetes. Also significant is the lack of adequate nutrition and medical care often a result of poverty. Depression is the primary mental disorder likely to be found among the aged. For elderly men, the suicide rate is four to seven times greater than the national suicide rate in the United States (Barrow and Smith 1983, 260, 240).

Obviously, health problems can be quite severe for some of the aged, but we should not overlook the larger number who are in good health and lead full, creative, and satisfying lives. Comedians George Burns and Bob Hope, photographer Barbara Morgan, and psychologist B.F. Skinner, all active into their 80s, remind us of the potential we have in old age.

Economic Problems

While the number of elderly who live in poverty has been reduced in recent years, finances remain a significant problem for the aged. Many live just above the poverty level and do not qualify for certain public assistance programs. Budget cuts have affected Medicare and other programs designed to help the aged. Social Security benefits may be curtailed when the Baby Boom generation reaches retirement simply because there will be so many people drawing funds. Even good financial planning for retirement could be undercut by periods of high inflation and economic recession. For example, if you worked during the 1960s, an income of $7,000 was considered a good one. However, if you planned your years of retirement to live on $7,000, you should today most likely fall below the poverty level.

Atchley (1985, 154) pointed out that more than half of elderly couples had incomes at a modest middle-class level or higher. Couples seem to be in better financial shape than unmarried older people. Many of the unmarried elderly are women who do not qualify for full Social Security benefits or for pension programs after the deaths of their husbands. Retired minority workers and women are more likely to be poor in old age. They are hurt by high rates of unemployment during prime years, lack of private pension plans, and lower-than-average wages when they did work. In fact, Black, Hispanic, and Native American elderly are more likely to face all of the problems we have discussed regarding aging. The general health situation of ethnic minorities is poorer than that of whites. Moreover, they are less likely to go to the doctor. They suffer more from infectious diseases associated with poverty and poor living conditions (Hendricks and Hendricks 1986, 374). See chapter 7 for a more complete discussion of problems faced by minorities.

The federal government's Social Security program will not meet all the needs of the aged. Experts warn people today not to look to Social Security income as enough to live on when they retire. Moreover, an even greater crisis will face the Social Security Administration, Medicare, and private pension and insurance plans in about thirty years when the large number of postwar Baby Boom workers begins to retire (Butler 1985).

Facing Death

All humans face death, yet young people find it much easier to ignore death; it seems very remote to them and they can avoid issues surrounding death. The aged see their friends and family die. As they enter their 70s, they know life will end soon. Although advances in medical care mean that, more than ever, a person can live a long life, the quality of life may not be improved and may actually decrease. This is a special problem if the person is bedridden or confined in a hospital or institution. Terminal illnesses can linger for years. For some of these patients and their families, death is seen finally as a blessing.

Because we live in a death-defying society, research on death was slow in coming. However, social scientists as well as those in the medical community recently have begun to systematically research the issues surrounding death and how to make dying easier for the patient and family. A pioneer in the field, Elizabeth Kubler-Ross (1969) found that the dying generally progressed through five stages. At first, the individuals engaged in **denial**. They refused to believe that they were truly dying. They wanted to pretend it was not happening. Second, after denial no longer sufficed, they felt tremendous **anger** at life and at the injustice of death, often venting the anger on those close to them. Third, they attempted **bargaining** with fate, the illness, or with religion. They would say that they would change their lives, become a better person if only they could live a while longer. Fourth, they often experienced a period of extreme **depression** after denial, anger, and bargaining proved unworkable. Finally, they came to an **acceptance** of death and gained a certain peace near the end. While recent research disputes the fact that everyone goes through these stages in an orderly manner, the major issues surrounding death are represented in these stages.

Dealing with death directly and openly allows both the patient and the family to express their fears and anger. Openness allows the dying person to get his or her personal affairs in order. Family members and friends have a chance to express their feelings and to slowly adjust.

The **hospice movement** which began in England and slowly spread to this country is evidence of increased concern for the social and emotional environment of dying patients. Americans began to realize that hospitals were not the best environment for someone with a terminal illness. Most people say they prefer to die at home, but less than ten percent do (Barrow and Smith 1983, 366). Death is hidden in traditional hospitals and represents failure. The hospice approach, on the other hand, promotes openness. Specially trained hospice workers visit the home regularly and provide support, advice, medical care, and encourage open discussion about death. Physical pain is minimized in any way possible through hospice care. After the physical pain is controlled, then emotional pain can be dealt with more easily. Hospice care is designed to be warm and personal.

Such trends indicate that American society is paying more attention to conditions of the elderly. However, we have not yet reached the level of care and concern found in some other countries.

· · · · · · · · · · · · · · · · · · · Questions for Summary and Review

1. Explain the historical traditions regarding sex roles in Western culture.
2. Distinguish sex role, gender role, and sexism. Give examples of each.
3. Explain how the socialization process reinforces sex stratification in society.
4. Describe and explain income inequality between the sexes.

5. What are the reasons for an increase in the proportion of the elderly in modern society?
6. Discuss and gives examples of ageism in society.
7. List and discuss the special problems faced by the elderly in modern society.

·························· **Key Concepts**

Acceptance (p. 188)
Ageism (p. 182)
Age norms (p. 182)
Alzheimer's Disease (p. 186)
Androgyny (p. 173)
Anger (p. 188)
Bargaining (p. 188)
Cult of true womanhood (p. 169)
Denial (p. 188)
Depression (p. 188)

The feminine mystique (p. 169)
Gender roles (p. 170)
Gerontology (p. 181)
Gerontophobia (p. 181)
Hospice movement (p. 188)
Medicare (p. 182)
Sexism (p. 170)
Sex roles (p. 170)
Sex stratification (p. 171)
Social Security Act of 1935 (p. 182)

References

1. Atchley, Robert C. 1985. *Social forces and aging.* Belmont, Calif.: Wadsworth.

2. Baker, M. A., C. Berheide, F. Greckel, L. Gugin, M. Lipetz, and M. Segal. 1980. *Women today: A multidisciplinary approach to women's studies.* Monterey, Calif.: Brooks/Cole.

3. Barrow, George M., and Patricia A. Smith. 1983. *Aging, the individual, and society.* 2d ed. St. Paul: West Publishing Company.

4. Bem, Sandra L. 1974. The measurement of psychological androgyny. *Journal of consulting and clinical psychology* 42:155–62.

5. _____. 1979. Theory and measurement of androgyny: A reply to the Pedhazur-Tetenbaum and Locksley-Colten critiques. *Journal of personality and social psychology* 37:1047–54.

6. Bogue, Donald J. 1985. *The population of the United States: Historical trends and future projections.* New York: Free Press.

7. Brooks-Gunn, Jeanne, and Wendy S. Matthews. 1979. *He and she: How children develop their sex-role identity.* Englewood Cliffs: N.J. Prentice-Hall.

8. Bulcroft, Kris, and Margaret O'Conner-Roden. 1986. Never too late. *Psychology today* (June) 20:66–69.

9. Butler, Robert N. 1978. Age-ism: Another form of bigotry, In *Social problems of the aging: Readings,* edited by M. Seltzer, S. Corbett, and R. Atchley, 42–51. Belmont, Calif.: Wadsworth.

10. _____. 1985. A generation at risk: When the Baby Boomers reach Golden Pond. In *Social problems 85/86,* edited by L. W. Barnes, 138–44. Guilford, Conn.: Dushkin.

11. Chafetz, Janet Saltzman. 1978. *Masculine, feminine or human? An overview of the sociology of gender roles.* 2d ed. Itasca, Ill.: F. E. Peacock.

12. Chalfant, H. Paul, Robert E. Beckley, and C. Eddie Palmer. 1987. *Religion in contemporary society.* 2d ed. Palo Alto, Calif.: Mayfield.

13. Colt, George Howe. 1986. The fading mind. *Life magazine,* (February):31–38.

14. David, Deborah, and Robert Brannon. 1976. *The forty–nine percent majority: The male sex role.* Reading, Mass.: Addison-Wesley.

15. Doyle, James A. 1989. *The male experience.* 2d ed. Dubuque, Iowa: William C. Brown.

16. Farrell, Warren. 1986. *Why men are the way they are.* New York: McGraw-Hill.

17. Friedan, Betty. 1983. *The feminine mystique.* New York: Dell.

18. Fischer, David H. 1978. *Growing old in America.* Expanded ed. New York: Oxford University Press.

19. Hendricks, Jon, and C. Davis Hendricks. 1986. *Aging in mass society: Myths and realities.* 3d ed. Boston: Little, Brown and Company.

20. Henslin, James M. 1990. *Social problems.* 2d ed. Englewood Cliffs, N.J.: Prentice-Hall.

21. Kanter, Rosabeth Moss. 1977. *Men and women of the corporation.* New York: Basic Books.

22. Kitto, H. D. F. 1957. *The Greeks.* New York: Penguin Books.

23. Kubler-Ross, Elizabeth. 1969. *On death and dying.* New York: Macmillan.

24. Lever, Janet. 1976. Sex differences in the games children play. *Social problems* 23:478–87.

25. Martin, Susan E. 1980. *Breaking and entering: Policewomen on patrol.* Berkeley, Calif.: University of California Press.

26. Meer, Jeff. 1986. The reason of age. *Psychology today* (June) 20:60–64.

27. *Newsweek.* 1984. A slow death of the mind. (December 3).

28. _____ . 1989. The brain killer. (December 18).

29. Nuessel, Frank H., Jr. 1982. The language of ageism. *The gerontologist* 22:273–76.

30. O'Kelly, Charlotte G. 1980. *Women and men in society.* New York: D. Van Nostrand.

31. Pleck, Joseph. 1976. My male sex role— and ours. In *The forty-nine percent majority: The male sex role,* edited by Deborah David and Robert Brannon, 253–64. Reading, Mass.: Addison-Wesley.

32. Richardson, Laurel. 1981. *The dynamics of sex and gender: A sociological approach.* Boston: Houghton Mifflin Company.

33. _____ . 1986. Another world. *Psychology today* (February):22–27.

34. _____ . 1988. Secrecy and status: The social construction of forbidden relationships. *American sociological review* 53:209–19.

35. Sapiro, Virginia. 1986. *Women in American society: An introduction to women's studies.* Palo Alto, Calif.: Mayfield.

36. Seavey. C. A., P. A. Katz, and S. R. Zalk. 1975. Baby X: The effect of gender role labels on adult responses to infants. *Sex roles* 1:103–9.

37. Schulz, Richard. 1978. *The psychology of death, dying and bereavement.* Reading, Mass.: Addison-Wesley.

38. Tasker, Peter. 1988. *The Japanese: A major exploration of modern Japan.* New York: Truman Talley Books.

39. Weeks, John R. 1984. *Aging: Concepts and social issues.* Belmont, Calif.: Wadsworth.

40. Welter, Barbara. 1978. The cult of true womanhood: 1820–1860. In *The American family in social-historical perspective,* 2d ed. edited by Michael Gordon, 313–33. New York: St. Martins.

41. U.S. Bureau of the Census. 1989. *Money income and poverty status in the United States: 1988.* Current Population Reports, Series P-60, No. 166, Advance Data from the March 1989 Current Population Survey. Washington, D.C.: U.S. Government Printing Office.

42. _____ . 1989. *Statistical abstract of the United States, 1989.* 109th ed. Washington, D.C.: U.S. Government Printing Office.

43. Whitehurst, Carol A. 1977. *Women in America: The oppressed majority.* Santa Monica, Calif.: Goodyear.

Section 3

Understanding Disorder in Social Life

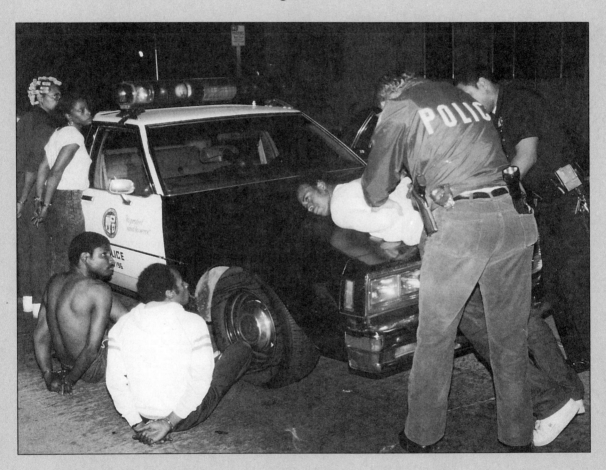

9 Understanding Crime and Deviance

• • • • • • • • • • •

Chapter Outline

Defining Deviance

The Relativity of Deviance

   The Relevance of Audience

   The Relevance of Time

   The Relevance of Social Status

   The Relevance of Situation

The Negative and Positive Functions of Deviance

Deviance and Social Control

Sociological Explanations of Deviance

   Anomie Theory

• Research Application 9.1 Academic Cheating on College Campuses

   Differential Association Theory

   Social Bond Theory

   Labeling Theory

   Conflict Theory

   Evaluating Sociological Theories

Major Types of Deviant Behavior

• Research Application 9.2 The National Crime Survey: What are Your Chances of Being a Victim?

   Violent Crime

     Murder and Aggravated Assault
     Sexual Assault

• Research Method 9.1 Nationwide Questionnaire: Date Rape on College Campuses

   Property Crimes

   White-Collar Crime

   Organized Crime

   Crimes Without Victims

   Mental Illness

Questions for Summary and Review

Key Concepts

References

•

> Picture a country where you never need to count your change; where the streets are free of litter, the walls free of graffiti; where no one feels compelled to vandalize public telephones; where people visit sports grounds not to engage in tribal warfare but to cheer good play; where there are no muggings ..., no recreational brawls on Saturday nights; where police are affable and courteous, and the pistols they carry are only fired a couple of times a year by the entire force (Tasker 1988, 71).

The above quote is a description of modern Japan, which has one of the lowest rates of crime in the modern world. There are fewer robberies in a year in Japan than in forty-eight hours in the United States even though the U.S. has just twice the population of Japan. There are fewer reported rapes in a year in Japan than in a week in the U.S. The Japanese, city and country dwellers alike, can leave their cars unlocked and carry around large amounts of cash with little worry of burglary or robbery. Japanese arrest rates are among the highest in the world, and ninety-nine percent of those arrested are found guilty (Tasker 1988, 71).

On the other hand, tax evasion, electoral fraud, and bribery of public officials are very common and rarely prosecuted in Japan. Large organized crime syndicates, called *yakuza*, make huge profits controlling pornography, prostitution, and loan-sharking (Tasker 1988, 74–79).

Emile Durkheim pointed out that deviance is normal; various forms of it occur everywhere. However, societies may differ dramatically in what they define as deviant or criminal and how they respond to it, including the amount of tolerance regarding certain behaviors. For example, the Japanese tolerate explicit pornography more than do many in the U.S. where pornography remains controversial. Societies also differ in the kinds of deviance they produce, as can be seen in the contrast of crime in Japan and the United States.

Sociologists remain intrigued with questions about deviance. Why does society single out certain behaviors as deviant, and how does that perception change over time? Why do some people defy the norms of their group, community, or society?

Defining Deviance

In the broadest sense, **deviance** means not conforming to predominant norms. It refers to behavior that violates the folkways and mores of a particular group or society. Deviance does not have to be negative. For example, if the norm of a group is moderate drinking on weekends, then the member who never drinks is deviating from the norm. Such deviance is often referred to as positive deviance.

All people violate norms. It is difficult to conveniently separate out a number of people in a society and call them deviant. However, society focuses more attention on deviance that is defined as negative, threatening, or immoral. For example, in describing deviants, sociologist Erving Goffman (1963, 144) wrote that they are:

> . . . the folk who are considered to be engaged in some kind of collective denial of the social order. They are perceived as failing to use available opportunity for advancement in the various approved runways of society; they show open disrespect for their betters; they lack piety; they represent failures in the motivational scheme of society.

Some people have more power and influence in determining what is considered deviant. Conflict theory in sociology assumes that judges, community leaders, religious leaders, leaders in the mass media, and politicians have more social power to define deviance.

Deviance encompasses a huge range of behavior. Perhaps the most significant type of deviant behavior is **crime**, behavior that violates laws. Yet even criminal behavior ranges from minor theft to first-degree murder. The study of deviance also encompasses much behavior that is not criminal. For example, it includes the study of mental illness and alcoholism, neither of which is strictly against the law.

A wealth of research exists in the study of deviance, and it illustrates the varieties of behaviors defined as deviant in our society. Sociologists have studied impersonal homosexual encounters in public restrooms (Humphreys 1970), pool hustlers (Polsky 1967), behavior in mental institutions (Goffman 1961), and adultery (Richardson 1988). Much of our discussion in this chapter will refer to crime, but you must remember that deviance encompasses far more than just serious crime.

The Relativity of Deviance

There are no absolutes in any sociological discussion of deviance. An important theoretical point of view in the study of deviance is known as labeling theory. This theory, particularly as developed by Edwin Lemert (1951) and Howard Becker (1963), states that no act or behavior is automatically deviant. The audience, time period, social status of those involved, and situation all influence whether an act is defined as deviant and how serious it is considered to be. The following sections discuss these four aspects of the relativity of deviance.

The Relevance of Audience

One of the important elements in the relativity of deviance concerns the audience. An audience includes anyone who witnessed the act or was aware of the act. Audiences may be strangers on the street, a family, a jury, a group of neighbors, or the public in general. Different audiences, particularly different subcultural groups, vary in their definitions of deviant behavior. Quite simply, the judgment of what is good or bad depends on those who observe and evaluate the act.

For example, in a newspaper account (*USA Today* 1985) of an incident in California, a Japanese immigrant attempted to commit a parent-child suicide, known in Japanese as *oyako shinju*. The woman walked into the sea with her two small children. The children drowned but the mother survived. In Japan, where this occurs about three hundred times a year, a parent surviving such an attempt would rarely be prosecuted, but in California the woman was charged with first-degree murder and could face the death penalty. The authorities in Santa Monica were deluged with calls and letters, mostly from the Japanese-American community, asking them to reconsider the charges and take into account the woman's cultural background. The judge eventually found her guilty but gave her probation and required her to undergo therapy.

This example requires us to remember that many different cultural groups live in the United States. These groups have potentially conflicting norms about what is and is not a serious violation, even regarding killing people.

The Relevance of Time

Another fundamental aspect of any definition of deviance is time period. Normative expectations change over time. Even in a short span of ten or twenty years, the standards and expectations of conduct can vary substantially in a modern, industrial society. For example, in the past ten years, certain groups including Mothers Against Drunk Drivers and Students Against Drunk Drivers have been relatively successful in redefining drunken driving as more serious than in the past. Similarly, cigarette smoking is now perceived as a much more serious and offensive behavior. Most public buildings such as courthouses and hospitals no longer allow smoking.

The definition of homosexuality as deviant has varied in degree over time (and certainly with regard to audience). For example, in the 1950s few people dared to openly admit to homosexual behavior. In the 1960s and 1970s, much more openness about homosexuality was observed, and the Gay Rights Movement became somewhat effective in reducing legal and social discrimination against homosexuals. The tragic disease, AIDS, triggered a near hysterical negative backlash against gays in the early 1980s, and homophobia—the fear and dislike of gays—increased. However, a recent national poll indicated that public attitudes are much more tolerant today. Most of those surveyed felt that gays should have equal job opportunities, and nearly half felt that homosexual relations between consenting adults should be legal. As one gay activist stated, "The world has been genuinely transformed in two decades" (*Newsweek* 1990, 21).

The Relevance of Social Status

Actors also will be perceived differently according to their social characteristics. Generally, higher status individuals are less likely to be labeled deviant or receive harsh reaction than are lower status individuals. The dress, manner, occupation, social influence, demeanor, and family background of an individual are important factors in whether or not the individual's actions will be labeled deviant.

William Chambliss (1973) made these points effectively in his article, "The Saints and the Roughnecks." Chambliss described the deviant activities of two groups of high school boys. The Saints were boys of good backgrounds from high-status families who were popular, well-known, and well-liked. The Saints committed many delinquent acts but were able to cover their tracks and were not perceived by others as deviant. Instead of simply skipping class, they developed elaborate con games to get teachers to excuse them from class. When one Saint said he had to be at a drama club rehearsal, he was believed because, after all, he was a good kid from a good family and the teacher did not expect him to lie. Although the Saints were actually involved in a wide variety of delinquent acts including truancy, drunk driving, serious vandalism, and malicious mischief, they were never arrested by the police or even perceived in any way as delinquent.

In contrast, the Roughnecks were a group of boys from working-class families who were not so well-dressed and not so well-liked, according to Chambliss. Partly because of their manner of dress, demeanor, and family background, teachers, police, and the community regarded them as troublemakers. They were not as outwardly respectful toward authority as were the Saints. People saw the Roughnecks fighting among themselves, shoplifting from the corner store, and skipping school. In comparison with the Saints' acts, the Roughnecks' acts were more visible to the community. They had fewer resources to camouflage their deviant acts. The Saints had cars and could travel to other towns to cause trouble, while the Roughnecks usually hung out on the street corner.

Chambliss indicated that the Saints committed more law-violating acts than the Roughnecks. Nevertheless, the Roughnecks were arrested a number of times. They did not do well in school, and the teachers labeled them difficult or troublesome students. In contrast, the Saints were seen by the teachers as good students despite their sometimes inferior schoolwork.

Chambliss's research documents the importance of social background, clothes, demeanor, reputation, and expectations—all related to social status—in defining a person's actions as deviant. Defense attorneys have long capitalized on the jury's expectations of what a criminal looks like by making every effort to get their clients to present their best demeanor before the jury by dressing in their nicest clothes and wearing conservative hairstyles.

A more recent example of how deviance is related to social status occurred in Forth Worth, Texas. A group of ten high school boys was responsible for pipe-bombing a student's car, shooting six bullets through the front window of a home, smashing out a car windshield, carrying weapons to school, and draping a mutilated cat over a student's steering wheel. The boys had about thirty weapons including ".357 Magnums, .45s, .38s, 10-, 20-gauge shotguns, deer rifles, an HK-91 semiautomatic British assault rifle, on which they had filed down the pin to make it automatic, and for tradition, a crossbow" (Breskin 1985, 70). They made pipe bombs and a rocket launcher. Apparently they had been responsible for a considerable amount of racist graffiti through which they proclaimed that they worshiped Hitler and would rid their school of scum.

By most accounts, the group of boys would be considered a dangerous juvenile gang, but they did not fit the stereotypical image of an inner-city juvenile gang. "They were well-off, from families comfortably middle-class to flat-out rich: their fathers were doctors and lawyers and bankers and ministers, their mothers given to the PTA . . ." (Breskin 1985, 68). They were excellent students as well as members of the football team; they had been appointed by the principal as hall monitors. One of the students was to be pictured in the yearbook as most outstanding senior male. The boys had formed a vigilante group naming themselves the Legion of Doom. Their victims were less well-off; some were minorities. The Legion of Doom members claimed their goal was to rid their high school of drug pushers, dopers, and thieves. The Legion members despised marijuana users but were themselves heavy drinkers (*Dallas Times Herald* 1985).

A storm of controversy was generated when the group was discovered. They made national news. Many students and community leaders defended the group, saying that they agreed with the Legion's goals but not with their methods. The penalties for the boys were light—weekend jail, probation, and community service. Their backgrounds, school achievements, and family influence contributed to defining the situation not as one of gang violence but as one of understandable pranks that got out of control. Many people could see no point in severely punishing these young men and ruining promising futures.

The Relevance of Situation

Often the situational context of the act is as important as the act itself in determining whether or not the act will be defined as deviant. For example, in recent years several women have killed their husbands who had seriously beaten them. In some cases, the abuse occurred over a period of years. Some juries have either found such women innocent or given them very light sentences because the women claimed they were acting in self-defense. Other juries have been unwilling to accept the self-defense argument and have given such women life sentences. In each case, the act was the same: a wife killed an abusive husband. The situations leading to the killings, however, were defined in a number of different ways. The definition of a particular situation, in turn, determined how people labeled the individuals involved. The situational context as well as the time period, the particular audience, and the social status of those involved strongly influence the definition of an act as deviant and how seriously the act will be viewed.

The Negative and Positive Functions of Deviance

Most people are accustomed to thinking of crime and deviance as indications of a sickness in society. Certainly deviance can have a negative impact. Crime, for example, undermines our sense of safety and trust. The terror of crime immobilizes people in all too many neighborhoods in the United States. We realize that anyone could be violently attacked or have his or her property stolen. Consequently, deviance can reduce the sense of security and community in society. Another negative impact is that crime and deviance cost us enormously in taxes to pay for police, courts, and prisons. These are the **negative functions of deviance**.

However, Emile Durkheim (1982/1895) encouraged us to see the **positive functions of deviance** for society. He observed that crime provides a dramatic opportunity for the society to collectively express moral outrage at the deviant which, in turn, can increase the cohesiveness of the group and its devotion to important norms. Also, the trial and punishment of a criminal serves to clearly publicize the important norms of the society.

Durkheim also suggested that criminal or deviant behavior can serve to bring about needed social change in a society by challenging unjust or outdated laws. For example, Martin Luther King intentionally violated many laws in order to bring attention to what he believed was the unjust nature of these laws. As a result of his actions and the actions of many others like him, the United States was forced to bring about more legal and social justice for blacks and to abolish the segregationist Jim Crow laws of the South.

Deviance and Social Control

Any discussion of deviant behavior inevitably brings about a discussion of societal attempts to control such behavior. Generally sociologists recognize three main types of social control.

First and most important, society attempts to control its members through the socialization process (discussed in chapter 4). In this process, individuals are taught what is proper according to their society so that they internalize these beliefs; they control their own behavior. Through **internalization** individuals become essentially self-governing. Internalized societal norms and beliefs are ingrained in a person; they become second nature. A cross-cultural example can help make this clear.

In parts of India and the Middle East it is not at all acceptable to serve food or to eat with the left hand. The left hand is reserved for bathroom functions. Americans in Pakistan rarely realize this and may very well put something to their mouths with the left hand. The revulsion felt by an Indian is real even if he or she knows that the norm is not known in America. Similarly, an American traveling in Pakistan may feel an equivalent amount of revulsion when seeing people urinate by the side of the road.

On one level, we can realize that people have different ways of life, but the strong feelings we experience when we see our norms violated indicate the strength of internalization. However, internalization of norms is not so perfect that an individual will not violate norms at some point in life. People are not so "oversocialized" that individual choice is completely overruled (Wrong 1961).

A second type of social control is termed **informal social control**. In this type, individuals are controlled by the groups to which they belong and by the reactions of others to their perceived deviant behavior. Groups use ridicule, hostility, ostra-

Participants in the fourteenth annual Lesbian and Gay Pride parade march along Fifth Avenue in New York.

cism, the proverbial cold shoulder, raised eyebrows, and other informal actions to keep group members in line.

Even among strangers, people fear social embarrassment. For example, when someone slips and falls while walking on an icy sidewalk, unless the physical injury is serious, the victim's first concern is whether anyone saw the slip, causing the social pain of embarrassment. Most of us have been ridiculed by others because we have violated the norms of the group, whether intentionally or not. The desire to avoid social pain is a powerful motivation for conformity.

The last type of social control is termed **formal social control**. In this case, society sets up a system of laws and attempts to induce conformity through the threat of institutionalized punishment. The threat of being caught by the police, of being publicly tried and convicted, of paying a fine, of going to prison, or of being put to death is the deterrent used in formal control efforts. The inducement to conformity is the fear of being officially punished.

While formal controls are effective in some circumstances, it is apparent that, in the United States, formal controls are the least effective deterrent to crime and deviance. Although they are not ineffective, formal controls are not as effective as internalized and informal controls. For example, most law violators do not believe that they will be caught, and some evidence, as we shall see later in this chapter, indicates they are right.

Sociological Explanations of Deviance

Over the years, sociologists have offered a number of explanations for deviant and criminal behavior. Some have concentrated on large-scale societal conditions and problems. Others have taken the opposite approach, focusing more on the individual and his or her immediate social environment and interactions with others. All of the sociological theories of crime and deviance have in common an emphasis on social forces and conditions as opposed to psychological or biological factors.

Psychological approaches typically emphasize mental or emotional states such as weak superegos or character disorders. Biological approaches have considered physiological disorders, brain chemistry, or genetic makeup as explanations for crime. However, sociologists have made considerable efforts in both theory and research regarding deviance. We will review four of the most important groups of sociological theories regarding deviant behavior in order to give you some understanding of how sociologists explain deviance.

Anomie Theory

Robert Merton (1967) developed an important sociological theory based on the concept of anomie. In his theory, **anomie** refers to a societal condition where some people are blocked from achieving the standard of success. Success is usually expressed by material possessions such as cars, houses, clothes, stereos, and other things. The proper means to achieve such things would be getting an education and a good job. However, not everyone in society can attain success. Chapter 6 on social stratification indicated that most Americans do not have high-status occupations and others cannot afford higher education. Similarly, not all students can make A's in college. In fact, the structure of the college system makes it impossible. Very few instructors could give all A's without suffering some negative reaction from the college's administrators. Consequently, a blockage to success is built into the educational system just as it is built into society.

In addition to blocked success, Merton said that too much emphasis on success without a corresponding emphasis on the proper means to achieve success is a cause of anomie. For example, American society may indeed put more emphasis on winning in sports than on the spirit of fair play, or more emphasis on grades than on the process of learning. Cheating in sports and cheating in the classroom are common results of this overemphasis on goals. Research Application 9.1 contains additional information about academic cheating.

Research Application 9.1

· · · · · · · Academic Cheating on College Campuses

Cheating on campus is in many ways a microcosm for the study of deviance in our society. It allows us to examine how the forms of social control operate and to examine some of the theories found in the study of deviance. Instead of asking, "What causes someone to steal?" you might ask your friend what caused him or her to cheat—or, you might ask yourself.

Various studies of student cheating in college, conducted both recently and in the past, indicate that a considerable amount of cheating does occur. Most of the recent studies found that about half or more of the students have cheated in some way during college (Haines et al. 1986a, 1986b; Singhal 1982; Baird 1980). In the most recent study of cheating, two researchers found that eighty-six percent of six hundred students surveyed at a large state university had cheated on exams, papers, or homework (Michaels and Miethe 1989, 876). Some researchers have suggested that student cheating is actually "epidemic" on campuses (Baird 1980).

As with all forms of deviance, part of the problem lies with how the behavior is defined. Students seem vague about their definition of cheating. For example, some say that looking on someone else's paper during an exam is cheating, but letting someone look on your paper is not. Stealing an exam is usually considered cheating, but often the use of old exams, stolen or not, is not perceived as cheating. Faculty and students also differ in their conceptions of what constitutes cheating. Since faculty and the administration hold more power, it is likely that they give the official definition of cheating, if one is given at all. Often, however, the teachers and the administration do not directly address the issue of cheating, allowing the vagueness of definition to continue.

A student cheater can be viewed as the classic example of Merton's deviant innovator, someone who will cheat or steal to get ahead. It appears that some students today are much more concerned with grades and the diploma than with the process of learning and acquiring academic skills. Michaels and Miethe (1989) found that pressure from parents to improve grades was an important motivation in cheating.

Regarding the three types of social control, much of the evidence indicates that informal controls—students sanctioning other students for cheating—are not at work with regard to cheating. In one study, fewer than ten percent of the students indicated that they would report other students for cheating (Haines et al. 1986a). Students as a group did not show much disapproval of other students for cheating; most said they ignored it. Furthermore, in some student groups cheating was actually encouraged. Formal controls also did not appear to be at work; the majority of those who admitted cheating said they were not caught. That leaves internalized control as the only source of control regarding cheating, and it does apparently operate to some extent for those who did not cheat.

If asked, most students will say that cheating in general is wrong, but many students will violate the standards they endorse. One sociological theory not discussed elsewhere in this chapter addresses this situation.

Sociologists Gresham Sykes and David Matza (1957) noted that those who violate norms often construct rationalizations or neutralizations both before and after the act, helping ease the guilt they experience for violating internalized beliefs. Sykes and Matza discussed five typical **neutralizations,** or justifications, used by people who committed deviant acts. Three clearly apply to cheating students. For example, a student might say that cheating in general is wrong, but in his or her particular case there was a legitimate reason for cheating. In the Haines study, a number of students attempted to justify their cheating by noting that the semester had been especially difficult or that he or she had been sick. Others argued that the school required too much work for any student to handle. Some students complained of being overloaded with both a job and classes. This neutralization is called **denial of responsibility.** The person violating the norm is saying, "It's not my fault."

Another technique of neutralization is called **condemnation of the condemners.** In this rationalization, the cheating student typically blamed the boring teacher, the uncaring teacher, the teacher who left the room during an exam, or the teacher "out to get students" as the reason for cheating. The teacher, or some other person likely to condemn the cheater, becomes the excuse for the cheater. The deviant tries to justify his or her actions by saying that those in authority positions are not respectable and are in some way responsible for the deviant behavior. Again, it is a way of saying, "It's not my fault."

A third type of neutralization, the **appeal to higher loyalties,** involves a conflict between what is expected officially and what is expected from friends. The friends become the higher loyalty regarding standards of cheating. A student might say, "I couldn't let my friend down; I had to help him in algebra." Members of sororities and fraternities may experience a sense of obligation to help fellow members. This becomes a higher loyalty.

Two other neutralizations listed by Sykes and Matza were not used by students in the Haines research on cheating. **Denial of the victim** occurs when an individual assaults or harms another person but claims that the person deserved it. For example, "He hurt my family, and now he has to pay." The last neutralization, **denial of harm,** means that no one was hurt even though the law was broken. For example, if someone smokes marijuana, he or she can claim that no one else is involved or is harmed. Apparently, cheating students didn't use this neutralization because it never occurs to them that harm could come from cheating.

Thus, cheating can be analyzed as a form of deviance like any other using sociological theories and concepts. In fact, studying cheating may be especially important today. Cheating occurs in a wide variety of contexts from income-tax preparation to corporate decisions to lie a little or to misrepresent something. "Across organizational settings, cheating has become a widely accepted means of achieving institutional rewards" (Michaels and Miethe 1989, 883). If cheating and other shortcuts to success are allowed to continue and grow, the organization or business will suffer along with the people they serve.

Merton outlined four types of deviant responses to this condition of anomie. Table 9.1 shows Merton's scheme. The first deviant adaptation to success blocked through legitimate means is **innovation**. The innovator wants the culturally approved goal, success, but uses deviant means to achieve it. The innovator steals or cheats to get money and success.

As mentioned above, if too much emphasis is put on grades and the diploma without the corresponding emphasis on achieving grades properly, college students who are not doing well might cheat to get better grades. In an anonymous survey of cheating in one of the author's classes, one student stated, "I plagiarized an English paper; the author said it exactly the way I wanted to say it. In America we are taught that results aren't achieved through beneficial means but through the easiest means." Another student wrote, "I cheated in college on a chemistry final that was comprehensive; my scholarship and grant were riding on my passing the class." Each is an example of deviant methods used to acquire socially prescribed goals.

The second deviant adaptation, **retreatism**, occurs when individuals simply give up any hope of achieving the goals set by society. Retreatists feel that they cannot make it. Many students who drop out of school have given up hope of reaching graduation. They have retreated. People can retreat into alcoholism and

● **Table 9.1** Merton's Deviant Modes of Adaptation to Anomie

Deviant Adaptation	Approved Goals	Approved Means
Innovation	Accepts	Rejects
Retreatism	Rejects	Rejects
Rebellion	Rejects and substitutes new goals	Rejects and substitutes new means
Ritualism	Rejects	Accepts

Source: Adapted from Robert K. Merton. *Social Theory and Social Structure*. New York: Free Press, 1967.

drug addiction; they can retreat into skid-row. Others choose alternative lifestyles far away from mainstream society. Perhaps the ultimate type of retreatism is suicide.

The third deviant adaptation, **rebellion**, occurs when individuals want to change the structure of society by challenging the system. Rebels want to institute new societal goals and new means for achieving them. For example, revolutionaries often violate laws in an attempt to institute a different political system. As noted in an earlier example, Martin Luther King intentionally violated laws in order to bring about social change.

Merton's last deviant adaptation, **ritualism**, occurs when an individual has lost sight of the goals altogether and becomes obsessed with doing things the right way. Although this may not seem deviant to us, imagine a college football coach who continually loses every game but does not seem disturbed by losing as long as the team acts properly, according to the rules. Many people get exasperated with such an individual.

Imagine working for a boss who knows he or she will never advance but insists that everything must be done properly and exactly according to the rules. The boss makes no exceptions and is obsessed with things being done properly even if it makes no sense to do so. The ritualist sees conformity as paramount. He or she has lost sight of what such conformity is supposed to bring in terms of success. In fact, conformity to the rules has become the goal of the ritualist. Conformity becomes its own reward.

Merton's theory has been criticized for several reasons. First, he assumes large-scale agreement on the goals and means in society; this assumption tends to overlook diversity and heterogeneity in modern society. Second, his theory does not tell us why people choose one particular form of deviant adaptation. Why do some become innovators and others become retreatists? Finally, Merton points out that most of us conform most of the time, even though a sizable number of us will not achieve the ideal of success; however, he does not explain how this happens. In any case, Merton's purpose was to illustrate how the structure of society can induce deviant behavior. By taking this societal approach, he showed less interest in the actions of individuals.

Differential Association Theory

Taking a different approach from Merton, Edwin Sutherland developed the **theory of differential association**. This theory focuses attention on the process of learning norms, values, motivations, techniques, and rationalizations that encourage deviance.

Sutherland and his colleague, Donald Cressey (1978), specified a number of important propositions in differential association theory. They asserted that deviant behavior is learned, primarily in interaction with others. Most of this learning takes place in intimate social groups. The process of learning deviant behavior is the same as any other type of learning process. This learning includes both motives and rationalizations for deviance as well as the techniques to commit deviant acts (Sutherland and Cressey 1978, 80–82). If an individual has been exposed to deviant orientations with greater intensity, frequency, and for a longer period of time than he or she has been exposed to conformist orientations, then the individual is likely to engage in deviance (Traub and Little 1985, 174).

The implication of differential association theory is that the family environment, neighborhood, peer group, school, and other socializing agents can teach a child deviant behavior just as easily as they can teach conforming behavior. For example, prostitutes tend to enter their profession because they have a friend, a group, or a pimp who encourages them (Bryan 1965, Davis 1985). New prostitutes serve a period of apprenticeship under someone more experienced, usually another prostitute or perhaps a madam or a pimp (Best and Luckenbill 1982).

Consider Malcolm Braly, a noted author who spent most of his life behind bars for drug offenses and a string of petty property crimes. Braly (1976) described his father as a liar and a cheat who stole from people who trusted him. His father was a con artist who often used phony names in new towns as he shifted his family from place to place. Not surprisingly, the first time a very young Malcolm was picked up by the police for stealing, he used a phony name. He had learned to lie well by watching his father in the intimate family environment.

Braly's father would often disappear for weeks at a time. Eventually, he deserted his family for another woman. Not surprisingly, Malcolm began to run away from his "trashed family," as he put it. In his adulthood, he also deserted a young son. In addition to the influence of his father, Braly (1976, 11) described how he began to steal seriously as one of a small gang of boys. They stole from back porches, garages, and eventually from inside peoples' homes. Braly's social influences transmitted attitudes favorable to crime.

Cultural transmission theories have been criticized for not being easily testable in research. It is difficult to add up deviant influences on an individual and compare them to nondeviant influences. Moreover, many individuals who grow up in neigh-

Prostitutes, like these teenagers in Boston, are almost always labeled deviant; their customers are rarely labeled as such.

borhoods with a high rate of deviant behavior and who have family members who are deviant do not themselves become criminal. For example, Malcolm Braly's sister was never in trouble with the law. Nevertheless, differential association theory remains one of the most important contributions of sociology in the understanding of deviant behavior.

Social Bond Theory

Criminologist Travis Hirschi (1969) is well known for his social bond theory. Hirschi does not ask the question, "Why do people commit crimes?" Instead, he asks, "Why do most people conform?" What stops people from stealing or cheating when, in many instances, such acts would be relatively easy? Hirschi's **social bond theory** suggests that the individual who has close social and emotional connections with law-abiding family members, friends, and who is actively involved with school or other mainstream institutions, is less likely to deviate. According to Hirschi, deviance occurs when there are weakened social bonds.

Hirschi theorized that the social bond consists of three elements. First, attachment to law-abiding others in emotional relationships provides the basis for internalization of societal norms. People with such ties do not want to disrupt their attachments by doing something that would cause disapproval. Second, involvement in conventional activities such as school-related functions, sports, and family occasions leaves less time for getting into trouble. The third element in the social bond is the belief in the rightness of the rules and moral precepts found in conventional society. If an individual's beliefs in the validity of social norms is weakened, then he or she is more likely to engage in deviant behavior.

Social bond theory adds a great deal to our understanding of deviance. However, it does not explain how people with weakened bonds choose among various kinds of deviance. In addition, many people in high-status occupations have strong social bonds to conventional society and still take part in illegal activities such as fraud, price-fixing, and insider trading (Barlow 1990). Also, recent research has not found a great deal of empirical support for Hirschi's theory. The social bonds to law-abiding family and school did not appear to deter most juveniles from committing delinquent acts (Agnew 1985, Haines 1989).

Labeling Theory

Labeling theory does not attempt to explain the origins of deviant behavior. These theorists assume everyone commits deviant acts at some point in life. Labeling theory focuses on the perpetuation of deviance as a result of being singled out and given the stigma of a deviant status. As an illustration, consider the situation of a young man in one of our university classes. He was a likable, intelligent student, if somewhat shy. As the semester progressed, he made more friends; he began to date a woman in the class. However, one of his classmates discovered that the student had spent a year in the state prison for possession of large amounts of cocaine and marijuana. The word spread.

Although no one knew if he continued to use drugs, it was not difficult to see how the students began to treat him differently. The young woman quit dating him because she felt her family would not approve. The other students, except for those involved in the drug culture, seemed less friendly to him. Several students appeared afraid of him. His ex-con status became his most important status, overshadowing his other attributes. It became a master status, as discussed in chapter 5. A master status is one that takes precedence over all other statuses the person may occupy.

The label, ex-con, carried with it a powerful **stigma**, "an attribute that is deeply discrediting" (Goffman 1963, 3). In conversations with this student, we heard about his difficulties in keeping a job as well as his repetitive feelings of rejection from other students, especially straight females. He was angry that he had the bad luck to get caught. Other students on campus, he said, used drugs frequently, but, because they had not been publicly labeled, they were treated as normal. He complained of his scarlet letter. The student drifted back into the drug culture and is now in a rehabilitation clinic for drug dependency.

Labeling theory can best be understood as an elaboration of Cooley's looking-glass self concept (see chapter 4 on socialization). Cooley pointed out that much of an individual's self-image is based on his or her interpretation of how others view him or her. Labeling theorists assume that we tend to live up to, or down to, the impressions others have of us and the image we have of ourselves. According to one of the founders of the labeling perspective, Howard Becker (1963), the critical variable in the process of developing a stable pattern of deviant or criminal behavior is getting noticed, caught, and publicly labeled as a deviant. You should note that labeling theory is more concerned with sustained deviance, as in a deviant career, in contrast to occasional deviance (Traub and Little 1985, 278).

Deviant behavior that goes unnoticed is termed **primary deviance**. For example, students who use drugs but are not known to others as drug users and have not been caught are primary deviants. If the deviant behavior is noticed and the individual is labeled over a period of time, **secondary deviance** occurs. Secondary deviance is essentially an individual's acceptance of and long-term continuation of deviant behavior (Lemert 1951). It means that, after public exposure and rejection, the individual tends to take on a deviant career. He or she incorporates the deviant label as a major part of his or her self-concept. As a result, the deviant behavior is perpetuated. The student in the example above had drifted into secondary deviance. The life of a deviant can become a **deviant career** in response to the exclusion by nondeviants and in response to a self-image of being deviant.

Imagine how different your life could be if you had been caught for some serious norm-violating act you may have committed. Others would tend to redefine you according to your new status of deviant. You, in turn, might redefine yourself and change your behavior in response. A deviant status, such as being known as a homosexual or an ex-convict or prostitute, is likely to become a master status, however unfair that may be.

It is significant that over time an individual can become self-labeling. Early in his autobiography Braly (1976, 4) wrote, "I was from any beginning I can recall, a liar, a sneak, a braggart, as show-off and a thief." He goes on to note that, "It is only now, some forty years later, that I begin to see how stealing cast me in my first successful role. I was more driven, hence less fearful, than my friends and this was sweet to a boy who had often been the butt" (Braly 1976, 12). Braly's criminal career in and out of San Quentin lasted until he was more than forty years old.

Conflict Theory

In a related way, the **conflict approach** focuses on the unequal way in which some groups more than others are singled out for deviant statuses; it also focuses on the lack of power some groups have to fight the deviant status and the system that labels them. Recall from chapter 1 that conflict theory finds its roots in the critical philosophy of Karl Marx who emphasized the inequality of economic class.

Conflict theory complements labeling theory in several ways. Conflict theory holds that groups with less social and political power are more likely to be labeled deviant. In addition, members of less powerful groups have little opportunity to influence the laws of the society. They have fewer resources to fight the labeling resulting from the attention of the police and the courts. Our prisons have a considerable concentration of people from lower classes and from minority groups. As we will see later in our discussion of white-collar crime, high-status people also commit a great deal of crime but are less likely to be detected and to receive harsh negative reaction from others in society.

Richard Quinney and other conflict criminologists argue that traditional property crimes threaten the dominant class (Masters and Roberson 1990, 173). People in this class have the most to lose if the system is threatened. In addition, they will design the system to protect their interests. Quinney (1973) points out that, "Criminal law is used by the state and the ruling class to secure the survival of the capitalist system, and . . . criminal law will be increasingly used in the attempt to maintain domestic order." The considerable use of criminal law to control drug use in our society is a case in point. Rather than channeling efforts into prevention and treatment of drug use, the United States government relies most heavily on border control, drug enforcement agencies, and prisons in an attempt to mount a war on drugs. Also notable is the concentration of efforts to control drugs used by lower-class or minority members of society while little effort is made to control prescription-drug abuse which is more characteristic of middle- and upper-class individuals.

Both labeling theory and conflict theory have received their share of criticism. Labeling theory is criticized for not attempting to explain the origins of criminal and deviant behavior. Both labeling and conflict theory are accused of being too simplistic by failing to take into consideration the vast complexity of factors involved in deviant behavior. Finally, labeling theory implies that punishment causes additional deviance. Opponents argue that not reacting to deviant behavior only reinforces that behavior precisely because that behavior goes unpunished.

Evaluating Sociological Theories

Each of the sociological theories discussed above has both merits and drawbacks in explaining deviance. All sociological theories of deviance are criticized for putting too much emphasis on social structure and societal processes and too little emphasis on individual factors. Individual factors include biological and psychological predispositions toward crime. In their controversial book, *Crime and Human Nature,* Wilson and Herrnstein (1985) argue that attributes such as IQ, age, race, and male hormonal level may be important in explaining criminal behavior. They also argue that individuals make a rational choice to commit crimes, something sociologists are less likely to emphasize. On the other hand, Wilson and Herrnstein recognized that the social environment is enormously important in perpetuating deviance.

While no one of the sociological theories provides an adequate explanation of deviance, each can offer insights that can be combined to more fully understand the social context of deviance. Anomie theory gives us an awareness of the extent to which our society emphasizes success and materialism and how that can contribute to deviance. Cultural transmission theories have helped us understand how crime and deviance are behaviors learned in the social environment. Social bond theory emphasizes our connections and involvements with conventional society as barriers to deviance. Finally, labeling and conflict theories alert us to the importance of social reactions to deviance, to the inequality in who gets labeled, and to the way deviance can develop into a lifetime career.

Major Types of Deviant Behavior

As mentioned early in this chapter, deviant behavior encompasses a wide range of acts in society. This section will familiarize you with some of the types of deviant behavior that our society considers the most serious and that sociologists have intensively studied. We will begin our discussion with various kinds of criminal activity in America. A chart of the eight most serious kinds of crime as defined and listed by the FBI in its annual report on crime in America, *The Uniform Crime Reports,* is found in Table 9.2. The *Uniform Crime Reports* is based on information collected and sent to the FBI every year by local police departments concerning the number of crimes reported and the people arrested. Another major source of data is known as the *National Crime Survey,* a U.S. Department of Justice nationwide survey concerning victimization. While the *Uniform Crime Reports* consists of re-ported crime and arrest statistics, the *National Crime Survey* asks people if they have been victims of various crimes. The *National Crime Survey* can indicate how much crime is not reported to police. Research Application 9.2 summarizes recent results of the *National Crime Survey.*

Research Application 9.2

• • • • • • • The National Crime Survey
What are Your Chances of Being a Victim?

Since 1975 the U.S. Department of Justice issues yearly results of the National Crime Survey. The survey, administered by the Bureau of the Census, consists of lengthy interviews of approximately 100,000 persons in 49,000 households, almost three-fourths of them conducted by telephone. The respondents are asked if they have been a victim of crime within a recent specified time period. The interviewers ask for a great deal of detail regarding the victimizations. The Department of Justice then analyzes the data and provides statistically projected rates of victimization for the entire United States. Some of the data for the year 1987 are given below.

Note that the National Crime Survey (NCS) cannot provide data regarding homicide. It also does not include data for kidnaping or for commercial burglary or commercial robbery. The so-called victimless crimes of drunkenness, drug abuse, and prostitution are excluded as well. Most of these crimes are not included in the NCS for financial reasons or because it is difficult to identify knowledgeable respondents (U.S. Department of Justice 1989, 1). As such, these exclusions make the NCS a less-than-perfect measure of crime in America, but it remains an invaluable source of data beyond the FBI *Uniform Crime Reports.* Also note that the National Crime Survey has never shown an increase from year to year in overall household crime since the Department of Justice first conducted the study in 1975.

Some of the more interesting results from the National Crime Survey include the following:

1. One in four U.S. households experienced a rape, robbery, assault, burglary, or theft in 1987. This figure is down from the rate of one in three in 1975.

2. In almost five percent of U.S. households, a member had been a victim of a violent crime in 1987.

3. High-income households, urban-area households, and black households were more vulnerable to crime. Hispanic households had a higher victimization rate than non-Hispanic households.

4. Households in the northeast U.S. were the least vulnerable to crime, while those in the West were the most vulnerable.

5. Younger persons (ages 12–24) had the highest victimization rates for crimes of violence and crimes of theft. Elderly persons had the lowest victimization rates for both violent and theft crimes.

6. Black males had the highest rate of violent crime victimization and white females had the lowest. For crimes of theft, there were no significant differences in victimization rates between white and black males.

7. White females were victimized more often than black females in theft crimes.

8. Persons with either the least (1–4 years of education) or the most (4 or more years of college) amount of education had the lowest violent-crime victimization rate. For theft crimes, people with some college had higher rates of victimization than those with less education.

9. Less than a third of theft victimizations resulted in losses of $250 or more.

10. Only thirty-seven percent of all crimes covered in the NCS were reported to the police. Almost half of all violent crimes were reported to the police.

11. The most common reason given for not reporting violent crimes to the police was that it was a private or personal matter.

12. The most common reason given for not reporting theft crimes to the police was that the objects were recovered or the offender was unsuccessful.

Source: U.S. Department of Justice. 1989. Criminal Victimization in the United States, 1987. Washington, D.C.: Bureau of Justice Statistics.

Violent Crime

For many Americans, violent crime is the most threatening and the most difficult crime to understand. Perhaps, too, many of us have faulty impressions of the kinds of violence we have in this society. Our perception of violence and the reality of violence are often far apart. Nevertheless, there is a great deal of violence in this society, more than in any other industrialized nation. Although murder is the least common crime in America, the U.S. murder rate is far greater than that for other industrial countries such as Canada, Japan, England, and West Germany. Each of us is roughly seven to ten times more likely to be murdered than is a European or a Japanese (Currie 1985; U.S. Department of Justice 1988). Much violence in America takes place within the family. This critical area of study, family violence, is discussed in chapter 12 on marriage and the family.

Murder and Aggravated Assault

Approximately 20,000 Americans are murdered every year. Most often, Americans are murdered in "crimes of passion." The FBI defines **murder** as "the willful (nonnegligent) killing of one human being by another" (U.S. Department of Justice 1989).

As you can see in Table 9.2, murder has the highest clearance rate of any of the FBI's index crimes. The **clearance rate** is the percentage of reported offenses that have been cleared by arrests. Clearing a crime means the police are certain they have caught the person who committed the crime and they have closed the case. It does not mean that anyone is necessarily punished for having committed the crime; the courts decide that.

It is not difficult to understand why police are more likely to catch murderers than any other kind of offender. First, the evidence tells us that most murders are committed by acquaintances, friends, neighbors, and family members of the victims. Murders are more likely to happen at home or in public places such as bars and restaurants where someone observes the offense. Most murders are not planned in advance but are the result of emotionally charged situations. The typical American homicide grows out of an argument, often over seemingly trivial matters, between friends and family members (Reid 1985, Luckenbill 1977).

The *Uniform Crime Reports* (U.S. Department of Justice 1989) also shows that murder predominantly is committed by males; 88% of those arrested in 1988 for murder were males. Nine out of ten female victims were murdered by males, and eight out of ten male victims were murdered by males. Although people of all ages are involved in murder, 45% of those arrested are under age 25 (including juveniles, those between the ages of 10 and 17). Of the general population, approximately 35% are between the ages of 10 and 30 (Bogue 1985). Significantly, the FBI *Uniform Crime Reports* also states that "murder is primarily a societal problem over which law enforcement has little or no control" (U.S. Department of Justice 1985a, 11).

In his study of homicides in Houston, Henry Lundsgaarde (1977, 111) provided a typical example of American homicide. The murderer, a 20-year-old male, and the victim, a 19-year-old male, were lifelong acquaintances living in the same neighborhood and were in a cafe-lounge late on a Saturday night. The written confession of the killer stated:

> Clifton came over and sat at the table where I was sitting. . . . Clifton asked for some of it (food) and I gave him two pieces of meat and a slice of bread. . . . and he asked for another piece and I gave him another piece. . . . he then reached over in my plate

●Table 9.2 *The Eight Index Crimes as Defined by the FBI*

Offense	Rate Per 100,000	Rate Per 100,000	Clearance Rate
	1979	1988	1988
Total	5,565.5	5,664.2	21%
Violent Offenses:	548.9	637.2	46%
Murder and nonnegligent manslaughter	9.7	8.4	70%
Forcible rape	34.7	37.6	52%
Aggravated assault	286.0	370.2	57%
Robbery	218.4	220.9	26%
Property Offenses:	5,016.6	5,027.1	18%
Burglary	1,511.9	1,309.2	13%
Larceny-theft	2,999.1	3,134.9	20%
Motor vehicle theft	505.6	582.9	15%
Arson	NA	NA	15%

1. The rate per 100,00 refers to the number of offenses reported to the police for every 100,000 members of the U.S. population for the given year.
2. The clearance rate refers to the percentage of known offenses for which the police are certain they have arrested the offenders and have closed the case.

Source: U.S. Department of Justice, Federal Bureau of Investigation. *Uniform Crime Reports.* Washington, D.C.: U.S. Government Printing Office. 1989.

and got another piece (without asking). I told him to put it back on my plate and he got mad and put it back. I got up from the table and was going over to another table when Clifton splashed hot sauce on my clothes. I asked him why he did that and he told me that he would do it again and about this time he got hold of the neck of the bottle like he was going to hit me with it. He came at me with the bottle and I pulled my knife out and as he grabbed me I cut him.

As Lundsgaarde reported, the victim, Clifton, actually died of multiple stab wounds. Interestingly, the offender was not indicted by the grand jury. We can only guess as to whether the jury interpreted the situation as self-defense or if the jury was influenced by the fact that the victim was known as a tough guy in the neighborhood.

The preceding example represents the typical American homicide. We are more likely to hear about sensationalistic cases involving random or mass killings by strangers, yet murders by strangers represent less than 25% of the known cases of murder since the FBI started keeping figures.

Sociologists have offered several explanations for the high rate of murder in this society. First, Americans, more so than other Western societies, have a long-standing cultural tradition of using violence as the ultimate means of solving interpersonal problems and arguments. Violence is a part of our value system (Reid 1985, 214). Americans value the right to own guns; in a family quarrel, the gun in the desk drawer is immediately available and lethal. Sixty percent of American homicides are committed with guns (U.S. Department of Justice 1989). Our mass media often portray heroes as extremely violent—the Rambo syndrome. Some groups in our society emphasize proving masculinity with aggression.

Thus, our history and value structure are, to a large extent, the major antecedents of American violence (Wolfgang and Ferracuti 1967, McCaghy 1980). Cultural transmission theory clearly applies here. American children grow up with violence. They learn that aggression is used to resolve disputes. Especially for boys, role models in the family, at school, and on TV tell them that they must not be sissies. They may have to fight to maintain a reputation. Sociologists see less of this in Europe or in Japan.

Sexual Assault

More than 92,000 sexual assaults were reported to the police in 1988, and the rate of reported rape has increased dramatically since the 1960s. Rape, also labeled sexual assault, is the most underreported of the violent crimes (U.S. Department of Justice 1989). The victim often feels that he or she will not be believed; he or she may not want to go through the humiliation of publicly dealing with the trauma of the situation. It is especially difficult to report rape when the offender is a family member. Acquaintance rapes, common on college campuses, are also unlikely to be reported. Acquaintance rape is discussed further in Research Method 9.1.

Research Method 9.1

· · · · · · · Nationwide Questionnaire

Date Rape on College Campuses

The most common kind of sexual assault on college campuses does not happen when a coed is walking alone at night and is assaulted by a lurking stranger. **Date rape,** *or acquaintance rape, is far more common. For example, Sarah G. was at a party at a male friend's apartment. Another friend, Jack, talked with*

Sarah at the party, and she liked him. After midnight, Jack offered to drive her home, and she agreed. Sarah said they got along really well, and they talked about a lot of things as they drove. It was a nice night, and he suggested they drive by the lake. Once at the lake, he kissed her. She did not resist. When he tried to go beyond kissing, she said "No." He grew very belligerent, and then he angrily pinned her to the seat and raped her. When he was finished, he acted as if everything were normal, and he drove her home. Like many victims, Sarah told no one, including the police. She couldn't believe that it had happened. He seemed so nice.

Researchers Mary Koss, Christine Gidycz, and Nadine Wisniewski (1987) were interested in discovering just how much sexual victimization occurs among college students. They designed a self-report questionnaire for both men and women to be administered during college classes. Although some institutions refused to participate, Koss and her colleagues gained the cooperation of 32 universities, colleges, and community colleges representing all regions of the continental United States. The researchers were able to administer the questionnaire to 6,159 students whose instructors allowed them to take class time. The institutions sampled, as well as the students, were representative of the overall national populations. Fifty-two percent of the students sampled were female and 48 percent were male. Most were single and white.

After an arduous, expensive, and time-consuming process of data collection, Koss and her colleagues statistically analyzed the data. They found that 53.7 percent of the women had experienced some form of sexual victimization including verbal and physical intimidation. One in 7 of the women, 15.4 percent, had been raped according to the prevailing legal definition. An additional 12.1 percent of the women had been victims of attempted rape (Koss et al. 1987, 166).

In Koss' study (p. 169) only 5 percent of the women who were victims reported it to the police, and only 5 percent sought victim assistance services. Forty-two percent never told anyone.

One of the most interesting results from the study was that 73 percent of the rape victims did not label what happened to them as rape (Koss et al. 1987, 169). Sociologists point out that situations are socially defined, and definitions of the same situations can vary. Because the women's situation did not fit the stereotype of being raped by a stranger in a dark alley, they did not call it rape. Like many victims, they felt ashamed and humiliated; they assumed they had done something to deserve being raped. They felt betrayed because they had trusted the dates and acquaintances. Rather than face the trauma of accepting it as rape and the idea that they couldn't trust some dates, they denied the rape had happened.

Koss and her colleagues discovered that, of the college men surveyed, 25.1 percent reported engaging in some form of sexual aggression, ranging from unwanted touching and fondling to rape. About 3 percent of the college men admitted attempting rape and 4 percent reported committing rape according to the legal definition—using force to have sex with a woman against her will— yet none of these men defined themselves as rapists (Koss et al. 1987, 166).

Again, behavior is situationally defined. In this case, the definition is influenced by gender-role expectations and stereotypes whereby college men are expected to "score" with women. Aggressive behavior is defined as appropriate by many men in order to persuade the female. Women, on the other hand, are expected to control the situation and not let it get out of hand. If it does get out of hand, then men define it as her fault. Moreover, stereotypes exist which foster the belief that women say "No" to sex when they really mean "Yes," or they will eventually say "Yes" if pressured enough.

College men, then, may be confused when a date says "No." Does she really mean "No"? When does pressure become force and, thus, rape? Women, given gender-role expectations, may find it more difficult to forcefully say "No," shout "No," or run for help. However, a recent study by Koss and Dinero (1989) discovered that rape victims could not be distinguished from nonvictims on the basis of any behavior or set of attitudes. "Most of the sexually assaulted women were dissimilar to unvictimized women primarily in that they had encountered a sexually aggressive man" (Koss and Dinero 1989, 249).

Gender-role stereotypes as well as stereotypes about rape cloud the issue of date rape. Acquaintance rape is a complex situation that is not easily defined by the offender or the victim. Because of the number of these rapes, many college officials are conducting seminars on the issue as well as setting up rape-crisis counseling centers on campuses. In addition, men and women on campus need to communicate with each other in order to clear the confusion about sex and dating.

It is doubtful that Koss and her colleagues could have obtained such detailed, nationwide data using any research method other than the survey. The use of a questionnaire, as opposed to interviews which are oral, also allows the respondent greater anonymity. A topic as sensitive as sexual assault requires that the researchers do everything possible to guard the anonymity of respondents. Koss and her colleagues did not even publish the names of the universities in order to protect identities as much as possible.

Of course, the use of questionnaires relies on the honesty of respondents and the willingness of people to cooperate. In addition, questionnaires lack the depth and insight of unstructured interviews or participant observation. Nevertheless, this study of acquaintance rape has helped increase awareness and dispel some stereotypes about sexual assault. In addition, this and other studies have spurred universities to face the issue and do something about it.

Sexual assault is unique among crimes in that our society tends to suspect that the victim is in some way responsible for the crime. It is a classic case of blaming the victim. Even today we tend to hold on to a number of myths about rape. These myths include:

1. the victims somehow invited the rape by what they were wearing, how they were acting, or where they were (as in a bar);
2. women say "No" when they really mean "Yes";
3. nice girls are not raped;
4. men cannot control their sexual desires;
5. women have an unconscious desire to be raped (McCaghy 1980, 128–29; Scully and Marolla 1984; Bart and O'Brien 1985).

Years of research on rape indicate that these beliefs are not accurate. Nevertheless, these myths give a set of excuses to rapists, add to the guilt and shame of the rape victim, and influence lawyers and juries.

Today sociologists generally agree on the following facts about sexual assault.

1. Rape is a crime of violence; the motive is not primarily sexual but derives from the desire to control, dominate, humiliate, and express anger and hostility toward the victim, a specific woman, or women in general.
2. Most rapes are planned by the offender.
3. The offender is most often a stranger.

4. Most rapes do not appear to be related to any seductive dress and manner of the victim; rather, she becomes a victim primarily for being in the wrong place at the wrong time. Women of all ages, backgrounds, and ethnic groups are victims of rape.
5. Rapists often report regular sex lives and many are married.
6. Most rapists are not psychotic nor can they be distinguished by a specific psychological illness. They may be insecure, unable to handle stress, unable to establish close interpersonal relationships with others, or they may be hypersensitive to rejection (Reid 1985, Bart and O'Brien 1985; McCaghy 1980; Bureau of Justice Statistics 1985).

Like murder, rape is primarily a crime by the young (under age 25) and the victims also tend to be young, although victims range in age from infancy to the late 80s.

Property Crimes

The major property crimes included in the FBI index crimes are burglary, larceny, auto theft, and arson. **Robbery** is technically considered a violent offense because it involves a direct threat to a person in order to get money or goods. Many robberies occur in convenience stores, gas stations, and grocery stores where a robber directly threatens a clerk in order to get money. **Burglary** is defined as breaking and entering to commit a felony. If someone breaks into your home when no one is there, a burglary has occurred. **Larceny** is simply theft which is a felony offense but does not involve the threat of force or breaking and entering. The most common form of larceny is shoplifting (for larceny to be classified as a felony it has to be over a certain amount, such as two hundred dollars).

Table 9.2 shows that the clearance rates for these crimes are quite low. Burglary and larceny are difficult to solve because there are rarely enough clues or a witness. The police, on average, clear these crimes less than twenty percent of the time.

Property crimes far outnumber violent crimes, but the sentences for property offenses are lighter because no direct personal harm to a victim is involved. The most common property offense is larceny. In 1988, there were more than a million arrests for larceny compared to about 16,000 arrests for murder and 28,000 arrests for sexual assault (U.S. Department of Justice 1989).

Those arrested for property crimes are most likely to be young males and usually from lower-class backgrounds. **Juveniles**—those under the age of 17 or 18, depending on the state—make up a significant proportion of these arrests. Referring back to conflict theory, it may also be that these people are more likely to be caught committing these crimes. Conflict theorists also point out that they have fewer resources to fight the criminal justice system. It is often suggested that these individuals have no stake in mainstream society and its norms. Many are part of a subculture that supports such criminal activity. Thus the theories of differential association and cultural transmission as well as Merton's discussion of anomie, particularly the response called innovation, apply to property offenders in our society.

White-Collar Crime

The most costly economic crime in America is white-collar crime. Estimates of its cost to society range from $80 billion to $231 billion, a far greater cost than that of street crime (Coleman, 1989, 6). **White-collar crime** is defined as "a violation of the law committed by a person or group of persons in the course of an otherwise respected and legitimate occupation or financial activity" (Coleman 1989, 5).

It is a mistake to think of white-collar crime as costly only in terms of dollars. "The National Product Safety Commission has estimated that 20 million serious injuries and 30 thousand deaths a year are caused by unsafe consumer products" (Coleman 1989, 8). Imagine buying a car that executives of the company knew was unsafe. In the mid-1970s, Ford Motor Company's Pinto was so poorly designed that, in rear-end crashes of over 25 mph, the gas tank ruptured. Any spark could ignite it. Ford executives denied the problem and later denied that they knew about it before making the cars. Internal memos proved otherwise. Apparently, the executives were more concerned about the cost to remake the car than cost in human life. It is estimated that 500 people have been killed, most burned to death, in the Ford Pinto (Bonn 1984, 246).

Producing unsafe consumer products is only one kind of white-collar crime. Income-tax evasion, bribery of public officials to obtain commercial advantage, influence peddling by politicians, and computer-based embezzlement are types of white-collar crime. White-collar crime may be motivated by individual gain, as when an accountant embezzles money from his or her employer, or it may be for the benefit of the company, such as false advertising.

These crimes occur in massive numbers in America. The most important study of crimes by corporations (Clinard and Yeager 1980) found that 60% of the 582 companies examined had at least one important known violation. More than 40% had multiple violations in the two-year period studied. The automobile and pharmaceutical industries had a particularly high number of violations.

White-collar criminals do not receive the punishment given to street criminals when caught (Coleman 1989, Simon and Eitzen 1990). We are not accustomed to thinking of corporations or corporate executives as criminals. We find it difficult to convict a well-educated, high-status person when he or she was acting for the benefit of the company or on the instructions of higher-ups. The access to well-known attorneys and the money to pay them, along with the public's difficulty to accept a high-status person as a "criminal," go a long way toward protecting white-collar criminals from the courts and from prison. The ability to influence the making of laws at the state and federal level also serves as a means of insulating white-collar offenders from effective formal controls.

Organized Crime

White-collar crime is sometimes called crime in the "upperworld"; organized crime is often called crime in the "underworld." **Organized crime** is defined as "activities by members of deviant formal organizations in pursuit of the organizations' goals" (Best and Luckenbill 1982, 71). The organizations' goals involve amassing huge sums of money. They do this by providing Americans with ready access to narcotics, prostitution, gambling, and loan-sharking. Organized crime activity includes predatory crimes like burglary, hijacking, extortion, business racketeering, and murder to further their goals. These organizations have also moved into legitimate business to cover their tracks, but organized crime is most known for providing illegal goods and services. The greatest profits come from drug smuggling and gambling operations (Bonn 1984, 332).

Over the years in America, organized crime has been called various names— the Mafia, the Cosa Nostra, the syndicate, or the rackets. The term organized crime is more useful because it is not limited to any ethnic or racial group and more aptly describes the nature of this criminal activity.

The key to understanding the nature of organized crime is not so much the range of illegal activities involved but rather the way the criminal activity is structured. You should note that our definition used the term formal organization (see chapter 5) to refer to organized crime. These deviant groups have structured, bureaucratic organizations such as those utilized in legitimate bureaucratic systems— a corporation, for example.

An organized crime syndicate is typically structured in a pyramid form with the boss insulated by underbosses who control lieutenants who control certain territories and certain activities. The lieutenants in turn control the street operatives who must carry out the day-to-day activities of the organization. Those at or near the top are well distanced from everyday criminal activity.

It is extremely difficult for law enforcement agencies to control organized crime. Those in organized crime have the financial resources to thwart criminal justice through the use of highly specialized attorneys and through bribery. Millions of Americans are willing to pay for illegal services such as gambling or prostitution. In addition, our criminal justice system is geared toward dealing with crimes by individuals, not by organizations. In this way organized crime is similar to crime committed by corporations.

The criminal justice system's bias toward crime committed by individuals is evident in the eight index crimes listed in Table 9.2 on page 209. None of the eight offenses directly reflects organized or white-collar crime. These index crimes receive the most publicity, and they are the crimes used to calculate crime increases and decreases over the years. They do not direct public attention toward organized or white-collar crime.

Crimes Without Victims

Some deviant acts are defined as crimes in our society because of moral concerns. These acts do not fit the traditional picture of crime as involving a perpetrator who injures a victim. Called **victimless crimes** or **public order crimes**, they produce no direct victims of the crimes other than the offenders themselves. Such acts include prostitution, pornography, gambling, and drug use. These acts involve "the willing exchange of socially disapproved but widely demanded goods or services" (Schur 1965, 8). Although there are no direct victims of these crimes, people in society essentially make a moral judgment that these acts should not be tolerated. Also, it can be argued that there are indirect victims of such crimes. A family whose breadwinner suffers from compulsive gambling or drug use certainly feels the effects. These effects might be financial, emotional, or both. A neighborhood having much traffic in prostitution or a proliferation of sex shops often experiences declining property value. Typically, other street criminals move in as well.

These types of crimes are especially difficult to control because there is no direct victim to complain to the authorities. Millions of Americans are willing to pay high prices for marijuana and cocaine. The people who complain are those who feel a moral outrage at these acts which they define as corrupt, degrading, and threatening to the "moral fiber" of the community or the society. Many people today complain about the use of drugs in the workplace. If drug use interferes with a worker's accuracy in constructing passenger jets in which we travel, then we must rethink the term "victimless."

Public order crimes are a continuing source of controversy. On the one hand, people argue that formal controls cannot be expected to control these crimes. For example, demand for illegal drugs exists in every city in America. Apparently a large number of people want marijuana and cocaine. It is extremely time-consuming to try to enforce these laws. Drug enforcement requires paying informants, setting up stakeouts, and spending days or weeks on surveillance. In addition, such laws may encourage corruption among law enforcement agents as well as offering an illegal and unregulated marketplace for organized crime (McCaghy 1980, 320–21).

In contrast, other people argue that society cannot tolerate behaviors that they deem morally unacceptable and that laws must be used to make the statement that these social-order crimes are undesirable. To them, marijuana and cocaine use are not only morally wrong but are disruptive to society as well. As another example, the use of children in pornography outrages many Americans today.

Moral entrepreneurs (Gusfield 1963, Becker 1963) are those people determined to influence the society by forcing a set of values on everyone through law. Moral entrepreneurs crusade to stop others from committing their "sins." In the 1920s the majority of Americans used alcohol, but a small group, mostly women, in Christian Temperance organizations was instrumental in getting the Volstead amendment passed which outlawed alcohol in America. Today, in the case of abortion, a significant segment of the society is determined to bring back laws to prohibit abortion. To them, it is a crime. To others, it is not. Once again, we are reminded that the definition of deviance is relative to the group.

Mental Illness

A recent survey by the National Institute of Mental Health (1984) indicated that as many as 20% of American adults suffered from some form of mental disorder according to standard psychological classifications. Included in these classifications were alcohol and drug addiction which afflicted more than 6% of adults. Another 6% experienced depression, while 8% had anxiety disorders such as phobias and panic attacks. People may argue that alcoholism and phobias are not really mental illnesses. Nevertheless, the fact remains that a fairly large percentage of Americans face relatively severe "problems in living" (Szasz 1971).

The various forms of mental illness in our society carry with them a powerful stigma. People may be just as wary of an ex-mental patient as they are of an ex-convict. It is unnerving when people do not act as we expect in our everyday routines. Not long ago, a student in one of our classes was wandering the halls stopping people at random to explain elements of the universe. Afterwards, people reacted by trying to avoid him at all costs, quietly telling others how weird he was or by ridiculing him. Now in the state mental hospital, the student was diagnosed as having schizophrenia, a serious mental illness characterized by delusions (I am Caesar or Captain Kirk) and hallucinations (hearing and seeing things others don't). About 1% of the adult population experiences schizophrenia, according to the survey discussed above.

The sociological perspective on mental illness suggests that it is not always easy, even for psychiatrists, to know exactly who is mentally ill and who is not. Researcher David Rosenhan (1973) had twelve "pseudopatients" (people who had no history of mental problems) commit themselves to various mental hospitals around the country by saying that they heard voices. Other than giving a false name, everything else they told was true. None of them was discovered; all were routinely

While mental hospitals have improved considerably since the days of the Insane Asylum they are still far from being comfortable places. Except for the most expensive treatment centers, both facilities and attention to patient needs are often lacking.

admitted to the hospitals with fairly severe diagnoses. Rosenhan told them to act normally while in the institution and to take careful notes of their experiences. The pseudopatients were amazed at how easily they were accepted as mentally ill. In a good illustration of labeling theory, the pseudopatients' behavior was reinterpreted in light of a deviant label. At one institution, a staff member wrote that a pseudopatient engaged in bizarre and extreme writing behavior. Only the other patients saw that the pseudopatients were not ill. Several pseudopatients were denied the right to leave the hospital; others were released in a few weeks with diagnoses of schizophrenia in remission.

Labeling theory is important as one sociological perspective on mental illness, but sociologists are also interested in other ways of looking at the problem. Rather than concentrate primarily on the individual who is experiencing some form of mental disorder, sociologists are more likely to examine demographic features and the social and cultural environment of those who experience problems. For example, we know that women are more likely to experience depressive and anxiety disorders, while men are more likely to have problems with drug and alcohol addiction and to experience personality disorders such as antisocial behavior. Single, never-married men are more likely to have mental and emotional problems than are married men, but marriage does not appear to be such a significant factor for women.

Social class seems to be one of the most important variables affecting mental illness. People in the lower classes are more likely to suffer from the most severe mental disorders and for longer periods of time than are those in the higher classes. Most sociological research indicates that the social stress of lower-class life is most likely to influence the high rate of mental illness, though it is also possible that the labeling process is more of a factor with those in the lower classes. It may also be that those people experiencing severe mental problems eventually "drift" down into the lower classes because they cannot cope with the demands of society. In any case, they are less likely to receive high-quality care available to more affluent Americans experiencing mental and emotional problems. (Goode 1984, 281–84).

In fact, the major question we face in our society today is how to treat the chronically mentally ill who have little or no money and who find it difficult or impossible to hold a job. Until the 1960s, the primary method was to house them in large state hospitals paid for by the public. In the 1960s, the advent of more sophisticated drugs made management of symptoms of mental illness possible for many. In addition, a pervasive view developed that mental hospitals were degrading warehouses for the unwanted. This view fueled the **deinstitutionalization** movement which drastically reduced the number of people in public mental hospitals. In 1955 more than 500,000 people were in mental institutions. By 1980, only 255,000 were in such places (U.S. Bureau of the Census 1985, 48). In the 1980s the opposite problem developed. When people are released from mental hospitals, where do they go and how do they live? Rather than being dumped into institutions, they have been dumped into the streets. Many may discontinue taking their drugs; few are monitored carefully. They can be seen in any urban area living off the streets, sleeping on sidewalks, and roaming the cities. They make up a sizable portion of the American homeless (Estroff 1981). As one author (Fustero 1984) wrote, when a winter storm comes, the media warn people to bring their pets in, but the homeless are left on the streets.

Questions for Summary and Review

1. How do sociologists define deviance, and why is it difficult to define deviance?
2. Discuss the major ways deviance is relative. Think of your own examples for each.
3. What are the positive and negative functions of deviance?
4. Discuss and give examples of the three major forms of social control.
5. Discuss Merton's four types of deviance. Give examples of each.
6. Summarize each of the major sociological theories concerning deviance. Compare and contrast these theories and point out the shortcomings of each.
7. Discuss the major types of violent crime. What factors contribute to the high rate of homicide in the U.S.? What are the myths and the realities concerning sexual assault?
8. Define, compare, and contrast white-collar crime with organized crime. How are they alike and how are they different?
9. Define and give examples of crimes without victims. Why do some people disagree that these crimes are victimless?
10. What are the major issues concerning mental illness in contemporary society?

Key Concepts

Anomie theory (p. 199)
Appeal to higher loyalties (p. 200)
Burglary (p. 213)
Clearance rate (p. 208)
Condemnation of the condemners (p. 200)
Conflict theory (p. 205)
Crime (p. 193)

Date rape (p. 210)
Deinstitutionalization (p. 218)
Denial of harm (p. 201)
Denial of responsibility (p. 200)
Denial of the victim (p. 201)
Deviance (p. 193)
Deviant career (p. 205)
Formal social control (p. 198)

References

1. Agnew, Robert. 1985. Social control theory and delinquency: A longitudinal test. *Criminology* 23:47–60.

2. Baird, John S. 1980. Current trends in college cheating. *Psychology in the schools* 17:515–22.

3. Barlow, Hugh D. 1990. *Introduction to Criminology*. 5th ed. Glenview, Ill.: Scott, Foresman/Little Brown Higher Education.

4. Bart, Pauline B., and Patricia H. O'Brien. 1985. *Stopping rape: Successful survival strategies*. New York: Pergamon Press.

5. Becker, Howard S. 1963. *Outsiders: Studies in the sociology of deviance*. New York: Free Press.

6. Best, Joel, and David F. Luckenbill. 1982. *Organizing deviance*. Englewood Cliffs, N.J.: Prentice-Hall.

7. Bogue, Donald J. 1985. *The population of the United States: Historical trends and future projections*. New York: Free Press.

8. Bonn, Robert L. 1984. *Criminology*. New York: McGraw-Hill.

9. Braly, Malcolm. 1976. *False starts: A memoir of San Quentin and other prisons*. New York: Penquin Books.

10. Breskin, David. 1985. Leave it to Beaver: A grim tale about some very nice boys who did some really mean things. *Rolling stone magazine* (September): 67.

11. Bryan, James H. 1965. Apprenticeships in prostitution. *Social problems* 12:287–97.

12. Bureau of Justice Statistics, U.S. Department of Justice, 1985. *Bulletin: The crime of rape*. Washington D.C.: U.S. Government Printing Office.

13. Chambliss, William. 1973. The saints and the roughnecks. *Society* 11:26–37.

14. Clinard, Marshall B., and Peter C. Yeager. 1980. *Corporate crime*. New York: Free Press.

15. Coleman, James W. 1989. *The criminal elite: The sociology of white collar crime*. 2d ed. New York: St. Martin's Press.

16. Currie, Elliott. 1985. *Confronting crime: An American challenge*. New York: Pantheon.

17. *Dallas Times Herald*. 1985. The violence of privilege: Fort Worth's Legion of Doom cuts class lines with hate (March 31).

18. Davis, Nanette J. 1985. Becoming a prostitute. In *Down to earth sociology*, edited by James M. Henslin, 171–79. New York: Free Press.

19. Durkheim, Emile. 1982. *The rules of the sociological method*, edited by S. Lukes, translated by W. Halls. New York: Free Press.

20. Estroff, Sue E. 1981. *Making it crazy: An ethnography of psychiatric clients in an American community*. Berkeley, Calif.: University of California Press.

21. Fustero, Steven. 1984. Home on the Streets. *Psychology today* (February): 56–63.

22. Goffman, Erving. 1961. *Asylums*. Garden City, New York: Doubleday Anchor.

23. _____. 1963. *Stigma: Notes on the management of spoiled identity*. Englewood Cliffs, N.J.: Prentice-Hall.

24. Goode, Erich. 1984. *Deviant behavior*. 2d ed. Englewood Cliffs, N.J.: Prentice-Hall.

25. Gusfield, Joseph. 1963. *Symbolic crusade: Status politics and the American temperance movement*. Urbana, Ill.: University of Illinois Press.

26. Haines, Christy L. 1989. Delinquency in two groups of youth: A partial replication of the Richmond Youth Study. Paper presented at the Southwestern Sociological Association Annual Meeting. Houston, Texas. March, 1989.

27. Haines, Valerie J., R. Clark, E. LaBeff, and G. Diekhoff. 1986a. Student cheating and perceived social control by college students. *Free inquiry in creative sociology* 14:13–16.

28. Haines, Valerie J., G. Diekhoff, E. LaBeff, and R. Clark. 1986b. College cheating: Immaturity, lack of commitment, and the neutralizing attitude. *Research in higher education* 25:342–354.

29. Hirschi, Travis. 1969. *Causes of delinquency*. Berkeley: University of California Press.

30. Humphreys, Laud. 1970. *Tearoom trade*. Chicago: Aldine.

31. Koss, Mary P., and Thomas E. Dinero. 1989. Discriminant analysis of risk factors for sexual victimization among a national sample of college women. *Journal of consulting and clinical psychology* 57:242–50.

32. Koss, Mary P., Christine A. Gidycz, and Nadine Wisniewski. 1987. The scope of rape: Incidence and prevalence of sexual aggression and victimization in a national sample of higher education students. *Journal of consulting and clinical psychology* 55:162–70.

33. Lemert, Edwin M. 1951. *Social pathology*. New York: McGraw-Hill.

34. Luckenbill, David. 1977. Criminal homicide as a situated transaction. *Social problems* 25:176–87.

35. Lundsgaarde, Henry P. 1977. *Murder in space city: A cultural analysis of Houston homicide patterns*. New York: Oxford University Press.

36. Masters, Ruth and Cliff Roberson. 1990. *Inside criminology*. Englewood Cliffs, N.J.: Prentice-Hall.

37. McCaghy, Charles H. 1980. *Crime in American society*. New York: Macmillan.

38. Merton, Robert K. 1967. *Social theory and social structure*. New York: Free Press.

39. Michaels, James W., and Terrance D. Miethe. 1989. Applying theories of deviance to academic cheating. *Social science quarterly* 70:870–85.

40. National Institute of Mental Health. 1985. *Mental health, United States 1985*. Washington, D.C.: U.S. Government Printing Office.

41. *Newsweek*. 1990. The future of gay America (March 12): 20–25.

42. Polsky, Ned. 1967. *Hustlers, beats and others*. Chicago: Aldine.

43. Quinney, Richard. 1973. *Critique of legal order: Crime control in capitalist society*. Boston: Little, Brown and Company.

44. Reid, Sue Titus. 1985. *Crime and criminology*. 4th ed. New York: Holt, Rinehart and Winston.

45. Richardson, Laurel W. 1988. Secrecy and status: The social construction of forbidden relationships. *American sociological review* 53:209–19.

46. Rosenhan, David L. 1973. On being sane in insane places. *Science magazine* (January 19).

47. Schur, Edwin M. 1965. *Crimes without victims: Deviant behavior and public policy*. Englewood Cliffs, N.J.: Prentice-Hall.

48. Scully, Diana, and Joseph Marolla. 1984. Convicted rapists' vocabulary of motive: Excuses and motivations. *Social problems* 31:530–43.

49. Simon, David R. and D. Stanley Eitzen. 1990. *Elite deviance*. 3d ed. Boston: Allyn and Bacon.

50. Singhal, Avinash C. 1982. Factors in students' dishonesty. *Psychological reports* 51:775–80.

51. Sutherland, Edwin H., and Donald Cressey. 1978. *Criminology*. 10th ed. New York: J.B. Lippincott.

52. Sykes, Gresham M. and David Matza. 1957. Techniques of neutralization: a theory of delinquency. *American sociological review* 22:664–70.

53. Szasz, Thomas. 1971. *The myth of mental illness*. New York: Harper and Row.

54. Tasker, Peter. 1988. *The Japanese: A major exploration of modern Japan*. New York: Truman Talley Books.

55. Traub, Stuart H., and Craig B. Little. 1985. *Theories of deviance*. 3d ed. Itasca, Ill.: F.E. Peacock.

56. *USA Today*. 1985. Mother who drowned kids pits justice against culture (October 18):3A.

57. U.S. Bureau of the Census. 1985. *Statistical abstract of the United States, 1985*. Washington, D.C. U.S. Government Printing Office.

58. U.S. Department of Justice, Federal Bureau of Investigation. 1985a. *Uniform crime reports, 1984*. Washington D.C.: U.S. Government Printing Office.

59. _____. 1985b. *Criminal victimization in the United States, 1983*. Washington, D.C.: U.S. Government Printing Office.

60. _____. 1988. *International crime rates*. Washington, D.C.: Bureau of Justice Statistics.

61. _____. 1989. *Criminal victimization in the United States, 1987*. Washington, D.C.: Bureau of Justice Statistics.

62. Wilson, James Q., and Richard J. Hernnstein. 1985. *Crime and human nature*. New York: Simon and Schuster.

63. Wolfgang, Marvin E., and Franco Ferracuti. 1967. *The subculture of violence: Toward an integrated theory in criminology*. London: Social Sciences Paperbacks.

64. Wrong, Dennis. 1961. The oversocialized conception of man in modern sociology. *The American sociological review* 26:183–92.

10 Collective Behavior and Social Movements

• • • • • • • • • • • •

Chapter Outline

●

Structured, patterned, recurrent—these words describe the major portion of our social lives. This book emphasizes how daily life is governed by routines set by the norms our society and culture prescribe for our statuses. Because of these routines, daily life is generally predictable.

However, at times certain events occur that violate the normative expectations. In situations of uncertainty, where no norms exist or where old norms are no longer adequate, people and groups may behave in ways that appear irrational. Their actions take a variety of forms, ranging from behavior that is inconsequential to behavior that threatens lives on a large scale.

At the lower end of this spectrum are acts that are apparently meaningless but that engross those engaged in them. In the eastern part of the United States during the mid-1980s, a gross TV wrestling program began to grow in popularity. Broadcast times were extended until much of Saturday morning programming on one channel was devoted to the matches. The program featured many interviews with the wrestlers/actors, dressed in outlandish garb, during which they hurled insults at one another. This program grew so popular that videotapes of the matches and models of the wrestlers found large markets.

Sometimes crowd excitement can bring riots. In Belgium in 1985, British soccer fans seated close to their rivals began to taunt and threaten the enemy of the day. As the taunting and the return of insults mounted, the crowd became more and more emotional. Eventually sporadic fights broke out and spread, until the stadium was a seething mass of violence. The crowd seemed to have no real objective but was merely reacting to the growing emotion and anger aroused by the verbal exchanges between the two groups. As the fighting escalated, several people were killed and many were seriously injured.

In the spring of 1990 an anti-abortion group, Operation Rescue, organized a demonstration at a women's clinic in Los Angeles. What began as an attempt to shut down the clinic, which was providing abortions, turned to violence when the protestors failed in their goal. A seven-hour siege, which capped a week of protests, turned into a scene of destruction and physical harm. Nearly 250 people were arrested that April Saturday as 350 police, some on horseback, tried to control the behavior of the anti-abortion protestors and the pro-choice activists who opposed them. While injuries appeared limited to cuts and bruises, the crowd did engage in behavior that deviated from personal and societal norms (Harris and Wride 1990).

Other such behavior is the result of fear and panic. In 1985 an Italian ship received a bomb threat while cruising the Aegean Sea. Members of the ship's crew panicked and threw large crates of merchandise containing more than $1 million worth of gambling equipment into the sea; they feared the crates contained the threatened bombs. It was all a hoax, but the resulting panic had real results for the crew members as well as for the owners of the merchandise.

At the far end of such behavior lies the actions of terrorists. For example, on Christmas Day, 1985, terrorists attacked innocent civilians standing at or near the El Al ticket counters in both the Rome and Vienna airports. In the end, their coordinated machine-gun fire and hand grenade explosions killed fourteen people, including an eleven-year-old American girl; more than one hundred people were injured. These attacks were seen as the work of a terrorist group aligned with the cause of extremist Palestinian factions.

Sociologists categorize all of these behaviors under one general term, **collective behavior**. Collective behavior refers to public opinion and rumor, fads, crazes, panics, riots, and, in its most organized form, to social movements. All of these behaviors represent attempts of groups of people to respond to social change or to create social change. Frequently, collectivities of people act in novel ways when their situation is ambiguous and old norms are no longer valid or appropriate. For example, people who avidly cheer television wrestlers may be attempting to adjust to the tensions of modern society by sublimating their own feelings of aggression. The swift changes in clothing fashions for teens are probably a way for them to try out the right to make decisions about their lives, decisions they did not make when they were still children.

Organized forms of collective behavior, as embodied in social movements, seek significant social change. At times, movements develop with opposing views. For example the Right-to-Life (anti-abortion) movement is in direct opposition to the Pro-choice movement which seeks continuation of the right of women to have abortions on demand. While the former movement has been successful, to some extent, in getting some changes in the Supreme Court's earlier abortion-on-demand stand, the pro-choice movement has been effective in making its case before the nation's voters. As a result, many candidates favoring the pro-choice stance scored significant election victories in the late 1980s.

Instances of collective behavior are often misunderstood because they are novel. Those engaged are acting in ways that defy the conventions of society, but the behavior is not irrational in their own minds. During rioting, objects are attacked and goods looted. At times these actions seem to have little relationship to the purpose of the group. For instance, during riots against the government in Panama City in 1957, the objects of attack were parking meters and traffic lights. While these items had little apparent relationship to the grievances of the people against the government, they served as symbols of governmental power. Similarly, during riots in urban ghetto areas the property damage and looting that occurs seems unrelated to the events that spawned the riot, but, again, they are symbols of those in power.

Collective behavior is one way of dealing with **social change**, or some significant alteration in the cultural or social norms, values, and structures of society. **William Bainbridge** (1985) stated that collective behavior can be related to social change in one of four ways. The behavior itself may represent change (new fashion). It may be an attempt to cause social change (the riots that brought attention to the problems of ghetto areas). It may be action aimed at preventing or resisting change (movements that advocate the shift back to conservative religious values, such as the Moral Majority or Liberty Foundation). Or, it may be the result of social change (the adoption by teenagers of fads which seem to give teens an identity in a rapidly changing world).

Types of Collective Behavior

Through time, people have witnessed many instances of behaviors that vary from the established patterns laid down by society. These behaviors take various forms: they may be simply novel patterns of behavior, or they may represent intense desires or fears. These behaviors also have different outcomes: they may result in a lynching, a bank run, a ghetto riot, a change in clothing styles, or a mass desire to own a Cabbage Patch™ doll.

In general, collective behaviors represent reactions to stressful situations and provide new cues for behavior. They differ from normal behavior in terms of degree of deviance rather than in terms of deviance itself (Vander Zanden 1990).

Four basic principles of collective behavior can be set forth (Bainbridge 1985): (1) the behavior is unusual; (2) a group of people must be involved in the action; (3) those involved must influence one another in some fashion; and, (4) the whole action must take place without advance planning. Each type of the collective behavior will vary in the extent to which it conforms to this model.

This section discusses six aspects of collective behavior: fashions, fads, crazes, rumor, panics, and crowd behavior. Organized, structured collective behavior is dealt with later in the section on social movements.

Fashions and Fads

Fashions and fads are instances of people seeking excitement or meaning for their lives by doing something novel or different. These novel ways of acting seldom seem to affect only single individuals. To act in a way that defies, even scorns, the older patterns appears to require the protection or support of groups. Thus, both fashions and fads are new forms of action which do not conform to established norms but which require conformity for those who practice them.

Fashions

Fashions are novel customs that last for a period of some length and are taken up by a significant proportion of the population. In the 1980s a number of new fashions arose. Some of these originated with the Yuppies (Young Urban Professionals). Among the new customs was a concern for health that led to the fashion of jogging. A number of food fashions that started with the Yuppies were taken up by many people who could not be called Yuppies. Thus, croissant sandwiches became popular at fast-food restaurants such as Burger King, and fashionable restaurants all over the country began to serve a Cajun dish, blackened redfish.

The Yuppie revolution began to fade away in the late 1980s. The young professionals caught up in Yuppie culture began to move back to more traditional forms of behavior. However, many of the fashions that resulted from that subculture remain as a part of the norms of our society.

Popular tastes in music are another example of fashion. The sound of the big bands became the fashion during the 1930s and 1940s. They were new and, to some extent, distasteful to older generations, but they represented an era, and they now have passed from fashion into one aspect of music in the United States. In the 1960s and 1970s, new kinds of music—rock and country/western—became new fashions (again, somewhat offensive to some older people). These have become another permanent part of our musical tradition. Thus, what appeared to be novel was taken up by a large portion of the population and was relatively lasting in its impact on music in the society. How and why such changes occur in popular-music fashion are questions addressed by those who study collective behavior.

Fads

Fads differ from fashions in several ways. They are adopted not by large groups of people but by a small part of the population. Fad behavior may be so bizarre as to show a contempt for established patterns of behavior. As a result, many fads are scorned by most people (Vander Zanden 1990).

An example can be found in the punk hairstyles affected first by unemployed, lower-class youth in England, perhaps as a means of dealing with the boredom and frustration of their lives. This fad was then taken up by young people in the United States. The hairstyles involve shaving parts of the head and dying portions of hair in different, unusual shades. One might see a young person on the street with part of the hair pink, another part blue, and other parts green. The hair may stick up in some places, be shaved in others, and be neatly combed in yet others. These young people clearly are drawing attention to themselves and seeking to shock conforming members of society. Young people have generally sought to establish their identity and individuality by engaging in some fad that separates them from the generation before them.

Means of entertainment can also be fads. In the 1930s, miniature golf entranced part of the population. A fad of the mid-1980s was a game called Trivial Pursuit®. At one time it was so popular that it was hard to find a set, and tournaments were played everywhere. The game is still played occasionally, but the intensity of the fad has diminished.

Musical entertainment and dancing styles can also be fads. Recently a Brazilian import, via France, has burst onto the scene. Described as a torrid dance involving a thigh-to-thigh two-step, the *lambada* is performed to a driving Afro-Latin beat. The fad for this new dance has resulted in two current movies, with five more planned, as well as the usual array of clothing, videotapes, and T-shirt logos (Simpson 1990).

Research Application 10.1

• • • • • • • Could You Love These Turtles?

If you are not caught up in the fad yourself, it is hard to understand how four cartoon-character turtles could become the source of such fascination and desire. Yet, as the United States entered the 1990s, the cartoon creations of Peter Laird and Kevin Eastman were much sought after by pre-teens.

As described in *Time* (Simpson 1990), the characters in question are slow-moving turtles transformed by radioactive material into human-size animals with the ability to speak. These teenage turtles are, as the story line goes, adopted by a rat named Splinter and tutored in one of the martial arts. Thus they come to be known as the Teenage Mutant Ninja Turtles®.

A mania for movies, videos, books, and other objects connected with these four creatures has occurred among kids. The youngsters are so eager to get toys based on the turtles that the company which produces them has trouble keeping up with the demand. For Christmas of 1989 they were the third best-selling toy, and the spin-off products from the cartoon and videos are almost endless. You can walk into a supermarket and purchase (for $2.50) a short book about Teenage Mutant Ninja Turtles' exploits, go to a Target store and buy T-shirts and bath towels emblazoned with their images, or simply listen to children repeat their key phrases (for example, "Hey, dude") or share in their craving for pizza.

They seem unlikely objects of such attention. Yet, like pet rocks, Cabbage Patch dolls, and other fads that have gone before them, the turtles attract a segment of the public—in this case, pre-teens—which becomes absorbed in them. Whether it is for a $12-dollar movie, one of several videos, or items of clothing, a ready public awaits the latest in the adventures of the "wisecracking, pizza-guzzling reptile masters of the martial arts . . ." (Simpson 1990, 59). To those not caught up with these turtles, the mania for them is irrational—but that is the story of fads. To the kids who adore the creatures, there seems to be no way to satisfy their appetite for more.

• • • • • • •

Clothing styles take faddish turns, too. "Texas chic" spread through the United States in the 1970s bringing on the fashion statement of the Urban Cowboy. Blue jeans, boots, cowboy shirts, and other forms of Western dress became popular with a few. The fad also included a craving for western style food—one could go to the Lone Star Cafe in New York or London and get a bottle of Lone Star beer and such Texas favorites as barbecue or chicken-fried steak. This fad was also short-lived; some of the restaurants remain, but the trend in clothing fashion has died out.

David Miller (1985) has separated fads into three kinds. One he refers to as useful-product fads. For example, when the use of citizens band (CB) radios was authorized by the government in 1958, businesses purchased them to make contact with delivery trucks, taxis, and so forth. By 1973 sales of these devices had increased by a factor of twenty, and owning a CB for recreational use had become a fad. Sales of CBs peaked in the late 1970s, and use of CBs returned mainly to the business sector.

A second kind of fad Miller refers to as a novelty fad. In 1977 a clever promoter conceived of the pet rock. Ordinary rocks were sold as pets. The marketing of the fad produced easy chairs, diplomas, and even burial plots for the rocks (Horton and Hunt 1984). About the same time mood rings became a fad. The rings supposedly changed colors as your mood changed. Both items briefly occupied the minds of many in the United States.

The third kind of fad Miller calls the activity fad. In the mid-1970s a practice called streaking was briefly popular. It involved individuals or groups running naked through public places, an act violating the mores of our society. By one estimate (Evans and Miller 1975), streaking incidents occurred on at least 123 colleges and universities. Both Wall Street and St. Peter's Square in Rome also were subjected to streaking episodes (Miller 1985, 144).

Fads are generally trivial in nature. They probably represent a desire to break away from the ordinary. They may be attempts to establish an identity (as in punk hairstyles), to amuse oneself amid the tensions of life (as in Trivial Pursuit), or to show disdain, even if only briefly, for the norms of traditional society (as in streaking).

Crazes

Crazes are distinguished from fashions and fads on the basis of the intensity and relative absorption of the people in the behavior. A craze is an obsession for those who follow it, involving more of their time, resources, and interest than is true for fads and fashions. Youngsters who spend most of their time and money playing video games are involved in a craze. The key features of a craze are illustrated in this game craze in that the players show feverish intensity in their attention to the games, investing great personal and financial resources in them.

Some periods of economic boom are actually closely related to the idea of a craze. In their usual course, such economic crazes follow a pattern of intense activity, upwardly spiraling prices, and the eventual bust. Although the economic downturn inevitably occurs, those caught up in the investment craze seem to feel that this is *the* opportunity that will be different. Thus, those who became involved in land investments in Florida in the 1920s were sure that this was the investment that would put them on "easy street" for life. Florida at that time was relatively undeveloped. However, the extension of roads and rail transportation to the area gave promise that significant growth would occur in this pleasant climate. People rushed to purchase land, and the value of property rose in almost geometric fashion; land was bought and resold, often without even being seen. The craze was to buy, sell, and repurchase land to make great profits. In the end, financial reality returned, and those who last purchased land were left with property that had far less value than the amount invested. The craze ended in financial disaster for some, but, during the year or so that it lasted, nothing would stop those who truly believed this was the path to financial success.

For most, the ownership of a Cabbage Patch doll was merely a fad—but for the 5,000 shoppers who nearly wrecked a department store in their desire to purchase Cabbage Patch dolls and accessories, it was a craze. Those shoppers sought the dolls more intensely than did people who saw them as a fad; they had a nearly obsessive craving to possess the object.

Rumor

Rumor is a very familiar term. We are all familiar with the many rumors that circulate through our school, our neighborhood, our church—indeed, through all groups of which we are members. By implication, rumors spread beyond the bounds of a small, informal friendship group. They pass among a number of people and usually arise in situations of uncertainty and even fear. Although we tend to think of rumor as false, this is not necessarily so. It is not truth or falsity that makes talk rumor but the channels through which the rumors are communicated.

As Turner and Killian (1987) point out, rumors arise at times when the normal channels of communication are, for a variety of reasons, disrupted. This means the information or definitions of a given situation come from unorthodox, even unreliable, sources that cannot be checked in the usual way. For example, during a flood or following a tornado people are cut off from their usual sources of knowledge. Telephones may not work, television and radio may be cut off, and people are often isolated from the larger society. In such a situation the only information available is rumors that circulate from group to group in the affected area.

In essence, rumors arise when we find ourselves in ambiguous positions. The standard norms and rules of the society do not fit the situation and there is little, if any, communication with standard sources of information. Uncertainty is the key feeling of those susceptible to rumor. When there appears to be no meaningful definition of what is going on, rumors circulate, they are the tools by which we can reconstruct a meaningful reality.

For many in the late 1980s and early 1990s, older standards of religious belief and behavior appeared to be challenged. While some leaders emerged to shore up the defense of the traditional faith, many wondered why the old ways were being challenged. Given the uncertainty of many and the shortage of reliable answers, rumors arose. One persistent rumor placed the blame on an individual.

Madalyn Murray O'Hair has been outspoken in her opposition to public support of religion for years. She began the legal procedures that led to the banning of the devotional reading of the Bible in public schools. Her opposition to religion became a focus for those seeking answers to the weakening of the traditional role of religion in society. She, and her followers, were seen as seeking to stop numerous forms of religious activity in the public arena.

Fifteen years ago a rumor circulated that O'Hair was seeking to ban the granting of licenses to any religiously oriented radio stations. The rumor was untrue. Its foundation was a proposed ruling that would curtail the licensing of educational radio stations, a category which included religion but was not limited to religious education. O'Hair actually had nothing to do with the action, yet for fifteen years the rumor has continued to persist, despite fifteen years of press releases seeking to quell it. The FCC continues to receive hundreds of thousands of letters monthly protesting the supposed action by O'Hair (Dart 1990). The rumor is stronger than the truth because, for some, it explains changes in the public presentation of religion that they see as threatening.

Another rumor addressing the same feelings of uncertainty and fear centers on the supposed influence of satanism in the society. The soap company Proctor and Gamble has battled for ten years to dispel the idea that its familiar trademark shows satanist influences. The half-moon and stars in the trademark were interpreted as symbols of satanic power. In a similar vein, rumors regularly arise around Halloween that satanic cults will capture and sacrifice blonde, female children. The rumors tend to be spread by members of fundamentalist Christian groups—again, people concerned about the irreligious path of contemporary society. The rumors have no basis in fact, but they are powerful because they make the situation meaningful to those who find themselves in an ambiguous situation.

Panics

Whereas in crazes the rush is toward something desired, **panics** represent the flight of groups from something they fear. A panic can be seen as the collective behavior of groups, irrational and uncoordinated, to avoid what they perceive as a threat (Vander Zanden 1986, 381).

The possibility of a bank failure, a flood, an earthquake, or a disease may be the source of the real or imagined catastrophe. A fire on the stage of the Iroquois Theater in Chicago led to a panic that killed several people. Although the fire was confined to the stage and was quickly extinguished, people crowded against the exits and crushed one another in their desire to get out of the building. Similarly, patrons waiting to get in to a Who rock concert in the early 1980s feared they would be unable to get seats when they got into the arena where the event was being held. As rumors of the shortage of space spread, the crowd panicked and began to push against the doors. In the ensuing crush several were killed and many injured.

A well-known example of panic created by rumor is the reaction to a 1939 radio broadcast entitled "War of the Worlds." The dramatic story depicted the invasion of the United States by creatures from another planet and took the form of standard radio news coverage. At the beginning of the broadcast, it was announced that the story was not true. However, not all heard those words. Most turned to the program about ten minutes after it began (Miller 1985, 99). Many who had not heard the disclaimer were sent into a state of panic. People all over the nation, particularly in New York and New Jersey (the supposed targets), were seized by terror and set out to guard themselves with shotguns, pistols, and whatever came to mind. It took considerable time and effort to calm people down. Rumor seemed more powerful than truth.

A case from the mid-1980s also illustrates panic and the power of rumor over truth. In 1980 and 1981, two medical researchers found evidence of diseases that occurred in young, gay patients but that were rare among young people in general. The findings of both physicians were reported to the Center for Disease Control in Atlanta, Ga. It was concluded that a new disease had entered the U.S. population. The condition came to be called AIDS (Acquired Immune Deficiency Syndrome).

In the beginning, AIDS was seen as a curiosity found only among homosexual males (at first it was known as GRID—gay related immune deficiency) and those who used drugs intravenously. It soon became evident that the condition was not limited to these small groups. It spread to women—particularly prostitutes—and to people who received transfusions of blood tainted with the virus. A number of hemophiliac children fell victim to the disease, and infants born to women who carried the AIDS virus also became AIDS victims.

AIDS is no longer considered to be a disease limited to homosexuals and drug addicts. It is a national public health problem. According to one U.S. Surgeon General's report (*Time* 1986b), it affects heterosexuals as well as homosexuals, whites as well as blacks, women as well as men, children as well as adults. Former Surgeon General Everett Koop anticipated that AIDS would increase as it spread among people not included in the groups originally considered at great risk. According to recent estimates, more than 90,000 cases of AIDS have been reported throughout the world, with about three-quarters of these in the Americas (Henahan 1988, 3377).

AIDS is spread primarily by sexual contact. The Surgeon General's report of 1986 warned against the danger of sexual contact with strangers and numerous partners. It also indicated that everyday contact with AIDS victims or carriers will not transmit the virus. The report stated that we would not contract AIDS by shaking hands, hugging, social kissing, crying, coughing, or sneezing. AIDS has not been contracted from swimming pools or by eating in restaurants where workers have AIDS or carry the HIV virus. It is not transmitted by sharing sheets, towels, dishes, or other eating utensils. It cannot be contracted from using toilets, telephones, or office machines. In other words, while AIDS is a major public health problem, it is only a threat through sexual activity, transfusion of impure blood, or sharing a contaminated needle.

Again, rumor seemed more powerful than truth. Even highly educated people, including many in the medical profession, still suspect that we are not being told the whole truth about AIDS. Recent surveys have found that almost one-half of the nation's population feel they might catch AIDS by sharing a glass with a victim, and that others have concluded it is unsafe to give blood. The assurance of the medical profession that AIDS is a difficult disease to catch has not allayed fears; it has instead aroused distrust of the medical profession.

Many victims of the panic concerning AIDS are hemophiliac children who were infected with transfusions of tainted blood. For them AIDS also means social isolation at an early age. In New York City, one school board decided that a seven-year-old girl who had AIDS would be permitted to attend public school. This decision touched off a lawsuit and a boycott that involved at least 18,000 children. In Kokomo, Ind., school board officials refused to let a seventh-grade student attend school because he was the victim of AIDS. This matter also led to a lawsuit, but the family had to move to another small Indiana town where the reception of their son was positive. In fact, the son became nationally known and a symbol of courage in the face of AIDS until his death in April of 1990. Still, in a small Massachusetts town, 700 parents were prepared to oppose the admission of a thirteen-year-old AIDS victim to the public schools.

There are other examples of panicky behavior in reaction to AIDS. Unwarranted fears of getting the virus by means of casual contact have appeared at both the workplace and the ballot box. In Massachusetts, technicians for the New England Telephone Company walked out of jobs for a day to protest the return to work of a colleague with AIDS. In California, a proposition was being considered which would give public health officials the right to quarantine all AIDS patients and carriers of the HIV virus (*Time* 1986b, 76).

Several points can be made from this example. First, the panic is based upon unfounded rumors about the means of transmitting AIDS. Second, the attempt of qualified medical professionals to dispel the rumors with medical facts is distrusted, sometimes with reason. Third, the panic that has resulted may have long-term effects for the nation. The development of a test for the presence of the AIDS virus, for instance, may lead to limitations of insurance for those shown to have the virus, to dismissal from the armed forces where testing for AIDS is now mandatory, or to refusal of employment.

Crowd Behavior

Crowd behavior is a common form of collective action and has been given much attention by sociologists. Herbert Blumer (1946) distinguished between two basic types of crowds: those which conform to the established patterns of behavior for the crowd, and those which do not. He divided each of the two basic types into two further classifications.

The first type of conforming crowd is the **casual crowd**. It simply consists of people who are gathered together in one place—for example, people walking through a shopping mall or people waiting for an elevator or bus. (The casual crowd is similar to the nongroup discussed in chapter 5.)

A casual crowd has no form or organization; people just happen to be in a given place at the same time. As another example, a group of people who have stopped to view a street performer as they walk through the park would be a casual crowd. Nothing brings them together other than the brief performance of the mime; when the performance is over, or when members of the group tire of it, the crowd breaks up. (They are not unlike the aggregate described in chapter 5.)

The second conforming crowd is referred to as a **conventional crowd**. Members of such crowds gather together for a specific purpose and behave in a conventional manner. They may assemble to see a movie or a sporting event, and they follow the prescribed patterns for the event they attend. Neither a casual crowd nor a conventional crowd is involved in collective behavior.

A useful way to think about the conventional crowd is to see it as an audience. Audiences are generally groups of individuals who have purposefully come together to listen to or watch some event—a play, a musical presentation, a sports contest. As Turner and Killian (1987) point out, much of the behavior of the audience is not, in fact, collective behavior in the sense of the term as used here. There is a patterning, for example, to the behavior of the audience at a classical musical event. Rarely does the audience applaud spontaneously after a particularly brilliant passage of music. Rather, the performance receives applause only at the end of the work, and this response is given regardless of the merit of the performance.

Similarly, religious congregations are conventional crowds and much of their behavior has become routine. Whether it is the formal routine of a liturgical church, such as the Roman Catholic or Episcopal churches, or the emotionally charged service of a pentecostal revival, members of the conventional crowd give the responses that are customary for that group. Even the expressions of emotion at a healing service take on a more or less routine form.

However, in the nonconforming types of crowds we find many examples of collective behavior. The first type is the **expressive crowd**. For example, in religious groups emphasizing emotional expression, the rhythmic preaching of the leader can arouse considerable feeling. As a result members of the crowd may begin to express their feelings by chanting, dancing, or shouting. Some of this behavior may be patterned for the group by former behavior, but the crowd behaves in a pattern that deviates from the way society in general expresses emotion.

By definition, the expressive crowd does not have an objective. It is not seeking any change in group members or the physical environment. Instead, its aim is to produce "mood, imagery and behavior" (Turner and Killian 1987, 97) in the group.

The feelings of great emotional release evoked by certain religious ceremonies provide a case in point. While the senior author was conducting a group of students through a lower-class section of Chicago, they stopped to visit with a group meeting in a storefront church. The group was actually a board meeting of the church, but the members quickly agreed to provide an example of their way of worship. The leader began to preach to us. As he preached his speech took on an increasingly rhythmic pattern and emotional tone. The congregation responded in kind. As the sermon went on, vocal expressions of approval ("Amen," "Yes, Lord") became increasingly frequent. Then the members began to clap in tempo and perform a kind of shuffling dance as they sat in their seats. Soon, however, they arose and the dancing became more real. Through vocal exclamations and bodily movements, congregation members were expressing emotions, and that alone was the point— the awakening of an emotional state which brought them release.

Other expressive crowds seem more spontaneous. For example, on Monday, January 27, 1986, thousands of Chicagoans came together along State Street to welcome the returning Super Bowl XX champions, the Chicago Bears. The crowd, which had only their love for the Bears in common, did not let below-zero temperatures bother them as they danced, cheered, and in other ways expressed their joy.

Other expressive crowds seem to originate out of deep frustration. In April of 1989 the world's attention was drawn to the crowd of students and workers gathered in Tiananmen Square in the heart of Beijing, People's Republic of China. The students gathered to express their frustration with governmental policies and their desire for greater freedom and the chance for democracy. Until the movement was crushed in June of that year, vast numbers of students gathered in the immense square and quietly expressed their desire for a more democratic government. Their goal was to express their feelings in order to influence government leaders as well as world opinion.

Millions of Iranian mourners flock to the grave of Ayatollah Ruholla Khomeini at Beheshte Zahra cemetery in Tehran to mark the seventh day since his death with another emotional outpouring.

The final type of crowd, the **acting crowd**, gathers and, after some cue, begins to take action against a group or object perceived as an enemy. Frequently the action takes the form of riots, looting, and other forms of damaging mob behavior. In the acting crowd, normative patterns of behavior, with their rules, values, and expected behavior, no longer have meaning. New norms—which may involve the legitimization of looting and damaging property—replace the older ones.

Turner and Killian (1987) raised the question of why the acting crowd acts rather than takes out its frustrations or anger in expressive fashion. They suggest that crowds act when they have the feeling that such action will produce results. That is, the crowd turns to action when there is a perception, true or false, that this behavior will in some way bring about change in the situation. As they pointed out, black crowds only moved from the more escapist expressive behavior to acting behavior when they believed they possessed power to make their actions count.

At times this may simply mean that a sense of power grants permission to act out feelings rather than to simply express them. During the evening of January 30, 1986, a rumor spread among the residents of the Little Haiti section of Miami, where 50,000 to 100,000 Haitian refugees live. It was rumored that the Haitian government of President Jean-Claude Duvalier had fallen. A celebration burst out as 1,500 refugees streamed into the streets to show their joy at the fall of the Duvalier government, but the actions of the crowd turned violent when a driver backed swiftly through the crowd, killing a forty-seven-year-old woman and injuring two men. The expressive crowd became an acting one. Five people were bitten by police dogs, and a policeman was hit by an object thrown by someone in the crowd. When the riot ended, seven residents of the area and six policemen had been injured (Associated Press 1986).

The next day, the official spokesperson for U.S. President Ronald Reagan announced that the Haitian government had collapsed. The celebration continued, although the crowd returned to merely expressing their joy. The announcement, however, was premature; Duvalier's government still stood.

A week later the Haitian government did collapse, and the dictator was flown to France where he was granted temporary asylum. Again, celebrations broke out among refugees in the United States; in Boston, the crowd turned to violence when some members rushed the Haitian consulate, destroying pictures of Duvalier and his wife. In this case fact, not rumor, brought about the crowd behavior (Associated Press 1986).

Groups may also gather to act when they have a traditional sense of empowerment. In England, in the spring of 1990, a crowd gathered on Whitehall Street, London, just outside the residence of the British prime minister, Margaret Thatcher. They were protesting a new means of property taxation which they felt favored the wealthy over the less well-to-do and poor. The so-called poll tax was levied equally on each person regardless of his or her wealth. The protest action was not atypical of a people who felt they had the power to influence governmental action. The crowd grew; as time went on, members of the crowd felt they were not being listened to and the actions became more violent. Eventually the crowd extended a mile up Whitehall into the theater district, and many people were injured as they resisted police attempts to break up the crowd.

Theories of Collective Behavior

As in other areas of sociology, there have been a number of explanations of collective behavior. The earliest theories rested on psychological explanations of crowds in unusual situations. One early explanation described collective behavior in terms of a contagious feeling among crowds which led people to behave in abnormal ways. A corollary to this concept was the idea that crowds were made up of people with similar frustrations and goals leading them to behave in ways that conflicted with normal standards. A later theory saw collective behavior as building through a series of value-added stages (Smelser 1963). More recently, collective behavior has been viewed as an attempt to solve problems that affect social groups, with emergent norms bringing structure to the group's efforts (Turner and Killian 1972).

Contagion Theory

Contagion theory grew out of the work of Gustav LeBon (1841–1931). At a time of rapid social change in his native France, LeBon perceived the crowd as a threat to the social order (Perry and Pugh 1978, 26). He thought that the feelings of power felt in groups, the anonymity of the individuals in crowds, and the power of suggestion in crowds led people to defy their previous socialization and engage in harmful and threatening behavior.

All members of a crowd were assumed to have the same motives and to act on the same impulse. Members of a crowd were perceived to undergo a single, massive transformation from ordinary human beings to cruel, savage individuals. Once caught up in the contagion of a crowd, these people were capable of performing acts that, as individuals, they would not imagine possible.

As LeBon saw it, a "mass-mind" took over the rational thinking of people in a mob. They imitated others in the group, behaving in deviant ways which played upon the suggestibility awakened by the crowd. Both the imitation and suggestibility reinforced the tendency of group members to behave in deviant ways. According to this theory, then, those who would never think of killing or destruction as individuals were changed by the mob into people capable of violent actions such as lynching, riots, and destruction of property.

One hot spring in Oklahoma, university students milled around their campus. There were no set final-exam periods, and many students had little to do. They began to merge at one corner of the campus where there was a women's dormitory. Small groups began to taunt the women living in the dormitory. The taunting soon turned into active behavior, with groups of men attempting to invade the dormitory for "panty raids." As the feeling of the crowd became more intense, the raids became more widespread. Soon the crowd became a mob that stormed the dormitory. The sporadic panty raids turned into a full-scale attack on the dorm, resulting in much damage and in fires. What began as mild teasing turned into a near riot because of the contagious transmission of feelings.

Value-Added Theory

A prominent theoretical approach to collective behavior and social movements is referred to as **value-added theory**. Neil Smelser (1963) drew upon economic principles of manufacturing to develop a framework by which collective behavior could be explored. The basic premise is that there are several stages in the formation of collective behavior and social movements. According to Smelser, each of these steps, in the order he outlined, was necessary before collective behavior would come about.

Smelser's theory listed six stages necessary for collective behavior to occur: (1) structural conduciveness, (2) structural strain, (3) a generalized belief that spreads and grows and that points to some particular line of action, (4) some precipitating factor or factors that intensify pain, (5) the mobilization of participants to follow the line of action suggested by the generalized belief, and (6) an attempt by opposing elements in society to control the growth and effectiveness of the movement. Eventually, Smelser dropped the concept of precipitating factors as a separate stage; he saw it as a part of the stage in which participants were mobilized.

It is easiest to see the focus of this theory when studying movements that continue over a length of time. For example, the theory can be applied to the movement known as the New Religious Political Right. There is structural conduciveness for such movements because we have a complex and differentiated religious situation in America. There are many groups with varying beliefs. Some hold very conservative (traditional) beliefs. Others, notably in the leadership of member denominations of the National Council of Churches, espouse liberal causes, such as abortion on demand, a new role for women in society, and opposition to military buildup. These opposing viewpoints result in structural strain as the conservative groups see the values they deem essential to society being threatened by the liberal wave in society.

As a result of structural conduciveness and strain, a set of generalized beliefs became common among some people: The National Council of Churches aided world communism, morality was being destroyed, the God-given role for women in society was being challenged, and a number of similar ideas. Two or more precipitating factors helped turn the concern from that of individuals to that of small groups: the Supreme Court decision upholding the right to abortion and the new attitudes toward sexual morality promoted by many groups, especially gay and lesbian factions.

Mobilization of the strain and generalized beliefs into a social movement came through the political activities of several conservative religious groups. Powerful leaders such as Jerry Falwell (The Moral Majority) and other television preachers founded organizations that supported candidates who could be relied upon to support the political ideals of the conservative movement (Hadden and Swann 1982).

Finally, attempts to control the influence of this movement were made. Television producer Norman Lear formed People for the American Way (PAW) to counter the New Religious Political Right. The liberal wing of Protestantism sought to challenge the conservative group's proposition that it and it alone spoke for the Christian position. Whether such attempts at social control were effective is unclear. The conservative movements have lost a great deal of financial support. However, poll data (NORC 1989) still indicate strong support for some of the conservative ideas that are seen by many as traditional to religion.

The value-added model provides one tool we can use to understand some of the complexity of collective behavior. Mainly it is useful because it points out that collective behavior requires more than simple discontent (Marx and Wood 1975). However, the approach is very limited. In a few cases, events do proceed according to Neil Smelser's predictions; for example, Jerry Lewis (1972) found that the Kent State riots over the bombing of Cambodia in 1970 followed the six stages. In some cases the stages occur but not in the predicted order, and in some cases all six do not occur (Milgram 1977). Russell Dynes (1970) suggested that the value-added theory simply provides us with a useful set of terms but that these terms only describe rather than explain collective behavior.

Emergent Norm Theory

Emergent norm theory dismisses many of the propositions of both contagion and value-added theories. It views the crowd not as a mass but as individuals who lack unanimity, having many different motives and actions. According to Turner and Killian (1987) a major problem with older theories of collective behavior is that they assume a unanimity of crowd feelings and action without explaining how this develops. Rather, they take it as a given. In some cases this may be true, but it cannot be assumed that all members of any crowd feel the same way about the issue in question and hold the same predispositions. In fact, empirical evidence indicates that crowds do not exhibit this similarity of thought and feeling. Instead they are characterized by a considerable degree of different thoughts, feelings, and attitudes.

Assuming that this perceived unanimity is merely an illusion, it becomes necessary to explain how certain norms and understandings of the situation become common to the crowd. Turner and Killian believe the norms or common understanding that develop in the crowd actually emerge from the specific situation. Collective behavior can thus be understood as the emergent definition of the situation which arises out of the interaction of the crowd. Out of the diversity of the crowd, a collective interpretation emerges as the various segments of the crowd react to build a common definition.

According to Perry and Pugh (1978), Turner and Killian identify at least five different types of members of the crowd: people who are (1) truly committed to the cause, (2) concerned but not fully committed, (3) simply getting satisfaction from being part of a group, (4) simply spectators, and (5) exploiting the crowd for their own uses. Following the concept of emergent norms, people do not find themselves so influenced by the thought of others that they identify with the crowd immediately and just follow the leaders like sheep without any set of norms guiding them. Rather, out of the diversity of the crowd new norms emerge which define the situation.

Even though collective behavior may have its origins in diverse opinions and motivations, meaningful definitions of the situation do emerge. As has been demonstrated in a number of group experiments (Sherif 1936, Asch 1956, to name two), crowds place a high priority on developing new, operative norms. As the activity of a crowd continues, normative expectations for members will emerge out of the crowd itself. These norms will be as effective in providing guides to behavior as were the traditional standards. They also will be effective in controlling and restraining behavior not deemed acceptable. Emergent norm theory, then, seeks to understand how new behavioral expectations rise out of the new conditions brought about by social change. Through this effort they seek to better understand the behavior of crowds.

In the late 1960s there was widespread killing of civilians, including women and children, in My Lai 4, Vietnam. These were acts against the general norms of society, even in wartime. The U.S. soldiers who attacked My Lai 4 suspected that Vietcong soldiers and supporters were disguised as villagers. As concern for their own safety increased, the troops, led by Lt. William Calley, began to round up the villagers. When the first civilians were killed, a new norm began to emerge in the group, a norm that saw the slaughter of civilians as the only way in which the situation could be resolved. Afterwards, many soldiers indicated their disgust at what had happened, but during the incident the norms against killing civilians were suspended as the new norm emerged. A dreadful act of collective behavior occurred not because of contagion or added value stages but because members of the group accepted the new norms put forth for them.

Social Movements

Social movements are collective activities that are planned and organized and that aim at achieving a change in the present structures of society. The aim may be to change only a small part of societal structures; for example, the Sanctuary movement seeks only to provide safety for people fleeing from Latin American governments. On the other hand, the aim may be to make a significant change in the total social system, as when the women's movement seeks to bring about equality for women in all facets of society. The aim may even be to return society to a previously held position, as when the pro-life movement seeks to prevent abortions and other forms of birth control and attempts to strike down the decisions that have legalized abortion on demand.

Social movements are a special case of collective behavior. They share many of the features of collective behavior. People who form movements hold deviant beliefs about what is needed in society and they sometimes use extreme methods, such as protest rallies, to draw attention to their causes. They experience a feeling of strain because of dissatisfaction with some facet of present social organization and patterns. The movements also tend to grow up spontaneously, as a few dedicated individuals assemble around the promotion of a solution to the problems they perceive in current social organization.

Social movements differ from other forms of collective behavior in a significant way, however: they become organized and develop plans for getting their solution adopted as part of the general social patterns. They are "collective enterprises to establish a new order of life" (Blumer 1951, 199). To establish a new order, it is necessary to establish an effective organization that develops plans and mobilizes resources over a significant period of time.

In contrast to other forms of collective behavior, social movements are characterized by a degree of continuity in seeking (or resisting) change in the social group of society of which its members are a part. However, it resembles collective behavior in general in that its membership is relatively undefined and is subject to considerable shifting. Similarly, leadership in social movements is not based on formal selection procedures, guided by rules and regulations, but on the ideas and personalities of individuals who take the lead in formulating and furthering movement goals. For example, Martin Luther King became a leader in the civil rights movement in the 1960s not as the result of an election but because of his actions and the persuasive power of his ideas and principles. Those joining in the movement looked to him as a leader not because of his official status but as a result of what he had done and what he was saying.

To summarize, social movements contrast with other behavior discussed in this chapter in two important ways. First, social movements are composed of people who are related to one another on an ongoing basis and who are involved in joint activities in which they act according to some plan. Second, continuity is fostered by an ongoing organization and supported by the relative stability in leadership and other roles.

Social movements do, in fact, tend to go through a series of stages. First, initial agitation brings the goal of the movement into prominence. Second, that goal gains legitimacy in the eyes of a significant segment of society. Third, the movement gains sufficient strength that some measure of organization is necessary, an organization that replaces the less restricted activities of the early stages of the movement. Fourth, some members of the movement react against what they consider the bureaucratization and stifling of the original spirit of the movement. Fifth, as a result, factions develop within the organization and new versions of the movement emerge.

Social movements may be seen as good or bad for society, depending on the judgment of those viewing them. They arise out of frustration with the present structure of society and seek to bring about a solution to social strain. They usually begin with an individual or a small group of people and expand as they gain strength.

The power of social movements has been seen throughout the history of the United States. Roberta Garner (1977) indicates that a number of social movements culminated in the American Revolution. Beginning with uprisings of the poor and farmers, dissatisfied with the agrarian policies of Britain, these movements accompanied dissent on the part of urban bourgeoisie and southern landowners. As dissatisfaction intensified with the Tea and Stamp Acts, the central movement became the Sons of Liberty. Eventually, a dual government was formed to act alongside official British rule. The Continental Congress was the most powerful figure in this government. Ultimately it guided the merger of the various social movements into the extreme form of the social movement known as the Revolution.

Social movements have continued to play a major role in the shaping of the United States. In a sense they have been benchmarks in the shaping of the nation. During the nineteenth century the abolitionist movement resulted in the granting of freedom to slaves and in a new chapter in intergroup relations, though not always a proud one. In the early twentieth century women made a major stride as they gained the right to vote as a result of the activity of the suffrage movement. In the mid-twentieth century a number of social movements led to dramatic changes in the structure of the nation.

The civil rights movement, dating back to the bus boycott in Montgomery, Ala., in 1955, was the first great stirring. It sought for blacks equal access to public accommodations and the right to vote. The movement began as a fight for the integration of blacks into the full life of society. Seen as the region in which even formal equality was not granted blacks, the South was the target of the efforts of young, educated blacks and mainly northern whites. It was a success in the sense that it forced the passage of the Civil Rights Act of 1964.

However, as Garner (1977) points out, it was not long before activists realized that the work of the civil rights movement needed to be carried further. The 1964 act did not provide the means for raising the low economic status of blacks. Now the focus of the movement moved to the urban centers of the North. At this time, the movement began to rely on black leadership more heavily than it had, easing many white members out of the organizations. The various segments of the movement took on new methods and new goals. Nonviolent protests were replaced with a more violent form of protest. The backing of liberal whites had been needed during the mobilization stages of the civil rights movement, but this support also defined the goals of the movement in assimilationist fashion (see chapter 7). After mobilization, blacks felt a new potential for power and sought different goals. To those

Marches, such as this one in Washington, D.C. in 1963, were a central part of the social movement which led to the Civil Rights Act of 1964.

ends, various groups—Black Muslims and Black Panthers, as examples—sought the right to cultural pluralism as an alternative to integration into a society based on Anglo-conformity.

The civil rights movement forced changes in some of the social and economic structures of the United States. It also spurred a number of other movements, principally student movements. (Recall the first transformation above.) These movements ranged from internal protests against college and university policies to far-reaching protests that were multiple in nature. Protests against the war in Vietnam questioned American foreign policy and created an atmosphere of strong political dissent. Other movements, such as the counterculture (hippies), called the whole social and economic structure of the country into question. Similarly the women's movement (see chapter 8), as it reemerged in the 1960s (see Research Method 10.1), has brought about radical changes in our society.

Research Method 10.1

• • • • • • • Historical Documents and Interviews

The Reemergence of the Women's Movement

In a recent article Verta Taylor (1989) challenges the notion that each new social movement suddenly emerges without any prior history. She suggests that this "immaculate conception" notion of movements is wrong and that the so-called new movements of the 1960s and 1970s were, in fact, rebirths of prior movements. Their emergence was not totally new but actually a revival of older attempts at social change when current political and social conditions were more favorable to these efforts.

She has studied the American women's movement as an example. According to her, a previous struggle for women's rights did not end when the suffrage movement won its goal—votes for women. Nor did the current movement just begin with Betty Friedan or the National Organization for Women (NOW). Rather, the demand for rights for women remained the goal of a number of women even after the suffrage victory, but, as the time was not conducive to success, went into a somewhat dormant period—that is, the demand was held in abeyance. The contemporary social movement concerning women's rights is the direct offspring of previous efforts and builds upon the resources and strengths of those efforts.

Taylor's central premise is that movements go into a holding pattern when the social and political environment is not receptive. However, when social and political opportunities are available the movement reemerges from its semidormant state and presents itself as a lively and viable social movement.

To support her thesis Taylor used historical data and interviews with leaders of the women's movement. She examined material found in archival collections as well as her interviews with women who had been active in the struggle for women's rights during the period of abeyance. She then interviewed leaders of the current efforts and traced the linkage between the older movement and the current efforts.

After examining the women's movement both in the post-suffrage era and in its current incarnation, she concluded that there is a direct link between the older organization and the current movement. From 1945 to 1960 feminist activity was, indeed, in a holding pattern. The social and political climate was not favorable. The stress on family life following World War II, which defined women who were childless as deviant, and the lack of employment opportunity for women were both factors which kept the movement in low profile.

Three groups continued to carry the banner of the movement though. The Women's Bureau of the Department of Labor sought improvement in working conditions for women but displayed little political power. The relatively conservative League of Women Voters pursued appointive positions and elective political offices for women. The third major group, the National Woman's Party (NWP), was more radical. As early as 1944 it tried to have an Equal Opportunities Amendment passed by congress. The women in this third movement suffered from marginality and alienated both men and women; but, according to Taylor, they were the basis for the reemergence of the later women's movement.

She concluded that, in fact, social movements do not actually die. They tend to scale down their efforts in unfavorable times, but they are probably never born anew. Instead they take new forms and show new organization. However, the new movement is not really new; it is in direct lineage with earlier efforts.

Turner and Killian (1987) outlined three basic approaches sociologists take in an attempt to understand how social movements arise, why they succeed or fail, and why the pattern of the movement goes in one direction as opposed to another. The three basic approaches are: (1) the grass roots explanation, (2) the resource mobilization approach, and (3) the collective behavior perspective.

Grass Roots Approach

This is the explanation that most closely follows a commonsense explanation. According to the **grass roots perspective**, social movements grow out of the dissatisfaction of a significant number of people with a situation they perceive as problematic. In other words, when there is a noticeable discrepancy between the ideal values of a segment of society and the reality as they perceive it, a group comes into existence working for a change.

For example, a number of individuals view abortion as morally wrong. They are alarmed at the extent to which legal abortions can be performed. Their real values, which define abortion as murder, are challenged by those who provide abortion on demand. According to the grass roots model, the Right-to-Life movement, opposing abortion, began as these individuals became more and more frustrated and communicated this frustration with others who shared their attitude. As this frustration spread to more and more people, a movement to fight legal abortion emerged. A core group of adherents of this attitude sought to increase the number of people who agreed with them and who would participate in the movement. As that number increases, so does the power of the movement and its effectiveness in opposing the abortion policy.

In brief, from this perspective, social movements grow out of the dissatisfaction of a group of people who seek a change in some current policy or situation. The movement is born from the frustration of individuals who band together to seek a common goal. Success or failure depend upon the effectiveness of the core of adherents in gaining strength and power.

Resource Mobilization Approach

Critics of the grass roots model suggest that wide-scale change cannot occur simply because some individuals are frustrated. That frustration can only be effectively organized when resources are available and strategically used in presenting the case to policymakers.

According to the **resource mobilization perspective**, social movements can only be effective when they are able to obtain sufficient resources to support their cause and when they are wise enough to use those resources well. Success of the movement depends less on the commitment of the adherents than on the planning and organization for the use of resources.

The mobilization stage is an essential part of the development of social movements. Jo Freeman (1983) has noted that, until resources and individuals are mobilized to act toward attaining the sought-after goals, no social movement can be developed.

There is disagreement about which sources best provide the resources needed to mobilize an emerging social movement. Charles Tilly (1973), for example, contends that group homogeneity and the preexistence of social networks are the most effective sources. Others argue that the usual sources of social movements—deprivation, discontent, and anxiety—need the resources of members who are not part of the deprived group (Jenkins 1983). Thus, efforts to obtain women's rights seemed to disappear during the Baby Boom era because there was no support for its goals from those who controlled political, social, and financial resources; the movement was in abeyance until a more favorable climate allowed it to reemerge (see Research Method 10.1).

The resources needed to undertake a social movement are seldom available to the oppressed. Thus, the civil rights movement, the anti-Vietnam War protests, the women's movement, and others have been supported by groups and individuals that do not directly feel the oppression (Snow, Zurcher, and Eckland-Olson 1980). Movements may begin within a group, but mobilization requires the assistance of those who have access to the necessary resources (McAdam 1982).

Returning to the example of the Right-to-Life movement, resource mobilization would view the existence and persistence of the movement as a result of resources, organization, and the effective use of both. It might well point out that the backing of powerful groups such as the Roman Catholic Church and conservative Protestant groups also play a large part in its success.

Collective Behavior Approach

As Turner and Killian (1987) pointed out, grass roots and mobilization approaches tend to view social movements from opposite points of view. The former contends that individuals come together spontaneously to pursue what becomes a common goal. The mobilization approach neglects the interests of the adherents while focusing on the organization and utilization of resources. Neither approach provides a total picture.

The **collective behavior approach**, as described by Turner and Killian (1987), provides a more balanced view of the emergence and operation of social movements. According to this view, social movements do begin as frustrations are shared with others, and plans for action that would relieve the frustration provide a focus for group formation. In order for this to occur, those joined together in this sense of frustration must develop a collective definition of the source of the problem they face and against which they will take action. With these two conditions met, a movement can take shape as individuals come together to eliminate the source of their grievances.

Such an approach is closely aligned to the emergent norm view of collective behavior. It views the eventual members and leaders of the movement as coming together with different interests and motives as well as with varying degrees of concern and loyalty to the incipient movement. Actually, social movements are viewed as in a constant state of change as definitions evolve out of the changing situations adherents face in addressing the problem. In that sense, social movements are seen as having a career—that is, a pattern of development out of which norms are developed and strategies of action are formulated.

Thus, the Right-to-Life movement is neither simply the result of individuals with like interests coming together nor the result of the mobilization and organization of resources. Rather, as those who are frustrated by the more liberal attitudes toward abortion come together, they do so with variant degrees of concern and motivation. The movement actually emerges out of the interaction of individuals with differing concerns as they act within the developing situation.

Types of Social Movements

In an earlier version of their work on collective behavior, Ralph Turner and Lewis Killian (1972) divided social movements into two types: value-oriented and power-oriented. **Value-oriented social movements** are concerned with matters of principle. They seek the improvement of the position of some segment of the society. For example, the civil rights movement sought to bring about an end to segregation and a fuller participation for blacks in the social structure of the United States. Similarly, the women's movement has sought a redefinition of the position of women in society, with equal rights and access to education, jobs, and prestige.

Power-oriented social movements are concerned with obtaining power. These include guerrilla movements seeking to control the government and establish a new regime, such as the various guerrilla movements in Central America and the Middle East during the 1980s. Other power-oriented groups seek what they see as an equitable share of power in their society. The goal of some (though not all) activist movements in South Africa is not to completely overthrow the white government but to have the black majority participate in determining national policies.

Social Movements and Terrorism

Today much of our attention is drawn toward the various social movements in the Middle East. Their number is unknown; their origins are often entangled in webs of conspiracy; and they exist under a number of names. Their chief weapon is terrorism, the results of which have become a worldwide concern.

The term **terrorism** is a negative label. We are quick to identify the activities of our enemies as terrorist while perceiving our own activities as legitimate. Thus, most Americans readily label any violent activity on the part of the Palestinians as terrorism. Our own attack on Libya in the mid-1980s, on the other hand, was viewed by most Americans as a legitimate activity to protect the rights of United States citizens and to stop terrorism. Arab countries, and most other countries, saw the attack as an act of terrorism. Similarly, Israel sees its actions against Palestinians as necessary to the preservation of its nation, and South Africans have used apartheid to maintain a way of life.

A reasonable definition of terrorism, avoiding the problems of labeling, is provided by Ernst Evans. He defines terrorism as "the use of violence to produce certain effects, including fear or terror, on a group of people so as to advance a political cause" (1983, 253). War might be seen as a form of terrorism, since acts of terror certainly occur; but war takes on a legitimation because it is seen as a political action taken by an appropriate authority. Again, this is a matter of definition. Palestinian terrorists may feel they have legitimate authority based in the "government" of the Palestinian Liberation Front; but most nations of the world fail to recognize this authority, so their actions are not considered those of war but of terrorism.

The violence that produces terror is most often used by revolutionary political groups in Latin America, the Middle East, and Ireland, but it also has been used in the United States. To the British, the colonists who attacked them from their hiding places must have seemed terrorists. The activities of the Ku Klux Klan have been notable instances of violent terrorism aimed at blacks, Catholics, and Jews. The cross burnings and lynchings that typified this group's activities in the nineteenth century and in the early twentieth century were used as political weapons to arouse fear in the groups they opposed. The goal of the Klan was to preserve the established white control. Groups seeking black power have also resorted to violent acts to achieve their goals.

Terrorism also became a part of the antiwar movement during U.S. military involvement in Vietnam. The movement began with a peaceful demonstration in Washington, D.C., in April, 1965. The demonstration was in protest of the actions taken by the Johnson administration in the war in Indochina (Evans 1983). Nonviolence was the rallying point for this loosely knit movement, even to the most left-wing factions, such as the Students for a Democratic Society.

However, nonviolence did not remain the sole tactic of the antiwar movement. Several events—including the assassinations of Robert Kennedy and Martin Luther King in 1968, the violent reaction of the police at the 1968 Democratic National Convention in Chicago, and the 1972 election of Richard Nixon as president—wrought a change in the minds of some members of the antiwar movement. A small faction of this movement, known as Weather Underground, began to advocate violence as the only way in which the aims of the movement could be achieved.

As the 1980s passed their midpoint, terrorism was very much alive in many parts of the world. Northern Ireland was torn apart by the terroristic activities of the Irish Republican Army and other groups seeking to cast off British rule. Wherever one went in Central America, there was some danger of terrorist attack. El Salvador and Nicaragua had for some years been the targets of organized terrorist groups seeking to overthrow their governments.

Terrorism and violence have reached their greatest extremes in the Middle East, where Palestinians fight Israelis, Moslem Lebanese battle Christian Lebanese, and Arab factions work against one another. Arab social movements are fragmented; until recently, much of their terrorist effort was aimed at other Arabs. This changed as the several groups recognized the need to strike at non-Arab targets in their efforts to construct a Palestinian homeland where they will wield power.

One Arab movement that has turned its terror on the Western world is Black June, led by Abu Nidal. Nidal created his own group upon breaking with Yasar Arafat because he felt Arafat was not pursuing Arab goals with enough diligence. Black June is an effective organization, within its limits. Young adherents are found throughout the Middle East and in many countries of Europe, where their presence is scarcely noted among the many Arab immigrants. Assassination threats made by this "evil spirit which moves around only in the night causing . . . constant night-mares" (*Time* 1986a) must be taken seriously.

How seriously they must be taken was demonstrated at Christmas 1985. In a coordinated effort, agents of Abu Nidal attacked the airports at both Rome and Vienna. Crowds of holiday travelers lined up at the ticket counters of El Al Air and TWA suddenly heard the sounds of gunfire and explosions. Terrorists, believed to be from Black June, killed fourteen people, including an eleven-year-old girl from the United States. More than one hundred were injured by gunfire and shrapnel (*Time* 1986a).

Nidal directed the assassinations of eight Palestinian officials who were con-sidered too moderate, other Middle Eastern diplomats, synagogue worshippers, and a journalist. The Israelis count 103 terrorist attacks during the past twelve years as due to Nidal's leadership of what he calls the Fatah—the Revolutionary Council. It is possible that more than 200 people have been killed by this group in just two years.

Black June is one social movement that takes extreme and violent steps to achieve the power it desires. Not all power-oriented groups use such tactics, but such groups have become more prominent in the last quarter of the twentieth century. Terrorist attacks continued in 1986 with the hijacking of a Pan Am plane at the Karachi (Pakistan) airport and the bombing of a synagogue in Istanbul.

The world was brutally reminded of this continuing terrorist activity by the Lockerbie, Scotland, air disaster in December of 1988. All 259 people aboard the plane as well as eleven people on the ground were killed when a plastic explosive, semtex, detonated on the plane. Scottish officials place the blame for the disaster on the Popular Front for the Liberation of Palestine—General Command. The same explosive was used to destroy a French plane over the Sahara in September of 1989, killing 170 people (*Time* 1990).

For Americans one of the most frustrating reminders of the results of terrorism in the Middle East is the hostage situation. Even as some hostages were being released in the early months of 1990, a number of others remained in captivity. A wide variety of terrorist groups operating under a general pro-Iranian Hizballah label continued to attempt to use Americans and Englishmen as ransom for their Shi'ite Moslem compatriots imprisoned in various parts of the Middle East (Lacayo 1990). Each group had a separate identity and different demands, but each repre-sented the attempt to bring about social change through acts of terrorism. The rest of the world watches the events with the horror that terrorism is meant to arouse.

We should not assume that terrorism is confined to the Middle East, of course. Portions of Central and South America have also seen terrorist activity. For example, the "killing fields" still exist in Guatemala. In 1989 a total of 522 people were killed in political violence in that country and 200 others were abducted. There is no real way of knowing how many have been killed in political violence in that Central American nation, but estimates run as high as 100,000 deaths and 40,000 disap-pearances (Freed 1990). Nor is such violence limited to one country. El Salvador, Nicaragua, and Colombia, among others, have a dramatic record of terrorist violence as groups within the countries attempt to bring about or resist social change through acts of terrorism.

········· **Questions for Summary and Review**

1. In what sorts of situations is collective behavior most likely to occur?
2. What are the characteristics of "collective behavior"?
3. How can we distinguish between fashions and fads?
4. How are crazes different from fads?
5. What are rumors, and what situations tend to give rise to them?
6. Under what circumstances do panics tend to occur?
7. What types of crowds can be distinguished, and how do they differ from each other?
8. How do contagion theory, value-added theory, and emergent norm theory each seek to explain collective behavior?
9. How are social movements different from other types of collective behavior?
10. What have social movements accomplished in the history of the United States?
11. What different approaches are offered to explain the rise and career of social movements?
12. How is terrorism related to the concept of social movements?

········· **Key Concepts**

Acting crowd (p. 233)
Casual crowd (p. 231)
Collective behavior (p. 223)
Contagion theory (p. 234)
Conventional crowd (p. 231)
Crazes (p. 227)
Crowd behavior (p. 231)
Emergent norm theory (p. 236)
Expressive crowd (p. 232)
Fads (p. 226)
Fashions (p. 225)

Grass roots approach (p. 241)
Panics (p. 229)
Power-oriented social movement (p. 243)
Resource mobilization (p. 242)
Rumor (p. 228)
Social change (p. 224)
Social movements (p. 237)
Terrorism (p. 243)
Value-added theory (p. 235)
Value-oriented social movement (p. 243)

References

1. Asch, Solomon E. 1956. Studies of independence and conformity. *Psychological monographs* 70:9.

2. Associated Press Wire Service. February 1, 1986.

3. Bainbridge, William Sims. 1985. Collective behavior. In *Sociology*, edited by R. Stark, 493–523. Belmont, Calif.: Wadsworth.

4. Bonta, Kenneth W. 1990. The arms merchants' dilemma. *Time* (April 2):29.

5. Berk, Richard A. 1974. *Collective behavior*. Dubuque, Iowa: Brown.

6. Blumer, Herbert. 1946. Collective behavior. In *New outlines of the principles of sociology*, edited by A. M. Lee. New York: Barnes and Noble.

7. _____. 1951. Social movements. In *Principles of sociology*, edited by A. M. Lee. New York: Barnes and Noble.

8. Dart, John. 1990. Rumor of atheist airwave attack persists. *Los Angeles Times* (April 14): S1, S8.

9. Dynes, Russell R. 1970. Organizational involvement and changes in community structure in disaster. *American behavioral scientist* 13:430–39.

10. Evans, Ernst. 1983. The use of terrorism by American social movements. In *Social movements of the sixties and seventies*, edited by J. Freeman. New York: Longman.

11. Evans, Robert R., and Jerry L. L. Millers. 1975. Barely an end in sight. In *Readings in collective behavior*, 2d ed., edited by

R. R. Evans, 401–15. Chicago: Rand McNally.

12. Freed, Kenneth. 1990. Killing fields of Guatemala persist despite U.S. effort. *Los Angeles Times* (April 14):A1, A12.

13. Freeman, Jo, ed. 1983. On the origins of social movements. In *Social movements of the sixties and seventies*. New York: Longman, 8–32.

14. Garner, Roberta Ash. 1977. *Social movements in America*. 2d ed. Chicago: Rand McNally.

15. Hadden, Jeffry, and Charles Swann. 1982. *Prime time preachers*. Nashville, Tenn.: Abingdon.

16. Harris, Scott, and Nancy Wride. 1990. Huge protest at abortion clinic turns violent. *Los Angeles Times* (April 15):A1.

17. Henahan, John F. 1988. AIDS' economic, political aspects become as global as medical problem. *Journal of the American medical association* 259 (23):3377–78.

18. Horton, R., and C. Hunt. 1984. *Sociology*. 5th ed. New York: Macmillan.

19. Jenkins, J. C. 1983. Resource mobilization theory and the study of social movements. *Annual review of sociology* 9:527–53.

20. Lacayo, Richard. 1990. Games captors play. *Time* (April 30):32,33.

21. LeBon, G. 1896. *The crowd: A study of the popular mind*. London: Ernest Benn.

22. Lewis, Jerry. 1972. A study of the Kent State incident using Smelser's theory of collective behavior. *Sociological inquiry* 42:87–96.

23. Marx, G. T., and J. L. Wood. 1975. Strands of theory and research in collective behavior. *Annual review of sociology* 1:363–428.

24. McAdam, D. 1982. *Political process and the development of black insurgency 1930–1970*. Chicago: University of Chicago Press.

25. Milgram, Stanley. 1977. *The individual in a social world*. Reading, Mass.: Addison-Wesley.

26. Miller, David L. 1985. *Introduction to collective behavior*. Belmont, Calif.: Wadsworth.

27. National Opinion Research Center (NORC). 1989. *General social survey*. Chicago: National Opinion Research Center.

28. *Newsweek*. 1986a. Aids in the classroom. 101 (September 8):10.

29. _____. 1986b. You're so vain. (April 14):48–50.

30. Perry, J. B., and M. D. Pugh. 1978. *Collective behavior: Response to social stress*. St. Paul, Minn.: West.

31. Sherif, Muzafer. 1936. *The psychology of social norms*. New York: Harper and Row.

32. Simpson, Janice C. 1990. Lean, green, and on the screen. *Time* (April 2):59.

33. Smelser, Neil J. 1963. *Theory of collective behavior*. New York: Free Press.

34. Snow, D. A., L. A. Zurcher, and S. Eckland-Olson. 1980. Social networks and social movements. *American sociological review* 45:787–801.

35. Taylor, Verta. 1989. Social movement continuity: The women's movement in abeyance. *American sociological review* 54 (October):761–75.

36. Tilly, Charles. 1978. *From mobilization to revolution*. Reading, Mass.: Addison-Wesley.

37. *Time*. 1986a. Carnage once again. 128 (Sept. 15)30–32.

38. _____. 1986b. A most explicit report. 128 (Nov. 3):76–77.

39. Turner, Ralph H., and Lewis M. Killian. 1972. *Collective behavior*. 2d ed. Englewood Cliffs, N.J.: Prentice-Hall.

40. _____. 1987. *Collective behavior*, 3d ed. Englewood Cliffs, N.J.: Prentice-Hall.

41. Vander Zanden, J. W. 1990. *The social experience*. 2d ed. New York: McGraw-Hill.

42. _____. 1986. *Sociology: The core*. New York: Random House.

11 Population and World Resources

· · · · · · · · · · · · ·

Chapter Outline

●

Two intertwined problems face our world. Social and technological changes have brought a lower death rate which has led to a population growth beyond earth's capacity to support it (Ehrlich and Ehrlich 1970, Brown 1990); and industrialization has further led to the depletion and pollution of our world's limited natural resources (Brown 1990, Brown and Young 1990, Postel 1990). While world food production grew to meet demand during the years following 1950, it appears to be reaching its limits, especially as one-fifth of our topsoil and one-fifth of our rain forests have been depleted. Added to this is the problem of atmospheric pollution leading to a deadly atmosphere and to warmer climates.

Such changes in the state of our world led the Council on Environmental Quality (CEQ) to paint a dismal picture of the potential quality of life in the next century:

> If present trends continue, the world in 2000 will be more crowded, more polluted, less stable sociologically and more vulnerable to disruption than the world we live in now. Serious stresses involving population, resources and environment are clearly visible ahead. Despite greater material output, the world's people will be poorer in many ways than they are today (1980, 1).

We have taken some steps to reduce our rate of population growth and to limit the pollution and waste of natural resources, but the world's problems of overpopulation as well as polluted and depleted resources have not gone away. The United Nations Fund for Population Activities predicts that the decade of the 1990s will see greater increases in population than had previously been forecast, with most of the population growth coming in the poor countries of the Third World that are least capable of supporting it (Lewis 1990). Recent investigations have revealed a hundred-square-mile hole in the ozone layer above Antarctica and, as a result of global warming, a four- to seven-degree increase in temperature in Alaska (Flavin 1990). The destruction of the ozone layer and global warming (the greenhouse effect) contribute to the destruction of natural areas, the depletion of resources, and an increasing number of animal species facing extinction (Brown and Postel 1987, 3,4; Jacobson 1989).

So far, we have been able to deal with only the simpler problems facing our world, while those less easily solved continue to grow (CEQ 1985). Threatened drastic changes in climate as well as the depletion of the ozone layer are vivid reminders that the destruction of the world's ecological balance presents serious issues for future generations. Throughout the world both economic and social progress are slowing, signaling our increasing inability to deal with these problems (Brown, Flavin, and Postel 1990, 12).

Not all reserachers see as inevitable the future painted by the Council on Environmental Quality. Some see our world as coming close to the exhaustion of its resources and seek a managed approach to both population and resource problems; others feel that technology will provide a solution that will enable us to reclaim polluted areas and expand our ability to hold a larger population (CEQ 1985).

In short, we live in a world that soon will be faced with the problems of finding and allocating depleted natural resources. As Lester Brown and Sandra Postel (1987, 7) indicate, we are crossing natural thresholds at an alarming rate, and those crossings are affecting our climate, our soil erosion rates, our land deforestation, and the acid level of the air we breathe.

Population

The world's population is now more than 5.25 billion and is growing by the astonishing rate of nearly 9,000 people per hour. The United States, with a population of approximately 248 million people, contains only 5 percent of the world's population. More than 90 percent of the world's population growth is occurring in the poorest nations—in Africa, in Latin America, and in India and other parts of Asia. The world's largest city, Mexico City (14.1 million population), is already seriously overcrowded; nevertheless, it continues to grow by more than 1,000 people each day. On the other hand, wealthier countries in Europe and North America show little population growth. As we discuss later, our population is rapidly becoming divided between the northern and southern halves of the world (Brown 1987a, 21).

Demography

What are the factors that lead the poorest, and often most crowded, nations to such extreme population growth? Why do modern, industrialized nations show little growth? What are the major causes of death in various nations? Will there be enough food for the people of the earth?

These and many other questions are the domain of **demography**, the scientific study of population. Demographers study not only population growth but also the characteristics of a population, such as its age and sex composition. Age and sex are important, for example, because a large number of young, fertile women may mean more births will occur. Demographers study how many people exist in a given territory, where they live, what groups they belong to, where they move, and so forth. The foundation of demography, though, is the calculation and study of births, deaths, and migration.

Births

The first dimension in the study of population is a count of **births** and the development of means to compare the number of births, from one time to another and from one place to another. The **crude birth rate** is the number of live births per 1,000 persons in a given year. This is calculated by dividing the number of births by the total population and then multiplying by 1,000:

$$\text{Crude birth rate} = \frac{\text{number of live births per year}}{\text{total population}} \times 1000$$

Calculation of the crude birth rate results in a relatively small number that can be easily used for comparison with other populations. For example, the crude birth rate for the United States in 1975 was 16 while it was 54 for Kenya in Africa. Using such a clear rate, we can easily see that Kenya had a far higher birth rate than did the United States.

Morning sun glimmers dimly through a thick layer of air pollution over the Paseo de la Réforma in Mexico City, Mexico.

Table 11.1 presents data on crude birth rates in a number of countries, as well as other demographic information. For the world as a whole the crude rate is 28. In the more developed countries, however, the rate is only 15 compared with a rate of 31 in the less developed nations. If China is excluded from this latter group, the rate is 35 (Population Reference Bureau 1989).

The crude birth rate does not always tell us everything we need to know about a population. Countries may differ in their percentage of women of childbearing age. Therefore we utilize a **fertility rate**. This rate is calculated like the crude birth rate, except that the number of live births is divided by the number of women in their reproductive years (ages fifteen to forty-four) in a population rather than by the total population:

$$\text{Fertility rate} = \frac{\text{number of live births per year}}{\text{number of women in reproductive years}} \times 1000$$

●**Table 11.1**   Fertility and Mortality Rates Among World Societies, 1989

	Crude Birth Rate	Crude Death Rate	Infant Mortality Rate
North America			
United States	16	9	10
Canada	15	7	8
Europe			
Belgium	12	11	9.7
Denmark	11	11	8.4
France	14	11	7.6
Spain	11	8	8.8
United Kingdom	14	11	9.1
USSR	20	10	25
Latin America			
Chile	22	6	19.1
Cuba	17	6	13.3
Haiti	35	13	117
Mexico	30	6	50
Puerto Rico	19	7	14.9
Nicaragua	43	8	69
Africa			
Algeria	42	100	81
Cameroon	43	16	128
Egypt	38	9	93
Ethiopia	44	23	155
Nigeria	46	17	122
South Africa	35	9	65
Asia			
Afghanistan	49	23	172
Bangladesh	43	15	138
India	33	11	96
Israel	23	7	10.7
Japan	11	6	4.9
Vietnam	34	8	53

Source: Population Reference Bureau, Inc. 1989. *1989 World population data sheet.* Washington, D.C.: Population Reference Bureau, Inc.

In demography such a rate is referred to as an **age specific rate**; it is adjusted to deal with a pertinent population—in this case, women who are able to bear children. Weeks (1989, 110) illustrates how using the age specific rate leads to a correct conclusion. During the depression of the 1930s it was thought that people were having fewer children, while during the Baby Boom era of the 1960s people were having large families. However, the crude birth rate alone predicted more births per 1000 women in 1935 than in 1967 (19 compared to 18). This was merely a result of the measure being used. Adjusting for age, the fertility rate did show the increase in births for the later period. With children and women not in childbearing years taken out of the equation, there were 88 births per 1000 in 1967 compared with only 78 in 1935.

Other subcategories are useful for different purposes. We would want a rate that is specific for certain socioeconomic statuses if we were interested in differences in childbearing by class. Region of the country and racial or ethnic backgrounds are also variables for which we might wish to have a specific rate.

Deaths

The second aspect of a population demographers need is an indication of the number of **deaths** each year, which can be measured and compared with the number of births. The **crude death rate** is the number of deaths per 1,000 population in a given year. Like the crude birth rate, the crude death rate (calculated in the same manner as the birth rate) results in a small, easily comparable figure.

In 1989 the crude death rate for the United States was nine and the crude birth rate was sixteen. From this we can see that our population is increasing as a result of natural births. In some European countries (see Table 11.1) the birth and death rates are quite similar, meaning there is little increase in population from natural births.

Most poorer nations, such as Mexico, have a lower death rate than do the United States and Western European nations. Mexico's low death rate may be due to its relatively young population. It is useful to calculate death rates specific to certain categories within the population, particularly within age and socioeconomic status groups.

Using crude or specific birth and death rates, demographers can determine the **natural growth rate**. This is usually expressed as the excess of births over deaths for a society as a whole or for certain segments of it. To determine the natural growth rate, you subtract the death rate from the birth rate and divide by ten. For the United States, the crude death rate of nine is subtracted from the crude birth rate of sixteen. The result is seven; our natural growth rate is 0.7 percent. By comparison, the natural growth rate of Kenya is 4.1 percent, or nearly six times the U.S. growth rate.

Migration

The third factor involved in determining the shape of a population is **migration**—people moving in or out of a society. For example, much of the population growth of the United States resulted from people coming to this country from other parts of the world (**in-migration**). In the nineteenth century, vast numbers of people came from all over Europe to the United States. Today, people continue to come from Europe and from Asia, among other places. In other countries, for example

Ireland, the population has at some time been reduced because a large number of people moved to other countries (**out-migration**).

When attempting to project population growth or decline for various regions, states, or cities in a society, it is necessary to estimate the amount of in-migration and out-migration. In the first part of the twentieth century, for example, blacks from the South began a steady stream of migration to the cities of the North. More recently there has been a large migration from the Snowbelt cities to the Sunbelt cities of the South, although this trend has slowed and even reversed in recent years.

Growth of World Population

The first humans roamed the earth in small tribes or groups, finding nourishment and clothing from hunting and gathering activities. For thousands of years, from the Old Stone Age until after the Middle Ages, the earth's population grew slowly, remaining at less than 1 billion (World Bank 1984, 3).

Since at least the nineteenth century, however, the world's population has increased dramatically. It is now about 5.25 billion, and some predict that it will reach more than 6.2 billion by the year 2000 (see Figure 11.1). Although fertility rates are expected to drop in both developing and developed countries, a continuing decrease in death rates will most likely offset the loss of new births, leading to a rapid rise in population.

●**Figure 11.1**   Population Growth and Distribution

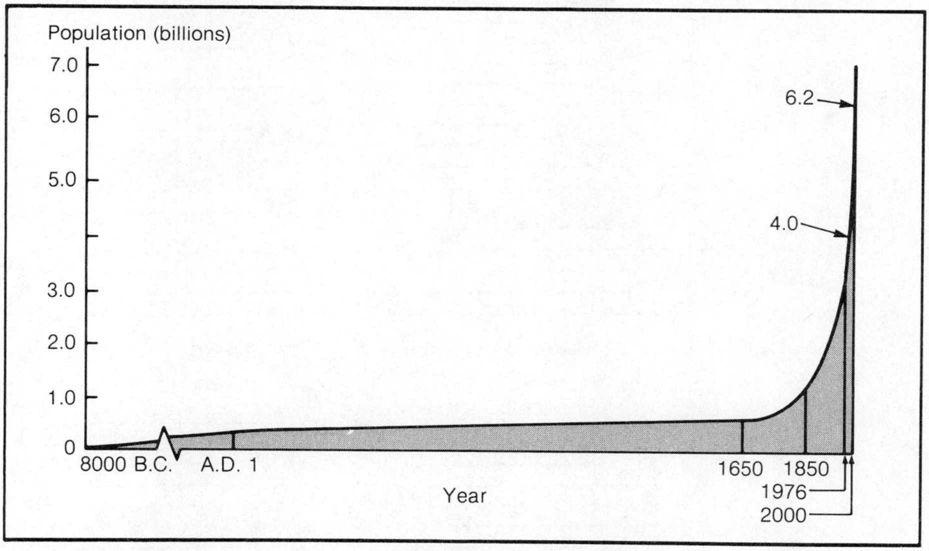

Population (billions)

7.0

6.2

6.0

5.0

4.0

3.0

2.0

1.0

0

8000 B.C.   A.D. 1   1650   1850

Year   1976

                                                        2000

Source: Population Reference Bureau. *World population growth.* Washington, D.C.: Population Reference Bureau, Inc., 1976.

Research Method 11.1

• • • • • • • **Population Pyramid: Birth Cohorts and Population Pyramids**

The following excerpt from Robert Weller and Leon Bouvier's book entitled *Population: Demography and Policy* (1981) illustrates the use of one demographic tool, the *population pyramid,* in following birth cohorts through the life cycle:

"The progress of birth cohorts through the various stages of the life cycle may be studied through the use of population pyramids. The pyramids shown below are based on projections of the U.S. population made by the Bureau of the Census. They assume a total fertility rate of 2.1. Note the indentation in the

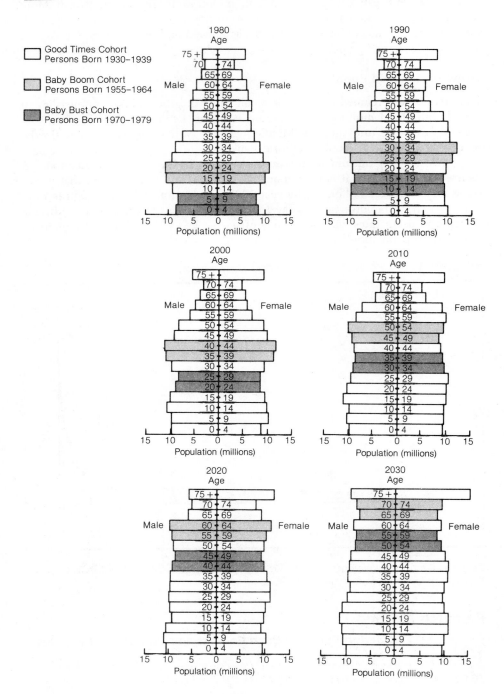

1980 pyramid at age forty to forty-nine. The people represented here were born during the 1930s, when the birth rate was lower than it was during either the 1920s or the 1940s. Also note the bulge caused by the baby boom and the way the pyramid slopes inward at the bottom because of the baby bust of the 1970s."

"Because these projections assume a total fertility rate equal to replacement level, the pyramid becomes more and more rectangular through time. The number of births increases slightly during the 1980s as members of the baby boom cohort pass through their twenties, which traditionally have been the prime years of childbearing. This increase is called an "echo" effect. The bulges represented by the baby boom and the echo effect continue to be present until the year 2030, when the baby boom cohort reaches age seventy and experiences very high mortality."

Art Source: U.S. Bureau of the Census (1977).

Since 1979 there has been some decline in the world's birth rate. However, the growth of the world's population has not dropped appreciably. It remains at 1.8 percent (Population Reference Bureau 1989). If this growth rate should remain constant, the world's population would double every 39 years; the world would have a population of 8.5 billion people in 2020 and 32 billion in 2089 if the present rate of growth continues.

According to the most recent U.N. projections, the population of the world will continue doubling in size until it levels off at about 10 billion, a figure that will be reached in the next century. The problem presented by such an increase in population is compounded by the fact that most of the 5 billion people added to the world's population will live in the poorest part of the world. The Indian sub-continent, parts of the Middle East and Africa, as well as Latin America will see the largest growth, and these are all areas which already have difficulty supporting their population.

Malthusian Theory

An English clergyman of the nineteenth century, Thomas Malthus, foresaw the possibility of tremendous growth in world population. He maintained that human populations would grow according to the amount of food available. He also contended that population growth would always be somewhat ahead of available food. Malthus assumed that population growth would come about as a result of a lower death rate accompanied by a continuing high birth rate. With these predictions, Malthus arrived at a **geometric theory** of population growth, also known as **Malthusian theory.**

Malthus suggested that human population does not grow arithmetically (1,2,3,4,5, etc.) but instead grows geometrically or exponentially (1,2,4,8,16, etc.). In contrast, food supply grows arithmetically. Malthus pointed out that the food supply would thus never keep up with the population.

An old Persian legend provides an example of the effects of exponential growth (Meadows et al. 1974). One day, a clever man presented a chess board to his king and asked only that the king give him in return, 1 grain of rice for the first square, 2 for the second, 4 for the third, and so on. The king agreed and ordered rice to be placed upon the board. The fourth square contained 8 grains, the fifth held 16, the sixth 32, the seventh 64, the eighth 128, the ninth 256, and the tenth 512. The twenty-first square gave the man more than a million grains of rice. By the fortieth square, the king needed a trillion grains of rice—far more than he had in his stores.

To put this in terms of population growth, consider the differences in two-child families and four-child families over three generations. Suppose a couple has two children who in turn have two children each (four grandchildren), and the four grandchildren in turn have two children each; the original couple produces eight great-grandchildren. Now suppose the original family has four children, who each have four children; if each grandchild also has four children, the original couple will have sixty-four great-grandchildren. As our population grows in this fashion we, like the king, are fast running out of resources.

It was 1800 A.D. before the world attained a population of 1 billion, taking from 2 to 5 million years to reach this level. However, it took only 130 years (from 1800 to 1930) for the second billion to arrive, and a third billion was added in only the next 30 years (from 1930 to 1960). Fifteen years later, in 1975, 4 billion people lived on the planet. At present the **doubling time** is 39 years. Doubling time is a popular term by which demographers indicate the number of years that it will take for the population to double itself, assuming growth continues at a steady pace (Population Reference Bureau 1989). For example, if you have a population of 50,000 with a 10-year doubling time, the population would be 100,000 in that 10 years. In yet another 10 years we would have 200,000 people, and so on. It is currently estimated that the earth's doubling rate is 39 years. If the world population is 5.25 billion in 1990, and growth is steady, by 2029 the population will be 10.50 billion.

The Demographic Transition

Malthusian theory, based on death rates alone, maintained that population growth would be cyclical—that there would be times of rapid population growth followed by decline. Thomas Malthus did not foresee the possibility of a steadily reduced mortality rate coupled with a lowering of the fertility rate; thus he did not predict the explosive population growth we have seen.

However, demographers now observe and report a decline in both births and deaths. This dual decline is the end result of the **demographic transition**, a drastic change in the world's population that is the result of many factors including industrialization (see Figure 11.2.). The demographic transition is really a description of three basic stages, or three dramatic shifts that took place as the world's static population began to grow (Weeks 1989, 73).

Research Application 11.1

· · · · · · · **A Divided World**

Completing the Demographic Transition

In the late eighties, the straightforward economic division of the world into the North and the South is yielding to a more significant demographic division based on differential population growth rates. . . . [I]n one set of countries, which contain nearly half the world's people, populations are growing slowly or not at all and incomes are rising. In the second group, populations are growing rapidly and incomes are falling, or risk doing so if rapid population growth continues.

Dozens of countries in the latter group, all in the Third World, have crossed key environmental thresholds and are now experiencing income declines. They need to slow population growth quickly lest they fall into the demographic trap. This will be particularly difficult because the economic and social improvements that normally help reduce family size are no longer operating. The urgent need to slow population growth under such trying circumstances presents a situation for which the experiences of other countries offer little guidance.

China narrowly avoided this demographic trap. Government projections in the late seventies showed that even if Chinese families averaged just two children, the country's population would still grow by several hundred million and would overwhelm support systems and resources, undermining the economy and reducing living standards. China's leaders saw the decline coming and took preemptive action to head it off. They adopted the only alternative—an unprecedented program to encourage one-child families.

The key to the Chinese success was a national effort to foster public understanding of the consequences of the demographic path China was on. Using the long-term projections, they calculated future per capita supplies of cropland, water, energy, and jobs. These numbers formed the basis of a broad public education effort on population policy. . . .

Attempting to slow population growth quickly when living standards are deteriorating is one of the most difficult, politically complex undertakings any government can face. Many nations face a demographic emergency. Failure to check population growth will lead to continued environmental deterioration, economic decline, and, eventually, social disintegration.

In this new situation, some policymakers are beginning to consider new approaches to lowering birth rates. Nigerian economist Adebayo Adedeji, Executive Secretary of the U.N. Economic Commission for Africa, urges research on "the use of the tax system as a means for controlling population growth and discouraging rural/urban migration." Such a recommendation, suggesting an unprecedented approach to Africa's population problems, indicates the urgency that some African decision makers are at last beginning to attach to escaping the demographic trap.

Source: Lester R. Brown and Edward C. Wolf. "Charting a Sustainable Course." In *State of the World 1987*, edited by L. Brown, New York: Norton, 1987, pp. 200–201.

• • • • • • •

Students of population (Weller and Bouvier 1985, and Weeks 1989 as examples) suggest that the demographic transition began in a **high growth potential stage**. At this time both birth and death rates were very high. Remember, however, that this stage held only the potential for considerable growth. If a significant change should occur in either birth or death rates, there could be considerable increase in population. For our planet, this was a time at which the world was poised for a great advance in population although it had not yet occurred. This condition probably lasted for several thousand years before the technology of the Industrial Revolution and modern means of sanitation made growth both a possibility and a reality (Weller and Bouvier 1981).

The second stage, the **transitional growth stage**, coincided with the Industrial Revolution. It began in about 1800 with a decline in mortality rates for the Western world. As a result of modern means of sanitation and medical care, people were living longer and there was a dramatic decrease in the number of deaths from acute illnesses such as measles and chicken pox. Thus, the potential of the first stage was realized. The birth rate did not experience the same decline, and world population

Figure 11.2 The Demographic Transition

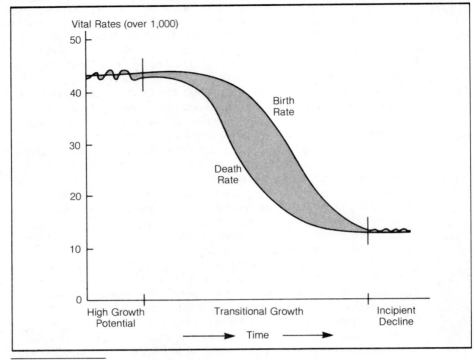

Source: From *Population: Demography and Policy,* by Robert H. Weller and Leon F. Bouvier. Copyright © 1985 by St. Martin's Press, Inc., and used with permission.

exploded. Toward the end of the period, however, death rates ceased to decline, birth rates fell in developed nations, and population growth almost stopped.

The third stage in the **incipient decline stage.** Both birth and death rates are relatively low in this stage, and population increases and decreases are largely a result of fertility fluctuations. This stage has been reached in many of the industrialized countries of the world, where birth rates have declined—except during the Baby Boom. Should this phase continue, population will decline over time. However, modern medicine may provide for a population increase as researchers discover ways to allow people to live longer.

Keep in mind that the demographic transition is only a model of population change. It may not be accurate in all cases, and it may not cover all possibilities The model does not account for what Lester Brown (1987, 36) refers to as a **demographic trap.** Brown suggests that this is the grim alternative that faces those who are unable to complete the demographic transition. Countries that stay in the transitional growth stage for a long period of time experience rapid growth in population, resulting in economic and ecological destruction, which may eventually force them back to the first stage of the demographic transition:

A typical developing country has ... been in the middle stage of the demographic transition for close to four decades. This high-fertility, low-mortality stage cannot continue for long. After a few decades, countries should have put together a combination of economic policies and family planning programs that reduce birth rates and sustain gains in living standards. If they fail to do so, continuing rapid population growth eventually overwhelms natural support systems, and environmental deterioration starts to reduce per capita food production and income (Brown 1987a, 36).

A Divided World

The story of world population is one of opposites. The countries of the world with the least income and lowest level of development are showing the greatest increase in population. Lester Brown (1987, 21) comments that, rather than speak of developing or developed nations strictly on the basis of economic conditions, we should look at their living standards. In doing so, we find that population growth has divided the world into two halves, one moving toward a better life, the other facing "ecological deterioration and economic decline" (Brown 1987, 21).

As can be seen in Table 11.2, slow-growth areas of the world have population growth rates of no more than 1.0 percent per year. The average population growth for these regions is 0.8 percent, yielding an annual increase of 18.6 million people per year. On the other hand, the rapid-growth regions have growth rates as high as 2.8 percent per year, meaning that these already poor parts of the world will increase in population by 65.5 million persons per year.

Population projections for specific countries are presented in Table 11.3. Among the slow-growth nations, China is predicted to have the greatest percentage increase—50 percent—and is expected to have approximately 1.5 billion people when population is stabilized. The United States population is expected to stabilize at 289 million, an increase of only 20 percent.

When we look at the population projections for the rapid-growth countries, we see a different picture. The smallest growth is predicted for Brazil, whose population will increase from 143 million to 198 million at the time of population

● **Table 11.2** Population Growth

Region	Population (million)	Population Growth Rate (percent)	Annual Increment (million)
Slow-growth regions			
Western Europe	381	0.2	0.8
North America	267	0.7	1.9
E. Europe and Soviet Union	392	0.8	3.1
Australia and New Zealand	19	0.8	0.1
East Asia*	1,263	1.0	12.6
Total	2,322	0.8	18.6
Rapid-growth regions			
Southeast Asia**	414	2.2	9.1
Latin America	419	2.3	9.6
Indian Subcontinent	1,027	2.4	24.6
Middle East	178	2.8	5.0
Africa	583	2.8	16.3
Total***	2,621	2.5	65.5

*Principally China and Japan.
**Principally Burma, Indonesia, the Philippines, Thailand, and Vietnam.
***Numbers may not add up to totals due to rounding.

Source: Lester R. Brown. "Analyzing the Demographic Trap." In *State of the World 1987,* edited by L. Brown. New York: Norton, 1987, p. 22. Based on information from Population Reference Bureau. *1986 World Population Data Sheet.* Washington, D.C.: US Government Printing Office, 1986.

● **Table 11.3** Projected Population Growth

Country	Population in 1986 (million)	Annual Rate of Population Growth (percent)	Size of Population at Stabilization (million)	Change from 1986 (percent)
Slow-growth countries				
China	1,050	1.0	1,571	+50
Soviet Union	280	0.9	377	+35
United States	241	0.7	289	+20
Japan	121	0.7	128	+6
United Kingdom	56	0.2	59	+5
West Germany	61	−0.2	52	−15
Rapid-growth countries				
Kenya	20	4.2	111	+455
Nigeria	105	3.0	532	+406
Ethiopia	42	2.1	204	+386
Iran	47	2.9	166	+253
Pakistan	102	2.8	330	+223
Bangladesh	104	2.7	310	+198
Egypt	46	2.6	126	+174
Mexico	82	2.6	199	+143
Turkey	48	2.5	109	+127
Indonesia	168	2.1	368	+119
India	785	2.3	1,700	+116
Brazil	143	2.3	298	+108

Source: Lester R. Brown. "Analyzing the Demographic Trap." in *State of the World 1987*, edited by L. Brown. New York: Norton, 1987, p. 23. Based on information from World Bank, *World Development Report 1985*. New York: Oxford University Press, 1985.

stabilization (108 percent). The largest growth is expected in Kenya, with an increase of 455 percent, and in Nigeria, with a growth of 406 percent. This devastating population growth is expected to occur in already impoverished nations that lack the resources to develop better economies.

Although population in the United States is not expected to increase dramatically, it will differ in general composition (see Figure 11.3). More of the population will be beyond normal childbearing years as we approach the year 2040. This trend is often referred to as the graying of America. There will also be nearly 50 percent fewer children under age five in the population (U.S. Bureau of the Census 1984b). Similar variations are expected in the age structures of other developed countries. In contrast, underdeveloped countries will have a far greater proportion of their populations between the ages of zero and fourteen.

The population of the United States is far more heterogeneous now than it has been. Anglos make up a smaller proportion, and this trend is expected to continue. By the year 2080, the population of the United States will be one-fourth black and Hispanic. This change in the distribution of the population will have dramatic effects on the society (U.S. Bureau of the Census 1984, 10).

Why are these minorities gaining in population relative to whites? There are, of course, several answers, but one can be found in the differential age distribution of the populations. As can be seen in Figure 11.4, for both men and women there are more blacks in the child-bearing years than there are for whites. In short, even if fertility rate and other factors were held constant, there would still be proportionately more black births. There is simply a greater proportion of black women

●**Figure 11.3** *Percentage of the Population in the Older Ages, 1940–2040*

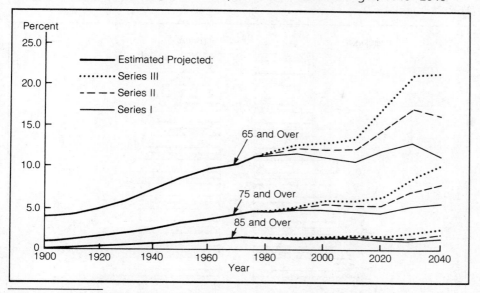

Source: From *Population: Demography and Policy,* by Robert H. Weller and Leon F. Bouvier. Copyright © 1981 by St. Martin's Press, Inc., and used with permission.

than white women in their child-bearing years. Such a difference, then, leads to the increased proportion of the population that is black.

Population Control

Population control seems a simple answer to the problem of overpopulation. It is certainly a direct approach. However, it is not an easy policy to put into action. Governmental policy alone cannot usually solve the problem; the cooperation of individual members of society and sufficient knowledge of birth control are also needed. There are both political and ideological problems. Conservative Americans may view such programs as government interference in their individual rights, while both Roman Catholics and those from conservative Protestant backgrounds see birth control as immoral.

One example of a government's enforcing birth control is found in the People's Republic of China. The government enforces a one-child, one-family rule through a number of penalties, including loss of pay, poorer housing, and lower status for those who disobey. In general this policy has worked fairly well; but the policy is not totally effective. In rural areas, many defy the policy and drown newborn daughters so they may try again for a son. The policy also has problems for those in urban areas as they attempt to deal with the growing problem of the aging in their society.

Looking at it as only a demographic matter, China's story is one of success in family planning (Jacobson 1989). However, the effectiveness of this planning may be blunted by China's past history. Because of past population growth in China, there is a large number of people in their reproductive years in that nation. For that reason, despite the one-child rule, population will continue to grow for at least the next three decades; thus, it is estimated that China's population will grow by

●Figure 11.4 Age-Sex Pyramid for the Black and White Populations of the United States, 1980

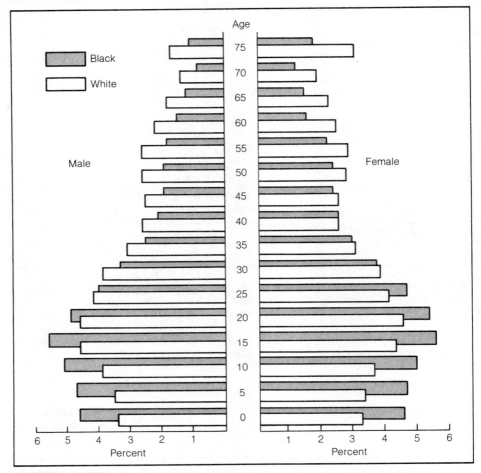

Source: Paul Zopt. *Population.* Palo Alto, Calif.: Mayfield, 1984, p. 125. Data from US Bureau of Census, 1980 Census of Population, Supplementary Reports, PC80–81, Age, Sex, Race, and Spanish Origin of the Population by Regions, Divisions and States; 1980. Washington, D.C.: US Government Printing Office, 1981, table 1.

50 percent, to 1.5 billion, by the year 2020. Even more stringent controls on population will be needed or the country will have to deal with the problem of such a high rate of growth.

Why do people in developing countries continue to have large families? According to the World Bank (1984), there are several reasons:

1. People obtain pleasure from their children.
2. At least in rural areas, children are a form of economic investment for the present and social security for parents in old age.
3. Families want a large number of children because they still fear high rates of infant mortality.
4. Cultural norms may encourage having a large number of children for religious and other reasons.

World Resources

World population is already straining the resources of "space ship earth" (Ehrlich 1968). Natural resources are being depleted and polluted. Some of these cannot be replaced, and others cannot be replenished in sufficient quantity to support the population.

Lester Brown and Sandra Postel (1987, 7–10) indicate that our increasing population, poor management of resources, and technology have brought us to the point of crossing natural thresholds. **Natural thresholds** are points at which our consumption of natural resources exceeds the ability of nature to replace them. For example, it is believed by scientists that pollutants that result from the burning of oil have damaged large areas of forests in northern Europe. If this damage increases, we will have crossed the natural threshold with regard to forestation, which will make it more difficult to cope with such natural occurrences as cold, drought, and wind.

Similarly, we are approaching the natural thresholds with regard to the quality of soil. Research shows that in a number of cases soils are so loaded with the acidity resulting from the burning of fossil fuels that their vital nutrients are depleted. When this threshold is crossed, large areas of soil will be damaged to such an extent that they may never again be useful for agricultural production.

Societies in every part of the world have become dependent on the rapid use of our depletable natural resources to maintain the present quality of life. In these systems, population is now reaching a level that cannot be supported. One example is the growing shortage of water for agricultural purposes. Throughout the world people are dependent on irrigation of land so that it can produce enough food. Whether we are talking about Egypt, northern China, or the western U.S. Great Plains, we are talking of areas that require irrigation to produce sufficient food.

Now it appears (Postel 1990) that we can no longer depend on irrigation to support the needed increases in food production. The advances in production previously gained through this method cannot continue to provide surplus. There is an economic problem; the money to finance new projects is not as readily available as it was. Even more basic, climatic changes, such as global warming, and overly rapid depletion of water resources have led to a severe shortage. Throughout the world there simply will not be enough water to grow the food required by projected increases in population.

Depletion of Resources

The early European explorers of the North American continent undoubtedly imagined they were seeing a never-ending supply of natural resources. However, as expansion and industrialization have progressed, the vast resources of the continent have been squandered to the point that many predict we will soon be without sufficient natural resources to continue life at its present level of quality. If population growth continues at its present rate, we will, at least in the short run, face severe shortages of most natural resources, including food, water, and other consumables. As one generation is succeeded by another, the resources needed for a secure and stable life will become harder and harder to provide.

For example, people who live on the South Plains of Texas are dependent for their water on the Ogalalla Aquifer, a giant underground reservoir that stretches over thousands of square miles. As the growing population of the South Plains, along with industry and irrigated farming, demand more and more water, the aquifer is gradually being depleted. It took thousands of years for the aquifer to develop, and it will not replenish itself quickly enough to continue to provide the needed amount of water. Only by importing water from other parts of the country will the people of the South Plains, and others, get the water they need for their very existence.

We can also look at the effects of agriculture on other parts of our resource system. Farming can lead to the destruction of land (Weeks 1989). Improper irrigation leads to soil erosion which results in the loss of valuable farmland. During the past two hundred years, one-third of the topsoil of the United States has been washed away. This damage has meant the loss of one hundred million acres of cultivated land. Other countries, particularly in South Asia and Latin America, face even more extreme loss of cropland (Brown 1987b). Recent estimates are that about one-third of all the cropland in the world is losing valuable topsoil at a rate that will endanger future productivity. It is estimated that as much as twenty-four billion tons of topsoil blows away or is washed off land in any given year (Brown 1989).

Topsoil erosion affects other natural resources, too. The eroded soil usually goes into a riverbed or lake bottom. Here it chokes out reservoirs. It can also turn large areas of previously agricultural areas into deserts. For example, the southern-most regions of the Sahara have been creeping into wide areas of farmland for years, turning previously tillable land into sand. Those studying the problem of land in western Africa have concluded that the land will not be able to feed the people in

Refugee children from Mozambique eat a badly needed meal at a settlement in South Africa.

this region unless some technological means is found. Even then it may be un-profitable to utilize the technology (Brown 1987, 26).

Pollution

The technology that has enabled us to sustain our world at a high level of quality is also the primary source for the pollution that is damaging our environment and natural resources. Technology not only consumes goods at a dramatic rate, it also produces shortages by contaminating air, water, land, and other natural resources. **Pollution**, the pouring of wastes into the air, water, and land, is a major threat to the continuing welfare of the United States.

While new problems, such as the greenhouse effect and the depletion of the ozone layer, make the headlines now, older problems continue to exist and, indeed, have been compounded. Neither air pollution nor acid rain, as we shall see, have ceased to be problems.

For a time there was optimism. Environmentalists in the Western world were able to make some improvements in the problems of a weary environment. However, these were neither sufficient nor long lasting enough to make the problems go away. Air pollution continues to devastate forests, agricultural produce, water sources, and even buildings in both Europe and on the North American continent (French 1990b). Evidence is growing that the Third World now faces serious levels of devastation as a result of pollution, too.

Ironically, some of the methods by which the Western world attempted to deal with pollution have caused even deeper problems. For example, when air pollution was first made a matter of serious concern one solution was to erect very tall smokestacks or chimneys. This took the pollution resulting from the burning of fossil fuels out of the immediate atmosphere. However, the sulfur dioxide and nitrogen oxide were still in the atmosphere and, as they drifted higher and higher, spread further into the environment causing the problem of acid rain.

Acid rain (moisture containing pollutants) is an increasing problem in Canada and the eastern part of the United States. Acid rain is caused by the pouring of acid-forming compounds into the atmosphere in either dry or wet forms. In eco-logically sensitive areas of the United States and Canada, the acid is generally derived from emissions of sulfur dioxide, nitrogen oxides, and hydrocarbons. Large quan-tities of these substances are discharged into the atmosphere every year. In the United States, about seventy percent of the emissions come from electric generating facilities. Automobiles and other vehicles emit a significant proportion of pollutants. In all, manufactured sources account for over ninety percent of all acidic emissions in the industrialized areas of eastern North America (CEQ 1984). In brief, what had been a local problem before the smokestacks were raised has become a national and international issue.

Pollution, like population, grows in geometric fashion (Meadows et al. 1974, 69). Even a little pollution now can lead to massive problems in the near future. Because pollution is rapidly destroying the natural habitats of wild animals and plants, a larger number of species in both categories will become extinct in the next twenty years; as many as twenty percent of animal and plant species could be lost to the world in this time.

Pollution also destroys the basic balance in nature. The result is a rippling effect in which the initial damage is multiplied by other aspects of our resource system. For example, during the 1970s the waters of Lake Erie were so polluted that people were unable to swim in the lake, and fish and vegetation died. In 1986 and 1987, pollution caused a red tide in the Gulf of Mexico that destroyed the shrimp that contributed to a major industry in south Texas.

As long ago as 1962, Rachel Carson published a book entitled *Silent Spring* (1970). In this volume, Carson spoke out with great emotion about the effect pollution was having on our environment. In particular, she was concerned with the way in which pollutants from industry and industrial by-products were being poured into our rivers, streams, and air. More recently our attention has been called to other problems which have further escalated the pollution problem. Issues such as the effects of modern, mechanized agriculture, global warming, acid rain, and the depletion of the ozone layer all contribute to the recognition that pollution is a problem that not only has not gone away but which is worsening. As an example, in the United States about 150 million individuals reside in places where the air is considered too unhealthy to breath. Still, industries are polluting the air with frightening amounts of toxicity.

In all of this, **global warming** (a result of the **greenhouse effect**) has arisen as the preeminent environmental concern. The old problems of air pollution have simply come to a head in the effects which the greenhouse gases have on the air we breath (French 1990b). The warming of our atmosphere will certainly be a central concern of the 1990s and the next century. For all practical purposes, the whole world is threatened by a change in its atmosphere which is irreversible and which has devastating consequences. Carbon dioxide has increased by one-fourth in the atmosphere while methane gas has doubled. In addition, chlorofluorocarbons (CFCs), which also contribute to the depletion of the ozone layer, add to the gases covering our globe (Flavin 1990).

The end product of pollution has been a serious assault on the **ecosystem** of our planet. This term refers to the interrelationship between various elements of an environment. Robert Lauer (1978, 534) suggests that the ecosystem concept emphasizes that all things in the world are dependent on one another for continuing existence.

According to the Council on Environmental Quality (1984), water sources in every state have had to be closed at one time or another. For example, in 1979 the Commission on Water Supply of Massachusetts found that one-third or more of the community water sources in the state were polluted. In January, 1980, California public health officials shut down the water supplies for 400,000 people in the San Gabriel Valley because of contamination.

The most common pollutant in the air is carbon dioxide. According to Sandra Postel (1987, 158–76), from the mid-1800s to 1985, the amount of carbon dioxide in the air increased. Carbon dioxide plays a special role in controlling the temperature of the earth. It is predicted that if the amount of carbon dioxide in the atmosphere should double, the world's temperature would rise by 1.5 to 4.5 degrees Celsius. The serious nature of the problem can be seen when we realize that carbon dioxide is one of the major waste products of our industrial civilization. As a result of the burning of fossil fuels, more than one ton of carbon dioxide for each one of us was added to the atmosphere in 1988. That is, an additional 5.66 billion tons of carbon dioxide polluted our atmosphere.

A companion problem to global warming is the depletion of the **ozone layer**; this layer has shielded our planet from the most harmful effects of ultraviolet rays from the sun. Two gases, the chlorofluorocarbons and halons, are chiefly responsible for the pollution that is eating away at this vital shield. First observed as a small

Photo released by Tass shows a helicopter flying past the damaged Chernobyl nuclear reactor. French officials testing veal from a Moscow central market have found it contained radiation nearly six times the newly adopted European Community standard level.

"hole" over Antarctica, the gap in the layer now appears to be larger in that region of the world and to have spread to other parts of the world. Most alarming is the fact that the holes now appearing reflect the result of gases released into the atmosphere just in the 1980s. Over the next forty years, according to Shea (1989), the presence of these gases in the atmosphere could result in from five to twenty percent more ultraviolet rays reaching the earth. Ozone is the *only* gas that shields us from the deadly solar rays; without this shield, human life will be impossible.

There is little doubt that our present air pollution poses serious health problems. On a global scale, the health of all humans is affected by what is in the air we breathe (French 1990). We can take the effects of pollution from automobiles as just one example. First, the carbon monoxide which is emitted interferes with the ability of our blood to absorb the oxygen it needs. As a result, our perception is impaired, our thinking and reflexes slowed, and we suffer symptoms of drowsiness. Second, nitrogen oxides make us more susceptible to such viral infections as flu while, at the same time, they irritate our lungs and causes bronchitis. Third, ozone affects the mucous membranes of our respiratory systems and increases coughing, choking, and the impairment of our lungs.

Another significant concern is the radiation poisoning that results from the destruction of nuclear reactors. In April 1986 a nuclear plant at Chernobyl in the Soviet Union exploded. Monitors in Sweden picked up the abnormal levels of radiation. Dr. Robert Gale, an American surgeon who volunteered his service to the Soviet Union, reported his reactions in *Life* (1986):

> Here was the largest group ever exposed to a reactor accident. So this was a bit of history, I thought, "These are the unfortunate ones who got doses of 200 to 1,200 rads. Not a small number are going to die in the next month...."
>
> As the days went on we saw patients with nausea—a common symptom of radiation exposure—vomiting, diarrhea, jaundice, loss of hair, confusion, high fevers. Some became comatose. In time 22 in the hospital died.

Christopher Flavin (1987) reports that the direct costs involved were very high. There were thirty-one deaths as of early fall 1986, and one thousand were injured. Many people (135,000) have been forced to evacuate, and people were still being evacuated in 1990. There was a direct financial loss of at least $3 billion and the figures keep mounting. At the end of 1986, the effects of the Chernobyl accident were being felt in Iceland, too, where residents were concerned about radiation effects on reindeer, their primary agricultural animal. What happened in a small city just eighty miles outside Kiev has affected almost every part of the world.

Another serious problem facing us today is **hazardous wastes**, those discarded chemicals and other materials that are toxic or poisonous to living beings. These waste materials are disposed of by industrial concerns and others. They may also be hazardous to health when they emerge in some fashion from where they were dumped.

The problem of unsuspected waste materials first surfaced in the Love Canal area of Niagara Falls, New York, in 1978. Chemical wastes had been buried in that area twenty-five years before by a chemical company. These wastes began to leak and reached into the backyards and basements of about one hundred homes and public schools. It was reported that eighty-two industrial chemicals and eleven substances suspected to be **carcinogenic** (cancer-causing) were surfacing in the neighborhood. The chemicals and other substances caused burns to children and dogs and also destroyed vegetation in the area. It was also indicated that the rate of miscarriages for residents of the area was a very high thirty percent and that one-sixth of the children born in one part of the Love Canal area were either mentally retarded or had birth defects.

Questions for Summary and Review

1. How would you summarize the problems facing our world with regard to population and the state of the environment?
2. What is meant by the term demography, and what different measures are used in its practice?
3. How is population affected by births, deaths, and migration?
4. How has the world's population grown over the centuries?
5. What is Malthusian theory?
6. How did the demographic transition occur?
7. What is meant by the demographic trap, and how does it lead to a divided world?
8. What attempts have been made to control population?
9. How are world resources being depleted?
10. What effects does pollution have on our lives?
11. What damage has been done to our ecosystem?
12. How have hazardous wastes affected our world?

Key Concepts

Acid rain (p. 265)
Age specific rate (p. 252)
Births (p. 250)
Carcinogenic (p. 268)
Crude birth rate (p. 250)
Crude death rate (p. 252)
Deaths (p. 252)

Demographic transition (p. 256)
Demographic trap (p. 258)
Demography (p. 250)
Doubling time (p. 256)
Ecosystem (p. 266)
Fertility rate (p. 251)
Geometric theory (p. 255)

Global warming (p. 266)
Greenhouse effect (p. 266)
Hazardous waste (p. 268)
High growth potential stage (p. 257)
In-migration (p. 252)
Incipient decline stage (p. 258)
Malthusian theory (p. 255)
Migration (p. 252)

Natural growth rate (p. 252)
Natural thresholds (p. 263)
Out-migration (p. 253)
Ozone layer (p. 266)
Pollution (p. 265)
Population (p. 249)
Population control (p. 261)
Transitional growth stage (p. 257)

References

1. Brown, Lester. 1987. Analyzing the demographic trap. In *State of the world 1987, edited by L. Brown,* 20–37. New York: Norton.

2. _____. 1989. Feeding six billion. *World Watch* 2(5):32–35.

3. _____. 1990. The illustration of progress. In *State of the world 1990,* edited by L. R. Brown, 3–16. New York: Norton.

4. Brown, Lester R., and Sandra Postel. 1987. Thresholds of change. In *State of the world 1987,* edited by L. Brown, 3–19. New York: Norton.

5. Brown, Lester R., Christopher Flavin, and Sandra Postel. 1990. Earth Day 2030. *World watch* 3 (2):12–21.

6. Carson, Rachel. 1970. *Silent spring.* Boston: Houghton Mifflin.

7. Council on Environmental Quality (CEQ). 1984. *Environmental quality— 1983.* Washington, D.C.

8. _____. 1985. *Environmental quality—1984.* Washington, D.C.

9. _____. 1980. *The Global 2000 report to the President.* Washington, D.C.

10. Ehrlich, Paul. 1968. *The population bomb.* New York: Ballantine Books.

11. Ehrlich, Paul, and Anne Ehrlich. 1970. *Population, resources, environment.* Belmont, Calif.: Wadsworth.

12. Flavin, Christopher. 1987. Reassessing nuclear power. In *State of the world 1987,* edited by L. Brown, 57–80. New York: Norton.

13. _____. 1990. Slowing global warming. In *State of the world 1990,* edited by L. R. Brown, 17–38. New York: Norton.

14. French, Hilary F. 1990a. Clearing the air. In *State of the world 1990,* edited by L. R. Brown, 98–118. New York: Norton

15. _____. 1990b. You are what you breathe. *World Watch* 3 (3):27–35.

16. Jacobson, Jodi L. 1989. Baby budget. *World watch* 2 (6):21–31.

17. Lauer, Robert H. 1978. *Social problems and the quality of life.* Dubuque, Iowa: W. C. Brown.

18. Lewis, Paul. 1990. U.N. says world population will reach 6.25 billion by year 2000. *The New York Times* 139 (May 15): A6.

19. *Life.* 1986. Witness to disaster: An American doctor at Chernobyl. 9 (August): 20–29.

20. Meadows, D. H., D. L. Meadows, J. Randers, and W. Beherens. 1974. *The limits to growth.* New York: Universe Books.

21. Population Reference Bureau. 1976. *World population growth.* Washington, D.C.: Population Reference Bureau.

22. _____. 1989. *World population wall chart.* Washington, D.C.: Population Reference Bureau.

23. Postel, Sandra. 1987. Stabilizing chemical cycles. In *State of the world 1987,* edited by L. Brown, 157–76. New York: Norton.

24. _____. 1990. Saving water for agriculture. In *State of the world 1990,* edited

by L. R. Brown, 39–58. New York: Norton.

25. Shea, Cynthia Pollock. 1989. Mending the earth's shield. *World watch 2* (1):27–34.

26. U.S. Bureau of the Census. 1984. *Statistical abstracts*. Washington, D.C.

27. Weeks, John R. 1989. *Population: An introduction to concepts and issues*. 4th ed. Belmont, Calif.: Wadsworth.

28. Weller, Robert H., and Leon Bouvier. 1985. *Population: Demography and policy*. New York: St. Martin's Press.

29. Zopf, Paul. 1984. *Population*. Palo Alto, CA: Mayfield.

Section 4

Understanding Social Institutions

12 Intimate Relationships, Marriage, and Family in Social Life

. . . .

●

The American family does not exist. Rather, we are creating many American families, of diverse styles and shapes. In unprecedented numbers, our families are unalike: we have fathers working while mothers keep house; fathers and mothers both working away from home; single parents; second marriages bringing children together from unrelated backgrounds; childless couples; unmarried couples, with and without children; gay and lesbian parents. We are living through a period of historic change in American family life (Footlick 1990, 15).

The above quote captures the main theme in the study of marriage and the family today—change. Like it or not, the modern institution of the family is quite unlike its historical counterpart. Our norms and values concerning the family have not changed as quickly as have the modern circumstances with which people must cope. Considerable tension exists between traditional attitudes and norms on the one hand and a postindustrial, complex, and rapidly changing society on the other. Such change is often disruptive, creating deep anxieties. Most modern societies, including Canada, western Europe, the Soviet Union, and Japan, are also having to cope with the sweep of social change in marriage and the family.

This chapter explores recent developments in love, marriage patterns, dual-earning couples, divorce, single-parent families, and stepfamilies. It looks at the diversity of family systems around the world.

Cultural Variation in the Institution of the Family

Some kind of family organization is found in all cultures. However, the definition of family must be very broad and flexible because family styles can be vastly different from culture to culture. Sociologically, the **family** is an institution through which people organize intimate relationships, sex, the bearing and raising of children, and kinship. To introduce the cultural variety in family living, the following sections briefly outline differences in family forms, marriage forms, and family authority patterns.

Variation in Family Forms

It is very difficult for us to step out of our culture and understand that our family form is not universal or any more natural than others. In the Western world we tend to think ethnocentrically of the family as a husband and wife living together, usually with children, in a home apart from other relatives. Known as the **nuclear family**, this form of family organization has been present in Western societies at least since the Middle Ages (Degler 1980).

The nuclear family is common in industrial societies requiring smaller, more mobile families which can relocate quickly according to the requirements of occupations and the economy. Japan, for example, has moved toward a nuclear family pattern as a result of modernization and industrialization. Today, living space in Japan is typically small and extremely expensive. Larger families are more costly in such an industrial society.

Nuclear families are also common in hunting and gathering societies where the family must be small and mobile, moving according to the requirements of the natural world (Gough 1983). A nomadic group relying on hunted animals and uncultivated vegetation must move as the animals move and go where vegetation is more plentiful. It is rare for them to have large families.

Although the nuclear family is established in the Western world, in many other societies the **extended family** system is the typical family arrangement. It is perhaps easiest to think of an extended family as any family arrangement that is not nuclear. In an extended family, more than two generations may live together in one household; grandparents live with parents and children, for example. Other relatives such as brothers, their spouses, and children may also live in the same household. In India it has been customary for centuries for the husband and wife to live with the husband's family. Likewise, an Egyptian woman described her living situation:

"Hamed (her husband) was on the river at the time, and I was living in his family's house with his two brothers and their wives" (Atiya 1984, 151).

Extended families are more common in less developed, agricultural societies where families have settled on the land and need more members to help work and support the elderly. Usually the land is passed from generation to generation, and the young have an incentive to stay at home. Many African and Middle Eastern societies have this tradition.

It is often said that the American family system has evolved from an extended pattern characteristic of agricultural life to a nuclear pattern more compatible with the industrial age. To the contrary, available evidence suggests that American households have always been relatively small and nuclear in orientation. Young couples tended to move into their separate households as soon as they were financially able (Degler 1980; Hareven 1983). Before the twentieth century, Americans most likely had a **modified extended family** system in which couples lived in separate households but were in close proximity to parents and other family members. If relatives moved away, they maintained close contacts with other family members by visiting and writing. This pattern is also relatively common in America today.

Variation in Marriage Forms

Marriage forms also vary considerably from society to society. In America we say marriages are based on personal choice and love. Such marriages are called **companionate**. In many other societies, however, **arranged marriages** are the rule. In arranged marriages, parents most often decide who their children will marry, and the decision is guided by economic, political, or kinship concerns. Love is irrelevant, or perhaps it is expected to develop after marriage. Traditionally in India, young people were not even allowed to see their fiancés prior to marriage. In Korea they were allowed a few hours of visiting prior to the marriage. Both Koreans and Indians

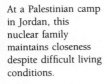

At a Palestinian camp in Jordan, this nuclear family maintains closeness despite difficult living conditions.

felt that such an important decision should not be left to the whims or emotions of young people. In other cultures, Egypt for example, parents might present several eligible mates to their son or daughter who then made a choice.

Marriage forms also vary according to the number of spouses allowed an individual. In Western societies, **monogamous marriage**—one husband and one wife at a time—is the rule. **Serial monogamy** refers to a series of one-to-one relationships, one at a time. Monogamy is the most commonly practiced marriage form in the world (Hunter and Whitten 1977, 115). However, many societies allow **polygamy**, permitting more than one spouse at a time.

Two types of polygamous marriages exist. The first, **polygyny**, permits the husband to legally have more than one wife at a time, and it is the most common form of polygamy. In the Blackfoot tribe of the northern plains of the United States, a man of success was expected to have several wives. Often he married sisters of his first wife (Hunter and Whitten 1977, 108). Polygynous marriages are also allowed in many Islamic nations. The Koran permits a husband to have four wives if they are treated equally. Nevertheless, today most Islamic marriages are monogamous; polygynous marriages appear to be limited to the small number of wealthy men who can afford to support a rather large household.

One might think that polygynous marriages would be full of conflict and jealousy. However, one researcher studying Nigerian women in polygynous marriages discovered that these women did not value husbands very much; they were not jealous of each other. In some cases, these wives had more freedom. "In losing part of their husband's economic and moral support, they also gain independence" (Ware 1979, 194). On the other hand, an Egyptian woman said that one could never trust her husband's other wives; "they can only wish each other heartbreak and misfortune" (Atiya 1984, 129).

The second type of polygamy, **polyandry**, allows the wife more than one husband. Polyandry is the least common form of polygamy, practiced in only a handful of societies. If members of a society are concerned about having a large number of children, polygyny may seem to make more sense than polyandry because, in a year's time, one man with several wives can have more children than a woman with several husbands. At best, she can have only one child every year or two. In addition, from our cultural standpoint, the question of biological fatherhood is problematic in polyandrous marriages. However, the Nyinba tribe in Nepal practices polyandry, and all of a woman's husbands are considered fathers of the children (Levine 1980).

Forms of Family Authority and Inheritance

Cross-culturally, families also differ according to patterns of decision making and authority. In **patriarchal** family systems, authority and decision making reside with the oldest male, usually the father. In **matriarchal** systems, which are quite rare, the authority resides with the oldest female. In **egalitarian** systems, husband and wife share authority and decision making in a relatively equal manner.

Patriarchal systems are most common around the world. Most of the major historical traditions influencing Western societies were patriarchal, including the ancient Greek, Roman, and Judeo-Christian traditions. Women were not legally allowed to own property, vote, get a divorce, get much of an education, or have wide opportunities for employment outside the home. It was the husband's duty to provide for the family economically and make the major decisions affecting the household. Ideally, the husband was the family's representative in the wider society while the wife took care of children and home.

A strong trend in modern Western societies is toward a more egalitarian approach to authority. However, it would be incorrect to say that it has become our dominant approach. More accurately, American families tend to have a blend of patriarchal and egalitarian authority patterns.

Societies also differ in how family name, kinship, and inheritance are traced. For example, in Western societies, children can inherit from both father and mother; children are considered related to both sides of the family. This pattern of inheritance is called **bilineal descent**. In some societies it is only possible to inherit relations and property through the father's family. Called **patrilineal descent**, this pattern is characteristic of patriarchal societies in which a woman cannot own property in her name. Everything is owned by her husband, so the children can only inherit from him. One leftover from patrilineal descent in our society is the taking of the father's last name. In a few societies, **matrilineal descent** occurs. Children can only inherit from the mother in this pattern.

Functions of the Family

As discussed in chapter 1, structural functionalists analyze institutions in society by attempting to discover the functions those institutions have for society as a whole. Functionalists assume that the family, as an institution, is a cluster of norms and practices organized to accomplish activity essential to the survival of the society. Most often, sociologists and anthropologists point to at least four functions that the family provides in most, if not all, societies (Ogburn 1950, Eshleman 1981, Strong and DeVault 1989).

Socialization and Social Placement

As discussed in chapter 4, the family is still considered the most important agent of primary socialization. It is the family's responsibility to provide the environment for the earliest and most crucial learning an individual experiences. The family is also an indirect source of socialization by establishing the social placement of an individual in social class, religion, social background, neighborhood, and other important shapers of a person's life. This does not mean that all families are successful; rather it means that society expects the family to accomplish much of the task of socialization.

Much socialization once left almost exclusively to the family has been taken over by other agents in society: schools, mass media, day-care centers, and peer groups. If the family cannot provide adequately for the children, then child welfare agencies take over. If the family cannot discipline and control the children, the juvenile court takes over. If the family has not prepared the children for school, Head Start programs are expected to make up the difference.

Some societies have experimented with socialization apart from the family. In Israeli collective agricultural settlements, called **kibbutzim**, almost everything is owned and operated by the commune. Centralized day-care centers in the kibbutzim are responsible for the majority of child care and socialization. The children do not live with their parents but visit them in the evenings and on holidays. Child-care nurses are responsible for the major care of the children. However, arrangements such as these are rare. In most cultures families are still expected to have a major role in socializing their children.

Reproduction

In line with its function regarding socialization, the family is usually the sanctioned setting for the birth of children. People in many cultures, Egypt for example, see the birth of children as essential to a family. In other words, the family, in whatever form, is responsible for providing society with new members so that the group and its way of life can be perpetuated.

Members of a society have a need to see that their way of life will continue, and they will encourage reproduction in an orderly and proper manner. For example, leaders in Western European countries expressed alarm at the continuing low birth rates in their societies compared with the high birth rates in Third World countries. These Europeans even suggested instituting policies to encourage reproduction so that they will not become such a small fraction of the earth's population (*Wall Street Journal* 1985).

Regulation of Sexual Relations

So far as we know, no society allows total freedom with regard to sexual behavior. While there is tremendous variation regarding what is acceptable from society to society, sex is generally permitted and sanctioned within the marital relationship. At the same time, sex with other family members, particularly between parents and children or between brothers and sisters, is discouraged (the **incest taboo**).

This does not mean sex is limited to the marital relationship; many societies including our own allow considerable freedom to people before they marry, and not all societies discourage extramarital sex. However, approving sex within marriage gives societies a legitimate channel for regulating sexual behavior.

Care, Emotional Ties, and Protection

The fourth major function of the family concerns the emotional needs people have for connection with others. The family is often the most important stay against loneliness. The family provides a socially structured environment where people can develop intimate relationships and can depend on one another. For example, small children must be given a caring and secure environment if they are to thrive. At times all of us are vulnerable to some extent, whether it is when we are very sick, very young, or very old. At these times we tend to rely on families to help us. Not all families fulfill this social obligation. As a result, we have constructed outside agencies such as Medicare, child welfare programs, and old-age homes to assume the function.

In fact, much evidence indicates that the family has actually lost a number of functions as societies have industrialized. Formal education has been turned over to the schools although it once was primarily a family function. The family once existed as an important economic unit, for example on a farm, with the family acting in concert to meet its needs in a self-sufficient manner. In the past, American families provided medical care for their members. Children were born at home, the sick were nursed at home, and people died at home. Today the hospital is the most common setting for these events. As societies have industrialized, the family's functions have been curtailed (Ogburn 1950, Cox 1990).

Diversity in American Family Forms

Our earlier discussions of cross-cultural variations emphasized the considerable variation in patterns of family, marriage, and authority. Even within our own society, we see considerable variety. Generally, Americans have a nuclear family, a monogamous and companionate marriage system, a mix of patriarchy and egalitarianism in patterns of authority, and a bilineal descent system. However, if you take a careful look at American households, in a statistical breakdown, you might be surprised (see Table 12.1).

As Table 12.1 shows, married couples with children under eighteen years old comprise only slightly more than one-fourth of the households in the United States. On the other hand, one-person households constitute nearly one-fourth of all households in the United States. About eight percent of all households have single parents with children under eighteen (U.S. Bureau of the Census 1989a).

Two experts on marriage and the family, Andrew Cherlin and Frank Furstenberg (1986, 217) predict that by the year 2000 three forms of families will predominate: traditional families made up of first marriages, single-parent families, and families of remarriages. This does not mean that the quality of family life will necessarily be poorer. It does suggest that the family is adapting to a postindustrial way of life and that this period of change may be quite disruptive and threatening.

Forming Intimate Relationships

The traditional image of the American family is no longer the only reality for many reasons. The remaining part of this chapter concentrates on analyzing the diversity and complexity in American families. We have organized the succeeding discussion by following the general life cycle of couples. We first discuss the process of dating, forming intimate relationships, and remaining single or getting married. We will then examine married life and five areas of compatibility. Developments in regard to dual-earning families, divorce, single-parent families, and stepfamilies, also are discussed.

●Table 12.1 Statistical Breakdown of U.S. Households, 1988 (in percentages)

	1988	1970
Married couples with children under 18	27.0%	40.3%
Married couples without children under 18	29.9	30.3
Other families with children under 18*	8.0	5.0
Other families without children under 18	6.6	5.6
One person living alone	24.1	17.1
Other (such as cohabitating)	4.4	1.7

Total households = 91,100,000

*Refers primarily to single-parent households

Source: U.S. Bureau of the Census, *Population Profile of the United States, 1989,* in Current Population Reports, Series P-23, No. 159. Washington, D.C.: U.S. Government Printing Office, 1989. p. 25.

Dating in America

Dating is the principal way Americans begin to establish intimate relationships. As Frank Cox (1990, 93) pointed out, every society has an informal or formal way of selecting mates. The American search for intimates is carried out informally through relatively unrestricted interaction among young people—no arranged marriages, no matchmakers, and no chaperones. Dating is a twentieth-century development.

Dating, or some form of close interaction, allows strangers who are attracted to one another a chance to get to know each other better. As Arlene Skolnick (1987) pointed out, this process involves exploring each other's lifestyles and attitudes to see if the two individuals are compatible and if they enjoy each other.

Finding people to date is often said to be the most difficult aspect of dating. The emphasis on looks and first impressions means that the self is on the line. Insecurities and fears of rejection are common (Skolnick 1987, 243–44). In their study of college dances at Yale University, Pepper Schwartz and Janet Lever (1985, 88) noted the importance of physical appearance: "All night long people are being approved or discarded on the basis of one characteristic that is hard, or at least painful, to discount—their appearance." The sociologists quoted a male student:

> It's such a superficial thing. You judge a girl there strictly by her looks. So you talk to a pretty girl while your eyes scan the floor for another pretty girl .... It's like looking at an object in the window. It's probably mutual.

Complicating getting to know the other person is the tendency to engage in **impression management** on dates. Borrowing from Erving Goffman's view of social interaction, Karp and Yoels (1986) suggested that dates strive to create an image most acceptable to the other. Each will try to discover what the other would like, then act it out. Each may conceal aspects of the self and the past to create a good first impression. It's not surprising, then, to hear someone complain, "Somehow you've changed," after getting to know the other person better.

Romance and Love

An important part of the dating process is finding someone to love. The emphasis on love can be found everywhere in American society. Turn on the radio and hear that you're addicted to love; go the movies and see Michelle Pfeiffer fall in love; or perhaps you'll notice the long racks of romance novels in the bookstore. An anthropologist unfamiliar with our culture might conclude that romance is the primary preoccupation of Americans. The anthropologist would be overstating the case, but not much. The desire for connection with another, for closeness, intimacy, and commitment, is an important part of life for many in this society. In the Western way of thinking, love draws us to one another and prevents loneliness and isolation. However, our word love has multiple meanings. We love our pets, cars, parents, music, best friends, and ice cream. Each object that we love is loved a little differently.

Consequently, it is necessary to make a distinction between **romantic love** and other kinds of love. Romantic love, while known in many cultures throughout history, is of special significance in Western culture. The Bible contains love stories such as Jacob and Rachel; Homer tells of Helen and Paris; and in ancient Rome, Ovid advised how to engage in the art of love through deceit and adultery. Most historians agree, though, that the concept of romantic love as we know it developed during the twelfth century in Europe. It was not originally associated with marriage.

In fact, the great and tortuous feelings of romance were saved for someone unattainable, usually already married. Ideally one loved the other from afar, even though adultery was clearly practiced (Hunt 1959, Cox 1990).

In romantic love the woman was an idealized object worthy of great devotion. Chivalrous traditions developed during the Middle Ages: opening doors for a woman, throwing one's coat for her to walk on, and jousting for her favor. Such traditions have survived today in reduced form. Opening doors for a woman is still a relatively common practice, as is seating her first and standing when she enters the room. Interestingly, in other cultures without the Western background of romantic love, such as Japan or China, women had to show deference to men; in Japan the wife had to walk several steps behind her husband. He was seated first and served first (Skolnick 1983, 216).

Today the ideology of romantic love is still expressed in our folklore. As it developed over the years, elements in this folklore of romantic love included: 1) an unrealistic idealization of the other person, 2) a concept of lovers as cosmic soul mates, 3) the idea that love conquers all, 4) a belief in love at first sight, and 5) love as an overpowering emotional attraction (Lantz 1982).

However, social scientists have pointed out that idealized romantic love is not the best basis for a lifelong marriage. Romance thrives on passion and mystery, things not always possible in a day-to-day relationship. Romantic love is often unrealistic. Under the sway of romance, one may very well be blind to problems in the relationship during its early phases (Cox 1990).

Companionate love, more akin to liking than to romance, is more characteristic of long-term relationships. As studies of successful marriages discovered, these husbands and wives considered each other best friends and could confide in each other. They like each other, considered marriage a long-term commitment, and agreed on aims and goals. They were more practical than romantic (Lauer and Lauer 1985, Scarf 1987). Nevertheless, the evidence shows that Americans are still very

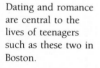

Dating and romance are central to the lives of teenagers such as these two in Boston.

much interested in romance, if not necessarily aware of its limitations (Cox 1990). The modern dilemma appears to be that we want intimate relationships, but many misunderstand intimacy due to the ideals of romantic love found in our cultural heritage.

Mate Selection

Regardless of the folklore and the media portrayal of romance in this country, there is little evidence that many Americans in the past married only in "blind, heedless passion." Rather than love at first sight, most research shows love and mate selection to be a more gradual process as one gets to know the other. People choose whom they will marry for practical reasons such as financial security, social status, and for children, as well as for love (Skolnick 1983, 220). In the marriage marketplace, two people make exchanges concerning appearance, money, personality, and social class (Strong and DeVault 1989, 139).

When it comes to mate selection, it is interesting to see how love is guided by a sense of who is a socially appropriate and attainable target. Even though we say we marry for love, Americans tend to choose marriage partners who are very similar to themselves. This pattern of marrying someone similar in social characteristics is called **homogamy**. Homogamous marriages have been prevalent in the United States since research on mate selection began in the 1930s. The social and demographic characteristics showing the greatest similarity among marriage partners are age, race, level of education, religion, and ethnic background. Like tends to marry like. Beyond these, similarities in attitudes and opinions, intellectual abilities, socio-economic background, and even height and weight are commonly found in American marriages (Buss 1986).

Related to the concept of homogamy is the fact that parents often exert influence on the choice of a spouse. Parents do this by approving or disapproving friends and dates, for example. Indirectly, the town or neighborhood parents choose to live in affects who their children are likely to meet as potential mates. If parents help pay for college and have some say in the choice of college, they may choose a college where their children are likely to meet acceptable partners. Obviously, affluent children are more likely to attend expensive, private universities. Thus, at college they are likely to meet and date other affluent children. The same holds true for students attending church-related schools.

A different school of thought on mate selection suggests that we are also attracted to people who are different from ourselves in terms of personality characteristics. Called the **theory of complementary needs** (Winch 1958), it states that people who are talkative and outgoing are more attracted to people who are quiet listeners. Shy people are attracted to friendly, confident people. The idea of the theory is that people search for mates who have qualities they feel they lack. The other person helps compensate for characteristics felt to be missing. When a person finds a complementary other, he or she feels more complete. This theory has not received as much support in research. Homogamy appears to be the dominant force in mate selection in the United States (Eshleman 1985, 318; Strong and DeVault 1989, 146).

Being Single

More than ninety percent of young people in this country expect to marry at some point in their lives. This percentage has not changed in nearly thirty years (Thorton and Freedman 1986). Nevertheless, as shown in Table 12.2 and Figure 12.1, one recent trend in the United States has been for more people to live singly. In Table 12.2 the categories of separated, widowed, divorced, and single comprise forty-three percent of all householders in the United States. Singlehood is one of the fastest growing living arrangements in this society. One estimate is that ten percent of men and twelve percent of women aged twenty-five to twenty-nine today may never marry, compared with only five percent of people over age forty-five today who have not married (Glick 1986, 24; Norton and Moorman 1989; U.S. Bureau of the Census 1989a).

The larger number of singles results partially from the higher divorce rate. Also, more people are choosing to remain single either for a longer period of time before marriage or for life. Because more women are going to college and planning careers of their own, many are postponing marriage (see Figure 12.1). Greater economic stability among these women allows them more freedom in choosing marriage and in choosing whom they will marry.

As sociologist Peter Stein (1976) pointed out, people labeled singles are not a homogeneous category. This category includes the divorced, widowed, and sepa-rated. It also includes unmarried adults living with their parents, living with but not married to another, and those involved in stable heterosexual or homosexual relationships. As a result singles have differing lifestyles, desires, and experiences. Many singles are young and expect to marry; others may be committed to their single lifestyles. Some have postponed marriage or have found limited opportunities to marry.

Two stereotypes are commonly associated with single life. One is that singles are lonely losers; the other is that they are swinging sexual athletes. Leonard Cargan (1983) examined these stereotypes in the lives of four hundred single and married people and found only elements of truth to them. For example, single people did report more feelings of loneliness than married people, but this was most apparent in the divorced group, not among the never-married. Those who had never married were the least likely to agree that living alone meant unhappiness. The divorced were most likely to see living alone as unhappy. According to Cargan, the average single person is unlikely to be a swinger. The swinger stereotype applied to less than twenty percent of the singles and was more characteristic of the divorced.

Most evidence shows people in our society to be more accepting of single lifestyles. Most Americans do not view singles with either pity or disapproval. Singlehood is not dreaded, but most young people would be bothered to some extent by failure to marry (Thornton and Freedman 1986).

●**Table 12.2** U.S. Household Breakdown by Marital Status, 1988 (in percentages)

Married, spouse present	56.9%
Married, spouse absent	1.2
Separated	3.7
Widowed	12.7
Divorced	11.5
Single (never married)	14.0

Total households = 91,100,000

Source: U.S. Bureau of the Census, *Household and Family Characteristics: March 1988*, in Current Population Reports, Series P-20, No. 437. Washington, D.C.: U.S. Government Printing Office, 1989. p. 111.

● Figure 12.1 Percent Never Married, by Age and Sex: 1970, 1980, and 1988

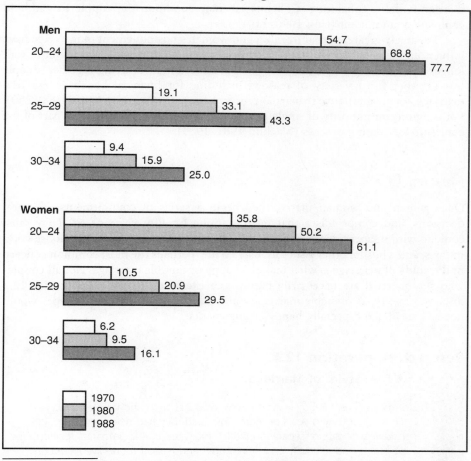

Men

20–24 54.7 / 68.8 / 77.7

25–29 19.1 / 33.1 / 43.3

30–34 9.4 / 15.9 / 25.0

Women

20–24 35.8 / 50.2 / 61.1

25–29 10.5 / 20.9 / 29.5

30–34 6.2 / 9.5 / 16.1

1970
1980
1988

Source: U.S. Bureau of the Census, *Population Profile of the United States: 1989,* in Current Population Reports, Series P-23, No. 159. Washington, D.C.: U.S. Government Printing Office, 1989. p. 27.

Single but Living Together

An increasingly prevalent aspect of singlehood is the choice to live with a member of the other sex, called **cohabitation.** The number of unmarried couples living together has been steadily increasing since 1970. The number of cohabiting couples has grown from a half million in 1970 to nearly three million in 1989, slightly less than four percent of household arrangements (U.S. Bureau of the Census 1989a, 1989b, 1989c). A nationwide study, financed by the National Institute of Health, found that thirty percent of single women in their twenties had lived with a man at some point (Tanfer 1987). A study of eighty-four married couples in Canada found that sixty-four percent of the couples had lived together to some extent before they married (Watson 1986, 39).

Most research on cohabitation has found that it is rarely a substitute for marriage. The majority of couples who live together do so for fewer than two years (Blumstein and Schwartz 1983). Moreover, recent studies indicate that couples who had lived together prior to marriage had a greater divorce rate than those who had married without cohabiting. Cohabitation may condition the couple to withhold complete commitment (Cox 1990, 110).

Relatively greater sexual freedom and women's postponement of marriage have influenced the cohabitation trend. The greater number of singles who prefer to wait longer to marry means greater numbers have the option of living together. People live together for a variety of reasons including for financial benefit, for a trial marriage, for an alternative to marriage, or for a prelude to marriage (Rice 1990, 250). For a significant minority of single people, living together has become a part of the courtship and dating process (Macklin 1981, 1983).

Married Life

Once a man and woman marry, they begin a series of commitments, changes, decisions, and compromises that may continue for fifty years or so. They must contend with finances, work, sex, children if they choose to have them, housework, in-laws, and a host of other issues in married life. Perhaps the most common concern in the study of marriage is what makes a happy or durable marriage. Not all couples who stay married are necessarily happy. For example, Research Application 12.1 discusses five types of stable marriages, although at least three of the types would not be considered especially happy arrangements.

Research Application 12.1
• • • • • • • Five Styles of Marriage

John Cuber and Peggy Harroff interviewed 211 men and women who had been married for ten years or more. They said they had never seriously considered divorce or separation, which indicated that their marital relationships were stable and relatively enduring. Cuber and Harroff found five recurrent themes in the marriages, which they labeled as follows.

1. **The Conflict-Habituated Marriage.** In this marriage style, much conflict and tension exist between the couple, but it is controlled. The fighting is intermittent and rarely hidden from the children, though they try to avoid quarreling in front of friends. In these marriages, both husband and wife realize that conflict and incompatibility are a way of life for them.

2. **The Devitalized Marriage.** Here the couple sees a large difference between how the marriage used to be and how it is now. They remember having a close, deeply loving relationship early in their marriage, but now they have grown apart and no longer find much satisfaction in the marriage. They spend little time together and long for days past.

3. **The Passive-Congenial Marriage.** While those in the devitalized marriage remember a happier time, those in a passive-congenial type have never been especially close, yet they experience little conflict or disruption. Often they direct their lives and energies toward careers or community service and retain more independence and freedom than other married people.

4. **The Vital Marriage.** A man and a woman in a vital marriage are intensely bound together. Sharing and togetherness are hallmarks of these couples; they are indispensable to one another. They spend a great deal of

time together and get genuine satisfaction from sharing activities and interests.

5. The Total Marriage. A couple in a total marriage are even more involved with each other than in a vital marriage. This kind of relationship was found to be rare. It was as if the two had become one. They spent even more time together and shared more interests and activities than a couple in a vital marriage.

Source: Adapted from John F. Cuber and Peggy B. Harroff, "Five Types of Marriage," in *Family in Transition,* edited by A. S. Skolnick and J. H. Skolnick. Boston: Little, Brown and Company, 1983. *pp. 318–329.*

This section of the chapter is concerned with compatibility in marriage. It looks at five major issues: money, work, husband-wife role expectations, sex, and marital violence.

Marriage and Money

Money and decisions about how to spend it are extremely important in marriage. The lack of money, unemployment, or financial irresponsibility can cause major problems for couples. Knowing each others' values and philosophy about budgeting and spending is important before two people marry if they are to avoid serious problems.

In a massive study of nearly 6,000 couples, including cohabiting and gay couples, sociologists Philip Blumstein and Pepper Schwartz (1983, 67–77) found that couples who were disappointed with their finances tended to be less satisfied with the entire relationship. They also found that couples who fought about money were more likely to argue about how it was spent than how much they had. If one spouse thinks money is to spend while the other thinks money is to save, then some compromise or agreement has to be reached. Those couples who fought about money were less likely to be together when the researchers conducted a follow-up study eighteen months later.

Money was an important factor in the balance of power in the marital relationships examined by Blumstein and Schwartz. Money brings with it power. For example, married women who worked and had relatively good earnings felt freer to spend money as they wished and felt less accountable to their husbands for what they spent. Having money of their own meant that wives were less dependent on their husbands. Wives who had no source of income occasionally reported feelings of resentment if their spending was watched over by the husband. One wife in the study said:

> We fight about money. `. . . I feel it's a personal insult when he starts yelling about how high the bills are. And yes, I do charge on them, but I have a legitimate alibi for every one of those charges (Blumstein and Schwartz 1983, 82).

On the other hand, when both spouses worked and kept their money separate, they were less likely to be bound together. They were less certain about the permanence of the relationship. Because they worried more that their relationships would not last, they were reluctant to pool their money; and when the couples did not pool their money, they were less interdependent and committed (Blumstein and Schwartz 1983).

Marriage, Work, and Dual-Earning Couples

The influx of wives and mothers into the labor force has been a major feature of American life in the twentieth century. The trend accelerated during the depression and World War II, slowed during the 1950s, then increased greatly. In 1979, for the first time, a majority of women were working outside the home. This does not mean that women were only homemakers prior to the decade of the 1970s. Women engaged in a wide range of productive work aside from paid employment. "As farm wives, for example, they raised and sold produce and dairy products. Women were the 'moms' in 'mom and pop' stores. They did piecework at home, took in sewing and laundry, and managed boardinghouses" (Lamanna and Riedman 1985, 389).

Nevertheless, we tend to think of the dual-earning couple as a relatively new phenomenon. Frank Cox (1990, 305) calls dual-working families "the real American family revolution." Today more than half of all women work and more than half of all mothers with infants and small children also work. They work primarily for the same reasons men work—for income, for self-expression, and for a sense of accomplishment. Most sociologists make a distinction between two types of dual-earning couples. In a **dual-worker couple**, both spouses work but the husband has the major career interest. In a **dual-career couple** both husband and wife are committed to careers (Coleman 1984, 338; Cox 1990, 336).

A number of problems are faced by dual-earning couples today. Our society has not yet made the full adjustment to both spouses working outside the home. Traditionally, the wife was expected to carry the primary responsibility for child care and housework. Today many women have added outside work to the duties of wife and homemaker without receiving enough additional help from their husbands. The shouldering of so much responsibility by the wife can be a major cause of stress for the marriage. One study indicated that employed wives work an additional five hours a day on household duties. Between ten and thirty percent of household chores was done by their husbands (Berheide 1984, 44).

A husband may feel a certain sense of deprivation when he no longer has the traditionally supportive wife waiting at home. He may feel inadequate in taking on additional parenting and household duties. Some husbands may be threatened by the wife's success; others complain of not having enough time to spend with their wives which in turn creates more stress in the relationship (Coleman 1984; Hochschild 1989). Research Application 12.2 discusses in more detail recent research concerning the issue of housework in a dual-earning marriage.

Research Application 12.2

• • • • • • • **Working Parents and the Pressures at Home**

The most revolutionary change affecting the family today is that sixty percent of couples with children are dual-earning. With both working, who is taking care of the children and the home? Or, as sociologist Arlie Hochschild (1989) asked in her research, who is responsible for the second shift of work—child care, cooking, cleaning, buying groceries, washing clothes, running household errands, taking the children to the doctor, and feeding the family pet. Are modern husbands and wives sharing the second shift?

Hochschild studied more than fifty working couples with children and used ten couples as intensive case studies, observing them in their homes, involving them in long interviews and informal conversations. She found that the majority of husbands, about eighty percent, did not share the work at home; some adamantly refused while others passively resisted helping but offered a sympathetic ear. Many husbands alternated between some cooperation and active resistance. When they did help, it was more in child care than in housework. However, they were more likely to take the children to the zoo than to bathe and feed them. Fewer husbands than wives washed toilets or scrubbed the bathroom (Hochschild 1989, 7–9).

The wives, on the other hand, felt much more responsible for child care and housework. Many repressed the conflicts and anger they felt after adjusting insurance claims or keypunching all day and coming home to cook and wash while their husbands watched television. However, most wives resented the double duty, and relationships with husbands deteriorated. One wife, who was responsible for all the child care and home duties, "half-consciously expressed her frustration and rage by losing interest in sex and becoming overly absorbed with Joey," their son (Hochschild 1989, 7).

The most common theme among the wives was exhaustion, both emotional and physical. They laughed bitterly at the media image of the slender, carefree career woman striding confidently, briefcase in hand. These working women hardly had time to get dressed in the morning and were always in a hurry, prodding the children to hurry up, "Let's go!" These mothers often bore the brunt of family anger because mothers are the ones who enforce schedules and make time demands (Hochschild 1989, 9).

Hochschild pointed out that husbands are inevitably affected by their wives' double duty. They are affected directly if they become more involved in child care and home duties. The husbands who shared work at home also reported exhaustion and strain. On the other hand, if husbands refuse to help much at home, then time with their wives becomes scarce, or husbands must contend with exhausted, stressed, and resentful wives. Hochschild noted that more than half of the wives had tried a variety of direct and indirect strategies to get their husbands to share household duties. In addition, sharing household duties improved the marriage considerably.

Ultimately, most modern societies including Japan and the Soviet Union are affected by the same revolutionary forces regarding the family. Working mothers are a major aspect of this revolution. The crux of the issue is that a tremendous contradiction exists between traditional family and sex-role ideology and modern social conditions. Married couples bear the weight of this contradiction because they have been socialized to accept outmoded ideologies about marital roles that do not fit today's social, economic, and demographic circumstances. It is a tension between tradition and reality, between patriarchy and egalitarianism.

All social classes and ethnic groups are affected in America, and it is unlikely that working women will return home in large numbers. The economy does not permit it. Finally, a tension exists between what Hochschild (1989, 205) calls "faster-changing women and slower-changing men." Women have more quickly adapted to the newer conditions and differ more from their mothers than men do from their fathers. The "female culture" has changed much more rapidly due to new economic forces and the push of the women's rights movement. No similar forces have operated on men. Nevertheless, the fact remains that the traditional division of labor at home is suited to the past, not the present.

• • • • • • •

In dual-career marriages a serious problem occurs when one spouse has a major opportunity for career advancement but is required to move to another city. Many couples resolve this problem by putting the husband's career first. More recently, however, a growing number are opting for **commuter marriages**, often seen as a temporary adjustment, in which the spouses live in different locations pursuing different careers during the work week.

Another problem for dual-career couples is deciding when to have children, if any. A career-oriented wife faces particularly painful choices with regard to children because pregnancy and child care are usually disruptive to her career. A child is rarely disruptive to the husband's career. It is not surprising, then, that the number of couples choosing to remain **child free** has increased in the past twenty years. One study found that about six percent of married women between the ages of eighteen and thirty-four did not plan to have any children (Pebley and Bloom 1982). In addition, others will delay having children until it is too late or will experience difficulty in having children. Many make a choice to focus their energies on other aspects of life.

If the dual-career couple does have a child and the wife chooses to take a long leave from work to be with her newborn, she loses seniority on the job; she will lose advancement in her work, and she may resent it. If she quits, the family income is reduced when expenses due to the child have increased, adding financial burden to the marriage. Women who have or plan to have children generally earn less than women without children, and the gap is widening. It is simply more costly for women to have children, particularly before they establish a career. It is little wonder, then, that women are delaying childbearing and choosing to have fewer children (Bloom 1986).

The inflexibility of the typical workplace in America means that all working mothers have to schedule everything around established working hours. The lack of adaptability by most employers to more convenient, flexible hours and work arrangements makes it difficult for working parents to get the children to and from school or the day-care center, adding to marital stress. The lack of after-school day-care options and the lack of quality day-care arrangements for preschoolers adds to the problem. Mothers who leave their young children in day care often experience guilt. In addition, day-care can be enormously expensive (see chapter 4 for more discussion on day care).

Most Western nations are facing the same dilemma regarding dual-earning couples. Some countries, particularly Sweden, have attempted to meet the needs of these couples through government programs. In Sweden, a home-help service provides helpers to assist families with child care and housekeeping. The service is mostly paid for by taxes and is available to all. It is free to poor families; others pay according to their income levels (Berch 1982). In the United States, workplaces and schools are beginning to change, but the adjustments appear to be slow in coming.

Husband-Wife Role Expectations

Men and women married today were probably socialized to have rather traditional views toward the roles of men and women in a marriage. The force of traditional definitions of marital roles, though fading, is still strong. The norms of husband as provider and decision maker and wife as homemaker and caretaker continue to guide couples. Power and dominance in marital relationships still tend to be found among husbands.

However, the sweep of social change in family life has meant that husband and wife roles are no longer clear-cut. Now the blueprint of tradition is not seen as the only way to be married. The change in the role of women in society has brought

Balancing work and family is often a creative process. This mother takes her baby with her to work so that she may nurse the baby.

about a weakening of tradition. The problem is crystallized when a couple enters a marriage with differing role expectations. For example, he may expect a rather traditional arrangement when it comes to cooking or housework while she may expect a more egalitarian arrangement. Sociologists have consistently found women to be less tradition oriented than men. In particular, working women, younger women, and women with more education are found to be more egalitarian in attitudes because it is to their benefit (Eshleman 1985, 117; Hochschild 1989).

When one or both of the partners reject tradition, the complexities in a marriage can be overwhelming because they have few norms to guide them. They cannot rely on parents as role models or on other guides to help them. The two must find their own way through experimentation, compromise, and occasional conflict. Anything "from cooking a meal to initiating sex to writing Christmas cards becomes a potential point of debate" (Blumstein and Schwartz 1983, 324).

Blumstein and Schwartz found that husbands tended to remain traditional in that they still felt their work was central to their lives and their major source of self-respect. Husbands' careers still tended to take priority, and they saw their wives' work as secondary. However, these men acknowledged that it was difficult to support a family on one income. On the other hand, wives had some choice in whether or not they worked but still fully expected their husbands to work. One highly significant problem to grow out of these role expectations is that women are still expected to do the majority of the housework even if they work outside the home.

Marriage and Sex

In recent years the astounding popularity of marriage manuals dealing with sex may indicate the extent to which Americans are concerned about sex in their marriages. In their study, Blumstein and Schwartz (1983, 193) pointed out, "Having sex is an act that is rarely devoid of larger meaning for a couple. It always says something about partners' feelings about each other, what kind of values they share, and the purpose of their relationship." Mutual satisfaction about the amount and quality of sex were found to be central to the well-being of the relationships. Blumstein and Schwartz (1983) suggested that other problems in the relationship, such as fights about money or children, divide the couple. They then are less likely to have sex. The lack of sex, in turn, becomes an important additional source of dissatisfaction. Consequently, a problem with sex is only one aspect of a larger problem facing a couple.

One of the major difficulties concerning sex is the inability to communicate feelings and needs. Couples who refuse to discuss sex or who feel that they cannot talk freely about it are less likely to be satisfied, and they are unlikely to solve sexual problems. Compatibility and mutual satisfaction are not automatic. On the other hand, sexual compatibility is rarely enough to maintain an otherwise incompatible relationship (Eshleman 1985, 392).

Marriage and Violence

Family violence has always been with us. Ancient Roman males had the legal authority to discipline, even kill, their wives. The expression "rule of thumb" supposedly came from English common law stating that a husband could beat his wife but only with a rod no thicker than his thumb. This rule was used in various states in the United States until the late 1800s (Gelles and Cornell 1985, 29–30).

Wife abuse is a known practice in many cultures around the world. Women are seen as the "appropriate victims" because violence toward them is common and tolerated not only in history but in the present as well (Dobash and Dobash 1979). For example, in Delhi, India, some 2,000 young wives have been killed by their husbands since 1979 because the wives' dowries were insufficient. Traditionally in India, the wife's family must meet the husband's financial demands at the time of the marriage. If they do not, the husband occasionally retaliates by burning his wife. Only a small fraction of the husbands are arrested or prosecuted. Today in India, dowry murders are more common among those in the middle class who are becoming very materialistic while, at the same time, losing traditional constraints of caste and religion. It is proving difficult for people in India to change centuries of tradition in which women held very low status (Bordewich 1986).

Only in the past fifteen years has our society attempted to define and come to grips with family violence. In the past, the general belief was that a family's behavior was no one else's business; what went on between husband and wife was strictly between them. (Child abuse is discussed in chapter 4.)

It is impossible to know just how much violence occurs between husbands and wives in our society. In interviewing a nationally representative sample of 6,002 individuals, Richard Gelles and Murray Straus (1988) found that three percent of the wives reported one or more severe, violent attacks in 1985. More than four percent of the husbands reported abusive attacks by their wives. However, abuse directed at wives is considerably more violent and damaging. These numbers do not reflect less severe acts such as shoving, slapping, and pushing. Rather, the figures refer to potentially more dangerous attacks such as choking, punching, kicking, stabbing, and shooting (Gelles and Cornell 1985, Gelles and Straus 1988).

Family violence is a complex situation, but certain factors are found to be consistently related to spouse abuse. Economic hardship, unemployment, lack of job satisfaction, poor housing conditions, and lower socioeconomic status are important factors. Unemployed husbands are twice as likely as employed husbands to beat their wives. Such economic factors can cause stress in a marriage which can translate to violence, particularly if the couple experienced violent childhoods. When the husband or wife dominates in power and makes all the decisions, violence is more common. Egalitarian households are the least violent. Finally, violent couples are more socially isolated. They have fewer friends and less social involvement outside the home than nonviolent couples (Gelles and Cornell 1985, 73–76).

In addition, if husbands receive little or no punitive response from police or courts, they are given the message that spouse abuse is not a serious act. Americans, particularly males, are often taught that violence is a means of resolving interpersonal disputes. (See chapter 9 for further discussion of violence in modern society.)

In her study of abused wives, Jean Giles-Sims (1983, 121–139) discovered six stages in the progression of violence among couples. First, in the dating and engagement stage, the woman often overlooked important signs of violence and loss of control in the man. His potential for beating her were present, but she glossed over or dismissed the signals.

The second stage consisted of the first violent incident. The wife believed that it was an isolated incident and would not happen again. She was willing to forgive; and, too, the wife was ashamed and embarrassed to report the incident, especially if she felt that the husband was the head of the household and had a right to discipline her. Unfortunately, it rarely ended with just one act of violence.

In the third stage, violence became an established pattern in the relationship. The husband used violence to dominate his wife. Because he could successfully get his way by beating her, he was rewarded for his violence. If she wanted to maintain the marriage and the family above all else, she continued to take the beatings. When she did complain to doctors or to the police, usually nothing was done to help her. Her husband would threaten her if she tried to leave. Also, the husband was often quite contrite and apologetic after he had beaten her. The wife was rewarded for taking the beating, and she could deceive herself into thinking that it would be the last time.

In the fourth stage, the wife was forced to make a choice; the beatings had become intolerable or the children were being threatened. In the fifth stage, she left the husband, often going to a shelter for battered wives or to friends for help. Finally, in the sixth stage, she had to choose whether to go back to her husband or to begin a new life on her own.

Many people find it difficult to understand why a woman would return to a husband who beats her, but consider her situation. She may lack education, skills, or job experience. She may be financially dependent on her husband and have no means of support for herself and her children. The fewer resources she has, the less likely she is to leave (Gelles and Cornell 1985). She may be afraid to leave if he has threatened her repeatedly. She may experience the abuse two or three times a year, and, in each case, after the abuse the husband is usually very contrite, begs for forgiveness, and swears it will never happen again. She may even have internalized the belief, often asserted by her husband and others, that she somehow deserved to be beaten. Her own low self-esteem makes it difficult for her to think she can make it on her own. These issues are illustrated by a battered wife quoted in Giles-Sims (1983, 116–118):

Then came the feeling of panic. I'm going to have to be on my own, look for an apartment, look for a job. I think that's mostly why . . . I was getting to the end of my three weeks of being at the shelter and I hadn't made a decision about whether I wanted to go home or not . . . . He (her husband) would whine and cry, and he'd fuss and say how much he loved me, how much he wanted me back. . . . I'm afraid of being alone, afraid of raising the kids by myself. I was really scared. . . . I'm lonely—very lonely. And I think that's why it looked so good, going back home.

Divorce in America

The United States has one of the highest divorce rates in the world and the highest ever in its history. Most of the increase in divorce has occurred in the past thirty years in this country, particularly during the 1970s. Table 12.3 shows the increase in divorce relative to the number of people married from 1960 to 1988. There is some evidence that divorce rates have recently leveled off and may even decline, but the future is uncertain (Norton and Moorman 1989). What is unique today is the apparent desire to get out of marital relationships that do not live up to expectations or do not meet the needs of both partners.

While divorce is common among all types of people in our society, it is more common within certain categories. For example, people who marry in their early teens are much more likely to get divorced than those who marry in their twenties. Those in the lower socioeconomic classes are more likely to experience stresses and difficulties in life, which is reflected in their higher divorce rates. Similarly, blacks have a higher overall divorce rate than whites. This is most often explained by a greater incidence of poverty and economic hardship among blacks. Divorce rates even vary according to region of the country. Rates are higher in the western and southern regions of the United States and higher in cities than in rural areas (Strong and DeVault 1989, 460–61).

Several factors can account for these variations. Some regions of the country, particularly rural areas, are more stable and culturally homogeneous. They have

● **Table 12.3** Divorced Persons per 1,000 Married Persons With Spouse Present, by Age, Sex, Race, and Hispanic Origin: 1988, 1980, 1970, and 1960

Year and Sex	Total	Race		
		White	Black	Hispanic[1]
Both sexes:				
1988	133	124	263	137
1980	100	92	203	98
1970	47	44	83	61
1960	35	33	62	(NA)
Male:				
1988	110	102	216	106
1980	79	74	149	64
1970	35	32	62	40
1960	28	27	45	(NA)
Female:				
1988	156	146	311	167
1980	120	110	258	132
1970	60	56	104	81
1960	42	38	78	(NA)

NA Not available.

[1]Persons of Hispanic origin may be of any race.

Source: U.S. Bureau of the Census, *Marital Status and Living Arrangements: March 1988*, Current Population Reports, Series P-20, No. 433. Washington, D.C.: U.S. Government Printing Office, 1989. p. 60.

greater reliance on primary-group relationships which can help in difficult, stressful times. Areas of the country with higher divorce rates tend to have more liberal divorce laws and a larger number of people living in poverty (Eshleman 1985, 583).

Like many aspects of social life, divorce can be viewed both positively and negatively. In a positive light, divorce is now an available option for those who do not wish to stay in unhappy, restrictive, or dangerous relationships. For example, it allows a woman to leave a man who abuses her or t' e children; and it allows a man the same. On the other hand, in a negative light, divorce brings with it considerable emotional impact and disruption. Many are divorced without wanting to be. Some people complain that because divorce is so common it undermines our willingness to make a complete commitment to relationships and family. Children may have a difficult adjustment to make when the parents split up. The burdens of single parents can be overwhelming.

The causes of a high divorce rate are varied, but most fit within the following seven categories:

1. Changes in the status of women, such as increased opportunities for them in the workplace, have made them less dependent on husbands. She is freer to leave him, and he is freer to leave her.

2. Economic and financial difficulties including unemployment and underemployment take a toll on marriages today. Economic problems are among the most significant sources of stress in marriages. Marital partners tend to blame each other for financial problems, and this increases the sense of friction and dissatisfaction.

3. The American trend toward increased individualism and self-gratification means that people are less likely to emphasize self-sacrifice for the family. Americans today are more likely to leave marriage because they see it as a barrier to personal goals and desires.

4. The liberalization of divorce laws has had a significant impact. Divorces are relatively easy and inexpensive to obtain. However, the laws were primarily a reflection of a growing set of values more compatible with divorce, such as individual fulfillment rather than self-sacrifice.

5. Divorce became more socially acceptable. Most churches in the United States do not condemn divorce, and divorced people no longer suffer the stigma of failure once common in this society.

6. Many people came to support the idea that one should not be trapped in a relationship which did not offer personal fulfillment, intimacy, and love. Consequently, many couples break up because one or both is on a quest for a more perfect union.

7. At the root of this quest lies the ideal of romantic love. When love does not conquer economic problems or alcoholism or boredom, we say we no longer love the other. This may be especially apparent among couples who married at a young age, particularly in the teen years.

It was not until 1970 that no longer being in love could be grounds for divorce. At that time California was the first state to institute **no-fault divorce laws**. These laws stated that, in effect, no grounds were needed to obtain a divorce other than one saying that there had been a complete breakdown in the relationship (Weitzman 1985).

It is likely that our divorce rate will remain relatively high in this country unless we see some fundamental changes in defining marriage, commitment, and romance. We have high expectations and needs when we enter a marriage in this society. We expect a great deal from one other person in emotional, physical, and economic terms. "Unfortunately, the more people expect from marriage—especially in terms of unrealistic expectations—the more likely they are to be disappointed" (Coleman 1984, 538).

Single-Parent Households

The long-term impact of the tremendous growth of single-parent households has yet to be completely understood in this society. We do know that single-parent households have become a common occurrence in our society in the past twenty years. Single parents head one-fourth of the households with children under age eighteen in this country. Among black families today, more than half are already headed by single mothers. Among white families, about fifteen percent are headed by women. It is possible that at least a third of the children born during the 1980s will spend at least some part of their childhood with only one parent (Footlick 1990, 16). Research Method 12.1 discusses the issues of divorce, single parenthood, and the effects on children.

Research Method 12.1

• • • • • • • Longitudinal Analysis: Tracing the Effects of Divorce on Children

Judith Wallerstein and Sandra Blakeslee (1990) recently published the first major study tracking selected families for a ten-year period in order to gauge the long-term effects of divorce. Wallerstein first began the study in 1971 in the California suburbs, and the first report was issued in 1980 (Wallerstein and Kelly 1980). She and her associates intensively interviewed members of sixty families individually, including 131 children, for six weeks around the time of the marital breakup. Each family member who could be found was also interviewed after eighteen months, after five years, and again after ten years. Wallerstein is in the process of research for the fifteen-year follow-up (1990, 321).

The sample of family members in Wallerstein's study includes slightly more females than males. Ninety percent of the marriages that broke up were first marriages, and the couples had been married for an average of eleven years. Most of the families were middle class or upper-middle class, although nearly thirty percent were working or lower class. Of the sixty families, eighty-eight percent were white, three percent were black, and nine percent were interracial. At the time of divorce, slightly more than fifty percent of the children were eight years old or younger, and about half were between nine and eighteen years old. The children selected for the study were emotionally healthy prior to the breakup; none had ever been referred for psychological or psychiatric treatment (Wallerstein and Blakeslee 1990, 321–22).

The in-depth and complex results of the study cannot easily be summarized. However, below are a few of the major findings relating to divorce and its effects on children (Wallerstein and Blakeslee 1990, 296–305).

1. Divorce is almost always a more devastating experience for children than for parents.
2. One-fourth of the children showed a severe and long-lasting drop in their standard of living. Very few received help from their fathers in attending

college, but they often did not qualify for financial aid because their fathers made too much money.

3. Over the years boys had a harder time adjusting than girls, although the girls often experienced the sleeper effect: they had a more difficult time establishing relationships in early adulthood.

4. About sixty percent of the children felt rejected by one or both parents. Many felt like leftover baggage.

5. Half grew up in the middle of chronic anger between their divorced parents. They felt used in a battle they never wanted. Half also saw their mothers or their fathers divorced again within ten years.

6. Adolescence was a particularly tough period for the children of divorce; many suffered severe emotional and psychological stress.

7. Almost half of the youth entered adulthood "as worried, underachieving, self-deprecating, and sometimes angry young men and women" (Wallerstein and Blakeslee 1990, 299).

Wallerstein and Blakeslee concluded that the effects of divorce are long-lasting, that people do not automatically recover, and that the conditions in the family after divorce were almost always worse than the conditions in the failing marriage. Finally, the children of divorce do not take marital breakups lightly, and they have a strong desire for enduring relationships. Those who did well had very supportive parents and role models who helped them rebuild their lives.

A longitudinal study, such as Wallerstein's research, is one of the most useful types of methods in social science. It is extremely important to trace events and circumstances as they affect people over time. A typical longitudinal study tracks a sample at intervals over ten or twenty years, sometimes longer.

Unfortunately, longitudinal studies are not as plentiful as other types of research for several reasons. Such studies are quite expensive and require financial support for long periods. The results are not immediate. It is also a painstaking and laborious process to keep track of hundreds of people in order to study them at selected intervals. The researcher must ask for a great deal of cooperation from research subjects. Finally, the researcher must be dedicated to the study for a large part of his or her life, as Wallerstein has been for the past twenty years. The ongoing results of the Wallerstein study, however, make it clear that her research efforts are changing the way Americans think about divorce and children.

. . . .

The most serious problem associated with single-parent families is the economic strain. Most families today depend on two incomes, and the loss of one can be devastating economically. More than half of single-parent families live below the poverty line, compared with fifteen percent for all families with children (U.S. Bureau of the Census 1989d). Poverty is much more associated with female single parents than with male single parents. The problem is particularly acute for black women, many of whom had children early and did not get the education or job skills necessary to provide economically for a family.

The inequities in the workplace and the lack of preparation of many women, given traditional sex-role expectations, to take on the breadwinner role are most often cited as the reasons for such poverty. For example, the kinds of work typically associated with women are more likely to be low-paying and lack opportunities for advancement and income increases, such as clerical work and public school teaching. For women without formal training or education, the conditions can be far worse. (See chapter 8 for a more thorough discussion of women's problems in the workplace.) In addition, divorce is usually much more financially disastrous for a woman. On the average, divorced women experience a severe drop in their standard of living the year after their divorce while men show an increase (Weitzman 1985).

In addition to financial difficulties, there are at least three other types of possible overload for single parents (Weiss 1979). One is **task overload** which is experienced when the parent has to fulfill the obligations of two parents. The parent typically has to work fulltime, maintain the household, handle all the finances, discipline and socialize the children, and carry out all the tasks of everyday life, often an overload for two parents. A second possible overload is **responsibility overload** where, with no one else to turn to, the parent feels overwhelmed with having to make all the critical decisions regarding the family. A third area of possible overload is **emotional overload**. This is particularly acute with regard to the children. The one parent must meet the needs children have for attention, for love, for interaction, and for play. Clearly, after a difficult day at work some single parents come home exhausted and unable to be emotionally giving to the children. Single parents have little time alone and may have trouble establishing new intimate relationships because they may already be overloaded.

This is not to imply that single-parent families have no benefits. In fact, Weiss (1979) found that single parents often developed stronger feelings of accomplishment and felt better than they would feel in a bad marriage. Many of the single parents noted that they had special relationships with their children that they probably would not have had if married.

Remarriage and Stepfamilies

Three out of four divorced people remarry, and at least half of them had children prior to the divorce. One in six families today is a stepfamily; nearly one in five of the nation's children are part of stepfamilies (U.S. Bureau of the Census 1989d; Rice 1990). Not surprisingly, most of the stepparents who live with their stepchildren are stepfathers. Courts most often grant children to the mother in a divorce, and when she remarries her children have a second father.

Remarriage does much to solve the economic problems of a single parent because it usually adds a second income, often from a male who tends to have more earning power. **Blending** two families into one, however, brings with it a new set of problems (Cherlin and Furstenberg 1986). Consider this situation. Susan is divorced from Jack, and their two school-age children live with her and see their father on alternate weekends. Recently Susan remarried, and her husband Richard has moved in with her and the children.

What do the children call Richard? They already have a "dad." Are Richard's parents their grandparents, too? Is Richard supposed to discipline the children even though they argue that he is not their real father? How do Richard and Jack interact? Are Richard's children from a previous marriage kin to Susan's children? Who should get more financial support from Richard, his biological children or his stepchildren? If Jack remarries, what do his children call his new wife, her children, and her parents?

The dynamics in blended families can become quite complicated. The questions above demonstrate the lack of clear ground rules and institutionalized guidelines for blended families, and this is a critical distinction (Cherlin 1983, Wallerstein and Blakeslee 1990). Our society is oriented toward first marriages and, consequently, there exists a lack of appropriate terms and models for those in subsequent marriages. In a blended family the stepparent is not replacing a parent but is an added parent, so what should he or she be called? The confusion regarding the stepparent's role in disciplining the children is another example, The children may resent attempts by the intruder to impose authority. They may resent his or her "taking the place" of the biological parent. In addition, numerous grandparents and **quasi-kin** such as the stepparent's children can add to the confusion (Cherlin 1983; Cherlin and Furstenberg 1986).

Stepparents are often just as confused as the children in a blended family. One study found that these parents typically mentioned three problem areas in dealing with the children. First, they complained of problems in attempting to discipline the children. The children were often rebellious and resentful toward stepparents. Second, stepparents noted that they often had trouble adjusting to the habits, routines, and personalities of the children. Stepparents often felt like outsiders. Third, they anguished over gaining love and acceptance from the children; instead, they often got criticism and rejection. These parents started out on an idealistic note, hoping for a true sense of family rather quickly. Most were unrealistic (Kompara 1980, Rice 1990).

On a more positive note, however, most research has shown that the people in stepfamilies do adapt in one way or another. Usually the process requires a good deal of work and compromise. In essence, the family members must restructure how they do things in order to accommodate a new parent. They develop norms, a shared history, and "a particular and reliable rhythm" that often resolves their problems (Papernow 1984, 361). However, the fact remains that family cohesion appears to be lower in stepfamilies than in families of first marriages (Rice 1990, 631).

A wide range of options has developed with regard to family arrangements and lifestyles in the twentieth century. The high divorce rate and the growth of single-parent households and dual-earning families indicate that the traditional family is no longer the dominant model of family life in this society. As we adapt to new values, increased economic pressures, and changes in the roles of men and women, it is inevitable that the institution of the family will also change. Concomitantly, as the family changes other institutions in our society such as the workplace and the schools most likely will have to change and adjust to accommodate our diverse styles of family living. The fact remains that Americans are highly committed to marriage and family, although the styles of marriage and family may be different from those in the past.

• • • • • • • • • • • • • • • • • • Questions for Summary and Review

1. Explain how the institution of the family is both universal and variable.
2. Define and give your own examples of the major family forms, marriage forms, and forms of family authority and inheritance.
3. Explain the diversity in American family forms. How common is the residential family with two parents and children at home?
4. What are the principal functions of the family? Explain each and how they operate in modern society.
5. Discuss the issues of dating, romance, and mate selection in modern society. Why is it important to distinguish romantic love from companionate love?
6. Explain why more people are single today and why young people are marrying at a later age than they did thirty years ago.

7. Discuss the five major issues of married life, and give examples of how these things affect couples in their everyday lives.

8. Why has divorce become so common in America? How has divorce changed the structure of American families? Be sure to address the issues of remarriage and stepfamiles.

9. What are the major problems faced by single-parent families? Explain what you think our society could do to aid single parents and the children of divorce?

Key Concepts

Arranged marriage (p. 274)
Bilineal descent (p. 276)
Blended families (p. 296)
Child-free marriages (p. 288)
Cohabitation (p. 283)
Commuter marriages (p. 287)
Companionate love (p. 280)
Companionate marriage (p. 274)
Dual-career couple (p. 286)
Dual-worker couple (p. 286)
Egalitarian family (p. 275)
Emotional overload (p. 296)
Extended family (p. 273)
Family (p. 273)
Homogamy (p. 281)
Impression management (p. 279)
Incest taboo (p. 277)
Kibbutzim (p. 276)

Matriarchal family (p. 275)
Matrilineal descent (p. 276)
Modified extended family (p. 274)
Monogamy (p. 275)
No-fault divorce (p. 293)
Nuclear family (p. 273)
Patriarchal family (p. 275)
Patrilineal descent (p. 276)
Polyandry (p. 275)
Polygamy (p. 275)
Polygyny (p. 275)
Quasi-kin (p. 297)
Responsibility overload (p. 296)
Romantic love (p. 279)
Serial monogamy (p. 275)
Task overload (p. 296)
Theory of complementary needs
    (p. 281)

References

1. Atiya, Nayra. 1984. *Khul-Khaal: Five Egyptian women tell their stories.* Cairo: The American University Press.

2. Berch, Bettina. 1982. *The endless day: The political economy of women and work.* San Diego: Harcourt Brace Jovanovich.

3. Berheide, Catherine White. 1984. Women's work in the home: Seems like old times. *Marriage and family review* 7: 37–53.

4. Bloom, David E. 1986. Putting off children. In *Annual editions, marriage and family 86/87,* edited by Ollie Pocs and Robert Walsh, 112–115. Guilford, Conn.: Dushkin.

5. Blumstein, Philip, and Pepper Schwartz. 1983. *American couples: Money, work, sex.* New York: William Morrow and Company.

6. Bordewich, Fergus, M. 1986. India: Dowry murders. *The Atlantic* (July):21–26.

7. Buss, David M. 1986. Human mate selection. In *Annual editions, marriage and family 86/87,* edited by Ollie Pocs and Robert Walsh, 60–65. Guilford, Conn.: Dushkin.

8. Cargan, Leonard. 1983. Singles: An examination of two stereotypes. In *Family in transition,* 4th ed., edited by A. S. Skolnick and J. H. Skolnick, 546–556. Boston: Little, Brown and Company.

9. Cherlin, Andrew. 1983. Remarriage as an incomplete institution. In *Family in transition,* 4th ed., edited by A. S. Skolnick and J. H. Skolnick, 128–136. Boston: Little, Brown and Company.

10. Cherlin, Andrew, and Frank Furstenberg, Jr. 1986. The American family in

the year 2000. In *Annual Editions, marriage and Family 86/87,* edited by Ollie Pocs and Robert Walsh, 217–222. Guilford, Conn.: Dushkin Press.

11. Coleman, James C. 1984. *Intimate relationships, marriages, and the family.* Indianapolis: Bobbs-Merrill.

12. Cox, Frank D. 1990. *Human intimacy: Marriage, the family and its meaning.* 5th ed. St. Paul: West Publishing Company.

13. Cuber, John F., and Peggy B. Harroff. 1983. Five types of marriage. In *Family in transition,* 4th ed., edited by A. S. Skolnick and J. H. Skolnick, 318–329. Boston: Little, Brown and Company.

14. Degler, Carl N. 1980. *At odds: Women and the family in America from the Revolution to the present.* New York: Oxford University Press.

15. Dobash, R. E., and R. Dobash. 1979. *Violence against wives.* New York: Free Press.

16. Eshleman, J. Ross. 1981. *The family: An introduction.* 3d ed. Boston: Allyn and Bacon.

17. _____. 1985. 4th ed.

18. Footlick, Jerrold K. 1990. What happened to the family? *Newsweek* (Winter/Spring special edition): 14–24.

19. Gelles, Richard J., and Claire P. Cornell. 1985. *Intimate violence in families.* Beverly Hills, Calif.: Sage.

20. Gelles, Richard J., and Murray A. Straus. 1988. *Intimate violence: The causes and consequences of abuse in the American family.* New York: Touchstone.

21. Giles-Sims, Jean. 1983. *Wife battering: A systems theory approach.* New York: Guilford Press.

22. Glick, Paul C. 1986. How American families are changing. In *Annual editions, marriage and family 86/87,* edited by Ollie Pocs and Robert Walsh, 23–26. Guilford, Conn.: Dushkin.

23. Gough, Kathleen. 1983. The origin of the family. In *Family in transition,* 4th ed., edited by A. S. and J. H. Skolnick, 25–42. Boston: Little, Brown and Company.

24. Hareven, Tamera K. 1983. American families in transition: Historical perspectives on change. In *Family in transition,* 4th ed., edited by A. S. Skolnick and J. H. Skolnick, 73–91. Boston: Little, Brown and Company.

25. Hochschild, Arlie, with Anne Machung. 1989. *The second shift: Working parents and the revolution at home.* New York: Viking.

26. Hunt, Morton. 1959. *The natural history of love.* New York: Knopf.

27. Hunter, David, and Phillip Whitten. 1977. *The study of cultural anthropology.* New York: Harper and Row.

28. Karp, David, and William Yoels. 1986. *Sociology and everyday life.* Itasca, Ill.: F. E. Peacock.

29. Kompara, Diane R. 1980. Difficulties in the socialization process of step-parenting. *Family relations* 29:69–73.

30. Lamanna, Mary A., and Agnes Riedmann. 1985. *Marriages and families: Making choices throughout the life cycle.* 2d ed. Belmont, Calif.: Wadsworth.

31. Lantz, Herman R. 1982. Romantic love in the premodern period: A sociological commentary. *Journal of social history* (Spring).

32. Lauer, Jeanette, and Robert Lauer. 1985. Marriages made to last. *Psychology today* (June): 22–27.

33. Levine, Nancy E. 1980. Nyinba polyandry and the allocation of paternity. *Journal of comparative family studies* 11:283–298.

34. Macklin, Eleanor D. 1981. Cohabitating college students. In *Single life: Unmarried adults in social context,* edited by Peter J. Stein, 210–220. New York: St. Martin's Press.

35. _____. 1983. Nonmarital heterosexual cohabitation. In *Family in transition,* 4th ed., edited by A. S. Skolnick and J. H. Skolnick, 264–285. Boston: Little, Brown and Company.

36. Norton, Arthur J., and Jeanne E. Moorman. 1989. Current trends in marriage and divorce among American women. In

Families in transition, 6th ed., edited by Arlene S. Skolnick and Jerome H. Skolnick, 106–122. Glenview, Ill.: Scott, Foresman and Company.

37. Ogburn, William F. 1950. *Social change*. New York: Viking Press.

38. Papernow, Patricia L. 1984. The step-family cycle: An experiential model of stepfamily development: *Family relations* 33:355–63.

39. Pebley, Anne, and David Bloom. 1982. Childless Americans. *American demographics* 4:18–21.

40. Rice, F. Philip. 1990. *Intimate relationships, marriages, and families*. Mountain View, Calif.: Mayfield.

41. Scarf, Maggie. 1987. *Intimate partners: Patterns in love and marriage*. New York: Ballantine Books.

42. Schwartz, Pepper, and Janet Lever. 1985. Fear and loathing at a college mixer. In *Down to earth sociology*, edited by J. M. Henslin, 86–93. New York: The Free Press.

43. Skolnick, Arlene. 1983. *The intimate environment: Exploring marriage and the family*. Boston: Little, Brown and Company.

44. _____. 1987. 4th ed.

45. Stein, Peter J. 1976. *Single*. Englewood Cliffs N.J.: Prentice-Hall.

46. Strong, Bryan, and Christine DeVault. 1989. *The marriage and family experience*. 4th ed. St. Paul: West Publishing Company.

47. Tanfer, Koray. 1987. Patterns of premarital cohabitation among never-married women in the U.S. *Journal of marriage and the family* 49:483–498.

48. Thornton, Arland, and Deborah Freedman. 1986. Changing attitudes toward marriage and single life. In *Annual editions, marriage and family 86/87*, edited by Ollie Focs and Robert Walsh, 30–36. Guilford, Conn.: Dushkin Press.

49. _____. 1989a. *Population profile of the United States: 1989*. Current population reports, series P–23, no. 159. Washington, D.C.: U.S. Government Printing Office.

50. _____. 1989b. *Households, families, marital status, and living arrangements: March 1989*. Current population reports, series P–20, no. 441. Washington, D.C.: U.S. Government Printing Office.

51. _____. 1989c. *Marital status and living arrangements: March 1988*. Current population reports, series P–20, no. 433. Washington, D.C.: U.S. Government Printing Office.

52. _____. 1989d. *Household and family characteristics: March 1988*. Current population reports, series P–20, no. 437. Washington, D.C.: U.S. Government Printing Office.

53. *Wall Street Journal*. 1985. Low birth rate in western Europe means big social economic changes are likely. December 20.

54. Wallerstein, Judith S., and Joan B. Kelly. 1980. *Surviving the breakup*. New York: Basic Books.

55. Wallerstein, Judith S., and Sandra Blakeslee. 1990. *Second chances: Men, women, and children a decade after divorce*. New York: Ticknor and Fields.

56. Ware, Helen. 1979. Polygyny: Women's views in a transitional society, Nigeria 1975. *Journal of marriage and the family* (February):185–195.

57. Watson, Roy E. L. 1986. Premarital cohabitation vs. traditional courtship: Their effects on subsequent marital adjustment. In *Annual editions, marriage and family 86/87*, edited by Ollie Pocs and Robert Walsh, 37–43. Guilford, Conn.: Dushkin Press.

58. Weiss, Robert S. 1979. *Going it alone*. New York: Basic Books.

59. Weitzman, Lenore J. 1985. *The divorce revolution*. New York: The Free Press.

60. Winch, Robert F. 1958. *Mate selection*. New York: Harper and Row.

Understanding Religion and Social Life 13

• • • • • • • • • • • • •

Chapter Outline

•

A small group of college students, members of the campus religious group from a midwestern university, are visiting Los Angeles. They are sure they know what religion is. It is largely the formal services of their hometown church, the various activities of their campus fellowship, and a somewhat varied set of beliefs that they have come to identify as correct. Their leader has plans to shake that certainty; the students will soon learn that there is much more to the concept of religion than they had imagined.

Walking through a low-income neighborhood, they stop at an unpretentious church building. A large group of people are present worshiping in their own way. This includes a service of faith healing; as the sick come to the front so that the minister may pray for them, the congregation becomes extremely emotional, chanting, dancing, and speaking in unintelligible tones. The students leave and walk further. They meet a group of shaven-head youth dressed in saffron robes, shaking cymbals. They are singing and chanting as they dance in a circle, performing a ritual of their faith. As it happens, this occurred in front of an impressive cathedral which the students entered. Inside, a stately procession is making its way down a center aisle through a somewhat sparse congregation to an elaborate, ornate altar. Although each in the procession is dressed a bit differently, each costume is ornate and displays some measure of artistic beauty.

New experiences await them as the students move into the Japanese section of the city. At a shrine they see infant clothing and baby toys pinned to posts for the use of babies who died shortly after birth. Before a copper statue, an elderly woman rubs the already shiny head of a Buddha and then steps back and folds her hands in reverence. Further on they see trees to which pieces of paper have been tied, papers which bear news of bad fortune that will be taken away by the Shinto gods.

We could take our band of students to many other experiences of religious behavior. The point is that all of these experiences, and many more, provide examples of the various ways people participate in the religious institution. As we study religion from the sociological perspective, we may understand how such a variety of behaviors fits this one term. By using our sociological imagination, we can observe the way in which people are religious and the way in which religious groups interact with other groups in society. We can see how religion, in its various forms, contributes to the stability and, at times, instability of the social world.

Religion in Sociological Perspective

Religion is a social institution concerned with the ultimate meaning of life and with the answers to questions that are unanswerable by natural means. It has been said to deal with the breaking points in life, such as death, illness, tragedy, or the feelings of powerlessness—events that we cannot readily handle. Religion frequently is seen as providing another realm of existence that transcends the everyday world in which we live. Religious beliefs and practices provide answers and consolation when we encounter experiences we do not recognize and questions we cannot answer.

Most or all of the religious groups in society hold a number of similar beliefs, and these beliefs form a common bond for society. They serve as a social glue that holds the society together, reinforcing its worldly norms and values with the authority of the transcendental world.

Sociologically, Emile Durkheim defines religion as

> ... a unified system of beliefs and practices relative to sacred things, that is to say, things set apart and forbidden—beliefs and practices which unite into one single moral community called a church all those who adhere to them (1947, 62).

This definition makes three points about religion: (1) Religion is always concerned with, and directed toward, things that are holy and worthy of awe (**sacred**); (2) religion involves beliefs and practices aimed at appeasing or obtaining favors from the sacred; and (3) religion is a group rather than an individual matter. Other sociologists have suggested a fourth aspect of religion: Religion is an institution that provides answers to questions about the ultimate meaning of life.

Milton Yinger (1970) believes that any belief system offering answers to questions of the ultimate meaning of life should be called religious. Thus, a number of belief systems might be seen as religious (Chalfant, Beckley, and Palmer 1987, 17); communism, Nazism, psychoanalysis, and other belief systems that do not refer to a supernatural realm might be included. However, religion in our society has typically included a supernatural element.

Still, as with all aspects of society, religion can be a changing thing, forming and being formed by shifts in the social fabric. In traditional societies, age-old religious customs serve to bind the community together. In the Western world, social change has occurred rapidly; the authority of custom has been lessened for most aspects of modern society, especially for religious life. Faith, and the practices that accompany faith, have seen numerous shifts since the Puritans first landed in North America, and these shifts have given a unique character to the religious institution in the United States.

Religion in Western Society

Dramatic changes occurred in the structure of Western society with the introduction of mechanical means of production. This changed aspects of society, including the way in which people thought and how they viewed sources of knowledge. These changes were associated with what is known as the Enlightenment of the eighteenth century and were accompanied by an apparent decline in religion. Early sociologists were concerned that this decline would lead to the destruction of societies as they had been known because it weakened the religious bond that held people to a society. Emile Durkheim (1947) saw the stability and strength of society threatened by these changes; Max Weber (1958) saw the "demystification" of the world as leading to individual loneliness and dehumanization.

This concern was based on the assumed rise of the secularization of society. **Secularization** may be defined as the continual reduction of the power and authority of religion. Some believe that, as society becomes more rationalized and complex, the institution of religion will be divested of its influence until it remains only at the periphery of society, in the most private sphere of life and as a token symbol in public ceremonies (Berger 1968).

Many students of religion were quick to pick up the theme of secularization. Religious attendance and participation have declined, particularly in England and in other European countries. Some sociologists in the United States (including Glock and Stark 1965) at one time saw traditional religion becoming a relic of the past. However, poll data (Gallup 1985; Wald 1987) and more intimate studies (such as Caplow, Bahr, and Chadwick 1984), do not support the theory that religion is dying in the United States. Traditional religious faith continues to hold a place of respect and confidence in the Western world (DeStefano 1990, Wald 1987).

Still, there are indications that some usual measures of being religious—membership in a religious group and attendance at services—have declined, and that religion is no longer seen as important as it once was. DeStefano (1990) reports that slightly more than half of Americans in 1989 (fifty-five percent) saw religion as an important part of their lives. Still, more than two-thirds are affiliated with a church or synagogue. In addition, more than forty percent of the people polled claimed that they attend religious services in a typical week. In short, there has been little change since the 1960s in the strength of religious faith in the country. Certainly, religious practice is stronger in this nation than in most of the Western world where only one-fifth or considerably less say they attend worship services on a weekly basis.

However, the levels of membership and attendance now, and in the 1960s, are significantly below those of the 1940s and 1950s. Whereas two-thirds of the population claimed membership in a church or synagogue in 1989, in the earlier time periods about three-fourths of the population claimed such membership. Further, there has been some change in level of church attendance. In 1987 and 1983, for example, only forty percent said they had attended services in the past seven days, while in 1958 and 1955 nearly one-half (forty-nine percent) claimed attendance.

The importance of religion to the lives of the American people is also slightly diminished. While over half of the population still considers it very important and another thirty percent see it as fairly important, in the 1950s and 1960s, seventy and seventy-five percent viewed religious faith as important in their lives. Indeed, in 1952 only five percent of those polled saw it as *not* very important, whereas fourteen percent gave this response in 1989 (DeStefano 1990).

These figures indicate that, while religion has declined somewhat in significance, it is by no means dying out. In fact, there is evidence all around us that religion may be more healthy today than at any time since it reached a high point in the 1950s and 1960s.

Some contend that, in viewing religion as waning in importance, researchers have taken too narrow a view of what constitutes religion. By confining it to traditional religious beliefs and participation in the activities of established churches, researchers ignore important aspects of what might be termed religious. They claim that religious beliefs and reliance on the sacred are, in various forms, still very much a part of today's world (Hammond 1985, Stark and Bainbridge 1985). While religion as expressed in the traditional churches may be declining, faith in some version of the sacred that gives meaning to our lives continues to be strong (Hammond 1985).

Functionalist and Conflict Theories of Religion

While functionalist approaches have been used most frequently in studying religion as a social fact, those following a conflict approach have also made significant contributions to our understanding. Functionalists, of course, see religion as contributing to the well-being and stability of society while conflict approaches note the ways in which religion inhibits change and can be used to reinforce a social system that is dysfunctional to many.

Functionalist Theory

The central proposition of the **functionalist theory of religion** is that, in all societies, customs and mores are tied together as a functional whole. This whole is aimed at solving various problems to ensure the maintenance of societal tradition, a task in which religion is deeply involved.

Emile Durkheim, a founding father of functionalism, sought to go beyond simplistic theories of religion. He wanted to find what had been common to the earliest of religions and was still found in later forms of religious expression. Durkheim asked how it happened that humans first came to make a distinction between what was sacred and what was not. He also asked how groups still form distinctive organizations around this separation.

In attempting to answer this question, Durkheim sought the most elementary form of religion. He thought it was the religious system of an aboriginal tribe of Australians, the Arunta. This tribe practiced a system of belief known as **totemism**. This belief system occurs in societies composed of clans united by kinship, real or fictitious (Hartland 1951). It is based on a ritual relationship to the totem. The totem takes the shape of a real thing, usually something from the animal or vegetable world. This image is the symbol of the clan and is prominently displayed.

For Durkheim, the true meaning of religion was in the totem. It defined the boundaries between the *sacred* and the **profane** (everyday events). It was inseparable from the clan. It had power, but not in itself; its power came from the clan. Thus it could be said that the sacred (totem) and the clan (society) were one and the same.

Durkheim's theory implies that every religious force comes from a power external to the sacred object itself. The religion of the Arunta is an expression of the individual's awareness of the Arunta social system. The individual feels the pressure of social reality and responds to this pressure with awe and reverence, creating an external power to be worshiped.

Religion can also be a force in shaping aspects of society. In *The Protestant Ethic and the Spirit of Capitalism* (1958), Max Weber contended that values and norms inherent in Calvinist Protestantism contributed significantly to the emergence of the capitalist economic system in Western Europe. He concluded that the religious spirit associated with this brand of Protestantism was significantly associated with economic behavior. He claimed that it was Protestants, more than Catholics, who owned the leading businesses and possessed the greater share of capital leaders, and that their religious beliefs were a vital factor in this prominence. The beliefs behind Calvinistic Protestantism had made a significant effect on social change in the economic area.

As Weber saw it, **Calvinism**, which emphasized the doctrine of God as all-powerful and all-knowing, viewed salvation as entirely the gift of God in Christ. Further, the all-seeing, all-knowing deity must predetermine one's eternal fate even before birth. That is, individuals are **predestined** to either heaven or hell at the time they are born. How are they to know which? The connection between religious belief and dedication to an economic system is made here. To some followers of this faith it seemed apparent that God would not want his elect—those destined for salvation—to suffer on earth; they would prosper in worldly things. To this end, the Calvinists worked hard, following the rational system of capitalism, so that they might prosper and thereby prove their membership among the elect. Because of a religious idea, they gave support to the development of the capitalist system.

From the functionalist perspective, Thomas O'Dea and Janet O'Dea Aviada (1983) outlined six basic functions of religion. First, religion provides support, consolation, and reconciliation for members of the group. As noted, religion provides a belief in the existence of a transcendent world to which individuals can turn for answers to the inexplicable. This means that religion can provide a source of support in the face of the uncertainties of life itself. At the death of a loved one, for example, reference to the transcendent realm can bring a sense of comfort and hope.

Religion can also be used to explain one's socioeconomic status. Those in high-status groups may feel that their wealth and position reflect the favor of God. As we have seen, Max Weber (1958) argued that the Calvinistic **Protestant ethic** saw wealth and property as signs of favor from God indicating that the wealthy were chosen by God for eternal salvation. This attitude still seems to prevail. Current attitudes toward the poor, attitudes which label them as shiftless and unworthy, are often still based upon this religious ethos.

Lower-status groups may also use religion to explain their position. They may disdain wealth and privilege in this world and believe that, in a future world, they will receive rewards beyond their greatest imagination.

Second, through religion, individuals find security and a firm sense of identity. In the established ideas of religious faith, individuals and groups find not only a sense of security but also a means of dealing with the ambiguities of the world. In their relationship with a transcendent world, they can find answers to the question of meaning in life and gain a sense of identity with the sacred.

Third, religion gives sacred support to the norms and values of society. In this case, religion has a conservative function. It contributes to the maintenance of the status quo. The force of the sacred tends to give added importance to the norms and values of the groups. Social values come to have a divine dimension as well as a societal one.

Fourth, religion serves a prophetic function. The term prophetic has its roots in the activities of the prophets of the Old Testament. The primary task of prophets was to call Israel back to the rules God had laid down for it. Similarly, religion functions to remind the group or society of its most basic ideals, and it calls for a return to basic religious norms and values. Many of the students who protested segregation in U.S. society felt they were shaping their society to agree with the values set down by its religious faith. Sometimes factions in the society can view matters differently. Some protested aid to the Nicaraguan Contras as contrary to God's will, while others supported aid as a way to express that same will.

Fifth, religion provides individual identity. In religion, individuals can find a secure idea of who they are and for what values they stand. This reduces much of the uncertainty associated with an individual's decisions, particularly in times when social values are rapidly changing. It has been found (Stark 1985) that religious behavior has little influence on individual decisions when there is consensus in society, as in the use of alcohol. Society legally approves of liquor use. However, where there is no clear direction from society, as in the use of drugs like marijuana or peyote, religious identity may be the deciding factor in how an individual will behave.

Finally, religion serves to give outward evidence of transitions in life. In Christian societies, for example, the baptism of a child marks the religious responsibility of the family to the child. It also symbolizes that a change has occurred in the life of the family—the family has gone through a transition. Confirmation, adult baptism, and the bar and bas mitzvah ceremonies of Christian and Jewish faiths make known to society, and to the individual, that the former child has now taken on a new status in life. The religious ceremony of marriage also symbolizes the new status of a person.

Conflict Theory

Conflict theory maintains that societies are dominated by power struggles. It asserts that the functionalist conception of a cooperative equilibrium as the basis of society is false. Instead, the confrontation of class interests is the central element of social reality. To ignore this fact is to blind ourselves to the realities of the essential forces that determine the shape of society. Further, viewing any element of society as inevitable and essential gives us too narrow a frame of reference from which to view society and leads to an easy acceptance of the status quo as good and right.

Karl Marx's description of the dynamics of class (see chapter 1) is basic to conflict theory. Marx saw religion as one of the institutions that had been co-opted by the dominant class in society. Friedrich Engels described religion as the opiate of the masses—that is, a sort of mental drugging of the proletariat, used by the dominant group to keep content those without access to important societal resources (Marx and Engels 1957).

The Marxist interpretation of religion may be summarized in two points (Winter 1977, 35). First, "god" is portrayed to the proletariat as a symbol of the class system of their society. Second, the working class is led to believe that the deprivation created by a capitalist society is the will of "god" and to look for rewards in some future existence.

Thus, conflict theory sees religion as useful to the ruling class and dysfunctional to those who are not members of the elite. For example, during the days of slavery, a religion developed that was helpful to slaveholders but not to slaves. The slaves believed that their suffering would eventually be rewarded in heaven. This religious belief led to patient, quiet slaves who served their masters well and obediently.

According to the **conflict theory of religion**, then, religion may lead us to believe that certain elements of society, such as the class system, are essential. In this view, religion helps the dominant group enforce the social order. Religion from this perspective is and always has been a counterrevolutionary force in human society. The demands and the struggles of the masses for concrete benefits, such as economic and social justice and freedom from domination by others, have traditionally been met with offers of "spiritual" rewards instead (Boughey 1978, 22–23).

However, religion must not be seen only as a tool for keeping the social system intact. It can be, as Gary Marx (1967) claimed, a force for protesting against the inequality of society. In his study of the black church in America he notes that, while a number of black congregations do fit the model of passive submission, this is not the whole story. He points to the fact that the black church, as a separate entity, came into being as a place where black people could meet with one another. In the church they not only worshiped but planned strategies to confront the system and to better their situation (Marx 1967, 64–72). A good measure of the success of the black church as a cradle for social change is found in the role played by black clergy in the civil rights movement of the 1960s. The black leaders of this movement, which was successful in gaining legislation promoting integration, were mostly ministers who had been reared in the black church and trained by its educational institutions. Far from making them passive subjects of the dominant social order, the black religious institution had provided the education, spirit, and style that would make such men as Martin Luther King and Jesse Jackson powerful figures for social change.

Looking at the other side of religion, Thomas O'Dea and Janet O'Dea Aviada (1983) note that the six functions of religion they identified also may be harmful to individual groups and to society as a whole. For example, in providing consolation to those who are greatly deprived and reconciling them to their status, religion may serve to maintain a situation that should be changed. Religion can also give a transcendental legitimacy to the present order. For example, some religious groups define the role of women in terms of past traditions; they turn to their beliefs to support this definition as God-given.

In discussing the functionalist and conflict approaches to religion we have been writing as if religion were a solitary phenomenon and that, as such, it interacts with society in only one manner. As we have been from the example of the black church, this is far from true. Actually, religion takes many forms and is expressed in a variety of ways. This variation is found in such matters as religious behavior, group organization, and stands on both doctrinal and social issues. We will look first at variations in religious behavior.

Varieties of Religious Behavior

Religious behavior varies in form and intensity. Sociologists have referred to the various types of religious behavior as dimensions.

Several factors are involved in how the individual experiences and expresses religion, and the several dimensions of religious behavior are not always consistent for any particular individual. People who are extremely religious in one respect may not be at all religious in others. For example, those who regularly attend Sunday services may have very low levels of commitment to the beliefs and values of their faiths. They may be attending only to boost a political career or to find new business contacts, and may know or care little about other aspects of their religious group.

Sociologists of religion have long debated the number of religious dimensions that exist. The most widely used list of dimensions suggests five different ways in which people are religious: experiential, ideological, ritualistic, intellectual, and consequential (Glock and Stark 1965).

The **experiential dimension** concerns feelings of having some measure of direct contact with the sacred. The lowest level of experience may be simply people's sense that the sacred has made itself felt to them. At the other extreme are those who feel they have been given the gift of the Holy Spirit (**charismatics** or **Pentecostals**). Members of some charismatic groups believe that the sacred has so filled their souls that they can step outside of themselves and speak in strange tongues.

Such strong emotional experiences were once thought confined to the poor in society. In recent years, however, a charismatic movement has been evident in many middle-class denominations including Catholics, Presbyterians, and Episcopalians. It has been suggested that the appearance of charismatic groups in such traditional congregations indicates that some members feel something lacking in their traditional worship which they find in the charismatic experience (Poloma 1982).

The **ideological dimension** deals with the set or type of beliefs held by the individual. Specific beliefs may vary among religions (as well as within them), but every religion sets forth some range of beliefs to which its followers are expected to adhere. For example, in the mid-1980s, the Southern Baptist convention was still divided over the beliefs expected of church members in that religious group. To many Southern Baptists, belief in the Bible as the literal word of God was essential to being a Christian. Others argued that more freedom should be allowed in what a Christian (particularly a Southern Baptist) should believe. These factions were debating the ideology that belief in the literal truth of scripture is necessary to be a Christian.

The ideological dimension tends to be measured along a liberal-conservative continuum, with those professing the greater number of conservative beliefs rated as high in ideology. Questions concerning belief in the Virgin Birth, the literal truth

Several hundred Moslem worshippers participate in a Juma service at the Roosevelt Hotel in New York. While Christian leaders bemoan the commercialization of Christmas, other religious groups are reporting revived interest in their own traditions in reaction to the relentless secular presence of the holiday.

of Scripture, and the need to believe in Jesus for salvation are frequently used to measure the level of ideology. As a result, liberal church members who believe strongly in many religious doctrines may be counted as nonbelievers because they do not believe in what is conservative. Such scales tend to favor the orthodox (established) view of religion.

The **ritualistic dimension** concerns activities and practices that are performed in the name of religious faith. Many of us think of rituals only in terms of elaborate ceremonies, such as those in the Episcopal, Catholic, and Orthodox faiths. Sociologically, however, a **ritual** is any routine or practice through which individuals attempt to relate to the sacred, strengthen their faith, call forth the favor of the sacred, or find comfort. It may, indeed, be the formality of a high mass, but it is also a number of other practices. Church attendance, membership, and participation are usually included in this dimension. Prayer, fasting, carrying a rosary, or even having a rabbit's foot handy are ritualistic behaviors. Having devotions at the breakfast table, attending a prayer breakfast, and crossing oneself before batting in a baseball game are ritualistic behaviors.

The ritualistic dimension is most often used to measure religious behavior. This is probably because it is easy to measure such things as church attendance, frequency of prayer, and actual membership.

The **intellectual dimension** involves the individual's knowledge of the basic beliefs, doctrines, and history of the religious belief system. An individual's knowledge of religion may be quite deep without any commitment to the beliefs or practices of the particular system. For example, professors of comparative religion usually know (intellectual dimension) a great deal about many faiths, but they may not believe (ideological dimension) in any of them or engage in any practices (ritualistic dimension) related to a specific faith.

The final dimension, the **consequential dimension**, concerns how all other aspects of religious belief affect how people act. Findings related to this dimension are mixed. When it is related to other dimensions, particularly the ritualistic dimension, contradictory results are reported. For example, when bigotry and church affiliation are compared, some have found a direct relationship between church affiliation and prejudice. Others claim that this relationship only exists for those mildly committed to the religious group (Gorsuch and Aleshire 1974). Still others (for example Chalfant and Peek 1983) have found that members of conservative churches, particularly Southern Baptists, continue to show prejudice even when they attend church regularly.

There is also much debate about the relationship between juvenile delinquency and religious behavior. Early reports (such as Hirschi and Stark 1969) indicated that individuals who display higher levels of religious behavior are no less likely to commit acts of juvenile delinquency than are those who show little or no religious involvement. Still other evidence has suggested just the opposite. The disparity may lie in the different ways in which studies measure both religious behavior and juvenile delinquency (Sloane and Potvin 1986).

A more satisfactory explanation is that group association has more to do with delinquency than does religious affiliation (Stark 1984, Peek, Curry, and Chalfant 1985). Rodney Stark (1984) suggested that we tend to behave like those with whom we associate in everday life. If our associates are highly religious, religious values will have a distinct effect on how we behave. If not, our religious behavior probably will not have great consequences for our everyday decisions.

The different religious groups in society expect somewhat different kinds of behaviors from their adherents. For example, while Southern Baptists and Roman Catholics hold many values in common, the expectations for each group are different. Why do these differences exist? Can we find clues to this question in studying the organization of religious groups in the United States?

Organization and Growth of Religious Groups

The religious group is essential to the formation and maintenance of beliefs, practices, and values (Chalfant, Beckley, and Palmer 1987). As it is only through the agency of the group that we become truly human, so it is only through interaction with the religious group that we become truly religious.

Although religious groups face different problems and solve them in their own ways, they share definite stages of organization as they grow. The emergence of a new movement is characterized by informal leadership and organization. New groups tend to begin through the leadership of strong individuals who use the power of personal gifts (a personal charisma) to attract supporters. This is known as **charismatic authority**. A new movement centers on such an individual or individuals, and their teachings form the basic creed of the group.

When the original leader dies or stops actively directing the movement, a second stage of growth is reached. At this point, memory of the leader's teachings become authoritative for the maintenance of group life, a process Max Weber (1958) referred to as the routinization of charisma. Teachings are written down and more formal policies are developed. The personal gift or charisma that inspired the new move-ment is set down in policies that guide the future of the movement, and **traditional authority** guides the group.

If a group continues into the third generation of leadership, it generally takes on an even more formal style of authority, **legal-bureaucratic** (see chapter 5). Rules and group structures become a part of the group's life. The movement is established; its policies are fully routinized, and there are official rules and channels for decision making.

We can see this development in many movements. The early history of the Christian faith provides one example. A small group of disciples were attracted to the charismatic teachings and person of Jesus of Nazareth. While Jesus was on earth, there were no formal doctrines; the movement was based on his teachings and actions. After Jesus was no longer with his disciples, the norms and customs of the church were guided by what were seen as the traditions Jesus had set. Thus, those who had been closest to him were seen as providing the guidelines of faith. The whole New Testament can be seen as an attempt to spell out the meaning of the traditions and teachings Jesus had left.

As the Christian movement grew and increased in size, it became necessary to implement more formal, bureaucratic rules. Especially after the edict of Constantine, which legalized Christian faith in the Roman world, an organization of rational rules, a hierarchy of offices, and regulations for the conduct of the church developed. The former small, charismatic movement had become a large, formal structure, and what had been charismatic inspiration had become routinized.

From time to time groups have felt that the "spirit" of the Christian faith was lost in established formalities and that renewal of the original charismatic feeling was needed. For example, in the Protestant Reformation of the sixteenth century, new movements protested what they saw as error in the Roman Catholic church's practice.

Another movement, known as the Campbellites by some, began as a protest association on the American frontier (Chalfant, Beckley, and Palmer 1987). Camp-bellites felt that the established religions of the Northeast had strayed from the true meaning of Christianity. Their goal was to reestablish a Christian movement that would not be bound by the structures and rules of traditional churches. At this stage, the movement centered on the charisma of the Campbells and others who felt as they did.

Taking no name other than Christian, the movement was without formal rules, doctrines, or decision-making methods. When the original leaders died, movement members relied on the tradition of what the leaders had taught. As the movement took hold and grew in membership and geographic scope, however, it became difficult for the group to obtain consensus. Arguments arose over how the Bible should be interpreted and what were the traditions left by early leaders. Eventually, the movement's unity was lost and it split into two major groups, partly over the question of whether instrumental music was appropriate in worship services.

One part of the movement, known as the Christian Church (Disciples of Christ), has moved most of the way toward a bureaucratic structure. While local congre-gations maintain their independence, formal relationships among congregations exist through boards and agencies that deal with programs beyond the congrega-tional level. The other section of the movement, The Church of Christ, still retains formal autonomy for individual congregations and much of the movement's original spirit. However, where congregations are large and numerous, as in parts of Texas, some bureaucratic measures have been introduced.

The different styles of organization that characterize the two parts of the Campbellite movement are part of a pattern that can be used to define different types of religious groups. These types provide a broad understanding of meaningful differences among groups.

Types of Religious Organization

In everyday language we refer to any Christian group as a church. However, significant variations exist in the style, operation, and life of different churches. Understanding these differences and their origins helps us to understand the various ways in which religious groups and their members relate to society.

Church and Sect

Ernst Troeltsch (1931) was the first to formally distinguish between religious movements. He divided religious groups into two polar types: the church and the sect.

For Troeltsch, the **church**, as seen in the Roman Catholic church of the thirteenth century, was a body in which the initial charisma had been completely routinized. The church was at peace with worldly powers, rejecting neither the values nor the authority of the secular order. While it sought to influence the secular world, it did so as an accepted part of social life. The church, then, was a religious group that compromised with and accommodated itself to the secular order. It was the only "legitimate" group, and all people born in its area were seen as its rightful members.

The **sect** is a group that reflects the opposite side of the relationship of Christianity with the world. Troeltsch felt that within the Christian faith there would always be a tension between the group's tendency to accommodate and its spirit of protest against the secular world. The spirit of protest is behind the formation of groups (sects) seeking a renewal of what they consider to be the original Christian spirit.

Contemporary Typologies

Although the historical models Troeltsch used no longer exist, the distinction he made between church and sect continues to be useful in understanding religious organizations. It alerts us to the continuing process of conformity with the secular world and renewed protest within religious groups. As a two-fold model it does not, however, account for the variety of religious life in the United States.

From a very early point in our nation's history, religious life has been characterized by a diversity of religious groups. Roger Finke and Rodney Stark (1989) point out that three groups—Congregationalists, Episcopalians, and Presbyterians— were the dominant religious groups as the American Revolution began; in less than eighty years, however, they had decreased numerically and upstart sects, or new religious groups, such as the Methodists and Baptists, began to have a greater influence on religious life in the nation. As religious tolerance became the rule in American society, aggressive groups protested the falsity of the established religions. Since the state sponsored no particular group, competition for believers was really wide open and any number of new groups was possible.

Pope John Paul II is greeted by bishops as he prepares to celebrate Mass in San Francisco. The Roman Catholic Church currently belongs among bureaucratic religious groups.

We can most usefully think of three general types of religious organizations in this nation. There are those groups which resemble the original three dominant groups and are comfortable with secular society; we will refer to these as **denominations**. Then there are the constantly growing number of groups that are heirs of the upstart sects in spirit of protest if not in doctrine; to these we apply the term sect. Finally, a third type of religious group is neither denomination nor sect. This type is less well-defined, and the groups so categorized vary considerably. The term **cult** is used for this group.

In dividing religious groups into these three types, we are speaking of each as an **ideal type**. This term, introduced by Max Weber, refers to an abstracted model of some aspect of society, such as an organizational form. In reality, no actual organization or other aspect of society fully conforms to the abstracted model or ideal. Rather, the model serves as a benchmark against which real groups can be measured. In our case no religious group is fully a denomination, a sect, or a cult.

However, individual cases come more or less close to the ideal type and therefore can be meaningfully distinguished from one another.

Denomination

The denomination is the most common organizational form of religion in the United States (see Table 13.1). Milton Yinger (1970) describes the ideal type of the denomination as one that appeals to only certain segments of the society. Its members tend to come from the upper and middle classes. In general, the denomination has accommodated itself to the values and norms of its society. Membership tends to be on the basis of being born into a family belonging to that group. The doctrines of the denomination tend to be liberal in their interpretation of Scripture. Worship services are formal and led by one or more trained clergy. The denomination is also tolerant of other religious groups, frequently engaging in joint worship services and transferring members to other denominations without questions.

● **Table 13.1** *Denominations and Sects*

Characteristic	Sect	Denomination
Size	Small	Large
Relationship with other religious groups	Rejects—feels that the sect alone has the "truth"	Accepts other denominations and is able to work in harmony with them
Wealth (church property, buildings, salary of clergy, income of members)	Limited	Extensive
Religious services	Emotional emphasis—try to recapture conversion thrill; informal, extensive congregational participation	Intellectual emphasis; concern with teaching; formal; limited congregational participation
Clergy	Unspecialized; little if any professional training; frequently part-time	Specialized; professionally trained; full-time
Doctrines	Literal interpretation of Scriptures; emphasis upon other-worldly rewards	Liberal interpretations of Scriptures; emphasis upon this-worldly rewards
Membership requirements	Conversion experience; emotional commitment	Born into group or ritualistic requirements; intellectual commitment
Relationship with secular world	"At war" with the secular world which is defined as being "evil"	Endorses prevailing culture and social organization
Social class of members	Mainly lower class	Mainly middle class

Source: Glenn, Vernon, *Sociology of Religion*, New York: McGraw-Hill, 1962. p. 174.

Again, remember that these characteristics represent an ideal type. Few groups match the ideal type completely, as there is wide variation found both between and within denominational associations. Some groups generally referred to as denominations are very close to a hypothetical middle point on the continuum between the denomination and its opposite, the sect.

Sect

Above all, the sect is characterized by protest. Frequently it is a body that has withdrawn from a more denominational group which is seen as having become too compromised with the world and as having lost the true faith. For example, the early Methodist movement was a protest against the established Church of England. However, as the Methodist Church accommodated itself to the dominant values of society, sectarian groups such as the Wesleyan and Free Methodists seceded to pursue what they saw as a truer version of the faith.

As can be seen from Table 13.1, it is convenient to describe the ideal type of sect as the opposite of the denomination. It is opposed to the world and refuses to compromise with secular values. It takes a literal view of the Scriptures and stresses doctrine based upon such an interpretation. Its services are informal, are often quite emotional in nature, and tend to be led by lay leaders, with no formal clergy and little structure. Its members come to the group through a conversion experience, and its members are drawn from the lower socioeconomic strata.

How do sects come into being? The theological answer would be that they develop as doctrinal protests against the impure ideology and practices of the denominations. But are the reasons for sectarian development based totally on religious grounds? It does not seem to be so simple.

A major sociological explanation for the development of sects is economic deprivation. We can generalize and say that most sectarian groups arise among the

Emotion is an integral part of the worship services of Pentecostal sects. In this tent meeting the aroused emotions of the worshippers are expressed in the waving hands lifted in the air.

poor, among the people cut off from the rewards of this life. Thus, sects are largely made up of people from the lower classes of society. Being cut off from mainstream society, the doctrines of the established (denomination) groups do not meet their spiritual needs. In other words, economic deprivation and its attendant problems are seen as the root causes of the development of new sectarian groups.

Deprivation theory is a productive approach to the development of new sects. However, remember that we can feel deprived for a number of reasons other than economic plight. A feeling of social marginality can induce feelings of psychic deprivation which may be alleviated by allegiance with a sectarian group that reduces such feelings. Similarly, cultural shock, as experienced by immigrant groups, is a form of deprivation. This sort of deprivation, in fact, may explain the growth of Pentecostal sects among Mexican immigrants to U.S. cities.

A common assumption is that sects that persist over two or more generations begin a movement toward a denominational style. The Salvation Army, the Church of the Nazarene, and other formerly sectarian groups have come to accept some compromise with the world's values. Even though the accommodation may be far from complete, these groups now exhibit denominational characteristics such as a trained clergy, toleration of other groups, and less emotional worship services.

Not all sects follow this path, however. Some sectarian groups maintain their initial spirit with only slight compromise. Milton Yinger (1970) refers to these groups as **established sects**.

An example is the Old Order Amish found in twenty states but concentrated in Pennsylvania, Indiana, and Ohio. William Kephart (1987) describes the Amish as riding in a horse and buggy and attired in plain, old-fashioned clothes. They see themselves as a particular people who have been called to stay separate from the world at large. They reject almost all of modern culture, refusing to use the auto, television, radios, electric lights, and many other such items. They also refuse involvement in political life and eschew the use of such worldly things as makeup and jewelry.

The separateness of the Old Order Amish appears to be one major way in which established sects avoid accommodation to the secular order. Such separation may be through the isolation of the Hutterites or through the strict asceticism of such groups as Jehovah's Witnesses. **Asceticism** involves self-denial such as not drinking alcohol, not dancing, or not wearing cosmetics when these acts are viewed as impure.

Cult

The term **cult** is difficult to define. In the sense of the term as used by social scientists, such a group is transitory and bears many of the features of the sect (see Table 13.2 for a comparison). Both sects and cults are in high tension with society (Stark 1985). However, while sects deal with the tension by returning to a purer form of the dominant religion, cults seek resolution of the tension in new or deviant religious traditions.

Cults draw their memberships from a pool of spiritual seekers who are attracted to one cult now, another later, and so forth (Wallis 1978, 91). These members turn to new groups that promise to help them resolve their own personal tension with the world and with those around them.

The cult is a tolerant form of religion and is not much concerned with membership figures. In this atmosphere of seeking and drifting, the ideologies of individual cults are very tenuous and group loyalty is low. Traditional religious cults are Christian Science, Scientology, and various forms of spiritualism.

●Table 13.2 Salient Dimensions of Sect and Cult in Social Scientific Literature

Variable	Sect	Cult
Membership requirements/ behavioral codes	High level of commitment, achieved status, selective conversion, proof of change of heart, formalized admission procedures, high standards of conduct demanded of members, asceticism	Minimal requirements, lack of official membership, low level of commitment
Social control	High degree of control	Low degree of control
Entry into group	Voluntary	Voluntary
Expulsion	Excommunication if doctrines not followed or transgression of rules	Expulsion almost impossible
Boundaries	Rigid, clearly defined	Difficult to distinguish; permeable
Orientation to world, perception of world	Deviant, ethically exposed to world as it exists, world torn between good and evil, apolitical	Deviant, indifferent to world in ethical sense, tolerant, oppositional in instrumental sense, apolitical
Cause of existence	Economic deprivation	Psychic deprivation
Manner of original emergence	Schismatic	Nonschismatic
Duration of existence	Generally short-lived	Generally short-lived
Organizational structure/ complexity	Hierarchical	Amorphous, loosely structured, evanescent, difficult to distinguish from cultic milieu
Religious leadership	Unprofessional ministry, priesthood envisioned	Priesthood rejected, charismatic leadership
Spiritual hierarchy	Dualistic	Monastic
Class orientation	Lower classes	Upper classes
Time orientation	Past	Present or future, a-historical
Institutionalization	Minimal to moderate, marginal group	Minimal, marginal group
Size	Usually small, but can be larger	Small
Composition of membership	Conversion aimed at adults though families become basic units	Adults
Socialization practices	Values transmitted to next generation	Little concern with socialization of children into group
Structural orientation, group interaction	*Gemeinschaft*, community oriented, intensive interaction	*Gesellschaft*, individually autonomous

(continued)

● Table 13.2   Salient Dimensions of Sect and Cult in Social Scientific Literature (continued)

Variable	Sect	Cult
Self-conception/ conception of others	Elite, the elect, claims unique status, exclusive group consciousness	Eclectic, polymorphic, many paths to truth, broad and tolerant, epistemological individualism, individual consciousness
Relation to dominant cultural tradition	Oppositional but related to dominant cultural tradition	Inspirational source outside of primary religion of culture, non-Christian
Belief system	Belief system stressing certain elements of traditional religious culture	Mystic belief system
Symbolic behavior	Attention paid to rite and dogma	Rite and dogma eschewed, ecstatic religious experience promoted
Psychological outlook	Psychology of persecution, pessimism, conflict consciousness	Optimism, psychology of success
Goal of group	Through personal perfection in a perfect, moral community in a world in God's image	Purely personal enlightenment, growth, salvation, etc.
Interaction with world, outside, culture, religion	Isolationist, no multiple memberships allowed, complete allegience	Isolationist tendencies but multiple memberships of (religious/ philosophical) groups regularly occur

Source: Barend van Driel and James T. Richardson. "The categorization of new religious movements in American print media," *1988 Sociological Analysis* 49:2 (Summer). pp. 173–74.

In the popular mind today, the term cult has come to have negative connotations. There is a tendency to call any religious group that is deviant or threatening a cult. To many, particularly to family members of those who have joined cults, these groups are so dangerous that any means of destroying them and bringing converts out of the groups is deemed valid. A vigorous anti-cult movement exists and is active not only in deprogramming cult members but also in seeking to destroy the cults through legal and other procedures.

A major problem today is that print media tend to use the term cult to refer to any sort of group that does not conform to society's expectations (see Research Method 13.1). This is particularly true when the group exhibits apparently bizarre and potentially threatening beliefs and actions (Melton 1986; van Driel and Richardson 1988). It is significant that a recent Gallup poll (*Gallup Reports* 1989, p. 45) indicates that almost two-thirds (sixty-two percent) of Americans report they would not want a cult member as a neighbor, a higher proportion than rejects any other set of people.

Research Method 13.1

• • • • • • • **Content Analysis: New Religious Movements and the Print Media**

Putting a label on something has social, even political significance. This is particularly true if that label has negative connotations. If the word we use to describe something implies that it is a bad thing, those who hear and accept the label will perceive the person, object, or organization named as threatening and dangerous.

The large variety of novel types of religious movements which appeared during the 1960s and 1970s appear to have suffered from such negative labeling. Accounts in the mass media of the activities of these movements not only attracted public attention to them, they also made the movements seem evil and damaging to their members. Regardless of the reality of allegations made against the movements, the label they were given automatically made them bad to some.

The label which the media most frequently used for the novel religious groups was cult. The term was almost always accompanied by a negative evaluation. The use of the term was sufficient to put a stigma on new religious movements and evoke violent reactions from much of the public.

Is this a valid indictment, or are the mass media being unjustly accused of creating a monster of these groups? To explore the extent to which the mass media are involved in the negative labeling process with regard to the new religious movements (NRMs), sociologists Barend van Driel and James Richardson (1988) employed the research approach of content analysis. They argued that, while social scientists use the term cult, as well as sect, in a neutral, nonjudgmental fashion, the media use the term cult in ways which bring up overpowering images of something threatening and dangerous.

In content analysis, available material—usually newspaper items, magazine articles, song lyrics, television programs, and the like—are examined to determine what images of a particular subject are being projected. In studying the image of the NRMs in the print media, van Driel and Richardson examined the content of newspaper headlines and stories concerning the movements over a period from November of 1973 to April of 1984. They looked at headlines and articles over five time periods evenly spread through the years chosen for analysis. The four major newspapers examined were: *The New York Times, The Washington Post, Los Angeles Times,* and *San Francisco Chronicle.* They also analyzed the contents of three national news magazines: *Newsweek, Time,* and *U.S. News and World Report.*

Since the term new religious movement covers such a broad spectrum of groups, the researchers selected specific groups to be included as NRMs. They examined headlines and articles which dealt with seventeen groups: The Unification Church, Church of Scientology, Hare Krishna (or ISKCON), Transcendental Meditation, Divine Light Mission, Children of God, Meher Baba, Bhagwan Rajneesh, Youth for Christ, Campus Crusade, Navigators, the Jesus Movement, the Church Universal and Triumphant, est. and Eckankar. The researchers also chose four marginal religious groups which are not generally considered NRMs: Christian Science, Jehovah's Witnesses, the Salvation Army, and the Amish/Mennonite groups. These served as control groups to be used in comparing the language used in referring to them with that used for the NRMs.

The researchers examined any article, headline, editorial, column, letter to the editor, or other printed material in the periodicals on the dates specified. They looked at both the headlines attached to the material and to the content of the specific material itself.

van Driel and Richardson found that accounts of NRMs in the print media consistently used the term cult, and to a lesser extent sect, in ways which effectively cast the movements in a negative light. The language was such as to connect the term with something that was dangerous and threatening. In fact, they found that almost all of the contextual units they analyzed furthered a popular negative image of the NRMs which was close to that of groups organized specifically to fight the groups—the anti-cult movement. In only one case did they find the accounts at all favorable toward the NRMs. Instead, the most frequently emphasized characteristic of NRMs was the idea that converts were somehow confined and deprived of their personal freedom by an authoritarian leader who utilized severe discipline to keep the "faithful" in line. They also implied that NRMs regularly used brainwashing techniques to bind the members to the movement and to build in them fear and hatred for the outside world in order to keep them separated from former friends and their families. In addition, the leaders of the NRMs were portrayed as interested only in the wealth they could accumulate from their followers.

The researchers did find some difference between the content of the material and the headlines which accompanied that content. The articles themselves were less harsh in tone while the headlines were more likely to use the term cult in a fashion implying the most negative of images. In general, the press favored the use of the term cult, though, and seemed to favor it because it conveyed an intriguing aura of danger that attracted readers.

Barend van Driel and Richardson concluded that there was great disparity between the ways in which social scientists and the press viewed the NRMs—even in their use of terms like cult and sect. The press was consistently negative and frequently implied condemnation of the movements. The authors pointed out that this was true in newspapers and magazines of national importance with highly skilled staff. They suggested that the negative interpretations of the new religious movements would be even more pronounced in more local and popular sources.

In summary, through content analysis the researchers confirmed the power of labeling. By giving a negative label to NRMs, the press created an image that led to negative evaluations and to fear of the groups on the part of the public.

Because the word cult has become such a pejorative term, many social scientists have adopted a new term, **new religious movements** (van Driel and Richardson 1988), for such groups. The term is obviously a broad umbrella under which many quite disparate groups are placed. Even so it is a useful term because it does not carry negative value judgments about the groups. Rather, it presents them for what they are—new expressions of religion—and allows us to evaluate each on its own merits.

New Religious Movements

Over the past several decades, many new religious movements have emerged. Some come from reinterpretations of Christian faith, others have borrowed their messages from Eastern religions, while still others have attempted to make religions from a variety of more secular beliefs. These groups deviate from established religious ideas, values, and practices; they conduct unusual worship services, hold doctrines contrary to our Judeo-Christian tradition, and exhibit nonconformist lifestyles. This deviation is sometimes horrifying, as in the suicides that occurred in The People's Temple group at Jonestown, Guyana. At other times it is threatening to the fabric of traditional family life, as in the case of the Moonies. Still other movements merely seem peculiar in their practices and threaten established norms and patterns.

These movements have little in common other than that they bear many traits of social movements (see chapter 10) and have been labeled as new religious movements. Eileen Barker (1984) suggested that there is great danger in taking a number of diverse movements and placing them under the same umbrella. The only generalization that can be made about the various groups is that each represents an attempt to proclaim meaningfulness in life in an age of considerable ambiguity.

There is some question as to whether these movements actually represent something totally new. Although their leaders, ideologies, and practices may be unique, similar movements have appeared at various times throughout the history of the United States. Revitalization movements have appeared at regular intervals, seeking to reestablish what they see as the true interpretations of Christianity or to bring a reevaluation of religious truth. A century ago, spiritualism was the new religious movement; this movement appeared so strange that those deeply involved with it were considered insane (Bainbridge 1984). In the nineteenth century, large numbers of patients in insane asylums were diagnosed as having "religious excitement." Thus, what looks new because its form is different may simply be an attempt to bring new vigor to religion through renewal or revelation (Lechner 1985).

A brief look at three such movements demonstrates their diversity. The **Unification Church**, better known as the **Moonies** after its founder, the Rev. Sun Myung Moon, is a well-known movement that is based upon a radical revision of Christianity. In fact, The Rev. Moon claims that when he was sixteen he had a vision and was told that he was the "Lord of the Second Advent"; as such, he was to complete the work which Jesus had not been able to finish. Although missionaries for the movement had been in the United States since 1959, it was not until Moon, himself, came from Korea in 1972 that the Unification Church began to gather strength (Melton 1986).

As the movement gathered strength it also attracted negative response from the media and public alike. The Moonies have been one of the major targets of the anti-cultist movement and have been continuously involved in controversy. Several aspects of the movement drew the anger of many. Moonies were seen as overly aggressive in both recruitment of new members and in their money-raising techniques. An active program of evangelism by members has frequently been interpreted as brainwashing that entrapped unsuspecting young people. The not-so-subtle appeals for money, especially through front groups, was viewed with suspicion. In addition, the movement was gathering extreme wealth for its leader, buying expensive real estate and even purchasing a Washington, D.C. daily newspaper company. The public doubted that the money was really being used for religious purposes, a doubt that seemed to be confirmed when Moon was convicted of tax evasion and spent thirteen months in prison during 1984 and 1985.

Another well-known movement is best known as **Hare Krishna**, although its official title is The International Society for Krishna Consciousness (ISKCON). It is a new religious movement in the United States, but its roots are found in a version of Hinduism practiced in Bengali in the fifteenth century. Most who join the movement must make a total commitment, much as Roman Catholic monks devote themselves to an ascetic discipline (Melton 1986).

Hare Krishna has been another prime target of the anti-cultists. The movement is highly visible and easily identified. Their saffron robes and shaven heads do cause them to stand out in a crowd. Further, they have been active in fund-raising in such public places as airports, at one time disrupting traffic at Chicago's O'Hare. They are also evident on the streets of many major cities as they conduct their *sankirtan,* a ritual involving dancing and cymbal playing. Like the Moonies, their converts have been targets of the anti-cultists and have been kidnapped and subjected to deprogramming (a sort of reverse brainwashing).

The third movement, **Satanism**, the worship of Christ's devil, is both old and new as a movement. Its roots can be traced to a classical Satanism known since the Middle Ages. It is said to conduct many rituals which are parodies of Christianity—such as the black mass which turns Christian worship upside down, as it were—as well as ceremonies of sacrifice, mutilation, and even rape of victims. Yet there is relatively little known of this version as it has no real history.

A sort of "public Satanism" (Melton 1989) is formalized in two organizations—the Church of Satan and the Temple of Set. Both of these groups, however, are small and relatively staid. While members may conduct rituals offensive to Christians, there is no evidence that members are involved in threatening or dangerous activities. Their numbers are small, and the groups maintain a very low profile.

Why, then, did rumor and controversy surround the groups in the late 1980s? As Bromley (1989) puts it, at that time Satanism became the "new American cult scare." Wild stories, based on isolated incidents (Balch 1989) raised the concern of many. One rumor in particular frightened the public. That was the claim that Satanic cult members were prepared to capture blond, blue-eyed girls on Halloween and sacrifice them. Although no such incident was ever confirmed, the rumor circulated several years in a row. There was no evidence to support the fear the mention of Satanism evoked.

According to Melton (1989) the facts that gave substance to the rumors were the actions of what he called "Satanic solitaries." These are individuals or small groups that appear from time to time using the symbolism of Satanism as part of their activities. There is no evidence of any relationship between either the individuals or the small groups. Satanism, for them, appears to be not so much an active faith as an excuse or justification for deviant behavior. Thus, while we are justly horrified by what is done by some in the name of Satanism, there is little to cause us to be afraid of a widespread, destructive movement aimed at harming innocent citizens.

What is the meaning of these new movements? The task of explaining their emergence and their attraction is as complex as the world of new religious movements. It is impossible to generalize. They appear to be a response to the increasing secularization of society (Wallis 1982) and to gain support from religious seekers who find them a way to serve a sacred cause in the face of a secular society. Rodney Stark and William Sims Bainbridge (1985) suggested that the secularization of contemporary society is self-limiting and that, when it has gone too far, groups form to reassert the sacred. As Harper (1988) suggested, the materialism of modern society has left many feeling spiritually bankrupt, and the secularized religion of the established churches is not filling the emptiness they feel. In addition, the new movements provide structures through which individuals can deal with an increasingly secular, alienating world.

Another suggestion is that these new religious movements are successors to the politically oriented movements of the 1960s. When political action failed to

provide meaning for many of those involved, they turned to novel religious movements. The fact that many members of the new religious movements had participated
in the countercultural movements of that time lends support to this argument.

Religion and Current Issues

Whether we are watching television news, reading a news magazine, or scanning the
daily newspaper, we frequently come across issues involving the religious institution.
The issues range from battles within religious groups to confrontations between religion
and the Constitution. This section looks at four issues: conservative growth and secularization, religion and politics, televangelism, and religion and women.

Conservative Growth or Secularization?

From the beginning, American society has focused on two conflicting world views:
the Judeo-Christian one and a perspective based on secular, humanistic thought.
The mainstream religious groups, especially liberal protestants, see Figure 13.1,
(the denominations that are now losing members) have attempted to be a bridge
between the two views. However, the tension between the two perspectives is slowly
pulling apart and polarizing our religious views.

●**Figure 13.1** The Families of American Religion

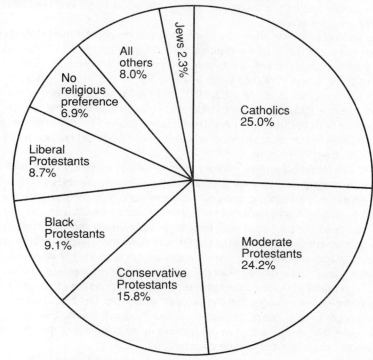

Source: Wade Clark Roof and William McKinney. 1987. *American Mainline Religion: Its
Changing Shape and Future.* © by Rutgers, The State University. Reprinted by permission
of Rutgers University Press. p. 82.

Beginning in the mid-1960s, mainstream churches began to lose membership not only in percentage of the population but also in absolute numbers. Newer, more conservative groups are becoming major actors on the religious stage. Figures provided by Roof and McKinney (1987, 82–84) present a picture of religious groups today. Liberal Protestants include such groups as the Episcopalians and Presbyterians while Moderate Protestantism includes Methodists, Lutherans, and Disciples of Christ. Conservative Protestants include Evangelicals, Fundamentalists, and such broad groups as the Southern Baptist Church. Among the various families of American religion, Catholics and Moderate Protestants form the largest groups (about one-fourth of the population each) while Liberal Protestants represent only 9.7 percent. The Conservative Protestants comprise 15.8 percent.

Research Application 13.1

• • • • • • • Are Baby Boomers Returning to Church?

As we have noted, many major mainline Protestant denominations have been suffering from dramatic drops in membership and declining attendance. As Roozen, McKinney, and Thompson (1990) reported, denominational leaders have consoled themselves, in the face of this decline, with the assumption that once the Baby Boom generation (persons born between 1945 and 1965) grew up and became established in careers and raised families, they would once again fill the empty pews of the congregations. Has this happened? Have the so-called Baby Boomers really returned to church life, reviving flagging interest in established, mainline religious activity?

In seeking to answer these questions, the three researchers used data from the General Social Survey of the National Data Program for the Social Sciences. They used two points in time for reference. Their early 1970s reference came from 1972, 1973, and 1974 data while a later group, or early 1980s reference point, used responses from the 1982, 1983, and 1984 surveys. In their analysis they divided the Baby Boomers into older and younger segments, the former being those born from 1945 to 1954. Their analysis focused on this older group because those in the younger cohort would not have been old enough to be included in the 1970s surveys.

To understand patterns of religious attendance and membership, as well as reasons for the patterns, they focused on three explanatory variables: family life cycle, educational attainment, and political orientation. They used *stage in the family life cycle* to test the assumption that young adults would return to church once they began to have their own families. In other words, they felt need to bring up their children in a religious faith would draw them back to the church. *Educational attainment* was considered important because level of education has been shown to be directly related to participation in religious, as well as other, organizations. *Political orientation* was seen as a potential explanatory variable since it was thought that the "liberal" attitudes of the 1960s had led young people to drop out of traditional religious participation and that the conservative shift evident today would possibly mean a reversal of that attitude and would bring them back to the churches.

The data did reveal that attendance at worship service increased for the older Baby Boomers from the early 1970s period to the early 1980s time. Regular attendance at worship, as reported by respondents to the survey, rose from only about one-third (33.5 percent) who said they attended regularly in the 1970s to

42.8 percent on the early 1980s surveys. It is interesting to note that during this same time period the attendance level reported in the surveys for the general population actually declined.

They concluded, then, that in a very general sense the optimism of denominational officials was somewhat justified—that at least part of the lost generation of church members identified as early Baby Boomers had returned. The best explanation for this return is found in the family life cycle. Four times as many older Boomers were engaged in parenting in the 1980s compared with the 1970s. Also, a significant number of these Boomers brought their children to the churches for moral education.

However, the authors cautioned that this is by no means the whole story. It certainly does not mean that everybody is back. In fact, the data showed that increased attendance occurred mainly for those who had never really left. The denominations have not recaptured those Baby Boomers who made a complete break with their childhood faith. Further, while attendance has increased, it still does not match the level of the parents of these older Baby Boomers. In other words, they may be attending better than they did ten years before, but they are not attending as well as the age group they are replacing in society. Thus, it would be overly optimistic to predict that denominations will see any increase in their net membership.

On the basis of their study, then, Roozen, McKinney and Thompson held out only mild hope for a revival among Baby Boomers. First, the increase in participation is relatively small and applies only to the older Baby Boomers. Second, the increase is found only among those not completely cut off from the church—that is, from those most easily won back. Finally, they suggested that the growing conservative trend, even more pronounced among the younger Baby Boomers, may lead to conflicts within the churches that could present them with new dilemmas.

Roof and McKinney (1987) claim that established religion, as seen in mainstream churches, is undergoing profound changes. New trends seem to be shaping the picture of American religion today, trends which are moving religious life in the United States away from a liberal faith to a more centered position. The bridge between secular values and religious faith appears to have fallen down. In a society characterized by moral and cultural pluralism, attitudes have polarized around the liberal and conservative positions—and the latter position is seen as growing in strength.

Kelley (1977) suggested that those churches that were growing in the late 1970s were both exclusivist and anti-ecumenical. Among the most successful of these were such groups as Jehovah's Witnesses, Evangelicals and Pentecostals, Latter-Day Saints (Mormons), Seventh-day Adventists, and the Southern Baptist Convention (see Figure 13.2). On the other hand, the typically mainstream churches—such as the Presbyterians, Episcopals, and Methodists—were losing church membership. Those groups most clearly identified with the mainstream culture were in trouble, while those who had distanced themselves from it were not (Roof and McKinney 1987).

The term fundamentals or fundamentalism was first used to denote Christian orthodoxy in the early years of the twentieth century. Significant numbers of conservative Christians were concerned with the effects of liberal trends in theology that seemed to destroy what they had always known as the Christian faith. By 1910 the clash between conservative and modernist ideology had erupted into open

●Figure 13.2   Membership Comparison: 1958–1975

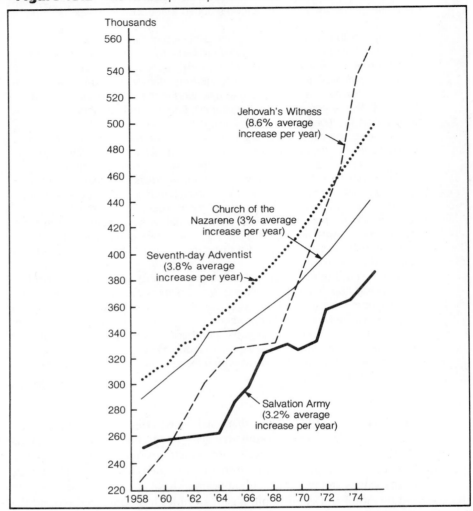

Note: U.S. population growth averaged 14% in 1960–69 and 1.1% in 1970–75.

Source: Dean M. Kelley. *Why Conservative Churches Are Growing.* Copyright © 1977. Reprinted by permission of HarperCollins Publishers.

controversy. Between 1910 and 1912, twelve paperback pamphlets, *The Fundamentals,* were published and fundamentalist faith defined (Goen 1959).

It is important, as Ammerman (1987) points out, to distinguish between evangelicalism and fundamentalism. While **evangelicals** are conservative Christians, they tend to place less importance on taking every word of Scripture as the literal word of God. Fundamentalists are more likely to stress beliefs about the immediacy of the second coming of Christ. In addition, they have resisted the cognitive style of modernity, often stressing separation from the secular world to the extent that is possible.

Fundamentalism was, in part, a social movement aimed at checking the onslaught of modernism (Hadden 1987). Among the many aspects of the secular humanism of modernism most opposed by fundamentalists was the teaching of the theory of evolution. Opposition to this theory was, in a way, one of the triumphs of this ideology. Laws were enacted forbidding the teaching of evolution in schools including state legislation which prohibited such instruction in any of the state's public schools.

Fundamentalism has had its dark period. In a small town in Tennessee, a biology teacher, John Stokes, chose to challenge a law forbidding the teaching of evolution. This so-called monkey trial became a national spectacle. While Stokes was convicted, the results of the trial were a hollow victory. The revealed Biblical ignorance of the prosecutor and bigoted attitude of the judge and townspeople seemed to demonstrate that fundamentalism was a simplistic doctrine. For liberal theologians and churches, the aftermath of the trial seemed a signal that the fundamentalist movement was thoroughly discredited (Hammond 1985).

However, fundamentalist doctrine was far from dead; it remained a fervent belief for large numbers of conservative Christians in the United States as well as elsewhere (Ammerman 1987, Hammond 1985, Hunter 1983). Under the surface of dominant Protestant liberalism, the followers of fundamentalist doctrine remained steadfast in their view of what constituted Christian orthodoxy. They waited, perhaps at times with little hope, for a time when their beliefs and values would again have a major influence on American thought.

Religion and Televangelism

Taking good advantage of this undercurrent in thought were a group of evangelists who used television as their principal means of ministry. Termed televangelists (Hadden and Swann 1981), they presented a message that incorporated conservative fundamentalist thought with other ideas and values concerning how society should be ordered.

The names and programs of these televangelists are familiar to most of us. Jerry Falwell is the fundamentalist leader of the "Old Time Gospel Hour" while Oral Roberts and his son Richard continue to conduct a ministry stressing both healing and economic success. Pat Robertson, who ran for president in 1988, conducts the ninety-minute talk show known as "The 700 Club." Two other televangelists, stressing Pentecostal ministries, held center stage for some time. Jim Bakker and his wife Tammy Faye hosted the "PTL Club," while Jimmy Swaggart conducted a modernized version of an old-time camp revival.

There was much dispute concerning the actual size of the audience reached by these programs, but the numbers were significant. The *Wall Street Journal* at one time suggested 130 million viewers each week. The strongest foes of televangelism said, however, that the audience was only ten million. It was reported that audiences were increasing, although it was contended that the viewers were downscale and already "sold" on conservative religion (Buddenbaum 1981).

Since the spring of 1987 the television ministries have been going through trying times. Dark clouds of doubt began to envelop telereligion when Oral Roberts made seemingly outlandish claims of a 900-foot-high Jesus that appeared to him to give him guidance. His credibility, as well as his ethics, was further damaged when he revealed that God had told him that he must raise eight million dollars for his medical school by March 31—or he would be "called home." Further doubt on his motives was raised when, having raised the eight million, he declared that was only a down payment on what God demanded to preserve Oral and his ministry.

The economic and ethical scandal of Oral Roberts's spiritual blackmail did cause many to begin to doubt the integrity of televangelists, and it confirmed the thoughts of those who had never believed in their sincerity. It remained, however, for sexual and financial scandals to bring about serious disruption in the world of televangelism.

In the spring of 1987 PTL host Jim Bakker was accused of having sexual relationships with a New York church secretary. It was also asserted that this was not a single instance of sexual straying, and some charges were made that he was involved in homosexual activity as well. At the same time it was revealed that his wife Tammy Faye had admitted herself to a California center for drug rehabilitation.

Bakker admitted the liaison with the New York secretary, to whom he had been paying blackmail for seven years, and resigned from the PTL ministry. At the same time he was viciously attacked by fellow Assemblies of God televangelist Jimmy Swaggart. Bakker claimed that Swaggart had actually engineered the revelation in an attempt to discredit Bakker's ministry while puffing up his own. While Swaggart denied this, he was certainly more than ready to cast the first stone and demand harsh punishment for Bakker. An audit of the PTL ministry revealed many irregularities and numerous financial problems. Above all, it showed that the Bakkers had lived a very high lifestyle: they owned a number of homes across the country, several Mercedes, and had received millions of dollars in salaries and bonuses from the ministry. Despite damaging information about the conduct of PTL, the Bakkers attempted to hang on to their possessions and salaries and sought a comeback. However, in 1989 Bakker was convicted of fraud and is now serving a forty-year sentence in prison.

Damaged but not totally bowed down, the ministries experienced a period of relative quiet and they may have hoped that the worst was over. However, in the early months of 1988 it was revealed that Jimmy Swaggart, who had been so quick to condemn Bakker, was photographed going into a New Orleans motel with a prostitute. Swaggart, shedding the copious tears that were so much a part of his ministry, confessed his sin to his congregation. He was ordered to step down from the pulpit for a period of at least three months by the Louisiana Presbytery of Assembly of God (AOG). In early April, from the steps of his ministry's headquarters in Baton Rouge, Louisiana, Swaggart announced that he and his ministry could not stand for such a penalty. Therefore he resigned from the AOG—shortly before he was given the sack—and tried to resume his ministry, without great success.

Religion and Politics

Although an established or state-supported religion is forbidden by the Constitution, the U.S. government has generally been friendly toward religion unless some activities appear to infringe on the rights of minority religions or nonbelievers. Religious groups are free to practice their particular beliefs with little constraint from the government; and religion, generally in terms of broad Christian beliefs, has made itself felt in a variety of political issues over time.

The absence of an established national faith has not left the country without belief in its sacred destiny. Sociologists and historians have spoken of the existence of a civil religion that is part of our national myth. Robert Bellah (1975, 3) defines this as "that religious dimension found . . . in the life of every people, through which it interprets its historical experience in the light of transcendent reality." Using symbols of our Judeo-Christian heritage, **civil religion** ties together our national history with a sacred purpose. It performs two functions for the society: it gives the social order legitimacy and it provides a higher standard with which to criticize social policy (Wuthnow 1988).

Religion is involved in political decisions in two ways today. The first has to do with prayer in public schools. The second is the continuing pressure by religious groups on governmental policy making.

School Prayer

The nonsectarian character of public schools in the United States has long been assumed, but the nonsectarian nature of our schools has not meant the absence of any religious elements. Prayer, Bible reading, and moral training have been a traditional part of school life, usually with a Protestant bias.

In recent years, however, such practices have been struck down by federal courts as a violation of the First Amendment to the Constitution. A recent example has been the attempt to forbid both silent prayer during the school day and equal access to school property by student religious organizations.

Those who support the right of schools to give time to prayer and to allow the use of school buildings for religious purposes have reacted strongly to the court decisions (Wald 1987, 128–29). They charge that the removal of activities such as school prayer leads to godless education. On the other hand, many who oppose public prayers contend that students have always had the right to pray silently if they wish. They contend that if open prayer is legalized, children who hold beliefs other than those who pray may be subjected to ridicule or forced to engage in activities in which they do not believe.

Political Pressure

Formally and informally, religious groups have influenced political decisions. The ability of religious groups to influence legislation seems somewhat dependent on the issue at stake. If the issue involves wide consensus in society, it probably will be put into effect, with the religious pressure providing additional support. However, if the issue arouses wide disagreement, the pressure of religious groups may have little effect.

Two examples illustrate this. When civil rights were a major issue in American society, many religious groups were involved in the pressure to enact legislation guaranteeing such rights. These groups had the support of very influential segments of society, and they merely added to pressure from those segments. Likewise, right-wing political groups have had major effects on issues that seem to have broad public support (Liebman and Wuthnow 1983).

In the past, established denominational-type groups led the involvement of religion in public affairs, working for both conservative and liberal policies. Jane Adams (1970) identified nine powerful groups in the church lobby in Washington. In the 1960s, the liberal voices of religion were those most frequently heard in the halls of Congress. They advocated not only civil rights legislation but, later, anti-Vietnam issues.

Today, however, we are hearing from more conservative groups, such as the Moral Majority (later known as the Liberty Foundation and basically abandoned) and NCPAC. These groups have organized to pressure legislators and the electorate to favor more conservative positions on matters ranging from pornography to abortion.

According to some, the efforts of these groups have not been as effective as their members claim (Simpson 1983, Shupe and Stacey 1982). However, their message seems to appeal to a large number of people. Although the Moral Majority was never known to but a few Americans (Shupe and Stacey 1982), it has managed to present a picture of power. This is probably because a large number of people agree with at least some of the positions taken by the Moral Majority and related organizations (Simpson 1983). The new religious right has taken advantage of the recent conservative trend in society to press its own views, such as opposition to abortion.

Religion and the Role of Women

All societal institutions, whether they mean to be or not, are involved in institutionalized patterns of sexism. Christianity in particular has been a major factor in the support of the traditional female role. Especially among those who take the Bible more literally, the doctrines of religious faith and the teachings of the Bible are seen as giving supernatural authority to the traditional role of women (Daly 1975). This has been especially true where family issues, such as male dominance and the right to abortion, have been involved (Conover and Gray 1983, Huber and Spitze 1983). As a result, a large portion of the religious community has fought against feminist concerns, such as the Equal Rights Amendment.

The Old and the New Testaments both reveal support for the traditional, subservient role of women. In the Old Testament, for example, women are frequently defined as the property of males (Driver 1976). One of the Ten Commandments forbids coveting the wife of a neighbor in the same way that it forbids coveting the other property of a neighbor. The Gospels portray Jesus as treating men and women as equals, but the Letters of Paul revert to the more traditional point of view. In sum, the religious ideology of the Judeo-Christian traditions tends to reinforce and give religious sanction to a sexist view of women. Insofar as groups take a literal interpretation of the Bible, they also are more likely to uphold the traditional view of women (Williams 1989).

Women have played a prominent role in the ongoing work of the church, but they have seldom played a significant role in policy decisions. Catholic women have always been active in the day-to-day activities of the church, but men have had the rule. As late as Mother's Day, 1990, Catholic women in Chicago boycotted services to protest the failure of that church to allow women a voice in its governance. Also, it is only in the twentieth century that Protestant churches have begun to allow women to serve on their official boards, and often the election of women to such office bears the marks of tokenism (Verdesi 1976). In religion or elsewhere, **tokenism**, is the hiring or appointment of a few minority members (in this case, women) to enhance the equality within an organization without increasing any of that minority's influence.

Concern over the appropriate role for women in the church becomes intense when the issue of ordination of women is considered (Lehman 1985). During the 1950s, several large denominations voted to allow the ordination of women to the ministry. In the 1970s, there was a significant increase in the number of women entering the ministry (Carroll, Hargrove, and Lummis 1983). Still, in 1977, only four percent of ministers in the seventy-six member groups of the National Council of Churches were women (Carroll and Wilson 1980). Eighty-three percent of women ministers are found in Pentecostal sects and in groups that devote much of their work to social service (for example, the Salvation Army). Only seventeen percent are found in mainstream denominations.

An increasing number of women are enrolling in theological seminaries. By 1978, one-fourth of those enrolled in such schools were women (Carrol and Wilson 1980). As these women graduate, however, they frequently have a difficult time finding employment as pastors. They generally are hired as assistants or directors of Christian education programs or for such positions as institutional chaplains. Finding the positions they desire is problematic partly because there is an oversupply of ministers in many denominations. When women are hired as pastors, however, they generally perform the role to the satisfaction of the congregations that employed them (Royle 1982, Lehman 1985).

Questions for Summary and Review

1. How do sociologists define religion? What are the implications of their definitions for our understanding of the meaning of religion in society?
2. How did changes in thought and changes in economic means of production affect traditional religious values in the West in the eighteenth and nineteenth centuries? What trends in religious activity have followed?
3. According to functionalist theory, how does religion support society? What are some of the specific functions performed by religion as functionalists view it? How do conflict theorists react to the assertions of the functionalists?
4. In what different ways do sociologists believe people practice their religious faith? What are the dimensions of religiosity that have been identified, and what does each dimension mean?
5. What is the typical growth pattern for new religious groups? What stages of authority occur as this pattern progresses?
6. Distinguish between the different types of religious groups. How do denomination, sect, and cult differ from one another?
7. Why do some sociologists feel that new religious movement is a better term than cult for novel religious groups? How do specific groups differ from one another?
8. How would you compare the strengths of liberal and conservative religion today? What role does fundamentalism play in our society today?
9. What is meant by televangelism? What effect have televangelists had on religious life, and what problems has televangelism encountered?
10. What has been the relation of religion to politics? How does civil religion play a role in American life? What political issues are important to religious groups and their members?
11. What has been the role of women in the Judeo-Christian tradition? How well is the church adapting to women in leadership roles? How does Biblical literalism affect the views of many on women and the church?

Key Concepts

Calvinism (p. 305)

Charismatic authority (p. 310)

Charismatics (p. 308)

Church (p. 312)

Civil religion (p. 328)

Conflict theory of religion (p. 307)

Consequential dimension (p. 310)

Cult (p. 313, 316)

Denomination (p. 314)

Established sects (p. 316)

References

1. Adams, James. 1970. *The growing church lobby in Washington*. Grand Rapids, Mich.: Eerdmans.

2. Ammerman, Nancy T. 1987. *Bible believers: Fundamentalists in the modern world*. New Brunswick, N.J.: Rutgers University Press.

3. Bainbridge, William Sims. 1984. Religious insanity in America: The official nineteenth century theory. *Sociological analysis* 45 (Fall): 233–40.

4. Balch, Robert. The social construction of Satanism: A case study of the rumor process. Paper presented at the annual meetings of the Society for the Scientific Study of Religion, Salt Lake City, October 1989.

5. Barker, Eileen. 1984. *The making of a Moonie*. London: Basil Blackwell.

6. Bellah, Robert. 1975. *The broken covenant: American religion in time of trial*. New York: Seabury Press.

7. Berger, Peter. 1968. *The sacred canopy*. New York: Doubleday.

8. Boughey, Howard. 1978. *The insights of sociology: An introduction*. Boston: Allyn and Bacon.

9. Bromley, David. Satanism: The new American cult scare. Paper presented at the annual meetings of the Society for the Scientific Study of Religion, Salt Lake City, October 1989.

10. Buddenbaum, Judith M. 1981. Characteristics of media-related needs of the audience for religious TV. *Journalism quarterly* 58:266–72.

11. Caplow, Theodore, Howard M. Bahr, and Bruce A. Chadwick. 1984. *All faithful people: Change and continuity in Middletown's religion*. Minneapolis: University of Minnesota.

12. Carroll, Jackson W., and Robert L. Wilson. 1980. *Too many pastors*. New York: Pilgrim Press.

13. Carroll, Jackson W., Barbara Hargrove, and Adair T. Lummis. 1983. *Women of the cloth*. San Francisco: Harper and Row.

14. Chalfant, H. Paul, Robert E. Beckley, and C. Eddie Palmer. 1987. *Religion in contemporary society*. 2d ed. Palo Alto, Calif.: Mayfield.

15. Chalfant, H. Paul, and Charles W. Peek. 1983. Religious affiliation, religiosity and racial prejudice. *Review of religious research* 25:155–61.

16. Conover, Pamela, and Virginia Gray. 1983. *Feminism and the new right*. New York: Praeger.

17. Daly, Mary. 1975. *The church and the second sex*. 2d ed. New York: Association Press.

18. DeStefano, Linda. 1990. Church/synagogue membership and attendance lev-

els remain stable. *Gallup poll monthly* 292:32–34.

19. Driver, Ann Barstow. 1976. Religion. *Signs* 2:434–42.

20. Durkheim, Emile. 1947. *The elementary forms of religious life.* New York: Free Press.

21. Finke, Roger, and Rodney Stark. 1989. How the upstart sects won America: 1776–1850. *Journal for the scientific study of religion* 28 (March):27–44.

22. Gallup, George. 1985. Religion in America, fifty years: 1935–85. *Gallup reports,* (May) No. 236.

23. *Gallup Report.* 1989. Cults lead list of groups unwelcome as neighbors. March/April: 45–46.

24. Glock, Charles, and Rodney Stark. 1965. *Religion and society in tension.* Chicago: Rand McNally.

25. Goen, C. C. 1959. Fundamentalism in America. In *American mosaic: Social patterns of religion in the United States,* edited by P. Hammond and B. Johnson, 85–93. New York: Random House.

26. Gorsuch, Richard, and D. Aleshire. 1974. Christian faith and ethnic prejudice: A review and interpretation of research. *Journal for the scientific study of religion* 13:281–307.

27. Hadden, Jeffrey K. 1987. Religious broadcasting and the mobilization of the new Christian right. *Journal for the scientific study of religion* 26:53–62.

28. Hadden, Jeffrey K., and Charles E. Swann. 1981. *Prime time preachers: The rising power of televangelism.* Reading, Mass.: Addison-Wesley.

29. Hammond, Phillip. 1985. Introduction. In *The sacred in a secular age,* edited by P. Hammond, 1–8. Berkeley, Calif.: University of California Press.

30. Harper, Charles L. 1988. The social construction of malevolence: Rethinking theories of the new religions. *Free inquiry in creative sociology* 16 (May): 3–13.

31. Hartland, E. Sidney. 1951. Totemism. In *Encyclopedia of religion and ethics,* vol.

II, edited by J. Hastings, 383–407. New York: Scribner.

32. Hirschi, Travis, and Rodney Stark. 1969. Hellfire and delinquency. *Social problems* 17:202–213.

33. Huber, Joan, and Glenna Spitze. 1983. *Sex stratification: Children, housework and jobs.* New York: Academic Press.

34. Hunter, James Davidson. 1983. *American evangelicalism: Conservative religion and the quandry of modernity.* New Brunswick, N.J.: Rutgers University Press.

35. Kelley, Dean M. 1977. *Why conservative churches are growing.* New York: Harper & Row.

36. Kephart, William M. 1987. *Extraordinary groups.* 3d ed. New York: St. Martin's Press.

37. Lechner, Frank J. 1985. Fundamentalism and sociocultural revitalization in America: A sociological interpretation. *Sociological analysis* 46:243–60.

38. Lehman, Edward. 1985. *Women clergy: Breaking through gender barriers.* New Brunswick, N.J.: Transaction Books.

39. Liebman, R. C., and Robert Wuthnow, eds. 1983. *The new Christian right.* New York: Aldine.

40. Marx, Karl, and Freidrich Engels. 1957. *On religion.* New York: Schocken Books.

41. Marx, Gary. 1967. Religion: Opiate or inspiration of civil rights militancy among Negroes? *American sociological review* 32:64–73.

42. Melton, J. Gordon. 1986. *Encyclopedic handbook of cults in America.* New York: Garland.

43. _____. Contemporary Satanic practice. Paper presented at the annual meetings of the Society for the Scientific Study of Religion, Salt Lake City, October 1989.

44. O'Dea, Thomas, and Janet O'Dea Aviada. 1983. *Sociology of religion.* 2d ed. Englewood Cliffs, N.J.: Prentice-Hall.

45. Peek, Charles W., Evans W. Curry, and H. Paul Chalfant. 1985. Religiosity and delinquency over time. *Social science quarterly* 66 (March):29–39.

46. Poloma, Margaret. 1982. *The charismatic movement: Is there a new pentecost?* Boston: Twayne.

47. Roof, Wade Clark, and William McKinney. 1987. *American mainline religion*. New Brunswick, N.J.: Rutgers University Press.

48. Roozen, David A., William McKinney, and Wayne Thompson. 1990. The "Big Chill" generation warms to worship: A research note. *Review of religious research* 31 (March):314–22.

49. Royle, Marjorie H. 1982. Women pastors: What happens after placement. *Review of religious research* 24:116–26.

50. Shupe, Anson, and William A. Stacey. 1982. *Born again politics and the Moral Majority: What social surveys show.* New York: Edwin Mellin.

51. Simpson, John. 1983. Support for the Moral majority and status politics in contemporary America. In *The new Christian right,* edited by R. Liebman and R. Wuthnow, 188–207. Chicago: Aldine.

52. Sloane, Douglas M., and Raymond H. Potvin. 1986. Religion and delinquency: Cutting through the maze. *Social forces* 65:87–105.

53. Stark, Rodney. 1984. Religion and conformity: Reaffirming a sociology of religion. *Sociological analysis* 45:273–82.

54. _____. 1985. Church and sect, in *The sacred in a secular age.* P. Hammond, ed. Berkeley: University of California Press, pp. 139–49.

55. Stark, Rodney, and William Sims Bainbridge. 1985. *The future of religion: Secularization, revival and cult formation.* Berkeley, Calif.: University of California Press.

56. Troeltsch, Ernst. 1931. *The social teachings of the Christian churches.* New York: Macmillan.

57. van Driel, Barend, and James T. Richardson. 1988. The categorization of new religious movements in American print media. *Sociological analysis* 49 (Summer):171–83.

58. Verdesi, Elizabeth. 1976. *In but still out.* Philadelphia: Westminster Press.

59. Wald, Kenneth D. 1987. *Religion and politics in the United States.* New York: St. Martin's Press.

60. Wallis, Roy. 1978. The rebirth of the gods? In *New lecture series,* no. 108. Belfast: Queen's University.

61. _____. 1982. The social construction of charisma. *Social compass* 29:25–39.

62. Weber, Max. 1958. *The Protestant ethic and the spirit of capitalism.* New York: Scribner.

63. Williams, L. S. Religion and sexism: Belief systems and Biblical bias. Paper presented at the meetings of the Southwestern Sociological Association, Little Rock, Ark., March 1989.

64. Winter, J. Alan, 1977. *Continuities in the sociology of religion: Creed, congregation and community.* New York: Harper & Row.

65. Wuthnow, Robert. 1988. Sociology of religion. In *Handbook of sociology,* edited by N. Smelser, 473–509. Englewood Cliffs, N.J.: Prentice-Hall.

66. Yinger, Milton. 1970. *The scientific study of religion.* New York: Macmillan.

Understanding Politics and Social Life 14

A somberly dressed politician strolls down the steps of the legislative hall. Blazing lights are turned on him as cameras focus on his progress and reporters thrust microphones in his face to catch anything that he might say. As he makes his way through this crowd, he stops now and then by the seats of various legislators. He makes a bit of conversation, obviously stressing issues about which he is concerned. He is engaged in buttonholing his colleagues in an attempt to ally them with his policies. He is, in short, politicking.

The scene is a familiar one to observers of legislatures in this country, both at the federal and state levels. What is unique is that it takes place not in the United States but in the Kremlin, the U.S.S.R.'s seat of legislative deliberation, and the politician is Mikhail Gorbachev, President of the U.S.S.R. and Secretary of the Communist Party. That he should need to use persuasion and influence to exercise power is a new thing in Soviet politics. A more open society, though, has led to a more open government; and Gorbachev's government is faced with a number of serious problems. Gorbachev—and his authority—is threatened by a number of issues. The economy has not improved, and Moscow, as well as the rest of the nation, is plagued by shortages of all sorts. Also, some of the Soviet states—Estonia, Lithuania, and Latvia—have declared their independence. Even more threatening to Gorbachev, as a politician, is the eventually successful struggle of his chief rival, Boris Yeltsin, to become President of Russia, the largest of the Soviet states.

This struggle to retain power is really all part of the day of a politician. The name of the game is politics, and the name of politics is power; or, as one political scientist put it more than fifty years ago, "Politics is the game of who gets what, when, and how" (Lasswell 1936). In this chapter we look at the societal structures that determine who gets what, when, and how.

Power and Authority

As we have already indicated, social institutions are those relatively stable complexes of values and norms by which societies deal with their basic problems of survival. In the case of the political institution, the issue is the way in which the social system distributes the use of power in the society. In the structure of society, the government is formally designated to have responsibility for the legitimate use of power. In theory, this power is used to appropriately channel the people's activities so the society can achieve its collective goals. In sum, the political institution is that complex of roles, role relationships, norms, and values which defines the appropriate use of power to preserve the order of society. For example, one part of this complex is law enforcement, delegated to police, sheriffs, and other government agents appointed to control crime and to assure civil peace. Only members of these groups can officially use force to meet this end. Others who attempt to do so, however well-intentioned or justified, violate the structures of society and may be subjected to punishment for their activities.

The establishment of government, then, means that power is not used in a random fashion. Rather, a structure of stable duties and responsibilities is provided that defines the relationships between powerful groups and individuals. In this way power is exercised in a society in a specified fashion that contributes to the establishment and preservation of order.

It should be clear, then, that power is a fundamental concept in the field of political sociology, the study of the political institution. An equally important concept, authority, signifies the way in which that power is legitimately used in the society. The study of politics and the government is centered on these two concepts (Orum 1988).

Power

What do we mean by power? Most sociologists begin to answer this question by citing the definition given by Max Weber that power is the chance that an individual or a number of individuals will be able to get their way, or realize their wishes, in a social situation even though they meet with the resistance of others (Gerth and Mills 1958). Dahl (1957) suggested an intuitive approach to the understanding of power. We can think in terms of the relationship between two individuals. A has power over B if A can get B to do something, even though B does not want to. This emphasizes the fact that **power** is a relation among people in which one actor—an individual or a group—can control the actions of another in that relationship.

Power is generally limited in scope. The boundaries of power are defined by the extent to which the probability continues to hold that A will be able to get B to do what B does not want to do. For example, your professor has the power to force you to take an exam which you do not want to take and even to write your answers in a Blue Book. However, the same professor cannot dictate what clothing you will wear while taking that exam, so the power of the professor is limited in scope. Similarly, in the political sphere you may be taken into custody by the police if you are suspected of breaking a law, but at another time the police cannot restrict your right to attend a movie of your choice or engage in other legal activity.

If power is the ability to get your way regardless of opposition and to dominate the actions of others, then power is force—the coercion of others to behave in a certain fashion. Such force may be used illegitimately or legitimately. If terrorists (see chapter 10) kill someone in order to coerce others to accept their views, that is an illegitimate use of power. If, on the other hand, the government of a Middle Eastern nation directs the police or army to seek out the terrorists and, if necessary, kill them, that would be a legitimate use of force. This legitimate use of power is referred to as authority.

Just as the legitimate power of the professor is limited, so also is authority limited, in general, to specified actions. For example, it was legitimate for President Bush to use his powers as president to formulate legislation to assist in the "bailing out" of the savings and loans institutions that were going under with such regularity in the late 1980s and early 1990s; that is within the scope of his authority as chief executive. However, it was not legitimate for then President Richard Nixon and his aides to suppress information concerning the break-in of Democratic Party headquarters at the Watergate apartments. The scope and delegation of authority are important aspects of political life.

Authority

Weber (1947) stressed that the continued existence of every social group is grounded in some form of authority. The grounding or delegation of authority in a society are provided by the basic values of the society's belief system. These values make power legitimate, turning it into authority.

The term **authority** implies that which is socially accepted and approved. As Robert MacIver (1965, 63) defined it, authority is the recognized right of certain individuals or bodies to set policy, make judgments where differences occur, and lead people in the fulfillment of socially defined goals. Gerhard Lenski (1966, 54) expressed the difference between the legitimate and illegitimate use of power nicely in noting that the former is the "rule of right" as opposed to the use of might.

Marger (1987) reminds us that the use and acceptance of authority are generally automatic and not consciously considered. As individuals internalize the norms of their society, they learn to comply with the dictates of authority as defined by those norms. As a result, for the most part we do not steal because we accept the value of honesty and recognize the authority of the police to arrest and the courts to punish us for such an action. What is significant is that we refrain from stealing even when there is virtually no chance of being caught; the norm guides our behavior in the absence of conscious restraints. How have we come to accept the values and recognize the appropriate authority? Weber (1947) describes three ideal types of authority which may be recognized and taught in a given society.

Charismatic Authority

Perhaps the oldest form of authority is that which Weber called charismatic. The term comes from a Greek word, *charisma*. It is used in the Bible's New Testament to refer to the gifts of the Holy Spirit, particularly to speaking in tongues and healing. Politically it has come to refer to the exceptional power an individual's personality has to command allegiance. Such charismatic authority is basically grounded on personal attributes of the leader. On the basis of these, the authority of the leader is recognized and the loyalty of people gained. Our immediate history provides several examples of such charismatic leadership.

In the U.S. the civil rights movement of the 1960s was clearly led by key figures whose charisma attracted people to their ideas and their leadership. Those familiar with that movement cannot think of it without remembering Martin Luther King. King held no formal office, other than pastor of a Baptist church, but he exercised an authority over a throng of followers, both black and white, that allowed him to direct political change. For many, to have heard him speak on the steps of the Lincoln Memorial in Washington was to accept the authority of his message and to join in the struggle to change the laws regarding civil rights.

Other charismatic leaders have been more directly connected to political power. For example, Adolf Hitler used the power of his personality to lead a minority party in Germany from its obscurity to domination of that nation and, for a while, much of Europe. Similarly, Fidel Castro was a folk hero in Cuba as he undertook a long but eventually successful guerrilla fight against the Batista government. Almost as if he were a prophet, he led his followers to a miraculous victory and was able to proclaim himself the ruler of the nation.

Hated as he was in the U.S., the Ayatollah Khomeini was for Iranian fundamentalists a charismatic figure who commanded their loyalty by the power of his personality (Hiro 1989). At a time when tension between the ruling shah of Iran and fundamentalist Shi'ite Moslem leaders was growing extreme, Khomeini became a leading voice of opposition to the Westernizing policies of the shah. He verbally attacked the shah personally on several occasions and was jailed in 1964. After he was released and deported to Turkey, he then fled to Iraq. He was eventually exiled to France, but even from that distance his voice was heard. His writings and his recorded sermons continued to proclaim "death to the shah." Eventually his leadership brought about the fall of the shah, and the Ayatollah became the religiously based leader of an Islamic Iran. The authority with which he forged a new government was based on his own charisma rather than on formal positions.

A major difficulty with charismatic authority is that it is basically unstable. If it is to continue beyond the lifetime of the original charismatic leader, and if the legitimacy of the movement is to be maintained, the authority must be transformed. Weber referred to this transformation as the routinization of charisma. In this process the qualities associated with the original leader are transferred to a different type of authority structure. More than the loss of the original leader is involved in a change in the authority based on charisma. The daily problems of any group or society must be faced and overcome. A more permanent, formal structure is needed. Weber described as options two other sources of authority: traditional and legal-rational.

The Ayatollah Khomeini, shown here returning to Iran to lead the revolution in 1979, had great charismatic appeal to the people.

Traditional Authority

Frequently the next stage after charismatic authority is that of tradition associated with the charismatic leader. As we pointed out in the last chapter (chapter 13), after Jesus was no longer with his disciples the movement he began relied on the tradition. This tradition was embodied in his logical successors, those who had known him and followed him personally. Their authority did not come from their own charisma but was, in essence, borrowed from his.

Not all societies directed by traditional authority began under charismatic leadership, but it is a common progression. While the original rulers of a nation, for example, may have gained power through their own charisma, the next generation of rulers is granted authority simply for the fact that they were the sons (and at times, daughters) of the original ruler. In this way kings, queens, shahs, and so forth, have received the mantle of authority. Even when the original regime was founded on the basis of the personality and teachings of a charismatic authority, traditional authority may fall upon successors who lack such personality but possess connection with the tradition that dictates their leadership. For example, Mao Tse-Tung rose to power in China as a revolutionary leader of the people; his successors have been the faithful who, though uninspiring, were loyal to his teachings.

It is difficult to find true examples of traditional authority in modern society. It continues to be the basis of authority in simpler society; however, elements of such leadership may remain even in the most complex of societies. The interest of many of the British in the activities of a largely ceremonial royal family is an instance of such traditional continuation. Though royalty is without power in that commonwealth, it does represent a connection with the traditions of the past.

Legal-Rational Authority

Far more typical of modern, complex society is authority based on legal-rational principles, especially as embodied in bureaucracies. The sources of legitimate power in this type of authority are the rules and regulations that surround a structure and the offices within it. The **legal-rational authority** of the leader is accepted because she or he has been elected or appointed to an office. Individuals accept the right of such leaders to make rules, enforce regulations, and provide guidance because the leaders hold offices to which such formal power is attached. Whether we like or dislike the current president or the administration's policies, for example, we accept his authority over those aspects of our lives for which his position empowers control.

The legal-rational approach to authority fits modern complex societies and their operation. Among other things it allows for an easy transition of power because succession of authority is spelled out in political rules. When President John F. Kennedy was assassinated, a new president, Lyndon Johnson, was sworn in within hours. The fact that Kennedy had been a young president with considerable personal charisma while Johnson lacked that spark was of no consequence. There was a rational, legal procedure to follow. Similarly, though Jimmy Carter was undoubtedly not thrilled to turn the office of president over to his Republican rival, Ronald Reagan, he nevertheless rode in the inaugural parade and participated in the peaceful transition of the authority of the office of president.

In considering these three sources of authority, it is well to remember that they are ideal types, just as the variety of religious groups discussed in chapter 13 were ideal types. That is, no single case fits perfectly into a given category; rather, any given system of rule will probably embody at least some elements of each type (Marger 1987). For example, some presidents of the United States, such as Kennedy and Roosevelt, have inspired people with their charisma while others have appealed to the nation's traditions to undergird their authority.

The State and Perspectives on the State

In modern societies the political institution is embodied in the **state**. That state is an entity encompassing a population that, to a greater or lesser degree, has some sense of a common identity. Rules and procedures are formalized, and the right to act on behalf of all the people or on behalf of a powerful group within the society is granted the state, which is the agent of societal order.

The State

Obviously, all societal institutions exercise a degree of authority within their particular arena. The state, however, holds ultimate authority. Basically, it is the one institution in society which holds a monopoly on the use of force to ensure compliance. When violence occurs, whether on a large or small scale, the state has the automatic legitimate right to use physical force to contain the situation.

As Marger (1987) points out, even when one's personal property is threatened, violence is not automatically sanctioned. If burglars break into your home and you shoot and kill one of them, you will have to answer to the state for that action. Even if you are eventually vindicated, your use of violence must be legitimated by that agent of society which has the monopoly on such force. Recent instances of citizens who committed acts of violence in what they considered self protection, only to find themselves indicted for murder, give evidence of the solitary control which the state has on the use of force. Even a police officer who kills someone in the line of duty must justify the death. Clint Eastwood's movie character Dirty Harry would not stand much chance in a real police department.

Types of States

Democracy may be defined as a form of government based on majority rule through an electoral system by which the members of the government are selected and in which citizens enjoy rights and privileges in their private and public lives. It is a political system which derives its authority from the consent of those governed and one which provides regular means for the routine replacement of its officeholders. Two concepts are central to the ideal type of democracy: equality and liberty.

Equality means that, simply on the basis of humanness, each individual has a moral right to take part in the governing process. Although a goal of true equality for all is never realized, the principle of equality is the important defining factor. It implies that the will of the majority, rather than the force of an individual, ultimately will determine the conduct of the government.

However, the majority is not always right and, not infrequently, the decisions of the majority may infringe on the lives of others. For example, after the Civil War the majority of voters in the South enacted Jim Crow laws (see chapter 7) which denied equality to blacks. Thus, the concept of liberty is added to equality in the ideal type of democracy. Liberty means that people have certain rights that cannot be taken from them—inalienable rights, as described in the Declaration of Independence. The phrase **civil liberties** expresses this democratic value. Civil liberties include our rights to freedom of speech, to be protected against the search and seizure of our property or person, the right to practice the religion we choose, and so forth. These rights are embodied in the first ten amendments to the U.S. Constitution—the Bill of Rights.

Scholars consider several factors favorable to the development and maintenance of a stable democracy. First, there must be viable political pluralism in the society; that is, citizens must have a real choice among policies of the society and among those who will execute the policies. Second, democratic government flourishes when economic and social conditions are stable. Finally, democracy remains healthy so long as there is a feeling in the society that such government is not only possible but also desirable (Kornhauser 1959, Gusfield 1962, Lipset 1963).

The validity of these factors can be seen when we contrast the situation of the United States with those of Latin American and African nations. From the beginning, the three factors cited were part of American life and, as the nation has grown stronger, the stability of its democratic tradition has become taken for granted. On the other hand, the instability, poverty and low educational level of Latin American and African nations make stable democracy difficult and give dictators—masquerading as democratic presidents—the opportunity to seize and maintain power.

Totalitarianism is a state organized in such a way that those in power have control over all aspects of the society's life, extending from the most public ceremonies to most of the very private activities of individuals. As a form of government, totalitarianism extends its authority to each aspect of social life. Government not only controls crime and regulates public order, it also oversees the media, the arts, and other aspects of life considered private in democracies.

Scholars have listed a number of characteristics of the totalitarian state. One of the more comprehensive portraits is that given by Carl Friederich and Zbigniew Brzezinksi (1965). They suggest six features. First, in a totalitarian state a compelling ideology exists which is used to control the public. Second, there is only one party and it is structured to prevent opposition. Third, the government has control of weaponry and, fourth, utilizes it to terrorize the public. Fifth, the state exercises pervasive control of the media as well as, sixth, all aspects of the economy. In other words, it is a society in which there is highly centralized decision making and the civil liberties of the populace are nonexistent. To accomplish this, all aspects of society must be controlled so that the entire public is mobilized toward the work of the totalitarian state.

China under Maoist rule is an example of a totalitarian state. Every aspect of the individual's life was under the control of the government. Dissenters, so-called intellectuals, were ridiculed, sentenced to jail, and forced to perform stoop labor for the government. Only the government's ideology, particularly during the time of the Red Guard, was permissible and guided people in how to think and in what they should do. Even as China's government seemed to loosen its grip on its people, totalitarianism was just below the surface. Even when the regulations against religion were relaxed, it was not a measure of liberation; rather, it was a means for bringing religion up from the underground and under the control of the government (Goldman 1986).

Authoritarianism is a modified form of totalitarianism. Authoritarian governments also permit little or no opposition to their official policies, but they do not attempt to extend this control to all aspects of social life. Debate on some issues is allowed, and the arts and other cultural media are not rigorously regulated. We find an example of this type of government in the U.S.S.R. of Gorbachev's reforms. There is still control, and the individual is expected to follow its policies, but the individual is allowed more decisions concerning personal life.

Theoretical Perspectives on the State

There are two polar views of the state. Functionalists see in it an inevitable and essential institution that has emerged as the life of a society becomes more complex. In this view only a specialized central entity, the state, could possible manage society's affairs. Even though elites are in control of the state, their control is for

As the communist countries have changed from totalitarian to authoritarian or democratic states, protest over individual and ethnic rights has emerged. Here *Czechoslovakian* flags are part of a memorial to those who suffered under communist, totalitarian rule.

the benefit of all. On the other hand, conflict theorists see the state as an instrument for the domination of the masses by the elites. That is, as society grew more complex the state operated on behalf of the emergent ruling class. It protected the interests of those who had managed to gain control of the surplus created by a more sophisticated economy.

The Functionalist Perspective

As it does when considering other societal institutions, the functionalist perspective sees the state as a necessary ingredient in the stability of society. Orum (1988) notes that such a view has its roots deep in the thinking of early social theorists such as Mosca (1939), Pareto (1970), and Michels (1962). All three theorists distrusted the masses or the public in that they believed the majority of people would constantly turn their allegiance to new elites.

According to these thinkers, history is simply the tale of successive elites taking control of the masses. As they see it, there is a split between the unorganized public and the organized groups that grasp the reigns of power. According to Michels, even where democratic principals are proposed, control is always in the hands of an oligarchy. These theorists did not see this rule by elites as wrong, rather they saw such rule as necessary in order for society to successfully operate and achieve its goals.

A more modern version of this approach is found in the theories of Talcott Parsons (1966). He presented a portrait of a society which is dominated by a few, but so dominated in order that the state can achieve "collective goal attainment." In the same way that functionalists view the social stratification system (see chapter 6), Parsons portrayed society as built on a harmonious consensus and organized for the greatest good of the most. The political subsystem operates to distribute power in such a way that society will achieve its goals and the interests of all will be served.

In this view the state plays several important functions for the benefit of society. First, the state establishes the laws and norms which provide order and direction for the society. Second, the state maintains necessary control over the society to protect citizens against the possibility of deviance which could be dangerous. Third, through its policy-making mechanisms, the state is responsible for giving direction to the society as a whole. Fourth, the state controls the economy so that it will remain stable. And, fifth, the state, with its legitimate use of force, is able to protect its members against the threat of other states or, at times, threats from within.

The Conflict Perspective

Conflict theory, which has strong roots in Marxian thought, holds that the state does not exist for the good of all but rather for the maintenance of the position and power of those who own the means of production (see chapter 6). As in the case of the analysis of religion's functions, conflict theorists would charge that all of the alleged obligations of the state seen as necessary by functionalists are, in fact, simply activities to protect the upper or ruling class. For example, the laws and norms that the state upholds are based on values that support the dominant elite, and social control is exercised in the interest of preserving these laws and norms regardless of their effect on groups other than the dominant group. Again, the so-called collective goals of the society are not those of the whole society but of only those that serve the interests of dominant elites.

The state arose from the need of the ruling class to make permanent the social arrangement of society that so benefits it. Therefore, the state is seen as an instrument of oppression of the masses, the products of whose labor is appropriated by the bourgeoisie. According to Marx, the origins of human alienation are found in this appropriation. Engels (1950) contended that the state exists expressly to cover up the contradictions of the ownership of property inherent in the capitalist order.

Even though contemporary ownership of the means of production is different than it was in Marx's time, the state still serves the interests of the dominant class. It is true that the corporation is now the central player in the economic game; and, with the rise of the corporation, the family-owned company of the past has vanished. However, even though the managers of the corporation are not its chief owners, they are more than randomly selected employees. Most ranking executives in corporations hold substantial blocks of stock in the company; thus, in company with the other major owners, they make up a new capitalist class that functions in the same way as the old capitalist class.

In the conflict view, the state will always serve the interests of those who control the means of production, in corporations or otherwise. From an instrumental point of view, the owners or executives are able to control those in strategic positions in the state through the exercise of pressure. Also, capitalist society is so structured that it is imperative that the interests of the capitalists be served; otherwise the process of the state would be undermined.

Political Behavior in the United States

While political institutions in all societies address the same basic problems, each solves them in its unique way. Each societal institution is influenced by its general culture, and each influences all other aspects of the society. Thus, the political institution of the United States bears the marks of its society's values and history. Thus, too, each facet of political life in the United States will bear the mark of our culture. We will look at four features of political behavior in the nation: the nature of political parties, the agents of political socialization, the influence of interest groups on political decisions, and the level of participation in political matters.

Political Parties

A political party is an organization that is formed in order to win control of the government through the electoral process. Its aim is to further its goals, or platform, through having its candidates elected to political offices.

LaPalombara and Weiner (1966) observe several broad factors which contributed to the rise of political parties as a means of seeking control of the government. First, a significant level of secularization was necessary since parties base their claims to loyalty on the fact that individuals must feel they (and not gods or fate) can make a difference in the society. Second, an extensive network of voluntary associations is needed to provide experience in action and a base for the support of parties. Third, there must be a communications network, including transportation, that will allow for contact between people in all parts of the society. These conditions seem to have come about in the nineteenth and twentieth centuries as did the need for organized political groups.

As we know them, political parties are basically products of the twentieth century (Orum 1988). Until then, politics was conducted among a small number of people within a rather limited area. In this century, however, politics is conducted on a mass basis and over large areas. Therefore, political parties are needed so that the contemporary political campaign, filled with party activity, can be conducted.

The situation of political parties in the United States is relatively unique. While there have been many political parties in the nation, some lasting only briefly, the two major parties—Democrat and Republican—form the basis of our two-party system. Candidates for small parties are regularly on the ballot in the United States, but they seldom win. In almost all cases, offices are won by candidates of the two major parties which control our electoral process.

This situation is peculiar to the United States. Few, if any, other countries have such a two-party arrangement. In some nations there are several major parties. For example, in the Netherlands five parties have significant influence on the outcome of elections; Italy has nine (Marger 1987). Why is the United States different? Several observers of the political scene suggest that it is due to the winner-take-all nature of the electoral outcome in the U.S. In other countries, like the Netherlands and Italy, legislative seats are awarded on the basis of the proportion of the vote a party receives. If your party gets ten percent of the vote it will, through proportional representation, have ten percent of the seats in the legislature. In the United States a party receiving only ten percent of the vote would be given no voice at all. Only those candidates who get the most votes, a plurality (or, in some cases, a majority) gain office. Therefore, it is to the advantage of politicians to band together in groups of sufficient size and scope to win the greatest number of votes.

Given the broad nature of the two political parties in the United States, how deeply involved is the average citizen? Studies indicate that people do not have a heavy intellectual or behavioral investment in the political parties to which they belong. In a major study of American voting behavior, Angus Campbell and associates (1960) found that, while three-quarters of Americans gave a preference for a particular party, only about ten percent were deeply committed to the party and its platforms. That is, only a small proportion of those identifying with a party had any significant commitment to the policies and principles for which it stood. Converse (1964) found that voters in the United States tend not to think in terms of the underlying agenda of parties but to vote on a more emotional basis.

Flanigan and Zingale (1987) noted that partisanship, or loyalty to one's political party, is shallow in the United States. Support of the Republican and Democratic parties has fluctuated widely. For example, when Eisenhower was first elected president only forty-two percent of Democrats voted for their party's candidate. When Goldwater ran against Johnson in 1964, sixty-four percent of Democrats supported their party's candidate. It is feasible to categorize those who identify with a party as strong, weak, or independent. For both Democrats and Republicans, slightly less than one-half of those claiming party affiliation describe themselves as "strong" members of the party. It is clearly this group that provides stable party support while those who describe themselves as "weak" party affiliates account for swing voting such as that described above.

There are signs of a shift in party identification in the United States. Voters are becoming more thoughtful concerning their politics. This has not led to stronger party identification, however. On the contrary, there is a growing disinclination for people to identify with either party. As Orum (1988) puts it, there seems to be a process of dealignment from political parties. Perhaps this is due to the higher educational level of the electorate as well as a breakdown of the older ethnic and class identifications which formerly resulted in stronger party identification.

Political Socialization

Political socialization is a process similar to all other forms of social learning and internalization. Through this process the values and norms that characterize the political system are passed on to the new generation. We learn what the norms and values of our society are and, as in general socialization, come to internalize and accept a particular way of doing things, "making them an integral part of one's way of seeing and making judgments about the political world" (Marger 1987, 217). For example, as Marger points out, Americans tend to settle almost everything through some modification of the democratic process. Wherever feasible we "vote" on the outcome because that is "the American way of doing things." This is what we have learned about settling differences of opinion in our lives, whether they involve a Little League team or the election of the nation's highest official.

How do we come to see this as the way to settle things? What agents produce this political socialization? Actually, as you would imagine, they are not unlike the agents of any other type of socialization. Family and religious groups certainly play a part. Indeed, it has been found that children profess an identification with a political party at an early age (Orum 1988). This preference is undoubtedly learned from parents. However, the identification is neither very meaningful nor long lasting. Evidence indicates that the family has little effect on the political world view of children—that is, on what political views they will eventually hold; this perspective develops much later. We may conclude, then, that the family plays a lesser role in political socialization than in other such processes. It appears that both schools and the mass media have more significant effects on our political views.

It has been observed that our public schools provide the most systematic, even deliberate, efforts at political socialization. This is not, of course, socialization to a particular party identification but to internalization of the norms and values of our American political heritage. The required history and civics courses of our school days were heavily laced with information that promoted our democratic and capitalist systems as essentially the only "true" ways of conducting political life. In some states, Texas for example, students at public colleges and universities must take four courses in American politics and history, courses which tend to strengthen faith in the existing system.

Perhaps the most interesting thing about political attitudes developed by our schools is in what is *not* taught about our societal life in the public schools. There is little mention, at least in public schools, of the acute inequalities of our economic world. The stratification system, which produces inequality at all levels of life (see chapter 6) receives virtually no attention. Instead, the view is taught that our system produces the greatest good for the most people, and taught to such an extent that even those who are disadvantaged accept the essential goodness of the system (Huber and Form 1973).

Another major player in political socialization today is the mass media, particularly television. Dye and Zeigler (1989) estimated that American children spend more time watching television than they spend in school; for American adults, about one-half of leisure time is given to viewing television programs. Television news is the source of information about the community and the world for two-thirds of the citizens of our society. The TV set has become our means of communication, reaching all segments of the society.

The mass media, then, and particularly television, are critical in the political socialization of the nation. This is especially true with regard to partisan issues. Through what is learned from the media, people come to interpret the events of the community and world and to form their political opinions. The media are able to shape our political beliefs and behaviors in two ways. First, they are our major source of information about what is going on in the world. Second, they build support for the dominant institutions and ideological system of our society. In these ways the media, and particularly television, become our political authorities. It is not coincidental that many favored a network news commentator, Walter Cronkite, over the candidates for either party in the last election. He was the figure that presented the image of political stability and trust to the nation.

It is significant that the media not only select what news we will have but also interpret it for us. As Dye and Zeigler (1989, 9) note:

> Events, people, and organizations invariably lend themselves to a variety of interpretations. Newsmakers try to find an angle on the story—an interpretation that affects the political implications of the story. ... By suggesting the causes and consequences of events, the media shape popular opinion.

Research Application 14.1

• • • • • • • Election '88: Media Coverage

If George Bush won the election, it must be the media's fault. That's the conventional wisdom that has poured forth from op-ed pieces, news talk shows, and "news analysis" articles ever since Election Day. TV news, we are told, was seduced by Bush speechwriter Peggy Noonan's sound bites, manipulated by media strategist Roger Ailes's photo-ops and attack ads, and shunted away from serious reporting by its own fascination with the horse race. Ever since the polls closed, the campaign has been depicted as a shallow and superficial process that manipulated, misinformed, and misled the electorate, an affair as nasty and brutish as life in Hobbe's state of nature (though not, alas, as short).

In a *New York Times* op-ed column, former network correspondent Marvin Kalb charged that television news was "so preoccupied with photo opportunities and sound bites, so manipulated by media experts, so driven by polls that it lost sight of its journalistic responsibilities. . . ." As a result "the overall tone of the coverage was shallow and distinctly timid." The bottom line: "TV news made no sustained effort to challenge Bush . . . ."

Under the headline "How the Media Blew It," *Newsweek* complained about the heavy horse-race coverage and the decision of reporters to censor themselves from criticizing Bush. Meanwhile, another *New York Times* op-ed piece by writer Mark Crispin Miller, complained of "TV's antiliberal bias." According to Miller, "Coverage of Dan Quayle was chilled." "Bush's background, too, was sanitized," and "reporters (bent) over backwards not to seem at all critical of Republicans. Finally, in a speech to his peers at the Washington Journalism Center, *New York Times* columnist Anthony Lewis cited numerous "press failures in the campaign," among them a "fascination with . . . process, not substance" and an "inability to deal with lies" coming from the Bush campaign.

These postmortems seem to be dissecting a different campaign from the one monitored by the Center for Media and Public Affairs this year. After analyzing all 735 general election stories that appeared on the ABC, CBS, and NBC evening news from August 19 through November 7, we found that the networks' coverage was notable for its balance, toughness, and focus on the issues—precisely the opposite of the critics' charges.

The charge of "horse racism" is a hardy perennial, but its bloom may finally be fading. In their study of television's 1984 general election coverage, Maura Clancey and Michael Robinson noted a shift away from the usual prevalence of horse-race stories. The new beneficiary of media attention was not policy issues ("enduring disputes about how *government* should behave") but campaign issues ("short-term concerns about how *candidates* or their *campaigns* should behave").[1] As table 1 shows, 1988 coverage was cast in the same mold. Campaign issues like disputes over Dan Quayle's National Guard service, negative ads and mudslinging barely edged out discussion of strategy and tactics as the most frequent topic of campaign news. Policy issues came in third, and horse-race news ran a distant fourth.

In fact the general election witnessed a dramatic reversal of the primary season in this regard. Throughout the primary campaign, over twice as many stories focused on the candidates' positioning for the nomination as their issue positions. This fall that ratio was nearly reversed, with 282 stories on policy issues and defense, and the economy were each covered in over 100 stories. Between forty and eighty stories apiece dealt with unemployment, drugs, taxes, the

●**Table 1** Top Ten Story Topics

Number of Stories

Campaign issues	339	The debates	103
Strategy and tactics	338	Vice presidential choices	23
Policy issues	282	Media coverage	22
Horse race	168	Past campaigns	20
The electorate	108	Reagan's role	18

environment, education, and the budget deficit. (Many stories covered more than one issue.)

Critics of this year's horse-race coverage usually focus on the profusion of poll reports, many of them commissioned by the networks themselves. The real issue here is the propriety of such coverage, not its preponderance. The horse-race coverage was heavily poll driven, but the polls didn't drive the issues off the air.

A Supine Press?

The other major complaint is that the networks let Bush and his image makers make patsies out of them. This passivity in the face of Republican skills at media manipulation allegedly gave Bush free rein to get his chosen message out each day. Thus, Kalb bitingly termed Roger Ailes a "de facto producer of the evening news," and *Newsweek* called for a return to "the days when reporters and editors picked the sound bites."

Once again, it is hard to square this portrayal with the data presented in table 3. This fall 1,137 judgments from all sources were aired on the personal character, public records, campaign styles, issue stands, or other attributes of George Bush and Michael Dukakis. The result was mainly bad news for both men. Negative judgments outweighed positive ones by the same two-to-one margin (66 to 34 percent) for both candidates. Even the number of evaluations was virtually identical—564 for Bush and 573 for Dukakis.

●**Table 2**   Top Ten Policy Issues

Number of Stories

Crime	142	Taxes	70
Defense	121	Environment	54
The economy	121	Education	46
Unemployment	77	Budget deficit	45
Drugs	74		

●**Table 3**   Good Press

	Bush	Dukakis	Number of Sources
Source			
All sources	34	34	1137
Partisans	32	35	795
Nonpartisan	38	31	342
Networks			
ABC	34	36	372
CBS	30	33	414
NBC	37	32	345
Topic			
Issues	31	27	221
Job performance	22	32	168
Candidate performance	34	36	418
Character	43	45	18
Time period			
Post convention (8/19–8/28)	75	26	78
Pre first debate (8/29–9/25)	23	28	288
Between debates (9/26–10/13)	28	31	216
Post second debate (10/14–11/7)	36	40	555

Media criticism outweighed praise by roughly the same two-to-one margin among both partisan sources (the candidates and their supporters) and nonpartisan ones (reporters, pundits, and ordinary voters) on all three networks, and on the major dimensions along which the candidates were evaluated—their issue stands, records in office, and performance on the campaign trail.

So Bush was *not* allowed to deliver his sound bites without challenge. On November 4, for example, he attacked Dukakis for financial mismanagement, while holding up a *Boston Herald* headline that read, "What a Mess!" CBS's Eric Engberg identified the *Herald* as a "pro-Bush Boston tabloid" and commented tartly, "Bush, without taking note of the fact that the federal deficit is now $155 billion, *acted* like an outraged prosecutor." Engberg closed by noting that the Bush campaign had "trotted out" some Massachusetts Republicans who said "with straight faces" that the vice president was surprised at this state of affairs.

Bush may have gotten the sound bite he wanted that night, but the *story* was about the act he was putting on, and the tone was one of unmistakable sarcasm. Similarly, in his September 15 report about an earlier Bush attack on the "Massachusetts miracle," ABC's Brit Hume commented acidly, "Bush says he wants a kinder, gentler America, but there's nothing kind or gentle about the way he's campaigning."

CBS's reporting was even more aggressive on September 16. After Bush claimed that Massachusetts had lost thousands of jobs, Engberg stated flatly, "Wrong!" He then rebutted Bush point by point. On October 19, ABC's Richard Threlkeld performed a similar vivisection on Bush's notorious "tank" ad that painted Dukakis as dovish on defense. Such stories could hardly have done more to inoculate viewers against the candidate's intended message.

Of course Dukakis didn't fare any better. The airwaves were increasingly filled with complaints about his dullness, arrogance, and disorganized campaign techniques. For every story that protested Bush's new-found pugnacity, another ripped Dukakis's ineptitude as a counterpuncher. On November 6, NBC's Tom Pettit summed up one line of criticism: "While Bush was burning up the campaign trail, Dukakis was fiddling with state functions." After a shot of Dukakis posing with children (and looking distinctly unpresidential), Pettit noted sarcastically, "Remember, this is the Democratic candidate for president." He then ridiculed the Massachusetts governor for "displaying keen knowledge of gardening" at an agricultural event where he talked about compost piles. Pettit concluded, "This is what you call a turning point. Dukakis discussing composting, while George Bush was out being ferocious."

If the coverage was anything but fluff and puffery, why the flurry of assertions to the contrary? First, there's the frustration factor. Part of the battle for the presidency is the struggle for control of the battlefield—the media agenda. The combatants are the candidates on one side, and the journalists on the other. Both sides win some and lose some, and journalists always come away licking some wounds.

Remember 1984, which saw practically none of this year's notorious negative campaigning? It was derided as an issueless exercise in feel-good politics. On election eve NBC correspondent Chris Wallace complained that Reagan had waged "a campaign long on glitz and short on substance . . . a cynical campaign, manipulative . . . (that) offered pomp and platitudes. . . ." Since 1972, television has set the rules for presidential politics. Journalists disdain those who play the game poorly and resent those who play it well.

The complaints, however, do have some basis in reality. Bush ran a better media campaign than Dukakis, which is not the same as fooling the media or getting good press. The issues mentioned most often on TV news—crime and defense—were Bush's key issues. And Dukakis was called a liberal on the evening news sixty-five times this fall, compared to only fourteen times during fourteen months of primary campaigning. The proportion of the public who found him "too liberal" nearly doubled from May to October. But it's not television's fault that the Democrats lacked a coherent media strategy or that Dukakis proved a poor pugilist.

The one time that Bush clearly benefited from good press was during and just after the Republican convention. His coverage in late August fulfilled all the conditions for the type of media breakthrough enjoyed by Jimmy Carter in 1972, Gary Hart in 1984, and Jesse Jackson earlier this year. By exceeding expectations he briefly dominated the field as a highly visible, viable, and desirable candidate. Why the sudden shift? The traditional convention honeymoon coverage was magnified by journalistic amazement that the 97-pound weakling of American politics had turned into a muscle-bound macho man. His media image and poll ratings soared in tandem as he kicked sand into his rival's face. It was a textbook demonstration of the power of positive viewing.

So, did television give Bush an unfair boost after all? We think not, unless the canons of media fairness are interpreted to require balanced coverage during every week of the campaign. Bush's good press plummeted even before Labor Day and ran behind Dukakis's the rest of the fall. At the time, moreover, notions of a media boost for Bush seemed absurd. The question being raised in late August was whether the media had done in the Bush campaign by its aggressive coverage of the Quayle controversy.

During the twelve days after his selection on August 16, Quayle was the subject of ninety-three stories on the evening news—more coverage than any presidential candidate but Bush had received throughout the entire primary campaign. Quayle's 21 percent positive rating from nonpartisan sources at the height of the controversy was nearly as low as we logged for Gary Hart during the Donna Rice scandal in May 1987.[2] (Quayle's image never recovered. His nonpartisan good press score rose to only 31 percent, compared to an unbeatable 100 percent for Lloyd Bentsen.)

Ironically, the Quayle affair worked to Bush's advantage by keeping him on-screen every night defending his running mate in a decisive, resolute manner that reinforced his new take-charge image. In addition it moved up the kick-off of the fall campaign. Bush roared out of the gate like an Oklahoma "Sooner," while Dukakis was still awaiting the traditional Labor Day starter's gun. In fact some of Bush's edge in good press derived from criticism of his opponent on precisely this point. As ABC's Jim Wooten noted on August 29, "The governor may remember in November what he didn't do in August."

Voter Perceptions

Finally, the media's role must be understood within the broader dynamics of how voters decide. The playing field was tilted in Bush's direction this year by the combination of peace, prosperity, and a still-popular president. And voters' perceptions are formed not only by the campaign drama but by the stage on which it is played out. Bush needed only to actualize this potential advantage by convincing voters that he was not a bumbling effete snob out of touch with their concerns. He accomplished this by focusing attention on his opponent's flaws rather than his own virtues.

George Bush has always had a media problem. Previous studies found that he attracted mostly negative press during the 1980 and 1984 campaigns, as well as the 1988 primary season.[3] He didn't convert many reporters to his cause this year, and his coverage showed it. Nonetheless, 1988 will be remembered as the year Bush succeeded in turning his media image from a threat into an opportunity.

1. Michael J. Robinson and Maura Clancey. "General Election Coverage Part 1." *Public Opinion*, December January 1985, pages 49–54 and 59.

2. "Quayle Hunt." *Media Monitor*, September 1988

3. Robinson. "General Election Coverage Part 1." Michael J. Robinson and Margaret Sheehan. *Over the Wire and on TV.* New York: Russell Sage, 1983. S. Robert Lichter. "How the Press Covered the Primaries." *Public Opinion*, July August 1988, pages 45–49.

Note: Data based on clearly positive or negative source evaluations on ABC, CBS, and NBC nightly newscasts 8/19–11/7/88

Source: Lichter, S. Robert, Daniel Amundsen, and Richard E. Noyes. "Election '88: Media coverage." *Public Opinion* 11 (5):18,19,52. Reprinted with the permission of the American Enterprise Institute for Public Policy Research, Washington, D.C.

Interest Groups

Voluntary associations—those groups one joins because one wants to—have played a very significant role in American life, including politics. One particular type of such associations is the **interest group.** These are groups or organizations with a specific interest and which seek to achieve a goal by influencing the outcome of political decisions. Dye and Zeigler (1989, 176) define interests groups as

> . . . formal organizations that try to achieve their goals by influencing public policy. Generally they equate their goals with the public interest. Whether they are good or bad groups depends very much on whether we like what they advocate.

The issue of the influence of interest groups on the political process has become increasingly important to Americans. Whereas few saw such groups as important in the late 1950s, by 1984 over sixty percent perceived them as having a great influence on political life. However, people make distinctions as to the influence of different interest groups. For example, in 1984 more than half of those surveyed saw labor unions (fifty-seven percent) and business (fifty-one percent) as having too much power over the political process. On the other hand, senior citizens' and farmers' groups were overwhelmingly seen as having too little power in the making of political decisions (Dye and Zeigler 1989, 177).

From this it should be clear that not all interest groups wield the same power. For one thing, interest groups have unequal access to the resources they need in order to influence political decisions. Those groups that can afford a **lobby**—that is, a highly organized presence complete with office, staff, and easy access to legislators—have the greater possibility of influencing the decision-making process.

Political action committees (PACs) are sponsored by a wide variety of groups and have the more successful lobbies in congress. They are a particularly effective form of influence group because they provide large campaign contributions. For example, in 1986 twenty-eight percent of all contributions to congressional campaigns came from PACs; nearly half of the support of incumbent House members (forty-nine percent) came from this source (Dye and Zeigler 1989, 195). The amounts of money contributed by the PACs are significant. In 1984 the American Telephone and Telegraph corporate PAC gave almost 2 million dollars to political campaigns while the Teamsters, through their PAC, provided about 4.5 million dollars. However, these sums are small when compared with the contributions of what Dye and Zeigler call the ideological and trade association PACs. Ideological association PACs that organized around Senator Jesse Helms brought more than 15 million dollars to the coffers of congressional campaigns, while such trade groups as the realtors PAC gave 5.5 million.

These investments in political campaigns must pay off since the PACs continue to make them. Does this mean that they are bad? Generally, the answer depends on what groups sponsor the PACs and how we feel about these groups. As noted, many Americans feel that some interest groups are too powerful and that the government is being run by these special interest groups. However, the extent to which people perceive this to be true for a particular groups depends upon the evaluation made of the group. Clearly this is an issue which must be given serious consideration in the future.

Political Participation

Perhaps because people in the United States are not deeply committed to the ideology of their political parties, participation in political life is relatively low. Even in the most common, and simplest, form of participation—voting—we lag far behind other nations. Whereas in other countries of the world, some of which make voting mandatory, as much as 85 to 90 percent of the electorate actually votes, only between 52 and 64 percent of those registered to vote in the United States actually do so— and these figures are for presidential elections in which the most people vote.

In an attempt to categorize different levels of participation in political life, Olsen (1982) divides people into six types. At the top are those he calls *leaders*. These are individuals who have great influence in the formal political system and also exercise some authority in economic and social matters. They have considerable impact on political life, depending upon the position they hold. Below them are the *activists*, members of interest groups, party leaders, and community workers who influence the government through lobbying and campaign financing. Depending upon the issue and their degree of involvement and resources, activists can have a considerable impact on decisions.

Less involved are what Olsen calls the *communicators*. These are politically concerned people who both talk and write about political matters. They express their interest in certain issues and, depending upon the effectiveness of the message they give, may have an important impact on the outcome of elections and other political decisions. Below them are what Olsen calls *citizens*, or those who actually vote regularly. Such individuals are usually well-informed about political matters and may have a collective, though not individual, impact upon policymakers.

The political *marginals* are only occasional voters but are individuals who may be mobilized for certain issues. Their contact with the political system is minimal and their activity is sporadic. They have virtually no impact on political decisions. Finally, the *isolates* are the nonparticipants who are apathetic and politically unaware. They have no impact on the system and are either withdrawn from or simply acquiesce in the political system.

Who are most likely to be found in these different categories? Not surprisingly there is a strong social basis related to participation, and those most likely to participate come from the more privileged segments of the stratification ladder. Verba and Nie (1972) estimate that socioeconomic status accounts for one-fourth of the variation in rates of participation in the political process. In addition, there are significant differences according to minority-group status, with blacks and Mexican Americans, for example, less likely to participate (a fact strongly related to socioeconomic status again).

Age has generally been a factor in voting. In the 1984 election less than half of those between ages 18 and 21 reported voting (45 percent) and just over half

(55 percent) of those from 22 to 24. On the other hand, over 80 percent of those between 45 and 75 got out to vote (Flanigan and Zingale 1987).

Research Method 14.1

• • • • • • • Asian-American and Latino Participation in Politics

Ethnic and racial groups have played an important part in the politics of the United States from the beginning of its history. While many of the older ethnic identifications have lost their relevance, newer minority groups may now be the basis of renewed ethnic politics. Uhlaner, Cain, and Kiewiet (1989) explored the role that such "new" minorities currently play in our political life and what we might expect for the future.

The two new groups with which these researchers were concerned are Latinos and Asian-Americans. Today Latinos represent forty-one percent of legal immigrants, and Asian-Americans account for thirty-six percent. How are these two minority groups involved in U.S. politics now, and what does the future hold? To answer such questions the researchers utilized survey data from a California sample.

California was deemed an appropriate site for the study of these minorities because both Latinos and Asian-Americans are well represented in the population of that state. Interviews were conducted in late 1984. The sample consisted of 574 Latinos, 335 blacks, 308 Asian-Americans, and 317 non-Hispanic whites. Among the information obtained from the sample were data about the extent to which members of the sample were registered to vote and voted. The investigators also asked about any campaign or other political activities in which the respondents were involved. The research model emphasized the political behavior of the Latinos and Asian-Americans as compared with that of the non-Hispanic whites and the "older-minority" blacks.

The findings indicated that both Latinos and Asian-Americans were significantly less likely to participate in political life than either non-Hispanic whites or blacks. In part this might be explained by the fact that a large number of the newer groups were not citizens and therefore not eligible for participation. However, it was found that this did not remove the differences. Even when only Latinos and Asian-Americans who were citizens were compared with the other groups, their participation remained lower.

However, the two "newer" groups were different from one another in political participation. For the Latino population, their ethnic status had very little direct effect on political activism of any sort. When demographic factors such as age, education, and income levels are introduced into the analysis, differences in participation between Latinos and the comparison groups virtually disappear. Culture accounted for only a tiny part of the difference in political participation.

For Asian-Americans, however, a quite different pattern was observed. The same controls that erased the differences between Latino participation and that of the white and non-Hispanic groups did little to remove the differential levels of political activity. Asian-Americans generally become citizens much sooner than Latinos, yet they do not participate at a higher level; so citizenship cannot explain the variant levels of participation for these two "newer" minorities. There must be other factors related to Asian-American status that can explain the difference.

One explanation advanced by the researchers was that Asian-Americans do not have the same incentive to participate in politics that other minority groups do. Blacks and Latinos tend to live in neighborhoods in which they constitute an overwhelming percentage of the residents. This is not true for Asian-Americans, who tend to be more widely dispersed throughout the general population. Therefore, even those Asian-Americans who seek and obtain political office do not represent an Asian-American constituency. Ethnicity just is not a major part of their politics. In other words, political activism will have little payoff for the Asian-Americans; they have no real opportunity to advance their status in society by climbing a political ladder as other minority groups have done.

A second explanation offered has to do with the history of Asian-Americans in the United States. Throughout most of their time in the country they were excluded from government and political affairs because they were not eligible for citizenship. Only in 1952, in fact, were barriers to naturalization totally removed. The period of exclusion served as justification for unequal treatment; indeed, Japanese-Americans were interned like criminals for the duration of World War II. There are two implications in this history. First, the short period of full citizenship for Asian-Americans means that there has been little time for full political socialization. Second, previous negative interactions with the political system, as expressed in government actions, may lead Asian-Americans to believe that they can best achieve their goals by looking in a direction other than politics.

But what of the future? It is suggested that both groups offer the established political parties significant opportunities. The party that is successful in recruiting members of either group will increase its power if it also concentrates on socializing its new minority members to be active, voting citizens. As the authors put it, it remains only to see which party will realize this first and be able to capitalize on it.

....

An analysis of the 1988 presidential election (Ladd 1989) revealed some interesting facts. First, some groups which had been identified with the Democratic party, at least since the days of the New Deal, defected in this or some previous election. In particular, the trend for Southern voters to turn to the Republican party continued. On the other hand, the older voter, long a substantial part of Republican support, was more likely to cast a ballot for Dukakis than Bush. It is also interesting that women were more likely to vote for the Democrat's candidate than were men, a change from a time when gender did not make a difference in voting patterns.

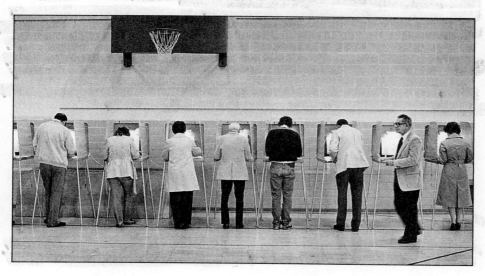

These Americans in Flint, Michigan, exercised their right to vote. However, less than half of all Americans eligible to vote exercise that right in presidential elections.

Second, the Democratic public philosophy has lost favor with voters, and this has been a major factor in making the Republicans the dominant party at least in the presidential election.

Third, there has been a dealignment from parties—that is, a weakening of voter ties to either of the major political parties.

Finally, the voter appears to have a split personality with regard to political affiliation. While the Republican candidate has won the presidency handily for five out of six of the past elections, the Democrats have controlled both houses of Congress for all but two years.

There is, Ladd reports, considerable evidence of group voting. For instance, Michael Dukakis won the black vote with eighty-six percent of blacks voting for him, compared with only twelve percent voting for Bush. Hispanics also continued to be Democrats. Whites, on the other hand, strongly backed Bush. Class differences in voting have declined, though. Low-income families were only marginally more likely to vote Democratic.

Looking at how other specific groups voted in the 1988 election, age did not play a significant factor in the results of the presidential or other elections. Voting figures are nearly identical for the various age groups, although both younger and older voters were slightly more likely to support Dukakis; even so, the support still constituted less than one-half of the total vote for these age categories (see Public Opinion 1989). Religion continued to make a difference. Jewish voters went for Dukakis with seventy-two percent, and more than half of Catholics (fifty-four percent) did also. Only thirty-eight percent of Protestants voted for Dukakis (this varies by the exit polls involved). As noted, black and Hispanic voters turned out strongly for Dukakis, with blacks slightly more likely to do so than Hispanics.

Models of Political Power in the United States

What is the shape of political power in the United States? Several models have been advanced. For some years a heated debate was carried on between those who took an elitist position and those who saw a pluralist view of our political life. The elitist perspective claimed that the key positions in government were under the control of a relatively cohesive group of power brokers. These represented, variously, the upper class or a combination of corporate, political, and military leaders. Elitist theorists see these groups as manipulating the masses in order to ensure that the state serves elite interest and institutions. The pluralist perspective, on the other hand, contends that participation in political decision making is far more widespread. Various interest groups and their leaders influence elected political officials and indirectly control the leadership elites through their influence. The state, then, is an arena where the various interest groups can produce a diversified position which will result in a political consensus.

Elitist Theories

Marger (1987) makes a distinction between classical elite theorists and radical elite theorists. The former are those political theorists we have discussed before—Pareto, Mosca, and Michels. In general they distrusted the masses, seeing them as too ignorant to rule themselves. For them, the masses are incapable of providing their own rule; elite rule is a necessity. It is not that the masses are oppressed by the dominant classes, but that the dominant must take over the responsibility of rule if society is to be stabilized.

The radical elite theorists take a quite opposite view of the relation between the elites and the masses. Far from seeing elite rule as benign and beneficial, they view the elites as ruling in their own interests. The elites are viewed as a cohesive group drawn from the upper echelons of society who rule in their own and their classes' interests, with a negative effect on society. They control resources for their own good rather than the good of the whole. This view has much in common with the conflict perspective discussed earlier.

The theory that an elite group controls the political process in American society has been given most eloquent voice in the writings of C. Wright Mills. In his book *The Power Elite* (1959), Mills focused on three factors in American society as it developed after World War II; these factors brought about what he considered a concentration of power in a small group of powerful people.

First, the small, family-owned business that had been the center of American business were rapidly being swallowed up by increasingly larger corporations which in turn controlled business and industry through their executives. Second, the federal government has come to play a much more significant role in all aspects of the life of the nation. And, three, beginning with the so-called Cold War of the 1950s, the military establishment has had a more influential voice in economic and political matters than at any previous time.

Mills contends that a very few people—his **power elite**—hold immense power over the American public and that these few form a more or less unified and cohesive group held together by economic, political, social, and cultural commonalities. This group is concentrated in the corporate, political, and military institutions. Members of the group change positions from one of these institutions to another with some regularity. For example, business executives become politicians, military leaders become corporate presidents, and politicians take up places in the corporate world. For example, at least since Harry Truman's administration, former presidential advisers have found lucrative careers in business, especially when it comes to influence peddling. These three groups operate essentially without effective control by the electorate or by any regulatory body.

Mills's conception of the power elite portrays decision making in the United States as a hierarchy of power on three levels. At the top is the power elite; at the bottom, the masses of the people. In the middle are members of Congress, organized labor, state and local political officials, and various pressure groups.

Marger (1987) reminds us that the most visible aspect of political life in the nation is at the middle level. That is, we observe the political game being played out by members of Congress, labor leaders, and representatives of various pressure or interest groups. It is this activity which the media reports. However, power at this level is relatively insignificant, in Mills's view; this level functions at the pleasure of the power elite, which directs what decisions are to be made.

Mills's conception of a power elite was based largely on theorizing. Other scholars have given the idea substance. For example, Floyd Hunter (1954) began his research with a study of the power structure of a southern city, Atlanta. He found that a relatively small number of business people actually controlled decision making in the community. The policymakers were the business executives who directed the implementation of their policies through such middle-level people as the editor of the newspaper.

Hunter then expanded his research to a national sample (1959) and corroborated Mills's assertion that a relatively cohesive power elite existed. He interviewed a sample of individuals who were named as key national figures and determined that about one hundred men could actually be considered top leaders in the nation. He found that these individuals actually knew one another and communicated concerning important national issues. In fact, he concluded that the important political issues of the nation were actually decided by the business executives more than by political leaders. Hunter concluded the corporation was the seat of real power in both local and national politics.

G. William Domhoff carried the power elite concept a step further. In a series of books reporting his research (1967, 1978, 1983), Domhoff looked at both local and national power. He argued that American society, at local and national levels, is actually controlled by a **ruling class**. In his analysis of power in American society, he emphasized the social nature of the ruling or governing class. It is a very cohesive group, held together by its common ties in the upper class. The infrastructure of this class is found in the interrelationship of social institutions, organizations, and social activities. These undergird the reality of an upper, ruling class.

In locating the members of this class, Domhoff found a primary source in the "Social Register." This relic of the past still lists about 65,000 families and single adults who are from the upper class. The register not only provides a picture of who is in this class but details their interconnectedness through private schools, social clubs, and other organizations. After cross-referencing the number of people who actually belong to this ruling class, he concluded that they comprise only from 0.5 to 1 percent of the American population. Yet this small group, as Domhoff views it, actually does rule. The political and military leaders to whom Mills ascribed authority actually serve the interests of this ruling class.

In his most recent work on the subject (1983) he concluded that this ruling class continues to exist. He based this on two sorts of evidence. First, he noted, if wealth and income are valid indicators of power, then the case for a ruling class is strong; these indicators have remained stable over the years of his studies and are concentrated in this tiny segment of the population. Second, if overrepresentation in corporate, foundation, and government positions is an indicator, the argument remains strong; those who belong to the upper class are the major holders of such positions.

There are several specific criticisms of the elitist theories (Marger 1987). First, it is argued that the inevitability of elites has not been proven. While there are always people with great power, it does not necessarily follow that these people represent a single group seeking to exercise power in its own self interest. Second, the evidence that there is a cohesion among the members of the group is only marginal. Members of the class actually come from a variety of different institutional areas including such facets of social life as politics, education, and the economy. Third, viewing the power of the elite as unbridled negates the influence interest or pressure groups have in our society. And, fourth, the view of either a two- or three-tiered power structure is entirely too simplistic to explain the complexity of our social life. For all of these reasons, some observers of political life contend that the views of many in the society are felt in the making of political decisions. That is, the political structure of the society is rooted in a pluralism that fits better with our democratic ideals.

Pluralist Theories

This has led some students of political life to take a very different view of power in the United States (for examples, Dahl 1961, Polsby 1963). They saw the political world as much more open than did elitist theorists. They denied that an upper class will rule simply because it exists. Rather, they found many different spheres of influence through which many people in the society may influence the government. For example, Dahl (1961) claimed that many different players emerged with regard to specific policy issues. Thus, he saw power as widely dispersed among several groups that were in contention with one another. Through this competition the many interests of the American public were represented.

Two other figures are important in putting forth the pluralist perspective. In his book *The Lonely Crowd,* David Riesman (1961) suggested that pluralism does exist in America and that our political structure can best be understood through the operation of **veto groups**. He defines these as interest groups with the capacity to block others from making decisions or policy. In reality Riesman views the American scene as so complex that structural constraints make it unlikely or even impossible for any group of decision makers to come together to form a cohesive group. He found no evidence of a strong and forceful leadership but simply a variety of pressure groups which counterbalance one another. No one of these can initiate and carry through action but can only block the others. Thus, political power is dispersed through a system of checks and balances.

Another pluralist theorist, Arnold Rose (1967), proposed that the American political structure should be viewed as one of "multi-influence." Focusing on power at the national level, he made two central points. First, not one but many power elites exist in American society, each with its specialized area of interest and influence. Second, any linkage between the power elites is only temporary and is limited to particular issues. Out of these multi-influential power elites comes a more democratic view of society in which, at times, issues are actually decided on a democratic basis.

Just as there are arguments against elitist theories of power, there are reasons to question the validity of theorists which suggest that we live in a pluralist society. First, following Marger (1987), it is questionable whether voluntary associations or interest groups can represent the interests of the individual. If such associations are small enough that all voices can be taken into account, they are probably too small to be effective in influencing public policy. Second, to the extent that such groups do have influence, they still probably represent only a small segment of the society. It is well established that those who join such associations are from the better educated and more financially stable elements. Third, even were such groups to work as pluralists contend, there would still be an unequal distribution of power. Certainly some groups, such as large corporations, are better supported and speak with a firmer voice than others, say, the elderly. Fourth, political institutions do not simply react to pressure from interest groups. Rather, interest groups tend to identify those matters which deserve attention. Homelessness, for example, has been with us for some time but it has only become an issue as politicians have made it one. Their response to groups concerned with the homeless is based on that decision to make it an issue, not on pressure from voluntary associations.

Synthesis

The arguments which elitist and pluralist theorists marshall against one another seem convincing, so much so that it is impossible to accept either position as providing a totally accurate picture of our society. Interest groups exist and do influence decision making; elite leadership groups exist, too, and they actually make the decisions in our democratic society, even though they are often in competition with one another (Marger 1987). Recognizing these facts, both elite and pluralist theorists have looked for some middle ground.

Two examples will demonstrate this attempt. The first is Dahl's concept of a **polyarchy** (1971, 1989). Translated literally from the Greek, the term would mean that there are many who rule in the society, and this is the way in which Dahl means it. There is competition between various groups, led by their own elites, and out of this competition for power comes the need to bargain and negotiate. The power of any particular group is held in check, and compromise becomes necessary. Thus, the rule of the elite is modified by the plurality of groups involved in the democratic process.

The second approach is that of Suzanne Keller (1963) who suggested the existence of **strategic elites**. In her view, modern society is so complex that no single group can possibly make decisions in all areas of social life. Therefore, critical decisions are referred to a number of groups having specialized interests, groups which she calls strategic elites. The groups function separately from one another but function to solve those problems which most affect their group.

In summary, then, neither elitist nor pluralist portraits of the U.S. political landscape are completely true, but there is an element of truth in each. There is clearly a considerable concentration of power at the highest levels, and elite groups are the major actors on the scene. Still, the voices of more common people are not totally silenced. The ruling or dominant class in society does strongly influence all political decisions; however, those decisions take into account the concerns of others in society as expressed by various interest groups. The latter may not represent all the people, but they do provide an opportunity for that lonely one-person, one-vote individual to be heard.

Questions for Summary and Review

1. What central issue does the political institution address?
2. What is power? How is authority a special kind of power?
3. What three sources of authority did Weber identify? How do they relate to one another?
4. What is the state? What types of governments do states have? How do totalitarian and authoritarian states differ?
5. What differing opinions are there on why the state exists?
6. What are political parties and when did they arise? What is unique about parties in the U.S.?
7. What is the level of participation in political life in the U.S.?
8. What are the agents of political socialization, and how effective are they?
9. What are interest groups and how do they affect political decisions in the U.S.?
10. Contrast elitist and pluralist views of the power structure of our society.
11. What arguments do elitist and pluralist theorists use against one another?
12. Why have alternatives been suggested to strict elitist and pluralist views?

·············· **Key Concepts**

Authoritarianism (p. 342)
Authority (p. 337)
Charismatic authority (p. 338)
Civil liberties (p. 341)
Classical elitist theory (p. 356)
Conflict theory of the state (p. 344)
Democracy (p. 341)
Elitist theory (p. 356)
Functionalist theory of the state (p. 343)
Interest groups (p. 352)
Legal-rational authority (p. 340)
Lobby (p. 352)
Pluralist theory (p. 359)
Plurality (p. 345)
Political action committees (PACs)
    (p. 352)

Political institution (p. 336)
Political party (p. 345)
Polyarchy (p. 360)
Power (p. 336)
Power elite (p. 357)
Radical elitist theory (p. 356)
Routinization of charisma (p. 338)
Ruling class (p. 358)
State (p. 340)
Strategic elites (p. 360)
Totalitarianism (p. 342)
Traditional authority (p. 339)
Two-party system (p. 345)
Veto groups (p. 359)

References

1. Campbell, Angus, Philip E. Converse, Warren E. Miller, and Donald E. Stokes. 1960. *The American voter.* New York: John Wiley.

2. Converse, Philip E. 1964. The nature of belief systems in the mass public. In *Ideology and discontent,* edited by D. Apter, chapter 6. New York: Free Press.

3. Dahl, Robert A. 1957. The concept of power. *Behavioral science* 2 (July): 201–15.

4. _____. 1961. *Who governs: Democracy and power in an American city.* New Haven, Conn.: Yale University Press.

5. _____. 1971. *Polyarchy: Participation and opposition.* New Haven, Conn.: Yale University Press.

6. _____. 1989. *Democracy and its critics.* New Haven, Conn.: Yale University Press.

7. Domhoff, G. William 1967. *Who rules America?* Englewood Cliffs, N.J.: Prentice-Hall.

8. _____. 1978. *Who really rules: New Haven and community power re-examined.* Pacific Palisades, Calif.: Goodyear.

9. _____. 1983. *Who rules America now? A View from the 80s.* Englewood Cliffs, N.J.: Prentice-Hall.

10. Dye, Thomas R., and Harmon Zeigler. 1989. *American politics in the media age.* 3d ed. Pacific Grove, Calif.: Brooks/Cole.

11. Engels, Frederick. 1950. The origin of the family, private property and the state. In *Karl Marx and Frederick Engels: Selected works in two volumes,* vol. II, edited by Frederick Engels , 155–296. London: Lawrence and Wishart.

12. Flanigan, William H., and Nancy H. Zingale. 1987. *Political behavior of the American electorate.* 6th ed. Boston: Allyn and Bacon.

13. Friederich, Carl, and Zbigniew Brzezinski. 1965. *Totalitarian dictatorship and autocracy.* 2d ed. Cambridge, Mass.: Harvard University Press.

14. Gerth, H. H., and C. Wright Mills. 1958. *From Max Weber: Essays in sociology.* New York: Galaxy.

15. Goldman, Merle. 1986. Religion in post-Mao China. *The annals* 433 (January):146–56.

16. Gusfield, Joseph. 1962. Mass society and extremist politics. *American sociological review* 27:19–30.

17. Hiro, Dilip. 1989. *Holy wars: The rise of Islamic fundamentalism.* New York: Routledge.

18. Huber, Joan, and William H. Form. 1973. *Income and ideology*. New York: Free Press.

19. Hunter, Floyd. 1954. *Community power structure: A study of decision makers*. New York: Doubleday

20. _____. 1959. *Top leadership U.S.A.* Chapel Hill, N.C.: University of North Carolina Press.

21. Keller, Suzanne. 1963. *Beyond the ruling class*. New York: Random House.

22. Kornhauser, William. 1959. *The politics of mass society*. New York: Free Press.

23. Ladd, Everett Carll. 1989. Election '88: The national election. *Public opinion* 11 (5):2–3.

24. LaPalombara, Joseph, and Myron Weiner, eds. 1966. *Political parties and political development*. Princeton, N.J.: Princeton University Press.

25. Lasswell, Harold D. 1936. *Politics: who gets what, when, how*. New York: McGraw-Hill.

26. Lenski, Gerhard. 1966. *Power and privilege: A theory of social stratification*. Garden City, N.Y.: Doubleday.

27. Lipset, Seymour Martin. 1963. *Political man*. Garden City, N.Y.: Doubleday.

28. MacIver, Robert M. 1965. *The web of government*. New York: Free Press.

29. Marger, Martin N. 1987. *Elites and masses: An introduction to political sociology*. 2d ed. Belmont, Calif.: Wadsworth.

30. Michels, Robert. 1962. *Political parties*. Translated by Eden Paul and Cedar Paul. New York: Free Press.

31. Mills, C. Wright. 1959. *The power elite*. New York. Oxford University Press.

32. Mosca, Gaetano. 1939. *The ruling class*, edited by Arthur Livingston. New York: McGraw-Hill.

33. Orum, Anthony M. 1988. Political sociology In *Handbook of sociology*, edited by N. Smelser, 393–423. Beverly Hills: Sage.

34. Pareto, Vilfredo. 1970. Elites and force. In *Power in societies*, edited by M. Olsen, 114–122. New York: Macmillan.

35. Parsons, Talcott. 1969. *Politics and social structure*. New York: Free Press.

36. Polsby, Nelson W. 1963. *Community power and political theory*. New Haven, Conn.: Yale University Press.

37. Public Opinion. 1989. Opinion roundup. *Public opinion* 11 (5):21–34.

38. Riesman, David. 1961. *The lonely crowd*. New Haven, Conn.: Yale University Press.

39. Rose, Arnold M. 1967. *The power structure: Political process in American society*. New York: Oxford.

40. Uhlaner, Carole J., Bruce E. Cain, and D. Roderick Kiewiet. 1989. Political participation of ethnic minorities in the 1980s. *Political behavior* 11 (3):195–225.

41. Verba, Sidney, and Norman Nie. 1972. *Participation in America: Political democracy and social equality*. New York: Harper and Row.

42. Weber, Max. 1947. *From Max Weber: Essays in sociology*, edited & translated by Hans Gerth and C. Wright Mills. New York: Oxford University Press.

Epilogue: Understanding People and Social Life

● ● ● ● ● ● ● ● ● ● ●

The havoc wrought by the violent forces of nature makes world headlines. Earthquakes, hurricanes, and tornados are often the big stories of the day. Such events are sudden, dramatic, and devastating. Horrified, people see the scenes of destruction and feel that awe of nature felt by the earliest humans. Despite advances in scientific knowledge and technology, people are still powerless before nature.

It is interesting, however, that the natural forces of change make international headlines more often than the social forces of change. Throughout the world the structures of societies are changing; the forces of change influence lives for not just a few weeks or a few months but for every day as long as people live. Modernization, innovation, cultural diffusion, and population shifts are not as immediately dramatic as an earthquake, though. People may get caught up in the everyday details of life and not step back and notice the incredible changes taking place in the larger culture.

Reconsider the usefulness of C. Wright Mills's sociological imagination in directing attention to broader social and historical concerns. Consider, also, one family and how social change has affected them.

Murray and Lois are in their late forties and have had three children. At times both have been very discouraged about their lives. Murray returned from the Vietnam War and went to college on a veteran's scholarship. He was the first in his family to finish college and felt that with his degree in business he would be able to move rapidly into a high-paying, prestigious job. Instead, he has worked for the same firm for twenty years and seems to be locked in a mid-level managerial position. As he considers his coworkers, he feels that some of them have been promoted over him without good reason. Sometimes he feels that his being white and male is no longer an advantage.

Murray often overlooks how much the economy has changed and how the hyperinflation days of the 1970s ate up much of his income. Even though he feels relatively poor, Murray still makes more than do half of all American workers. He is more fortunate than thousands of blue-collar Americans who experienced long periods of unemployment, many of whom had to be retrained for different jobs.

Murray's wife, Lois, went back to the university after her children were in school, taking courses in marketing. Now, ten years after completing her degree, she feels underemployed. Despite her credentials, she is really little more than a glorified clerk in a bank. The men who manage the business continue to bring in other men to fill the more influential and better paying posts. Lois wonders why her education has not paid off better than it has.

Lois is like sixty percent of all American wives—she works. Her life is far different from her mother's, who worked as a nurse only after her husband's death. However, the business world has not fully adjusted to the influx of women in such large numbers. Some employers hold on to old attitudes that some jobs are women's work and some are men's. Murray, too, continues to expect Lois to maintain her role as homemaker just as she did before she went to work.

Lois and Murray often worry about their children. Their youngest, Bryan, seems uninterested in school. He spends most of his time alone in his room or with one or two friends. He appears to be attracted to various cults, and his parents worry about drugs. Bryan says he has no desire to go to college and makes few plans for the future.

Their daughter Kimberly married young and had twins. Now divorced, she and the children have returned to live with Murray and Lois. Kimberly is struggling to attend school while working twenty hours a week. Erin, the older daughter, graduated from college and is determined to have a successful career in public relations. She has lived with a man for a year or two, but she feels that marriage and children would derail her career plans. Last year she admitted to her parents that she had an abortion because she was not yet ready for a child. Her parents were deeply troubled.

The lives of Murray and Lois have been disrupted in many ways by changes in social values during the past twenty years. Religion has always been important to the couple, and they support its more traditional values, so they are dismayed at Erin's abortion, Kimberly's early divorce, and Bryan's flirtation with cults. They are distressed by Bryan's lack of interest in education, career, and the future. On the other hand, they are somewhat ill at ease with Erin's single-minded concern with her career; they hope she will decide to marry and have children.

Politically, Murray and Lois have changed their attitudes. During the 1960s they were followers of the liberal policies of Kennedy and Johnson. Now, however, they find the more conservative decisions of Reagan and Bush more comfortable.

In this text we have tried to show the connection between personal lives and larger events. The things that disrupt the lives of Murray and Lois are not isolated events affecting only this couple. The sociological imagination stresses that personal troubles are part of a larger scheme of public issues. What is troubling Murray and Lois is that the norms and values they learned as young people no longer seem to hold true. Rather, their world has been affected by social change, perhaps more dramatic and rapid than at any other time in world history. Indeed, future historians may look back on our time and note that social change during this time had an even greater impact upon individual lives than did those brought about by the Industrial Revolution (see chapter 1).

Sociologists define social change as significant alterations in the patterning of behavior in a society. It involves a change in cultural definitions of reality, which results in shifting definitions of the roles we play in society, from those in the smallest groups to our positions in large institutional patterns such as the family, religion, and political life. Such change is disturbing! It causes discomfort because it challenges what people have come to define as reality itself; but such change is inevitable, particularly in rapidly moving, postindustrial societies like the United States.

Sociologists have taken opposing views of this change. Some theorists have portrayed it as the essential companion of human progress. In this view change is part of an evolutionary process by which societies are able to deal with increasing structural complexity. Indeed, according to this view we may be able to trace the future of any society by looking at its past in relation to the development of other societies.

Other students of social change, however, do not see any such inevitable pattern to these alterations in social life. Rather, they contend that there is a cyclical nature to the life of a society and that changes are the result of swings of the pendulum which almost always overcorrect for the problems which arise in the existing order.

The several theoretical perspectives discussed in this book—functionalism, conflict theory, and symbolic interactionism—differ in how they interpret societal change. All, however, accept the fact of such change as an inevitable part of ongoing social life.

While functionalists know that some change is necessary, their analyses tend to suggest that it should be as minimal as possible. From this point of view, only those adjustments necessary to maintain the equilibrium or balance of the present order should be made so that society can continue its familiar path with only little interruption. Thus, problems of massive unemployment should be handled with aid programs that provide basic help but do not affect the existing economic structures of the society.

Conflict theorists, on the other hand, view change as an essential response to changing social needs. Inequities that exist in the social order demand a response that can only be meaningful if basic aspects of social structure are altered. For example, the problems of minority groups call for significant responses to their needs such as affirmative action plans and laws requiring the integration of housing, among others.

Those who concentrate on the interaction of groups as part of an ongoing process of definition and redefinition know that change will occur. It is the inevitable product of group life in which people reshape the meaning of social life. Thus, the definition of the roles of wife and mother have been reinterpreted through such interaction to meet the changing patterns in the labor force as more and more women become fully employed.

As we have seen throughout the book, sociological research—however pursued—is affected by the theoretical perspective underlying the methodological approach. We have also seen that we can learn something from each of these special views of society. Research conducted from each of them aids us in our quest to understand people and social life as they react to the impact of the social forces of change.

In this book we have examined the various aspects of how the forces of social factors affect each of our lives. The established organization of a society is one such force. The various features of social organization provide us with a web of statuses and accompanying roles for playing our "parts." We behave as we do—as men or women, children or adults, laborers or professionals—on the basis of these social definitions. However, these prescriptions for our behavior are constantly shifting. Our culture provides the script for our lives but, as in a movie in the middle of production, the script is subject to rewrites and to the interpretations of the actors. As the lines of the movie change we all undergo socialization or resocialization aimed at restructuring our behavior. Whether the new socialization will actually cause an individual to change the way a role is played will depend on a number of factors, but, again, they will be social factors such as the impact of the social groups to which we belong.

Take Murray and Lois's younger daughter. She does not play the role of woman as did her mother. Rather, she is responding to forces of change which permit and encourage women to be more active in the world of work and which shift the task of child rearing to an option for today's woman. Her parents do find this disturbing, just as they found the easy divorce of Kimberly problematic, but it is part of the social change of our time with which they somehow must deal. The primary and secondary groups to which they belong may help or inhibit their adjustment to their daughters' ways of life as well as to their son's as they provide or withhold support for the new role definitions.

Alongside the forces of established social organization are social forces of relative disorder which actually demand that social change take place. For example, deviant behavior has been seen by some—especially conflict theorists—as the reaction to a social order that is not responsive to the needs of significant groups of people who are a part of the society. Because of this it is no longer adequate to simply provide for the smooth functioning of the society. In this perspective, deviant behavior is not the result of personal pathology to be resisted and constrained but is the signal of needed change if the society is to continue as a viable answer to the needs of social life.

In studying collective behavior we have looked at what happens when customary behavioral patterns are not available to meet the needs of a changing situation. While, as we have noted, much collective behavior is trivial in nature, in its most organized form—the social movement—it is a serious, organized attempt to alter in some basic fashion those aspects of society which adherents to the movement see as in need of change. In our lifetimes, each of us has seen numerous examples of how such movements have changed our lives, from the civil rights movement of the 1960s, to the anti-Vietnam protests of the 1970s, to the women's movement of the 1980s.

In the 1990s several movements are gaining strength which are concerned with two aspects of the major environmental problems we face—overpopulation and pollution. The world's population strains resources already diminished by the devastation of pollution and the destruction caused by the methods of industrial production; significant numbers of people across the world now call for change in the definition of appropriate use of our natural environment. They hope to reduce the effects of these twin sources of difficulty and to reverse the long-standing abuse of our natural world.

In spite of those forces which encourage social change, our social life must still be dominated by the outlines of social structure if group life is to remain viable. For good or ill, each society strives to maintain itself. To do so, it must address the basic problems of group life, solutions for which are embodied in the networks of roles and norms sociologists refer to as institutions. In this book we have examined what might be seen as the three most basic institutions: family, religion, and politics. The traditional outlines of these institutions are powerful and conservative in nature; but they are also subject to the forces of change as they react to altered conditions in the social world.

For example, the model of the family that Murray and Lois have taken for granted is no longer applicable to the demands of contemporary society. As we have seen, that model is based on a pattern that was adapted to an agricultural economic mode. As our society has moved through industrialization to a postindustrial society, the role patterns outlined in this model in many respects have become outmoded. With two-career families the rule rather than the exception, how wives and husbands fulfill their roles may be dramatically different than it was for the farm family of the early decades of the twentieth century.

Similarly, religion, which in some form lends a sacred nature to these older family patterns, is undergoing change. It has not, as early social scientists thought, vanished in a sea of secularization, but it is no longer dominated by the more liberal mainline denominations of the past; fundamentalists and other conservatives are increasingly influential in our religious life. In addition, new religions as well as religious immigrants from Moslem countries now make up a significant part of the religious landscape. In reality, belief in the sacred remains a significant factor for the people of our society. However, the shape of the sacred and the forms by which it is approached are more varied than they were as recently as World War II.

Finally, political life is also constantly shifting. The liberal agenda that dominated our government from the days of Franklin Roosevelt, John Kennedy, and Lyndon Johnson has been replaced by a more conservative approach, not unlike that of the days before the Great Depression of the 1930s. In any case, whether our political life is characterized by liberalism or reaction, those who play the game face a more intelligent and skeptical electorate. We are so much better informed about our politicians and we can make judgments with greater knowledge. Yet, even in the face of this expanded knowledge, there remains a dispute as to whether our political life is guided by the pluralistic, democratic model enshrined in our constitution or is in the hands of a power elite. Here we must ask the question of whether the technological change that has led to the increased impact of the mass media has resulted in a more open system or whether it is simply another tool by which we are manipulated by the dominant powers of the society.

Throughout the book an underlying theme has been the need to employ the sociological imagination in order to fully understand the world in which we live and the significance of both personal and larger events we experience. We hope that, as you finish the book and the first course in sociology, you will have come to appreciate the importance of using this imagination in interpreting what is happening to you, to those around you, to the nation, and to the world. Each of these levels of social life is as much influenced by social forces as it is by the dramatic surges of natural power. In fact, the very subtlety and persistence of these forces allow them to have a deeper, more lasting influence on each of our lives.

Whatever path you follow when you have finished your formal education, knowledge and an appreciation of these forces will give you an advantage over those who have never learned to look at the world with the sociological imagination. Very few of you will go on to be professional sociologists, but all of you will need to be armchair sociologists in order to deal most effectively with what is going on in your business, your family, your government, and all aspects of the social world in which you live. Lawyer, doctor, or merchant chief, all can profit from the peculiar perspective sociology takes on the world. We trust that you will be better able to do so because of this course, whatever path your life may take.

Index

· · · · · · · · · · ·